BALTIC
SEA

Stutthof

P O L A N D

Auschwitz

ECHOSLOVAKIA

A

H U N G A R Y

AN UNCERTAIN HOUR

Also by Ted Morgan

Maugham: *A Biography*

Churchill: *Young Man in a Hurry, 1874–1915*

F.D.R.: *A Biography*

Literary Outlaw: *The Life and Times of William S. Burroughs*

AN UNCERTAIN HOUR

**The French,
the Germans, the Jews,
the Barbie Trial,
and the City of Lyon,
1940-1945**

TED MORGAN

William Morrow and Company, Inc.
New York

Library of Congress Cataloging-in-Publication Data

Morgan, Ted, 1932–
   An uncertain hour: the French, the Germans, the Jews, the Klaus Barbie Trial, and
the city of Lyon, 1940–1945 / by Ted Morgan.
      p.   cm.
Bibliography: p.
Includes index.
ISBN 0-877-95989-7
   1. World War, 1939–1945—France—Lyon. 2. Morgan, Ted, 1932—
3. World War, 1939–1945—Personal narratives, French, 4. Lyon
(France)—History. 5. Jews—France—Lyon—History—20th century.
6. World War, 1939–1945—France.   I. Title.
D802.F82L9454 1990
940.53′44—dc20   89-34066
                                                                                        CIP

Printed in the United States of America

First Edition

   2   3   4   5   6   7   8   9   10

BOOK DESIGN BY BRIAN MOLLOY

This book is for my father,
Gabriel de Gramont, 1908–1943

CONTENTS

ILLUSTRATIONS

The illustrations in this book are the work of the German artist Joseph Beuys (1921–1986). Raised in a strict Catholic family in the town of Kleve near the Dutch border, Beuys joined the Hitler Youth and then the Luftwaffe, and became a dive-bomber pilot in 1941. Stationed in Nazi-occupied Crimea in 1943, his JU-87 was hit by Russian flak. He tried to make his way back to his base in the middle of a snowstorm, but crashed in the no-man's-land between the German and Russian lines. It was too late to jump, and when the plane hit the ground, he flew through the windshield and into the snow. The tail of the plane flipped over and buried him in the snow, where he lay for days, unconscious. German search parties stopped looking for him, but a band of nomadic Tatars found him and took him back to their tents. He awoke days later to discover that they had covered his body in animal fat to regenerate warmth, and then had wrapped him in felt as an insulator to keep the warmth in.

Beuys returned to postwar Germany with severe injuries and combat fatigue, and began to produce sculpture and objects that were his own postmodern "Horrors of War." Felt and fat, which had a particular life-saving meaning for him, figured prominently in his work, as in the grand piano wrapped in felt, or the Fat Chair, an ordinary kitchen chair with a big wedge of fat on it. Beuys isn't trying to tell the story of his wartime experiences in his art, but to my mind, he conveys a more powerful sense of what war is and what war does than traditional military artists who paint battles. To take the illustrations one by one:

Chapter I, Lyon '87: Fat Chair.
Beuys intended this chair to be a humorous object, to show the dual nature of fat as a warm liquid and a cold solid, a paradox that is compounded when fat is placed on the chair in an orderly, right-angled wedge. For me, the fat seems to represent the accretion of history.

9

Chapter II, The Funny War: Sledge.
With its flashlight and blanket, Beuys's Sledge suggests a military strategy of flight.

Chapter III, Vichy: Sunrise and Sunset.
To Beuys, this work was based on the passage from raw matter to ordered form through the sculptural process. What I see in it is a transitory state caught between sunrise and sunset, as in the short span of Vichy.

Chapter IV, Sonderbehandlung: Flag.
Beuys was thinking of the red flag of a revolutionary train crossing Eurasia, whereas I am reminded of the deportation trains from France.

Chapter V, Lyon '43: Bathtub.
For Beuys this bathtub refers to "the wound or trauma experienced by every person as they come into contact with the hard material conditions of the world through birth." In 1977, when this object was stored in the museum of Leverkusen, outside Cologne, the town's Social Democrats held a party in the museum and appropriated it as a beer cooler. The artist sued and collected $94,000 in damages. In the context of my book, this object has an obvious connection to the *baignoire* that was used by the Gestapo in the Hotel Terminus.

Chapter VI, Lyon '44: Object to Smear and Turn.
I feel there is something menacing and dangerous in this object, reminiscent of the situation in France in 1944.

Chapter VII, Last Train to Auschwitz: Tramstop.
Tramstop is a vertical sculpture made from the iron barrel of a field cannon, positioned upright. At the base (not shown) are clustered four primitive seventeenth-century mortar bombs. Emerging from the mouth of the cannon is the head of a man with a pained expression, archaic and unheroic, somehow both active and passive. This man, seen here in full face and profile, armless and constricted, sunken eyes and mouth frozen open, represents to my mind the archetypal camp inmate.

Since then, at an uncertain hour,
That agony returns.
And till my ghastly tale is told,
This heart within me burns.

—COLERIDGE, *The Rime of the Ancient Mariner*

LYON '87

Lyon, May 11, 1987, 1:05 P.M.: Judge André Cerdini said, "*Je demande qu'on introduise l'accusé*" ("I ask that the accused be brought in"). We were finally going to see him, this man who had fled Germany thirty-six years ago, finding refuge in Bolivia, a country unlike most others in that the annual take of its drug barons was four times the national budget. When the prisoner came into the glass booth, the attending police officer unsnapped his handcuffs, which made a small clicking sound that seemed to bridge the distance between imprisonment and freedom. He shook hands all around, with his two interpreters, with his lawyer and his lawyer's secretary. It was force of habit for the French, and yet it was startling to see this gesture of cordiality between the war criminal and the compatriots of his victims, as if to say, no hard feelings. He was seventy-three and he looked it. You could see the outline of the bone at the front of his skull, above the eyebrows, through the skin. One of the French newspapers described him as having "the emaciated face of a predatory bird."

When he was asked his name, he gave his Bolivian pseudonym, Klaus Altmann, and his residence as La Paz: "*Ich bin* Klaus Altmann." He had in fact arrived in France with a Bolivian ID card and driver's license, owing to the unusual circumstances of his removal from La Paz. He had been tried twice in France for war crimes, in absentia, in 1952 and 1954, and was found guilty. It was for these crimes that an extradition request was made in 1974

15

(after he had been discovered in Bolivia), when Georges Pompidou was premier. The French were told that extradition could be obtained for a price, in this nation where everything had a price, but in the margin of the report on his desk, Pompidou wrote one word: *non*.

In 1982 there was a new regime in Bolivia, more favorable to deportation. In January 1983 he was arrested on the pretext of an unpaid debt. A few days later, he was taken to the airport and placed on a plane to Cayenne, the celebrated penal colony (until 1946) and island capital of French Guiana. From Cayenne he was flown to Lyon* and imprisoned to await trial. The airfare from La Paz to Lyon added up to a planeload of arms, three thousand tons of wheat, and fifty million dollars, which the Bolivian president came to Paris to collect two weeks later. In the retrieval of war criminals, a bounty-hunter mentality has sometimes prevailed that says: Bring them back any way you can. For why should such men be allowed to live out their lives peacefully in some cocaine republic? Why should time and distance protect them from settling their accounts?

Judge Cerdini proceeded to pick nine jurors by dipping his hand into a jar and pulling out numbers. It was hardly a jury of his peers, for his peers would have been fellow SS officers, or at the very least fellow Germans. Perhaps they were his peers in the sense of being fellow humans, since he was being tried for crimes against humanity. As the jurors took their seats, flanking Cerdini and his two sidekick judges, known as "assessors," the prisoner scrutinized them as he must in the past have scrutinized his captives, searching for the guilt in their eyes.

It is one of the achievements of our time to have proclaimed the crime against humanity. There are those who say that humanity, like surgery, has advanced thanks to war. At the Nuremberg trials, where this new crime was written into law, it was used only twice, against Julius Streicher, for having urged the extermination of the Jews, and Baldur von Schirach, Hitler Youth leader and *Gauleiter* of Vienna, for having sanctioned the massacre of Jews on the eastern front. The message conveyed by the crime against

*In this book I have kept the French spelling, without the final "s," for the cities of Lyon and Marseille.

humanity was that there are different kinds of atrocities. To kill ten thousand civilians in a bombardment is a war crime. To deport children in the name of a state policy of extermination is a crime against humanity.

There was also a practical aspect. The crimes being judged had taken place in 1943 and 1944, while the statute of limitations for war crimes in France was twenty years. But the statute, which was based on the notion of forgive and forget, did not apply to crimes against humanity. Some crimes could not be forgiven or forgotten, and these crimes were, in the French phraseology, *imprescriptible*. Parricide, less frequent these days, used to be in that category. Desertion in time of war still was.

So the trial of "The Nation, France, against Barbie, Klaus" could only have taken place if the accused was charged with imprescriptible crimes. The vast Salle des Pas Perdus (Hall of Lost Steps, or waiting room) of the principal Lyon tribunal had been converted into a courtroom for the occasion. Light streamed in through six high semicircular windows. Armed gendarmes patrolled the roof. Behind and above the judges there was a bas-relief of Justice crowned and throned, holding a rod in one hand and a book in the other. Reporters interviewed spectators in the back of the court. "When I saw him come in it gave me goose bumps," said one. "He doesn't at all have a face that corresponds to his character," said another.

Two days later, on May 13, Barbie refused to continue appearing at his trial, claiming, with some justification, that he had been kidnapped. Since the game was rigged, he was not going to play. The trial could go on without him, like a performance of *Faust* in which the leading character leaves the stage before singing his first aria. The courtroom artists closed their boxes of colored pens. The glass enclosure for the accused now looked like an empty aquarium. You could already see the headlines: BARBIE BOWS OUT.

At the press center that day, I met a Russian historian, Lev Bezinenski, whose field was the Third Reich. As a young man in the Red Army in 1943, he had served as interpreter when General von Paulus surrendered at Stalingrad. He had also attended the Nuremberg trials, where he had seen Göring, prior to his suicide, testifying that he had not been informed about the death camps.

When I asked Lev Bezinenski what he thought of Barbie's refusal to appear in court, he said: "It's not right that a man who tried to destroy democracy should now be taking advantage of democratic justice." In the Soviet Union, he said, where he had attended many trials of war criminals, there was usually a military tribunal, and the accused was not permitted to absent himself. Almost invariably, he was found guilty and sentenced to death by firing squad. Nor was there any statute of limitations on war crimes. In fact, if you had been tried once, you could be tried again if new facts came to light. In Smolensk in 1946, he had attended the trial of a collaborator who was sentenced to five years because there were no witnesses. The man served his time and was released, but later, when witnesses were found, he was retried and sentenced to death.

Walking back along the Saône River from the press center to my apartment in *vieux* Lyon, I passed the courthouse. A French television commentator was standing on the steps, talking to the camera: "The ancient capital of the resistance has a rendezvous with its past," he said. And of the counterresistance, I thought, all those who were working for Barbie. If you remembered the resistance, you also had to remember the black market, the "olive gray" girls, and the stores advertising their "Aryanism" in order to get the Wehrmacht clientele. It was all part of the legacy. Of course the great majority of Lyonnais, like people elsewhere in France, were "those who watch while others act." You couldn't blame them. Not everyone wants to be a hero or a villain.

Try to imagine June 1940. A stillness in the streets. No church-bells ringing. A native son says that for the first time he can hear the Rhône River. Smoke clouds rising from the gasoline reserves of Port-Rambaud. The Place Bellecour turned into a parking lot for German tanks. Every morning a band concert, but attendance is sparse. With the armistice, Lyon is relieved to find that it is in the unoccupied zone. Posters on walls announce the imminent departure of the German troops.

That is of course why the resistance got started in Lyon. From July 1940 until November 1942 there were no Germans in the unoccupied zone. Also, Lyon was eighty miles from the Swiss border. And finally, Lyon was a city older than the Christian era, with an esteemed tradition of rioting and insurrection. Lyon had seen them come and go, the Romans with their aqueducts, the early Christians with their martyrs, the Merovingian kings, the Saracens, Charlemagne, the monarchy, and the republics. Behind its placid bourgeois façade, Lyon had always been seditious. The craft guilds revolted against the clergy in the thirteenth century. The working classes lynched the unsurers in the sixteenth. When the Jacquard loom transformed the silk trade, the textile workers rose up against their employers in the eighteenth. During the revolution of 1789, Lyon rebelled against the Jacobins in Paris, and 1,684 Lyonnais went to the guillotine in four months' time. Only the death of Robespierre saved the city from destruction. So the history of Lyon was a history of libertarian conspiracies of which the resistance was merely the latest. The hook-nosed puppet Guignol, known to every French child, bastinadoing the judges and the gendarmes, originated in Lyon. When the workers revolted, it was, in the words of Guignol, because they didn't want the herring's tail, and they didn't want the herring's head, they wanted the entire herring.

Outwardly, there was something a little morose and smug about the city. It seemed more Swiss than French in its bourgeois virtues and its distaste for any form of excess. It was a citadel of old money that was never flaunted. It was a place where people did not like you to see the newspaper they were reading because it might give away their political leanings. It was a city where you might be "invited" but you were rarely "accepted," a city of masonic-like social cells and hidden circuits. Very little was out in the open. A love of clandestine association went hand in hand with a passion for independence.

This also had something to do with Lyon having always been in the shadow of Paris. When I called one of my Parisian cousins in the middle of the trial, he said, "Here, no one is interested." What he meant was, "There is no point in paying attention to anything that does not take place in Paris." Lyon had made its peace with Paris by accepting the role of dowdy and charmless maiden aunt. Paris wore its diamonds; Lyon kept them in a safe-deposit box. Paris dined out on indiscretions; Lyon ate alone and kept its secrets. Paris slept around and caught the clap; Lyon slept around, but used a *capote anglaise,* condom, (or, literally, English riding coat). Paris had the Louvre; Lyon had the Museum of Banking. Paris had its *vespasiennes,* circular outdoor urinals with four or more stalls, conveniences for a happy-go-lucky population, while Lyon had its single-stall outdoor *pissoirs,* which went with a love of privacy. Paris had Maxim's; Lyon had its *bouchons,* with four tables and no sign, where the food was better than the food at Maxim's, although it was advisable for the untrained palate to shun such local dishes as *tablier du sapeur* (fireman's apron), a fatty slab of meat. Another Lyon dish was *poularde demi-deuil* (pullet in half-mourning, so named because of the sliced black truffles inserted between skin and flesh), which seemed somehow to sum up the city's blend of epicureanism and gloom.

When Georgette Léon and her mother arrived in Lyon as Jewish refugees in 1941, Georgette was taken to a Dominican convent. The Mother Superior told Mme. Léon that there was no room for her little girl. Mme. Léon told the Mother Superior that she was lacking in Christian charity. "I am sorry, *madame,*" said the Mother Superior, "but the province is not Paris." And there you had the heart and kernel of Lyon—the pride and sanctity of being provincial, of turning a drawback into an advantage. Lyon was the city of the hidden hand, closed to outsiders. Being a Lyonnais was an enviable condition which made it unnecessary to know the rest of the world. It was enough to love Lyon, maker of sausage and silk, city of seventeen bridges, where the Rhône and Saône rivers joined to head out to sea, indicating a capacity for making opposites compatible, as in the sign in the window of a bistro: RESTAURANT OUVRIER, CUISINE BOURGEOISE (Working-class Restaurant, Middle-class Food). Mme. Récamier, the great courtesan of the Directoire, was said to have been "a good Lyonnaise," because "all her life she distributed dividends without touching her capital."

Lyon didn't mind being second, just as the Crédit Lyonnais didn't mind being the second biggest French bank. The mothers of Lyon told their sons, in school "Don't be first, be second," because if you were first you were in the spotlight's glare. The Lyon dynasties were substantial but obscure, like the Morels, whose name had been Morelli when they came from Tuscany in the sixteenth century to start a silkweaving shop. They prospered, and put their money into real estate, until they owned practically the entire suburb of Ecully. When the city decided to renovate the Chartreux neighborhood, Joseph Morel graciously donated the necessary land to create a spacious square at the intersection of Tourette and Chartreux streets, which became the Place Morel and, in 1945, the Place Théodose Morel, after the resistance hero who was killed in March 1944 on the Plateau des Glières. This was an example, not only of the way the resistance cut across class lines, but of the Lyon dynasties' capacity for renewal, for they did not automatically espouse pro-Vichy or pro-German views.

Klaus Barbie knew Lyon well, having served there for twenty-one months, and having prowled the city making arrests. Aside from his native Germany and his adopted Bolivia, Lyon was the place where he had spent the most time. He knew it far better than I did. I had spent roughly half my life in France, and had often driven through Lyon on my way from Paris to my grandmother's house in Aix-en-Provence in the days before the highway, but I had never stopped there. And now Barbie, who had arrested and imprisoned so many, was himself a guest in Saint-Joseph Prison, sitting in his cell and waiting for the eight o'clock news to tell him what had happened that day at his trial.

Except that he was brought back to the courtroom for confrontations with witnesses whom he had arrested and interrogated. It was a way of tying up the loose ends of history. These men and women of Lyon, now as old or older than the accused, had been arrested, had in some cases been tortured, had been deported, and had survived; and now, forty years later, they were being given the chance one seldom gets, the chance to come face to face with the man responsible for their suffering. The formal surroundings of the tribunal, the Corinthian columns, the sculpted griffons on the walls, the judges' ermine-fringed red robes became the setting for a reenactment of wartime tragedies. And when the judge asked one witness, "What is your profession?" she replied, "I had five children." And when he asked another witness about her arrest, she said, "It was the difference between seeing an accident and being in the accident." She had been confronted with Barbie in the course of the trial preparation in 1984, and Barbie had said at the time, "This lady has been to the movies and is telling you the plot of the movie she saw." Now, at the trial itself, Barbie's lawyer, Jacques Vergès, was echoing this line of defense by complaining that Barbie was being accused of everything that had gone on in Lyon during the war years. "Next thing you know," he said, "they'll say he stole the Eiffel Tower."

And yet there was no equivocation among the witnesses. They all said they recognized Barbie *formellement* (absolutely). He stood there saying nothing while those who had been deported finally had their day in court. "Look at him," said Lucien Margaine, his face lined, his hair white, "he doesn't even look German, they were tall and blond. He told me, 'You will be N&N [*Nacht und Nebel,* night and fog, meaning no return],' with the same expression he has now."

"What do you have to say?" Judge Cerdini asked Barbie, who replied: *"Nichts."*

"For an SS," Lucien Margaine said, "that's a pretty poor performance."

"That face—those glacial eyes," said another witness, Mario Blardone. "I want to look him in the eye." He advanced toward the accused, and had to be restrained.

"In my soul and conscience," said Vincent Planque, "I can tell you: that's him."

"He still has that air of *faux-jeton* [literally, counterfeit coin, or someone who is not what he appears to be]," said Robert Clor.

André Courvoisier, who had been a radio operator for the Buckmaster network, was caught and questioned by Barbie, who said to him: "You're working for the British, you poor imbecile— where I'm going to send you, it will be worse than death." And it had been worse than death, but André Courvoisier had come back, and now it was his turn, and he spoke directly to Barbie rather than to the judge, saying, "I recognize you and I'll tell you why—the deep-set eyes, a jackal's eyes."

But Barbie did not respond, and finally the prosecutor, the equable, wavy-haired Pierre Truche, said: "I want to talk about another Barbie, the Barbie who in 1933, mourning his deceased father and brother, became a prison visitor. How did this young man become an SS? Now you know that you will never return to Bolivia, and that is why you should reply. This trial will come to a close, and people will ask: 'Did he have anything to say?' One of your own grandchildren will ask. They will wonder whether you were ever sensitive to human misery. They will wonder how the young man of twenty who did social work became a pitiless SS.''

And yet, in spite of Barbie's deaf-and-dumb act, those days of confrontation were illuminating. For each witness who faced Barbie went through a ritual of recognition, bringing about a shift in time, a flashback to the days of occupation. And seeing that happen in the courtroom gave me a small window of awareness, thanks to which I was able to understand why I had so badly wanted to cover the trial. I realized that I needed to fill a gap in my personal history. Because in 1940 when the Germans invaded, I was in France with my family. And in June when the armistice was signed, my father, who was a pilot in the French Air Force, went to London and joined de Gaulle, while my mother took my brothers and me to the United States. When my father was killed in 1943, I was sitting out the war in Washington, D.C. I had missed the occupation years, and in retrospect I had always felt a bit like a deserter. I had missed those great events, which I was now able to experience thanks to the testimony of these witnesses. For one generation fights the war, and the next generation is left to study the debris.

Barbie was an underling, but the trial raised many vexing issues—those of obedience, of reasons of state, of ends and means, of the occupation of one people by another and the abuse of their human rights, including the right to resist. There was a cleansing clarity in resistance: The country was occupied, which was unacceptable. But there was also a murky side, in terms of private agendas and treachery. Why were more accredited journalists here in Lyon than at Nuremberg? Why were young people, most of them students, standing in line every day for hours waiting to occupy the one hundred seats reserved for the public? Because the French had to look into this particular mirror, however distorted. Because there was a generation of young people that was still picking up the tab for World War II.

Jury deliberations began on July 3 at 5:38 P.M., and while the jury was out I unfolded in my mind the great map of human suffering displayed at the trial, ranging from Lyon to Warsaw, to Munich, to Berlin, the train platforms, the cattle cars, the hundreds of stories of death and survival, of ID cards, and borders, and barbed wire. I knew that the prosecution had made its case. Barbie was guilty a hundred times over, not only of the three crimes against humanity he was charged with, but of a great many war crimes that fell under the statute of limitations. He was guilty, for example, of the raids on the Jewish welfare office and the children's home in Izieu, of signing the telexes reporting the raids, which, we were told by experts imported from Germany, meant that he was responsible for those operations. And, in the case of the August 11, 1944, train to Auschwitz, he had been observed by several witnesses in the courtyard of Montluc Prison, in charge of rounding-up prisoners for deportation. He was guilty because he was an officer in the SS, a corps that by experience and training was privy to the coded language of deportation. The SS men were initiates. They knew that deportation meant death. When the Nazi leaders spoke in veiled terms of work camps and family reunions, when Hitler said that those who laughed at death would soon stop laughing, they understood. Barbie understood, having told those he interrogated, *"Fusillé ou déporté, c'est la même chose"* ("Shot or deported, it's the same thing"), and *"Là ou vous allez c'est pire que la mort"* ("Where you are going, it's worse than death"). Barbie made a startling answer when he was asked what Nazism meant to him. "Camaraderie," he said, showing an unchanged and remorseless loyalty to the principles of his SS training. It was too bad, I thought. Israel had reestablished the death penalty in order to try Eichmann. But France had no death penalty. And the irony was that the architect of the abolition of the death penalty was Robert Badinter, the minister of justice, whose father, Simon, had been one of the victims in the raid of the welfare office on the Rue Sainte-Catherine. This was vengeance in reverse, where the son of one of Barbie's victims had saved him from the guillotine.

It was true that Barbie had committed these crimes, but it was also true that the victor wrote the history, drew up the indictments, and picked the jury. The conduct of the trial, in its pretended adherence to the judicial principles of the French Republic, was a necessary travesty. For in fact there was an enormous presumption of guilt. It could not be otherwise, for how could a war criminal, already found guilty twice in absentia, be presumed innocent? And it came out in various ways—in the remarks of Judge Cerdini, for example, who said on the trial's first day, during the squabble over the use of the name Klaus Altmann, "I can understand that the name of Barbie must be heavy to bear." And in the remarks of the witnesses, one of whom, a former resistance leader, addressed the jury: "I hope you will have the courage to do your duty." And it came out in the prosecutor's summation, when he asked the jury to give the defendant a life sentence. "How am I going to explain to my readers," Stanley Meisler of the *Los Angeles Times* wondered, "that the prosecutor asked the jury for a specific sentence before a verdict had been reached?"

Summing up for the defense, Jacques Vergès told the jurors: "And remember, it's not like in the United States, where juries are locked up in a room and are not allowed to read newspapers or watch television or listen to the radio. Because here in France you are considered grown up enough to read and watch and listen to whatever you like."

Maybe so, I thought, but not grown up enough to deliberate without three judges in attendance. For Cerdini and his two assessors deliberated and voted with the jury. One of the Lyon reporters, Gérard Schmitt, told me that in the forties the French criminal justice system had experimented with a jury-of-your-peers approach, but there had been so many acquittals that they had to bring back the judges. With three judges voting, in addition to nine jurors, and with a two-thirds majority required, it only took five jurors and the three judges to reach a guilty verdict, so acquittals were rare. But the point that Vergès was making was that the French government television channel had the previous four evenings shown the film *Shoah,* an examination of the death camps, and Vergès thought that this was a form of jury tampering, that the film had been deliberately programmed to coincide with the end of the trial and the jury deliberations.

The jury was out for six and a half hours, filing back into the courtroom shortly after midnight on the morning of July 4. Barbie was brought in, seeming to appear in the glass booth as if he had come up through a trapdoor, in this great Hall of Lost Steps, with two thousand eyes upon him. He smiled at his daughter, Uta Messner, sitting in the front row of the press section, and then listened to a long recitation of the crimes he was guilty of. I had to remind myself that this elderly bald fellow with the bent head, weary eyes, and humble body language, whom I might have wanted to help across the street had I seen him standing on a corner, was an evil man, as he stood, silent and without expression, listening to the verdict with his hands in his jacket pockets. He was sentenced to life imprisonment, which in France means twenty years, and he would be freed when he was ninety-three years old, if he lived that long.

Judge Cerdini asked Barbie if he had anything to say, and he replied, speaking for the first time in French, in his gravelly, accented voice: "Yes, *monsieur le président,* I have a few words to say. . . . I never had the power to decide about deportations. I fought the resistance, which I respect, sometimes harshly. It was wartime, and today the war is over." But the war is never over, not for the victims and their families, and not for a nation's collective memory, which is sometimes known as history. I can myself remember certain things . . .

THE FUNNY WAR

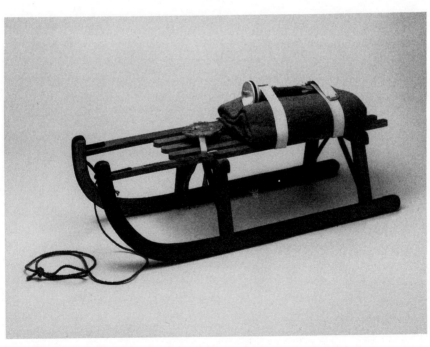

Photograph permission of Hirschl & Adler Gallery

When I was a boy growing up in Paris in the thirties, my father had a friend named Thierry de Martel, a famous surgeon in his early sixties. He had removed my father's appendix when my father was a boy. When I was four, in 1936, he removed mine. There was a complication, in that my appendix was touching my liver, and my father told me that Thierry de Martel had saved my life.

On June 14, 1940, a Friday, the Germans entered Paris. My father, a pilot stationed in Orléans, was in the capital on official business and went to see Thierry de Martel at the American Hospital in Neuilly. "This is intolerable," he kept repeating to my father, "this is intolerable." He said he had been to see the American ambassador, William Bullitt, to ask him whether he should leave Paris or remain at his post. Bullitt had told him to stay. The next day, Thierry de Martel locked himself in his office and injected himself with cyanide. I have often wondered why a man would commit an irreversible act because of events which were bound to change.

Years later, I had a talk with my uncle Gratien. "You know," he said, "there was another society doctor, Henri de Mondor. On the same day, June 14, he went into his study and started work on a book about Mallarmé [the symbolist poet]. You could call it two forms of patriotism." I said that I did not think suicide was a form of patriotism. "That's because you don't understand the logic of despair," Gratien said. "In any case he had cancer and didn't have long to live."

I read somewhere that the two things rats hate most are swimming and having their whiskers cut. If you throw a rat in the water, it will barely manage to swim but will probably make it back to shore, if it's not too great a distance. If you clip a rat's whiskers, it will stumble around like a drunk, but again it will manage. But if you cut off a rat's whiskers and then throw it in the drink, it will drown. In other words, you can die of bad news. Thierry de Martel died of bad news—cancer plus the occupation.

Primarily, the word "occupation" means how you spend your time, as in "gardening is one of my many occupations." In French, it specifically means profession. You ask someone his occupation, and he tells you "plumber" or "doctor." The word also means being busy, as in "I have some out-of-town clients on my hands and I'm very occupied." A busy signal on a French telephone is an "occupied line." In the toilet doors on trains and planes, the little windows don't read *Open* or *Closed,* but *Occupied* or *Free.* The opposite of being occupied is being free. Americans don't really know about this because America has never been occupied.

Another friend of my father's, Colonel Brunschwig, was a *gueule cassée* (broken face). In 1917 they had started rotations on the Somme, because the men in the trenches were going into shock under the artillery barrages. When Brunschwig came up to the line, the mocking and mutinous outgoing soldiers made sheep noises—*baaa, baaa.* It had nothing to do with courage. There came a moment when you cracked. There were men who would charge a machine-gun nest over open ground, but who broke under the artillery barrage, because there was no respite.

In any case, in the spring offensive Colonel Brunschwig was leading his men across some farmer's shell-pitted muddy field when the whistling started, followed by bursts over their heads. These were shells that exploded before hitting the ground with a spurt of yellow sparks and sent black curls of heavy shrapnel flying in all directions. In the midst of giving orders and deploying his men, Brunschwig realized that he could no longer see. He put his hands to his face and felt the blood, but could not see it because he was blinded. His hand ran down his face, feeling for his jaw, but there was no jaw. The lower part of his face had been sheared right off.

There were so many face wounds in those World War I battles that the Val de Grâce Hospital in Paris had a special ward for the *gueules cassées,* Ward 5, familiarly known as *les baveux* (the droolers) because many of the patients had no jaws or lips and wore towels around their necks to drool on. All the severe face wounds ended up on this ward, regardless of rank. In fact, few of the droolers ranked higher than captain, and Brunschwig was the only colonel.

Brunschwig himself had lost an eye and there wasn't much left of his face below his nose, but he was one of the better-looking specimens. He decided that he was goddamned if he was going to play the victim. He and the others had to learn not only to live with their torn faces, but to be proud of them. They were told to get used to being stared at, and having children point at them, and their presence being the cause of embarrassed silence. Not to mention the reactions of their wives and girlfriends. They were told that they formed a fraternal order of the disfigured. Someone on the ward thought up a grimace contest, with prizes for those who made the ugliest face. The motto these men with no mouths adopted was: *Keep Smiling.*

Brunschwig and the others were guinea pigs for plastic surgeons. After many operations, eyelids were sewn on, cartilage was inserted in his nose, and a piece of his tibia was used to make him a new jaw. He grew a bristly moustache, but his face still seemed to drop away beneath it, and he spoke as though his mouth were full of cotton.

The *gueules cassées,* became walking reminders of France's sacrifice in the Great War. This was what the *patrie* had demanded. Clémenceau asked that a *gueule cassée* be present at the signing of the Treaty of Versailles. After the war in the *Chambre Bleu Horizon* (thus named because so many veterans had been elected to Parliament who had worn the "Horizon Blue" French Army uniform), there was a *gueule cassée*. The cult of the fallen and the maimed became an important part of national life. The tiniest French village had its *monument aux morts* (monument to the dead) in the main square, giving employment to hundreds of sculptors. Veterans' groups proliferated, since each category of wounded wanted to remain distinct from the others. You had the *Aveugles de Guerre* (those blinded by war), the *Grands Invalides* (as opposed to minor invalids), and the *Ailes Brisées* (broken wings, or disabled aviators), among others.

All these groups competed for pensions, which were so important in post-World War I France that the minister of war was also the minister for pensions. It was natural for the *gueules cassées* to form their own veterans' group, and to claim that their pensions should be higher, for there was no worse mutilation than that of the face (unless it was having your balls shot off, but that was a group whose members did not go public). The *Gueules Cassées* (now capitalized) became an association of five thousand members who turned their handicaps into assets. "We are not like the others," they said, " and no one else went through what we did." They were admired because war had made their faces indistinct.

Each summer in Paris, during the big Quatorze Juillet military parade, Colonel Brunschwig led a detachment of fifty *Gueules Cassées* down the Champs-Élysées. In the summer of 1937, when I was five, my father took me to see the parade and sat me on his shoulders for a better view. He had arranged for Colonel Brunschwig to give us some signal of recognition as he passed. I saw coming toward us a group of men wearing uniforms and navy blue berets, stepping smartly, their decorations, pinned to their chests, flapping slightly with each step. There were six rows, with eight men in each row, and Colonel Brunschwig was leading them, preceded by a flag carrier; and as they came abreast of my father, Colonel Brunschwig boomed out the command "*Teeeeete drrrrooooiiiittte*" ("Eyes right"), and they all swung their heads around in our direction, and they were quite close, because we were right on the edge of the sidewalk, and there was one who looked as though a buzz saw had taken off the front of his face, with two little rubber tubes where his nose had been, and another one, whose face had the granular consistency and grayish-yellow color of oatmeal. The one carrying the flag had a triangular leather mask over the center of his face. At that time, at the age of five, I wasn't at all horrified, for I found myself wondering if their children would look like them, and I tried to imagine boys and girls without jaws and noses, or with a deep socket where an eye should be. It seemed entirely plausible to me that disfigurement might be hereditary.

Over the years, the memory of those men parading has come back to me fairly often, perhaps because of the contrast between their erect carriage, the way they held their heads and marched in step, and then, when they came closer, their smashed faces. They had every right to curse the nation that had sent them into senseless battles, but there was no *Phantom of the Opera* vindictiveness in them. They were proud men, proud in the knowledge that they had done their duty, proud that the proof of their valorous conduct was there for all to see, and proud that they had turned their deformities into emblems of gallantry. In terms of what was to come, and in terms of unjudging and unconditional patriotism, it was a rare sight, because I don't think that after World War II there were any more *Gueules Cassées* in the Quatorze Juillet parades.

As Colonel Brunschwig saw it, the wars between France and Germany were episodes in one prolonged and cyclical conflict that he called the "Hundred-Year War." In the opening phase, the war of 1870, the French declared war on Prussia, for foolish, comic-opera reasons. Prussia was a supplier of crowned heads to Europe, and the Spanish throne was vacant, but France was ready to go to war to prevent a Prussian prince from ruling Spain. King Wilhelm I of Prussia backed down, but France went to war anyway because he refused to sign a guarantee.

The French at that time had conscription by ballot, like a lottery, and if your number came up, you could pay somebody to take your place, somebody who was poor or unemployed, somebody who was young. In war the important thing is not who wins or who loses but who does the dying, and in the war of 1870, you could hire someone to go to war and die in your place. On the other hand, it was the last war in which the chief of state personally led his troops into battle. Napoleon III, like his uncle the other Napoleon, climbed on a horse, even though he was sixty-two and in serious pain from a gallstone, and went to war. Whatever has been said about this man who governed France for twenty-two years, that he was an *arriviste* who had arrived, that he had a velvet fist in an iron glove, at least he had the guts to fight the war he had started. The emperor was in the field, Kaiser Wilhelm and Bismarck were in the field, and the Prussians wrapped it up in a month.

On August 30 the Germans attacked on the Meuse, as they would again in 1940, and the Emperor and his army retreated along the river to the little fortress town of Sedan, seven miles from the Belgian border. There the emperor made his stand on September 1. The battle was over in a single day because of superior Prussian artillery. The emperor's long reign was ended. All that remained was the ceremony of surrender, and Napoleon's note to William began, "Sir, my brother." War between the French and the Germans would never again be so brief, so ceremonious, and so decent. When the two rulers met, the one about to be sent to Germany in comfortable captivity, the other returning in triumph to be crowned emperor, there were apologies all around. The French fought on until the following January, when an armistice was signed. Bismarck realized his dream of a united Germany. As he put it: "You don't go to war because your cause is just or because you are angry but because you can beat the enemy."

But "Paris goes her own way," wrote Victor Hugo. "A coach passes, flying a flag; it comes from Paris. The flag is no longer a flag, it is a flame, and the whole trail of human gunpowder catches fire behind it." The war with the Germans was over, but a war between Frenchmen broke out when the people of Paris, infuriated over the peace terms—the loss of Alsace and Lorraine, and war reparations that would impoverish the nation—rose up against their government and formed the Commune. In the few months that the Commune lasted, hostages were shot and the Tuileries and other emblems of the Napoleonic regime were burned. When encircled Paris surrendered in May 1871, twenty thousand Communards were shot, a record for legal savagery, creating a long-lasting divisiveness in French society. As the painter Renoir put it, "They were madmen; but they had in them that little flame which never dies." The Communards were the fathers of all future French resistance fighters.

After 1870 there were many French families with a father or a grandfather who had fought the Prussians and who told his stories to his children and grandchildren. Those children and grandchildren grew up thinking of revenge. The cession of Alsace-Lorraine meant war to perpetuity. A famous man of the period said, "Think of it always, speak of it never." There were plenty of reminders. In French towns where troops were garrisoned, every Saturday the regiment paraded, band in front, performing the *retraite aux flambeaux* (torchlight retreat). Quatorze Juillet was the most important day of the year. Flags everywhere—garlands—lights. Children sang patriotic songs of revenge. Normal French families, sitting around the dinner table, spoke of it, saying: "We'll get them—to Berlin."

But while the French wanted a return engagement, the best military minds were German. At the turn of the century, Count Alfred von Schlieffen, Chief of the German General Staff, was already planning the next war. His idea was to send the bulk of the German Army through the Liège–Namur gate in Belgium and then press westward toward the Channel and south to Paris. "Let the last man brush the channel with his sleeve," von Schlieffen said. Of course you would be violating Belgian neutrality, and you would be taking the risk of bringing the British in, but that was small change if you could achieve a quick victory. When von Schlieffen died in 1906, his last words were: "Keep the right wing strong."

The French High Command saw a copy of the Schlieffen Plan, but refused to believe that the Germans would attack through Belgium. The only one who took it seriously, General Michel, was dismissed as a crackpot and replaced by Marshal Joffre, who was convinced that the German attack would come in the east through Lorraine. Joffre had his own plan to attack Germany through Alsace and Lorraine and on to Berlin. Thus, in 1914, both sides attacked from different directions. The Germans, following the Schlieffen Plan, burst through Belgium, which the French had left virtually undefended, while the main French Army was in the east, "chasing cuckoo clocks in the Black Forest," as a German general later put it. In September 1914, von Kluck's horsemen came to within twenty kilometers of Paris, within sight of the tiled roofs of suburban houses and the tip of the Eiffel Tower.

What saved the French was the British Expeditionary Force, five divisions under Sir John French. Joffre carried out a skillful retreat by train, and the British and the French stood and fought on the Marne, and von Schlieffen's quick victory was turned into four years of slogging in the trenches, with northern France occupied. The French knew in their hearts that they could not have won without the British nor, in 1917, without the Americans. The wars would be fought, invariably, on French soil, but would be won with the help of their two allies. Bismarck had said a very wise thing, as early as 1880: "The most important political fact in the world today is that the North American continent speaks English."

It was a matter of numbers. Forty million French were no match for sixty million Germans. As Georges Clémenceau liked to say, "I've got nothing against the Germans, there are just too many of them." In 1918 a victorious France regained her two lost provinces, and settled once again inside her natural borders. But France was in a state of shock, having lost two million men, one third of the male population between the ages of twenty and fifty, more than twice the number of British deaths. France was a nation of widows and orphans, growing up on the *Assistance Publique* (welfare).

The essential fact was that between the end of World War I in 1918 and the start of World War II in 1939, there elapsed twenty-one years, which was just enough time for the returning soldier to produce a son born in 1919 who in 1939 would be sent out as cannon fodder, just the way his father had been.

In France the period between world wars was divided into the *après-guerre* (after World War I), and the *avant-guerre* (before World War II). It was, in retrospect, a brief intermission between wars. All France wanted was to be left alone to heal her wounds and work out her civilized way of life, but the outside world intruded. The French mood was isolationist. Europe was in turmoil, but why should France become involved in other people's problems? On this, the left and the right were joined in wishful thinking. Léon Blum, the head of the Socialist party, said that Hitler had no chance of coming to power. Old Hindenburg was the champion of democracy. Marcel Déat, the right-wing demagogue, wrote a celebrated editorial, "Why Die for Danzig?" Pacifism, born of colossal losses and war-weariness, went right across the political spectrum. You could only ask so much of a people. The unspoken thought was: One more like the last one and France is finished as a nation.

The military expression of this "never again" state of mind was the Maginot Line. To build a great system of fortifications along the Franco-German border was an announcement of peaceful intentions. It signaled that "We will never attack our German neighbor, but we will defend ourselves against invasion." It also seemed like the answer to the manpower shortage, according to the theory that one man behind fixed defenses is worth three attackers. Even Churchill the Great Attacker observed: "Having regard to the disparity of the population in France to that of Germany, the Maginot Line must be regarded as a wise and prudent measure."

André Maginot, a wounded war veteran, was minister of war and pensions from 1927 until his death in 1932 as a result of eating bad oysters at a New Year's banquet. Having experienced life in the trenches, and seeing before him daily the pension claims of the disabled, Maginot was conditioned to adopt and sponsor a defensive strategy. His words defined the nation's state of mind: "We are always the invaded, we are always the ones who suffer, we are always the ones to be sacrificed."

Work on the line began in 1927, and Maginot fought and lobbied to obtain the necessary funds from a reluctant Chamber of Deputies. By March 1936 the forts were fully garrisoned. The French were proud of their steel and concrete wall. It appealed to their fondness for marvels of engineering. There were incessant newspaper stories about life in the bunkers. Underground trains carried the soldiers from their battle stations to the mess. They were said to be kept so far below ground they didn't know whether it was summer or winter.

What was happening outside France did not matter. In the Spanish civil war, tanks were used by Italian troops under General Berganzoli. They broke through the enemy lines, but were held up for logistical reasons. This confirmed the French General Staff in its opinion that tanks were worthless. And it confirmed the German General Staff in *its* opinion that Italians were worthless. Guernica showed that dive bombers had a serious effect on enemy morale, but that lesson too was lost on the French. Instead, they were told that on one side of the border there was the Maginot Line, and on the other side there was the Siegfried Line. Soldiers on both sides were friendly and sometimes played soccer in no-man's-land.

In fact, the Maginot Line was an exercise in self-delusion. This was because the line stopped where it was most needed, along the two-hundred-mile-long border between Belgium and France, the German invasion route in the Great War. At great expense, after years of labor, a continuous fortress had been built along the border with Germany and Luxembourg to the east, where the Germans had not attacked, while the long Belgian border, from Luxembourg to the English Channel at Dunkirk, where the Germans had attacked, was left virtually undefended. Why had the French reinforced the area where they were the safest? It was as if they were cooperating with the enemy, as if they were stage-managing the kind of invasion they wanted.

The official reason was that it was too expensive to continue the Maginot Line along the Belgian border to the sea. But for national security, for the defense of French territory, the money could have been found. Another reason was that France had a treaty with Belgium that if Belgium were attacked, France would come to her defense. If France extended the Maginot Line, she would be sending a signal that she had no intention of backing up the Belgians, but planned to sit snugly behind her fortifications. As the minister of war in 1928, Paul Painlevé, said: "We cannot build impregnable defenses in the face of our friends the Belgians."

This explanation, too, was specious, for the Belgians could have been told that border defenses did not signify any change in the French commitment. The true reason lay elsewhere. It lay in the unspoken but visceral certainty that France could not fight alone. The British had to be brought in, and the only sure way to do that was for Germany to violate Belgian neutrality again. And it happened, just as it had happened before. The classic invasion route was left open, the Germans attacked through Belgium with a modified version of the Schlieffen Plan, the British sent over an expeditionary force, and the French threw their mobile forces into

Belgium. The difference this time was that Germany had an army that moved at the speed of a tank, twenty to twenty-five miles an hour. The French did not even have time to retreat. The Germans broke through to the Channel in one week, attacking the hinge of the Franco-British front, because, of course, they would retreat in different directions—the British from Dunkirk and across the Channel, and the French south to Paris. In the meantime, the main Panzer thrust came across the Ardennes, where the weakest French force, under General Corap, an army of draft dodgers, forty-five-year-old reservists, and men who shot themselves in the foot, was defending the vital Meuse front. The French were stretched thin along the border, and the Germans attacked en masse at one point. Once again, they captured Sedan, where in 1870 the emperor's reign had ended. And once again, as in 1914, they moved close to Paris. But this time the Anglo-Americans did not save them, at least not right away.

So, once again, a four-year cycle began in which the Germans invaded, parts of France were occupied, and a number of children were born of French mothers and unknown fathers. And at the end of each cycle there were women with shaved heads walking the streets, as if the ones in 1945 were the daughters of the ones in 1918. And the Germans arrived in the northern provinces with plans for annexation that had been drawn up in 1914 and dusted off. It was a form of compulsive repetition. And it was possible for a man to have lived through all three episodes, to have been born, say, in 1856, to have been a teenager in 1870, to have fought in World War I, and, as an octogenarian, see France invaded once again in 1940. Marshal Pétain, who had pronounced the Ardennes "impenetrable," was such a man.

In August 1939 Arthur Koestler, the Hungarian-born author of *Darkness at Noon,* was vacationing with his English girlfriend in the Riviera town of Roquebillière. One day he went to the town hall and saw green and yellow posters calling up men in Categories 3 and 4 to join their regiments within forty-eight hours. The widows of 1914, still in black, looked at the posters with an expression of satisfaction. Sitting in the sun on a wall outside town was a company of soldiers, dangling their legs, rolling cigarettes, and throwing stones for a black mongrel dog to recover. The dog was named after the prime minister of France, Édourd Daladier, and the soldiers shouted: "Go on, Daladier, hurry up, run, old one, you've got to earn your steak." The soldiers were grumbling. They were sick of being mobilized. "Don't tell me we're going to fight because the Germans want a town in Poland," they said. They grumbled about the disorder in the fortress where they were stationed. The damp concrete gave them rheumatic pains. More than half the shells in the munitions depot were the wrong caliber. Their uniforms were made with cheap materials. They ate *singe* (literally, monkey, figuratively, corned beef hash), while the Germans had fresh pork sausage and goulash and tins of butter.

In October Koestler was arrested in a roundup of foreigners and sent to the labor camp of Le Vernet, thirty miles from the Spanish border. On January 17, 1940, he was released. They had opened the gate to let him in, and now they opened it to let him out. How simple it was. In Paris on May 10, he heard that the Germans had taken Sedan. It was like a chair breaking under you, he thought. The rumors were flying thick and fast. German paratroopers had landed in the Place de la Madeleine. Gamelin, the French Commander in Chief, had shot himself. Koestler had a conversation with a French officer, who said: "The extended Maginot Line? Never existed. Some blockhouses, that's all."

"But for years you have known that Hitler has adapted the Schlieffen Plan and that the attack will come through Belgium."

"So what? To know is one thing, to act another."

"But since the war began, you have had nine months to build the extension."

"You don't say. Suppose they didn't want to?"

And suppose some of the gentlemen on the General Staff preferred Hitler to Blum, Koestler wondered. Even though Blum was no longer in power, it was an ingrained state of mind.

My father could have stayed in Washington, where he had arrived in the fall of 1937 as air attaché in the French embassy. He had been taking flying lessons and had his pilot's license, and in September 1939, when war was declared, he took us all back to France, my mother, my two brothers, and me. He was mobilized as a pilot and stationed in Orléans while we stayed in Paris with relatives. On May 17, 1940, he was summoned to the Foreign Ministry on the Quai d'Orsay and told that he had been appointed consul in Chicago. The Germans had crossed the Meuse, and the men in the ministry wondered how long it would take them to reach Paris. These civilized, cultivated men of the world, trained in the high tradition of French diplomacy, who spoke several languages, were trying to come to terms with the unthinkable, defeat and occupation. "I knew something was wrong last year," one of them said, "when I visited one of the Maginot forts and the commander received us in his slippers." "My daughter is seeing a young man," another said, "who told her that if his regiment was moved to the front he would fake an appendix attack. The army is full of malingerers." "It's sad," the first man said, "when you start seeing French place names in the communiqués." "After all," the second one said, "no one expected the Belgians to hold the Albert Canal."

The order had come down that day to destroy the archives, and they began discussing the best way to do it. "Let's throw them into the Seine," one man said. "No, let's pile them up on the lawn, douse them with gasoline, and set fire to them." Which is what they proceeded to do, almost casually. Men in shirt-sleeves threw green folders out the windows, onto the lawn in the ministry courtyard. A fire was lit, and soon thick black columns carried charred bits of paper over the Paris rooftops, treaties, memorandums, position papers, reports, years of diplomatic correspondence, all up in smoke.

Afterward, my father joined his colleagues in a nearby café. "All of Europe will laugh at us," one of them said. "What can you expect," another one said, "when everyone knows that victory does not pay. Nineteen-eighteen was much worse than 1870." My father turned down the Chicago appointment and went back to Orléans, and wondered, in the remaining weeks of the war, why the planes remained on the ground.

It was clear there was no real will to fight. It was all happening too soon. The young men in the streets, after checking the numbers on their military booklets against the numbers on the mobilization posters, were heading north again, crossing the countryside toward Nancy and Metz, drinking red wine out of the bottle in train compartments, exchanging snapshots of their wives and kids. And for what? For men with bad habits. The habit of thinking you were governing by rotating cabinet assignments. After the war started, the *remaniements ministériels* (cabinet reshuffles) continued, always with the same shabby crew. As the war closed in, with the swift defeat of Poland, and the alliance between Stalin and Hitler, the ministers worried whether they should take this post or that post, like a dog chewing its tail. Clémenceau had said, "I need balls," but who had them in 1939? President Albert Lebrun was a limp rag, who let things happen and then complained that they had happened. "Lebrun cries when a cloud covers the sun," said Pierre Laval. Daladier, the prime minister, was just as bad. Everyone complained about his inertia. They said there were more air force generals than planes.

When Paul Reynaud replaced Daladier on March 20, Daladier had to be kept in the cabinet for political reasons. They took a man who was no good as prime minister and made him minister of war. All they could think about was their political combinations. There was a complete incompatibility between the two men, so that in May, on the eve of invasion, the government was crippled by personality conflicts and little fits of pique. Reynaud said at a cabinet meeting on May 9 that Gamelin was not up to the job of Commander in Chief, but Daladier, just to be contrary, replied, "We can't change horses in the middle of the stream." Privately, Daladier said: "When Gamelin speaks, it's like running sand through one's fingers."

Then there was the habit of accumulating cabinet posts—Laval and Daladier, when prime ministers, were their own foreign ministers—and the habit of paying secret government funds to journalists and influence peddlers, and the habit of conducting boudoir intrigues. Joseph Paul-Boncour, the French delegate to the League of Nations, wrote his mistress, Magda Fontanges, "When I think of your lovely body, I don't give a damn about Central Europe." Too many of these men had digestive ailments and disorderly private lives. It was as if one of the instruments of public office was a highly visible mistress—Paul Reynaud had Mme. de Portes, Daladier had the marquise de Crussol, André Tardieu had Mary

Marquet, and Georges Mandel had Béatrice Bretty, the last two being actresses in the Comédie Française. In 1938 Mme. de Portes wanted a divorce from M. de Portes, but under French law a divorce could not be granted until after three years of separation. Only the minister of justice could change the law. The trouble was that Reynaud *was* the minister of justice. Mme. de Portes urged him to change ministries so that another, newly appointed and friendly minister could change the law. And it was done. Georges Bonnet, the foreign minister, replaced Reynaud at Justice, and Reynaud became minister of finance. Bonnet faithfully performed his little task, and the separation time was reduced from three years to one in a law dated November 29, 1939.

In May 1940, Reynaud, with his ministers and his bishops, had gone to the cathedral of Notre Dame to pray for the salvation of France. "I believe in a miracle because I believe in France," he had said. The French were locked into their defensive mentality, which consisted of sitting in their forts. They still sometimes used carrier pigeons rather than telephones. The Germans, by contrast, were full of surprises. The paratroopers who took the first two bridges on the Albert Canal had trained for months, rehearsing a single task, the taking of bridges. The corps of paratroop engineers who took the supposedly impregnable Belgian fort of Eben Emael that dominated the Meuse River had rehearsed attacks on forts for six months. They were dropped from gliders on the roof of the fort with flamethrowers, collapsible ladders, and two tons of explosives. The Germans had specialized units with precise objectives. The French had an amorphous mass of defenders, thousands of bumbling and unprepared Duponts and Durands (Smiths and Joneses).

How futile any heroism seemed. Near the Belgian city of Dinant, in May, some troops were blowing the bridges on the Meuse. At the Pont d'Yvoir, the electrical detonator did not work. A column of German tanks appeared over the rise. A Belgian lieutenant, René de Wispelaere, ran from cover and lit the fuse. The bridge was blown, but the lieutenant was killed by shellfire. And my young cousin, Philippe de Gramont, a lieutenant with an armored unit on the Meuse, was holding a village surrounded by Panzer tanks, and was asked to surrender. He refused. A minute later the tanks opened fire and he was killed. Why? For Reynaud and Daladier? For Mme. de Portes? And why was my father, in Orléans with his escadrille, waiting for flight orders that never came?

On May 14 Ambassador Bullitt cabled: "The German tanks crossed the Meuse as if it did not exist. They ran through the French anti-tank defenses which consisted of railroad rails sunk deep in concrete and protruding from the ground as if the rails were straw. . . . Reynaud said: 'At this moment there is nothing between those German tanks and Paris.' "

The French had more fighter planes than the Germans, 2,122 to 1,356, but the French High Command did not know what to do with them. They had never thought in terms of a defense coordinated with air power. They were holding planes in reserve because they believed it would be a long war like the previous one. They had not foreseen the Germans' combined used of tanks and planes. The question, Why did the Germans have an overwhelming victory in the air when the French had more fighters? was answered after the war by the commander of aviation in the northern zone, General d'Astier de la Vigerie, who said: "Almost every evening I had to pick up the phone and take the initiative to inform the army commanders that I had a certain number of planes without missions the next day, adding, 'Have you any to give them?' Their reply was invariably the same: 'We thank you very much but we do not have any use for them.' "

Said an officer who had fought in both wars: "It's just like Charleroi in 1914." The *fuyards* (fleeing soldiers), heading south, were running into reinforcements, heading north. They had to be rounded up and herded into barracks. Generals had to be replaced in the field, the most shameful thing that can happen to an officer in wartime. General Corap, commanding the Ninth Army, was replaced on May 15 by General Giraud, whose first order from his new headquarters in Maubeuge, a few miles from the Belgian border, was: "It is prohibited to spread pessimistic rumors." Four days later Giraud was captured, and that was no rumor. Giraud by then had realized that the Ninth Army had ceased to exist, without having really fought. Entire units dissolved at the approach of the Panzers. Entire units raised their hands and "went *Kamerad*."

Not everybody ran. Charles de Gaulle, then still a colonel, was in command of the 4th Armored Division, in the region between Laon and Rheims, about eighty miles east of Paris. His style of command was distance, hauteur, and silence. Reviewing his officers, he told a major with wine-reddened cheeks: "Tomorrow you will go on sick call." To his Chief of Staff, Lieutenant Colonel Rime-Bruneau, he said, "I don't want any advice." On May 15 he set up his headquarters in the village of Corbény, on the Laon–Rheims road. The next day, de Gaulle was out on the road, where he saw the columns of refugees and *fuyards* in uniform mixed in with the civilians. His sense of shame turned into a sense of resolve that whatever happened, he would continue to fight. The next day he ordered motorcyclists out on reconnaissance and told them, "Keep going until you are fired at."

On May 17 he moved 179 tanks and 47 armored cars north twelve miles to the strategic crossroads at Montcornet, and a de Gaulle–Panzer tank duel ensued. As the tanks blazed away at each other, the colonel thought: "You succeed, you're a hero, you fail, you're a *couillon* [asshole]." De Gaulle was plagued by poor maintenance and repairs on the tanks, by refueling problems, and by not having the infantry and air cover that the Germans had. He had to pull back, but he had done something quite remarkable. He had attacked when all the other French units were retreating, and he had taken 120 German prisoners. Two days later, he turned his force west, toward Crécy on the Serre River, and again destroyed some enemy tanks, but was stopped by German artillery and dive bombers. Running across his fellow officer, the colonel commanding the 322nd Artillery Regiment, de Gaulle said: "Congratulations! Pretty work! Your men took to their heels." The colonel replied: "My men are dead; the survivors are at your command."

De Gaulle, who had been operating pretty much on his own, and who had deliberately failed to stay in touch with the commander of the Sixth Army in his zone, was finally ordered to pull back south of the Aisne River, where the French were trying to establish a defensive line. In four days he had lost seventy-three tanks and thirty-three armored cars. One of his tank crew chiefs, Sergeant Major Nommay, was captured by the Germans and taken before a Wehrmacht colonel, who rose from the table where he was sitting and shook the French noncom's hand, saying: "You are soldiers! This is the first serious resistance we have met since Sedan.''

There were other pockets of resistance in the collapsed front. André Devigny was a twenty-four-year-old lieutenant from a modest farming family in Savoie. It struck him on the troop train leaving Paris that the men were singing the "Internationale" as often as the "Marseillaise." It also struck him that many of the generals were *grands mutilés*. His division commander, General de Juvigné, had a metal hook emerging from his right sleeve. Devigny's infantry unit was sent to Belgium, and when the front broke, he rounded up some strays near the town of Wassigny, thinking he would make a stand. He had about thirty men and a machine gun, and he placed them in combat position in some bushes along a railroad track. On May 17 Devigny saw the formidable German war machine approach, planes overhead providing cover as the tanks moved up, followed by the infantry. The column slowed down as they entered a village, and Devigny's group opened fire. Then he saw the tank turrets swing in his direction, and they ran for the woods. They reached a river, where it turned out that not one of his men knew how to swim. They were more scared of the water than of the enemy. But they had to keep moving because they were behind German lines. Devigny led the way across the river. French troops on the other bank opened fire, and despite his cries of *"Français,"* he was shot three times in the legs and buttocks, and was evacuated to a hospital in Bordeaux. It was a completely demoralizing experience. He had seen men from a regiment with the motto *Peur de Rien* (Afraid of Nothing) sewn on their tunics drop their guns and run.

It was all happening much too fast, and no one in the government seemed to know anything. Reynaud said it was impossible to govern because he could not find out what the High Command was doing. Had the bridges been mined? No one knew. Were there any French troops between the Germans and Paris? No one knew. Daladier grudgingly conceded at a cabinet meeting that two French divisions had caved in under the pressure of the Panzers and planes. On the evening of May 15, Bill Bullitt was in Daladier's office looking at the big General Staff map on the wall. They were trying to find the village of Liesse and trying to take in the fact that once again the Germans were on French soil. But Paris was still Paris, Ambassador Bullitt reported. The outdoor stamp market on the Champs-Élysées was functioning as usual. In the playground, children rode the eight ancient donkeys and sat happily in the sunshine watching the Punch and Judy show.

When Gamelin told Bullitt that the Germans had taken Rheims, Bullitt called President Roosevelt. FDR asked him what had happened to the French Army. Bullitt answered, "The French Army died twenty years ago. All of this generation of France's field officers were lost in the First World War. Every time I should be speaking to a forty-year-old French major, I am talking to a seventy-year-old officer who has been called up from the reserves to take the place of his son, a lieutenant killed twenty-five years ago."

And what was Reynaud thinking about? A cabinet reshuffle. On May 17 he finally moved Daladier from Defense, which Reynaud took over himself, to Foreign Affairs. He got rid of the somnolent Gamelin, replacing him with the peppery little Maxime Weygand, said to be the natural son of King Leopold II of Belgium. He brought in Marshal Pétain, "the victor of Verdun," as vice-premier, or premier-in-waiting. But the principal topic among the ministers in the new cabinet was not how to beat the Germans, but when to leave Paris and where to go. It was an inescapable geographical fact that the capital was one hundred miles from the Belgian border, an easy two hours' drive. At the rate the Germans were advancing they would be in Paris any day. General Pierre Hering, in charge of the defense of Paris, advised the government to leave as early as May 16, for if the ministers were captured, the war was as good as over. Where to go? What about Clermont-Ferrand? What about Bordeaux? On June 9 they decided on Tours, on the Loire, one hundred miles southwest of Paris, surrounded by historic castles. Presumably, the French Army, pushed back from river to river, would regroup and make a stand on the Loire.

And so you had the spectacle of a movable government, one step ahead of the invader, with its little army of civil servants, its aides and typists, its files and seals, a government on the run, a road-show government. This gypsy caravan of cars drove south on June 10, four days before the Germans entered Paris, with the ministers, traveling of course with their mistresses, alive to the contrast between the unchanging splendor of the countryside and their own painfully fragile and transient situation.

The government remained in Tours for only four chaotic days. Various ministries set up shop in castles that were miles apart, feudal fiefdoms cut off from one another because all calls had to be relayed through the Tours post office. President Lebrun was at the castle of Cangey, completely isolated, kept informed of nothing. The Ministry of Information had no information. Reynaud was at the castle of Chissay, with a big map of France spread out on the floor of the great medieval hall, on his hands and knees trying to follow the progress of the Germans. Why were they advancing so fast? Other ministries were in the castles of Azay-le-Rideau and Langeais. As Yves Bouthillier, named minister of finance in the June 5 *remaniement,* put it: "We were beyond pain, beyond measure, beyond the still-to-be-born, beyond fifteen centuries of history. We were in Renaissance castles in the country." On June 11 it was suggested that the French population be urged to remain where it was. "But how can we order others to do what we have not done ourselves?" someone sensibly asked.

In point of fact, the population had not waited to be asked. There were already millions of Frenchmen on the march, in what came to be known as *l'exode,* which must go down as the finest example of collective hysteria in a nation known for reasonableness, practicality, and a sense of proper limits. The French were the greatest stay-at-homes in all of Europe. They did not emigrate to other countries. They did not even leave France on vacations. The only way a lot of them had ever been abroad was as prisoners of war. They were attached to their soil, to their comforts of home, and they had a touching habit of giving cute names like *Mon Rêve* or *Nous Deux* to their modest little houses. But now they began to act in a completely irrational manner, for it was much safer to stay at home than it was to be on the road, where the Germans bombed and strafed civilians. Your house might be looted in your absence. You were leaving the secure familiarity of your *foyer* (hearth) for the risks and vagabondage of the refugee life.

Yet the French left by the millions, in a sort of grass-roots abdication, fleeing the invaded area like people fleeing a flood for higher ground. It was a form of despair, like Thierry de Martel's suicide, but contagious, spreading from town to town. *Exode* equaled not only defeat but groundless and mindless fear. As Jean Giraudoux, a great writer but in 1939 a not-so-great high commissioner of information, later put it: "Because the Picardie was emptying into the Beauce, which was emptying into the Rouerge, everyone thought that the secret was to push the French into each other until there was only one left, inaccessible and invincible, who would save all the others."

It began with the Belgians. The French could not close their borders to the Germans, how could they close them to the Belgian refugees? Like the French, the Belgians had been through it before. As one of them put it: "I stayed home in 1914." And another one said: "We'd seen a movie on German atrocities"—the atrocities of the first war. The Belgians left places with an unlucky past, places that had been destroyed in 1914. As for the French in the path of the invasion route, first they experienced the arrival of the Belgians and then that of an enemy who was not supposed to be there. For years they had been brainwashed with the powerful myth of the Maginot Line, a wall that had the shape of France itself. And now the impregnable became pregnable, and people were saying: "All we know is that we were lied to."

In a snowball effect, as people saw refugees coming through, they joined them. Retreating soldiers rang doorbells and said, "Save yourselves, they're here." When the Germans crossed the Meuse, the panic spread. Now soldiers joined civilians, a ragtag army on the march, but in the wrong direction. Big northern cities like Lille and Roubaix emptied like sinks. It was a nation in flight, bumper-to-bumper on the north–south roads. Cars ran out of gas. Drivers without maps lost their way. Rumors were repeated by thousands of mouths into thousands of ears: "Enemy agents are encouraging the soldiers to flee," as if the soldiers needed encouragement. "There's one dressed like a nun, hiding a submachine gun under the habit."

As they advanced, the Germans opened the doors of the prisons and the insane asylums to add to the confusion. In the great heartland city of Lyon, where thousands of refugees were arriving, a local businessman, Georges Villiers, was fixing up the buildings of the Foire de Lyon to house them. A man came up to him and said, "I have something serious to tell you. I am a convicted murderer. I was in Clairvaux Prison awaiting sentencing. When the Germans arrived they opened the doors and here I am." Villiers said: "I'm trying to get things in shape around here. You have shown that you can make decisions. I'm putting you in charge of the clean-up brigade. Find some brooms."

On June 8 gendarmes on bicycles arrived in Rouen, pedaling furiously and shouting, "The Germans are in Isneauville—get the fuck out, they'll be here any minute." Then they burned the city's gasoline dumps, the fire and smoke adding to the panic. At about the same time, Arthur Koestler, leaving Paris for Limoges, was amused by the variety of vehicles on the road—a Paris By Night bus, a fire truck from Maubeuge, a butcher's delivery van from Soissons, a dairy truck from Rouen, an ice-cream merchant from Évreux, a streetsweeper with rotating brushes from Tours, and in between, thousands of small Citroëns and Peugeots. Everything that could move on four wheels, from hearses to Rolls-Royces, was on the road.

There was a sort of hierarchy of flight. First the rich left with their big cars and their chauffeurs. Anne Dubonnet, of the *apéritif* family, a girl my age, told me years later that she and her parents had left in the family Hispano-Suiza with bills of large denominations sewn into the doll she was carrying and rolled up in the hollow stems of her father's golf clubs. Then came small cars with mattresses on top, then people on bicycles, or pushing wheelbarrows, or on foot.

On June 10 the government left Paris, giving the good example, and the next day all the roads out of Paris were clogged. People said, "If they leave, we'd better leave." The roads were jammed with stalled cars, exhausted horses, and cyclists off their bikes. Between the cars, there were people on foot, and horse-drawn carts, and brewery horses, and plowhorses. There was a woman pushing a bicycle, with a three-year-old girl sitting on her coat on the handlebars, and a ten-year-old boy sitting on the luggage rack over the back wheel.

Those who stayed in the towns and villages were hostile to the few troops who wanted to keep fighting. Why ask for trouble, a battle, shelling? At a town on the Indre, the officer in charge wanted to blow up the bridge, and the *ancient combattants* (old soldiers) assembled and marched to the bridge in military formation and vowed to stand on it until the French troops left, to prevent the destruction of their landmark seventeenth-century bridge.

By June 14 the Germans were in Paris and heading south. On that day, René Cerf-Ferrière, a thirty-eight-year-old veteran of the first war and holder of the *Croix de Guerre,* was mobilized as a reservist and summoned to Montargis, a town due south of Paris and a few miles north of the Loire, for his orders. The Nationale 7, a main north–south road, which went through Montargis, was bumper-to-bumper with cars topped with mattresses, as protection from strafing. There was no more Joffre, thought Cerf-Ferrière, to say, "the hour is over for looking backward." There was a captain behind a desk. "What are the orders, my captain?" Cerf-Ferrière asked.

"You have a bridge to defend."

"A bridge on the Cléry River, my captain. The Cléry is nine feet wide. The bridge is a mile away from the *Nationale 7.*"

"The orders are to defend the bridges."

"The Cléry is a foot deep right now. A tank will have no trouble crossing it with or without a bridge."

"Are your men armed?"

"With hunting rifles."

"Very good. Find some empty bottles, like Perrier bottles. Requisition some gasoline. Fill the bottles, stop them up with a rag, light the rag, and throw the bottles at the tanks."

"But my captain, gasoline—."

"Those are my orders—good-bye."

It was slow going, heading back in the sea of mattresses, each a whitecap bound for sunnier shores. Cerf-Ferrière rounded up his men, reservists like himself, and they filled about thirty Perrier bottles with gas and headed toward the bridge, hunting rifles slung over their shoulders. Cerf-Ferrière wondered what to do. Follow orders or tell the men to go home? A car stopped and an officer got out. There was a woman in the car. "Have you seen my unit," the officer asked, "the Thirty-fourth Infantry?" A captain who'd lost his unit? In the entire 1914–1918 war Cerf-Ferrière had never heard of that. He took his *Croix de Guerre* out of his pocket and said, "In my day, captains were at the head of their troops, not in cars with their wives." "You'll hear from me," the officer said, then got back into the car and drove off. That did it. Cerf-Ferrière told his men that it was pointless to defend the bridge with hunting rifles and Perrier bottles. As for him, he was leaving. They could do what they wanted. Some of them called him a deserter. That was their right, he reflected, as he walked home.

After my father had come to Paris on May 17 and seen the Foreign Ministry archives go up in smoke, he had sent us south to the village of Ustaritz in the Basque country. From a friend at the American embassy he had obtained visas for us. Ustaritz was in the Pyrénées, about ten miles from the Spanish border. We were poised for departure. My mother put me in the Catholic school, a big red house on a hill. My brothers, who were three and four, stayed home. On June 14 my uncle Armand, my father's half brother, came to visit. He was a man in his sixties, a well-known physicist, who in the first war had served as liaison officer with the British troops. He had four sons, all mobilized, and he had heard that two of them had been taken prisoner. Two things he said that afternoon I still remember. He was showing me on a map the route he had taken to get to Biarritz, where he was staying, and pointing out the different towns. "The inhabitants of Épinal are called Spinaliens," he said. "The inhabitants of Tournus are called Tournusgeois." Many years later, I wondered whether he had been telling me that the French have a penchant for needless complications.

The second thing was about the Germans, based on his World War I recollections: "The Germans were very correct. They plundered correctly, they arrested innocent people correctly, and they shot them correctly."

In the meantime, in the world of important events, the gypsy government on June 14 left for Bordeaux, the old city of wine traders on the Gironde River, which had served as provisional capital in the two previous wars. They took back roads, because of the influx of refugees, and arrived shaken by the sights along the way. It was a total rout. Groups of soldiers wandered over the countryside without their officers. The population, like the government, was on the road, without a fixed address. It was all they could do to keep the government caravan together, for at one point they almost lost the Ministry of the Colonies, which had taken a wrong turn. In Bordeaux there was keen competition for hotel rooms. The one consolation was that the food was good and the wine plentiful. Once again the ministries had to find temporary homes. Foreign Affairs settled into the Lycée Longchamps, where the man with the *chiffres* (codes) guarded his strongbox.

In the next two days, over the weekend of June 15 and 16, the Reynaud government unraveled. Reynaud himself was close to nervous collapse. He was fixated on the idea that everything would be all right if only the Americans sent him some planes. He was badgered by the unspeakable Mme. de Portes, who, according to one of the Foreign Affairs men, Jean Chauvel, looked like the maid on her day off. Reynaud began equivocating. He proposed to Weygand that the men lay down their arms in the field, as the Dutch had done, without a formal armistice. Weygand in the meantime was busy blaming the British. "You can't lead an army from London," he said. "When I had Ironside on the phone I would gladly have slapped his face." Weygand told Churchill that the British were lucky to have a built-in antitank ditch—the Channel. And yet it was the irrepressible Weygand who predicted on June 15: "In three weeks' time England's neck will be wrung like a chicken." To which Churchill would reply, in a speech more than a year later: "Some chicken! . . . Some neck!" The smell of Anglophobia hung in the air. On June 4 Pétain had told Bullitt that the British would fight to the last Frenchman. It was a way of rationalizing defeat to say "England dragged us into the war and now they won't fight." Laval constantly complained about British hypocrisy, dishonesty, and stupidity.

Reynaud was planning to leave for Washington as French ambassador. His two cabinet secretaries, Dominique Leca and Gilbert Levaux, went ahead of him, reaching the Spanish border on June 22. The *Guardia Civil* opened their trunks and found Mme. de Portes's jewels and eighteen million francs' worth of gold. Reynaud's henchmen had absconded with the government's secret funds. As Ambassador Bullitt wrote President Roosevelt, "The situation was horrifying since it would be most difficult for him to prove that he had not given Leca orders to do what he had done."

Six days after this incident, on June 28, Reynaud and Mme. de Portes were driving from Bordeaux to a country house in Sainte-Maxime. Nervous and tired, Reynaud abruptly slammed on the brakes; a valise in the back was hurled forward and broke Mme. de Portes's neck, killing her.

At the June 15–16 meeting, the cabinet was divided into those who were for and those who were against an armistice. A leader of the latter group, the minister of the interior, Georges Mandel, who in the first war had been Clémenceau's aide, lost his temper at the afternoon cabinet meeting on June 16, saying, "There are brave men and there are cowards; there are those who want to fight and those who do not want to fight." Camille Chautemps, like Pétain a vice-premier, and a member in good standing of the *République des Camarades* (Republic of Cronies), having been a minister in seventeen governments, replied, "I have no lessons to learn from Monsieur Mandel," which was a coded reference to Mandel's being a Jew. Chautemps said that the city of Blois had been bombed, that there were two hundred victims, and that the killing must be stopped. This feeling was echoed by the generals in the field, who said the army was being cut to pieces and asked for an armistice. At ten that evening, Reynaud convened the cabinet again and said almost offhandedly: "Marshall Pétain is forming a government." President Lebrun closeted himself with Pétain and told him: "Well, now, you must form a government." Like a man pulling a rabbit from his hat, Pétain pulled a list from his briefcase and said: "Here it is." He had been taking job applications all the previous day. It was the 107th government of the Third Republic, and eleven of the seventeen ministers had been in the Reynaud government. The usual squabbles over portfolios followed. Weygand vetoed de Gaulle as undersecretary of war, which was just as well, since de Gaulle left for London on June seventeenth and made his celebrated radio broadcast on the eighteenth. Nor did Weygand want Laval as minister of justice. Laval didn't want to be minister of justice. He wanted Foreign Affairs, which had been given to the pro-armistice and anti-English Paul Baudouin. So, Laval was not even a member of the first Pétain cabinet.

In Bordeaux Pétain's first deed was to ask for an armistice, at 12:30 P.M. on June 17, in a classroom at the Lycée Longchamps, where a microphone was placed in front of him. "With a heavy heart I tell you today that it is necessary to stop the fighting." What could be plainer even though no papers had been signed? All over France, soldiers lay down their arms. *Guerre finie! Krieg fertig!*

His second deed was to order the arrest of the former minister of the interior, Georges Mandel. One of Pétain's political advisers, Raphaël Alibert, a paranoid intriguer with fanatical royalist views, told him that after the formation of the new government Mandel had distributed weapons and money to gunmen and told them to assassinate several ministers. This was a ludicrous accusation, but Pétain believed it. At lunch on June 17, at the Chapon Fin restaurant, where *le tout* Bordeaux convened, two gendarmes marched up to Mandel's table, where he was sitting with the plump and bejeweled Béatrice Bretty. One of them put his hand on Mandel's shoulder and said, *"Monsieur,* follow me." "Will you let me finish my cherries?" Mandel asked. "No, *monsieur,* follow me." He downed his cognac, kissed Mme. Bretty's hand, and left. The charges were proved groundless, and Mandel went to see Pétain to ask for a written apology. "It is regrettable in such a serious situation," he said in his usual blunt way, "for France to be governed by a man who is the puppet of his entourage." All in all, an inauspicious beginning.

When Reynaud, with great relief, turned over the government to Pétain, he wasn't looking that far ahead. Basically he wanted a general the Germans would respect to negotiate the armistice, and what better choice was there than the victor of Verdun? Pétain was an icon you could take from the mantelpiece, dust off, and wind up. In France he was universally loved. For the right, he was the old soldier, traditional and conservative. For the left, he was the symbol of the Republican army, the man who had ended the mutinies of 1917, the man whose first reform had been to see to it that the soup got to the men in the trenches piping hot. The stomach first, strategy second.

The key to understanding Pétain was the year of his birth, 1856. He had lived forty-four years in the nineteenth century. He had lived through the war of 1870 and the Dreyfus case. He embodied an ample portion of the French past. Precocious he was not. He had graduated from the French military academy, Saint-Cyr, 403rd in a class of 412. He was slow in getting promoted, remaining a lieutenant for ten years and seemingly stuck in the ranks of captain and colonel. By 1916, when his hour struck at Verdun, he was sixty. When the war was over, he was a great hero. Streets were named after him, and he sat for an equestrian statue. In his personal life, he was a hit with the ladies. Among his wartime memorabilia were trunks full of love letters. One of his mistresses, Mlle. de Baye, was known as the duchess of Verdun because she had spent her nights at the front.

Pétain's career could be called the triumph of the senior citizen. For when he was received into the Académie Française he was seventy-three, and when he began his political career as minister of war in 1934, he was seventy-eight. He was a beautiful old man, with a straight back, clear blue eyes, a pink complexion, and a white moustache worthy of the Gauls. He was not Nordic- or Germanic-looking, nor was he Latin-looking. He was the essence of Frenchness. The Socialist prime minister Léon Blum, who named him ambassador to Spain in 1939 when he was eighty-three, called him "the most humane of our military leaders." At that time, Colonel de Gaulle wrote in his diary: "Poor Marshal! He's so far gone in senile ambition he would accept anything." De Gaulle also wrote: "Pétain is a great man who died in 1925."

In a sense he lived in the past, refighting old battles and reliving old loves. His apartment in Paris was like an annex of the Army Museum. Everything but the tenant was under glass. The level of his ideas was almost embarrassing, as in "The Chinese, they're yellow, aren't they?" and "The family is good. Alcoholism is bad." Yet Pétain had a long experience of men and the world, and while passing for Olympian and benevolent, he had a hidden side that was cunning and devious.

In 1940 he was eighty-four, and he had an embalmed quality that seemed to set him above factions and party quarrels. In fact, he was in excellent health. To demonstrate his physical vigor, he was photographed lifting a little girl as she held on to his horizontally placed cane with both hands. His masseur said, "His body is like marble," and "He pisses like a fountain." As for his capacity for work, Laval remarked: "Who's talking about work? We need a flag. A flag doesn't do any work. You stand in its shade."

Pétain fit right into the France of 1940, a defeated nation with a stable social system. He had endured, and now the nation would have to endure. And so Pétain came to power, for which he had a great though hidden appetite, and the first thing he did was ask for an armistice. The Poles, who sent men on horseback against German tanks in the last cavalry charge of modern warfare, did not ask for an armistice. The Norwegians, whose ski troops were strafed in the snow by German Stukas, did not ask for an armistice. The Belgians, who blew up their canals and bridges, did not ask for an armistice. Holland and Luxembourg and Greece and Yugoslavia, none of them did either. Only France! Such was Vichy's original sin, according to the theory of the lesser evil. There was always a greater evil than the one that was being committed. It was better to ask for an armistice than continue the slaughter of the French Army. It was better to give up the foreign Jews if that spared the French Jews. In French the slang word for coward is *veau* (calf), and this might be seen as the reasoning of the calves.

On June 15 in the city of Chartres, sixty miles southwest of Paris, there were 800 inhabitants left in a population of 23,000. Those remaining were the elderly, the infirm, and the unscared. Everyone with wheels was gone, and a lot of others had followed on foot. The shopkeepers had pulled down their metal shutters. The bakers had doused their ovens. Fortunately, thought the forty-one-year-old prefect Jean Moulin (a prefect was like a provincial governor, in this case, of the Eure-et-Loire *département,* of which Chartres was the capital), there were not that many mouths to feed. In any case, he had stocked three tons of canned food and eight hundred kilos of bread.

Everything was cut off, gas, water, electricity, and telephones. It hurt Moulin's professional pride to have to show the Germans a city in shambles. He found volunteers to bury the dead who had been piled up in the morgue of Saint-Brice Hospital. On the great circular Place des Épars, with its statue of Marceau, a hero of the Napoleonic wars, Chartres' two main hotels, the Hôtel du Grand

Monarque and the Hôtel de France, were jammed, though the employees had fled. Entire families lay on mattresses in the lobbies and people crowded the stairs. Moulin told them to stay put, there were no more trains or buses. He had to listen to their sob stories. One woman had lost her son. Another had been robbed of six thousand francs. At the Hôtel de France a man had found the key to the wine cellar and was selling the contents at the democratic price of twenty francs a bottle, whatever the vintage— twenty francs for the Château Lafite, twenty francs for the Clos Vougeot, twenty francs for the hundred-year-old brandy—the best bargains of the war.

Moulin looked inside the cathedral, the city's Gothic glory, with its sublime rose window. It too was full of refugees, who reasoned it was the only place that wouldn't be bombed. "It smells bad in here," Moulin thought. "I'd rather risk a bomb than stay in this stinkhole." He had officially broken into two bakeries, where he found plenty of flour, yeast, and salt. Now he stopped by one of them to say hello to the volunteer baker, and he asked to look into the oven, where the loaves were browning. There at least, he thought, was something clean and good and useful. Moulin disliked the baker, who was pro-German and said things like, "The *Boches* are ordinary guys like you and me." But what could he do? He couldn't find anyone else. When he got back to the *préfecture,* he was told that deserting soldiers had stolen his Citroën.

Moulin's prefectoral career had taken him all over France, but he was originally from the city of Béziers, which was about as far south as you could go, a few miles from the Mediterranean. He was an olive-skinned Latin, with straight brown hair combed back, round brown eyes, and a clear, open, intelligent face. You could see that he was the kind who does well in exams. His father, Antoine, a high-school teacher, had been a friend of the great Provençal poet Mistral who wrote in the lilting Provençal language, which, eclipsed by French, was dying out, and Mistral had told Antoine Moulin: "Beans will always be beans, and the frying pan will always be the frying pan."

Born in 1899, Jean Moulin finished law school and became a model civil servant, the youngest *sous-préfet* in France at the age of twenty-six. On one occasion, he delivered a baby in a mountain village. On another, he participated in a bobsled race. All in the line of duty. The only shadow in his life was a bad marriage, for he fell in love with a flirtatious nineteen-year-old girl who often left him alone to pursue a singing career in Paris. After two years he obtained a divorce on the grounds of desertion, and he did not remarry.

Politicians often borrowed bright young men from the prefectoral ranks to serve in their cabinets, and in 1936 Moulin was tapped by Pierre Cot, who was minister of aviation in the Popular Front government of Léon Blum. The question then was what to do about the Spanish civil war. Officially, the spineless, left-wing Popular Front backed away from sending arms to the anti-Franco left-wing Spanish government. But Cot and Moulin were both strongly anti-Franco, and Moulin took charge of a secret program to sell planes to the Republicans which were ostensibly sold to Finland and Brazil. He also recruited volunteer pilots who signed three-month renewable contracts with the Spanish government. Thus, Jean Moulin was part of an underground network of French aid in the fight against Franco.

It was a disheartening experience to be in a government where the fossils called the tune. On one occasion Pierre Cot was urging the formation of a paratroop corps before the council of War, and Pétain, who was presiding, said: "We need soldiers, not tumblers." Moulin returned to his prefectoral career in 1937, and was posted to Eure-et-Loire in 1939.

And now, at 6 A.M., on June 17, Moulin stood in the *préfecture* courtyard in his uniform, flanked by the bishop in his cassock and the mayor in his tri-color sash. "The *préfecture* is open," thought Moulin. "The major services, such as the post office, are open. The German's can't say, as they have said everywhere in their posters: ABANDONED POPULATIONS, TRUST THE GERMAN SOLDIER." An hour later he turned the city over to Colonel Baron von Galtlingen, the new *Feldkommandant* of Chartres. The exchange was polite, even cordial.

That evening, a German officer came to tell Moulin that the colonel wanted to see him. What about? Moulin asked. Women and children have been massacred and raped by French colonial troops, the officer answered. A protocol establishing their responsibility had to be signed by the colonel and the prefect. Moulin said he was convinced that black troops were incapable of such actions, but followed the officer to a house in the Rue du Docteur Maunoury. There, another officer, not the colonel, showed him a statement that said, "In their retreat, black troops went along a railroad track near which, 12 km. from Chartres, the bodies of mutilated and raped women were found." "How do you know they were our men?" Moulin asked. "Because they left some of their equipment behind," the officer said. "How do you know they committed those crimes?" asked Moulin. "The victims were examined by German specialists," the officer responded. "The violence they were subjected to offers all the characteristics of crimes committed by Negroes."

Moulin's smile, which seemed to say, "Call that proof?," enraged the Germans, and the short blond officer who had come to fetch him and who spoke good French, said, "Sign, or you'll find out what happens when you mock German officers." Moulin did not move, and was struck from behind with the barrel of a gun.

This was an interesting moment, because it represented the moment when resistance begins. A man is asked, or ordered, to do something, and he refuses to do it. He knows he is taking a risk, but deep in his gut he cannot comply. He is faced with a moral choice, to give in or not to give in. And if he is a willful, stubborn man, and knows that he is being asked to do something shameful, he refuses to be shamed. Such a moment did not always come in so dramatic a manner. For Edmond Michelet, a teacher in Brive-la-Gaillarde, it came when he happened to read these lines by the poet Charles Péguy: "In wartime he who does not surrender is my man, whoever he is, wherever he comes from, and whatever his party." For André Maurice, a poacher and smuggler in the Jura Mountains who began to help Jews get into Switzerland, it was a sort of professional challenge: "The urge was stronger than I was. It gripped me like the wish to catch a pike or trap a hare. Time and time again, just to irritate the Germans." For the resistance leader Yves Farge, the moment came in Lyon that June when he was on a tram that stopped to let a German motorized column pass. A fellow passenger said in a loud voice, "At last the French are going to learn what order really is." Farge got off the tram in front of the Grand Hotel, where women were waiting to see the German officers come out. He said to one: "You're too old to be a whore." And that for him was the beginning of resistance.

The German officers knocked Moulin down and started kicking him. He told them they were a disgrace to their uniforms. "It's not going to help you to obtain my signature by force," he said. The short blond officer was working himself up into a rage and burst out: "You're just a *raisonneur de français* [French argufier]. You're a nation of degenerates, of Jews and niggers." The tall dark one who had kicked him had a fox terrier beside him, and he started whipping Moulin with the dog's leash. "So you want proof," the blond one said. The two officers pushed him into a car and drove south on the road to Châteaudun, and then took a left to Saint-Georges-sur-Eure. "I should be afraid," thought Moulin, "but it feels too good to breathe fresh air." They reached the hamlet of La Taye, and beyond it, a railroad track. In the courtyard of a farm, under a lean-to, were nine bodies so mutilated you could not tell the men from the women. "Here is our proof," the blond officer said. "Here is what your niggers did." "It's not hard to see," Moulin said, "that these poor people, whose bodies are full of shrapnel, are the victims of bombardments." They took him into a small hangar where he saw something that had once been a woman, without arms or legs, the face a shapeless mass, the hair matted with blood. "Her limbs were chopped off by the blacks," the blond German said. They drove him back to Chartres, where again he refused to sign. They put him in a room with a black prisoner of war. "Now that we know you love niggers we thought you'd like to spend the night with one," the blond officer said. During the night, Moulin had a moment of despair, a lack of faith in his body's ability to take punishment. What if they beat him to the point where he agreed to sign? The floor was covered with broken glass from a bombardment. He picked up a shard and cut his throat, and felt the warm blood running down his chest. Several hours later, two German soldiers looked in and took him to the hospital. The nuns saw that he was not badly hurt and bandaged the cut. As he was getting dressed, the blond German officer came in and told the nun, Sister Henriette,

"You didn't know your prefect has special tastes. He wanted to spend the night with a black, and this is what happened." Afraid of adverse publicity, the Germans took Moulin back to the *préfecture,* where he wrote in the register: "Fifteen hours [3 P.M.]. The mayor of Chartres is asked, in the absence of the mayor of Saint-Georges-sur-Eure, to bury the bodies of nine victims of the bombing of La Taye. There is no question of atrocities imputed to the Senegalese."

In the midst of the general collapse of the French Army, what had happened to the military tradition of never surrendering? To all those slogans and pithy phrases? *On tiendra* (We will hold). *La garde meurt mais ne se rend pas* (The guard dies but does not surrender). The spirit was still alive at Saumur, the cavalry school founded by kings in the eighteenth century, whose motto was *De Materiam, Splendescam*—"Give me the opportunity, and I will shine." Saumur turned out some of the best cavalry officers in the French or any other army. Its Cadre Noir, composed of the best riders, competed in the Olympics and in horse shows around the world. On May 16 King Leopold had sent the royal Belgian stable to take refuge in Saumur. All the king's horses, as well as the princes' Shetland ponies, were unloaded from freight cars.

Saumur happened to be in the direct path of the German advance. It was on the Loire, which, after the Seine, was the second line of defense, about forty miles west of Tours, where the government had camped out. In the Ninth Army battle plan, the Saumur Cavalry Schol had been given a forty-kilometer line of defense along the river, with four bridges to hold. Colonel Michon, commander of the cadet corps, had 2,190 men under his orders, including 786 cadets, young men of nineteen or twenty who had been in uniform for about a month. Green as grass, they had never fired at anything but a target.

On June 12 Weygand ordered a general retreat. On June 15 the Saumur sector was ordered to fall back on Montauban, which was way to the south, about one hundred miles from the Spanish border. Then on June 17, Pétain told them all to stop fighting. But Colonel Michon argued that the school must stand and fight. He had a battle plan, which was to position his troops at the four bridges, and he wanted to carry it out. Don't take my battle away from me! The cadets barely knew how their weapons worked, but Colonel Michon was a man possessed.

The mayor of Saumur, Robert Amy, had visions of the town's total destruction, and was doing all he could to stop the colonel. What, after all, was the use? The Germans were upon them. They had already crossed the Loire both up and downriver from Saumur, and a battle would have no effect whatever on the outcome of the war. So Mayor Amy was driving very slowly through the streets of Saumur in a car with a loudspeaker attached, and telling the townspeople: "There is nothing to fear, Saumur will be declared an open city." The mayor's words were based on a government decision that all cities over twenty thousand would be open cities. Saumur itself contained about fifteen thousand, but if you counted the suburbs, it qualified. In the meantime, Colonel Michon was deploying his men at the four bridges and giving them little pep talks about what a wonderful thing it was to die for France. Colonel Michon told the mayor that he was planning to ignore the open-city provision.

On June 18 Mayor Amy managed to get through to the general in Poitiers who commanded the Ninth Military Region. The general was in a testy mood and said: "I can't change the orders, and I don't give a damn about the open-city business." "Well, at least, *mon général,* allow me to evacuate the population." "No, *monsieur le maire,* Saumur will not be evacuated." "My God," thought the mayor, "they have picked Saumur as the one place in France where a last-ditch battle will be fought." But he never considered disobeying the general's orders. Once again he drove around town with his loudspeaker, and this time the message was: "The population is advised that anyone leaving Saumur will have his home or his office requisitioned." There was, however, one exception. The eight hundred thoroughbreds belonging to the Cadre Noir were evacuated.

Colonel Michon's troops had deployed along their forty-kilometer line, taking position at the bridges and on a little island in the Loire at the entrance to Saumur. On the night of June 19–20, with the Germans approaching, they blew up the Saumur bridge, and the smell of gunpowder hung over the river, its gray waters slowly moving westward out to sea, away from the Germans. On the morning of the twentieth, a motorcycle with a sidecar stopped on the other side of the Loire, and two Germans got off, carrying white flags. They intended to ask for the surrender of the city. The cadets on the island, perhaps not seeing the white flags, perhaps overeager to engage the enemy, opened fire and killed both men. Within minutes, an artillery barrage began to pound the city, whose inhabitants took refuge in their cellars. Commanding the cadets on the island was Lieutenant de Buffevent, pacing up and down, a riding crop in his hand. "My father was killed in 1918 carrying this riding crop and I will be carrying it when I am killed," he said. The cadets answered the artillery barrage with 75mm recoilless cannon and 81mm mortars. They took some losses. One cadet told the lieutenant: "It's very hard to keep fighting next to a dead man." But the day turned to night and the Germans did not cross.

At dawn the next day, June 21, the sleepy cadets awoke and rubbed their eyes. Bare-chested German soldiers in short pants, their rifles slung over their shoulders, were crossing the river on dozens of small rafts. They had built them during the night from doors and oil drums, and they were using shovels for oars. The cadets were outnumbered, and after some fighting that lasted through the morning, it was over. Lieutenant de Bufevent had directed the firing, and when the submachine gun of one of his men jammed, he dropped to his knees to try to fix it, with his riding crop under one arm, and was shot and killed with the jammed weapon still in his hands. The Germans took the island. The cadets put down their weapons, lit cigarettes, and refused to raise their hands.

Upriver, at the bridge at Gennes, motorized and armored cadets attacked German tanks and put several out of commission. The Germans were startled to see the French attacking at this late date. In the town of Saumur itself, the cadets took up position on cafe terraces, on the bandstand in the Place de la République, and in the town hall with its medieval stained-glass windows, to the mayor's horror. But that battle did not take place, for on the afternoon of June 21, Colonel Michon received the order to pull out. He was disappointed, so badly did he want to die on the spot with his boots on, but he obeyed.

The general commanding the German division summoned Mayor Amy to his headquarters in nearby Chinon. "One of my officers who came with a white flag to ask for surrender terms was killed," he said. "This is a violation of the laws of war. We must have reprisals." Mayor Amy said he knew nothing about it, but that he was a veteran of World War I with four citations. At that the German general's tone changed, and he rose and stood at attention. Men who are fighting on opposite sides in a war are enemies, but men who have fought on opposite sides in a previous war are colleagues. "We despise the *Kaninchen* [rabbits] of this war," the general said. The officer who drove Mayor Amy back to Saumur said, "I used to come here often for the horse show. Sad thing, war."

Fifty cadets were killed in the battle of Saumur, and were buried in local cemeteries. One thousand cadets and instructors were taken prisoner. On July 2 they were set free because they had acted courageously.

When General de Gaulle made his broadcast on June 18 vowing to fight on, not many people were listening. The French had tuned in to radio Bordeaux for amistice bulletins. The broadcast was considered so unimportant by the BBC that it did not even make a recording of it. In the big cities not yet invested by the Germans, however, notably Lyon and Marseille, the newspapers printed excerpts of the speech. The word went around that there was this crazy general who had flown to London and was asking other Frenchman to join him. My father heard about it and decided at once to leave for London. He was disgusted with the mismanaged campaign and the way Pétain had caved in. He turned up briefly in Ustaritz to say good-bye to us, and to give my mother our passports with the American visas. Then he went to Biarritz and found a fishing boat that took him to England.

The arrival of the Germans in the Midi, the sunny south of France, was a first. In the previous war they had not gotten past the Marne, occupying only northern France. But on June 19 they entered Lyon, and the prefect, Émile Bollaert, wore a black tie as a sign of mourning. Lyon was an open city, but not everyone was notified. The Senegalese troops in the northern suburb of Limonest fired on the Germans and paid for it dearly. Reports on

German conduct were mixed. They were said to have massacred the Senegalese, against whom they had a grudge for having in the previous war cut off German ears and other appendages for trophies. But in Valence, farther south, they had Sunday Mass said for the French and German dead. (The war was called the *drôle de guerre* [funny war], but there were 100,000 French dead, which was not so funny.) And in a village near Valence, it was said that one of the German twenty-wheel trucks carrying heavy artillery had stopped on a dime to avoid running over the hairdresser's poodle.

The Germans arrived in Ustaritz, which was really about as far as they could go without invading Spain, on or about June 24, I can't remember the exact date. I'm also not sure why we hadn't left ahead of the Germans. I guess my mother was waiting to hear whether my father had made it to England. I do remember that it was early evening, but still light, when I heard the sound of boots hitting cobblestones, and I went to the balcony and saw a Wehrmacht unit, fifty strong, in gray-green uniforms marching down the street, not goosestepping exactly but marching with an exaggerated high step. My brother George had been slow to speak, confused by our trans-Atlantic crossings. Just when he had begun to speak French, we left for Washington, and he had to start learning English. As a result, he exercised his right to remain silent. But at that moment, as I watched the Germans march down the street of our insignificant Basque village, suddenly George was beside me, a four-year-old with big eyes and bangs, dressed in a sailor suit that came from a fashionable Parisian children's clothing shop, Le Petit Navire, and he began shouting at the top of his voice, *"Sales Boches! Sales Boches!"* I was so startled I did not react, but my mother ran out and pulled him back inside. She was so angry that she slapped him, for it was entirely plausible that troops hailed in this manner might respond with their rifles.

When I went to school the next day (the school year in France lasts through June), the Germans had taken it over as their headquarters, and I went home quite pleased at this turn of events. There were two German soldiers sitting outside in the garden, and one of them offered me some chocolate, which I accepted. My hand just reached out and took it, independently of my brain.

My mother told me that these two soldiers had been billeted in our house, and to be polite to them, but not to accept anything they might want to give me. I did not tell her that I had already succumbed, that I was a collaborator, accepting gifts from the enemy.

After the armistice was signed, the southern part of France was declared an unoccupied zone, and the Germans pulled out, singing in their trucks as they rolled out on a fine day in early July. A few days later we left for Spain, which was ravaged by its civil war. I had never seen such poverty. The streets of San Sebastián were full of beggars. One of them had had an arm amputated, and he pushed the stump in our faces as we walked down the street. At the restaurant, our table was next to the big plate-glass window, and a boy about my age pressed his face to the window and watched me eat. We continued through Spain and Portugal to Lisbon, where we waited a couple of weeks for a boat to America, and we spent the rest of the war in Washington. In retrospect, I'm sorry we didn't stay in France and live through the occupation years. It was one of those rare times when everyone was faced with a moral choice, even though the choice most people made was "life as usual."

As for my father, he reached London and joined the Lorraine Squadron in the RAF. In 1942 he was sent to South Africa to a training school for bomber pilots. On the way home his ship was torpedoed off Mozambique and he spent two days in a lifeboat. In a letter to his mother that I recently found, he described the experience: "We were in a small, slow boat heading around the Cape and we must have been an ideal target. We never saw him, but he did his job very conscientiously. First he fired a torpedo at the starboard bow, then he went around and hit the other side in the middle. Fortunately he took his time and by the time the second torpedo arrived we were already in the lifeboats. The second torpedo blew up the boiler and the ship sank in two minutes. After picking up the wounded, the lifeboats headed toward shore as night fell. But the sea was choppy and we were all separated. A plane appeared in the distance, causing great excitement in the lifeboat, but flew out of sight without seeing us. It was heartbreaking. We were hungry, cold, and soaked through. Sharks followed us and the sea got ugly. We had to drop the sail and row across the waves to keep from capsizing. It was very discouraging to row without advancing. But in the morning we raised the sail again. Fortunately we had with us a young man from Tahiti who had been in the copra trade in the islands and who lived on his boat. He turned out to be an admirable pilot. The spotters in the bow were too optimistic and constantly saw lights that did not exist. Water splashed into the lifeboat and we constantly had to bail. There was a panic close to mutiny when the sea got choppy and some of the sailors wanted to drop the sail and throw out the floating anchor. But we insisted on going toward shore in spite of heavy waves. That night a passing firefly gave us hope. I thought I saw Arab houses brilliantly lit, but it was a mirage. When the sun rose, I seemed to see far off a grayish line. I didn't say anything, not wanting to raise false hopes. But the line became more visible, others saw it, and we realized it was the shore. It's an unforgettable impression to see land. It makes up for all the misfortunes of shipwreck. I am writing this in front of a good fire in the RAF mess on a base where we are flying to become accustomed to conditions in England.''

My father took part in eight bombing missions over Germany. Then, on April 10, 1943, while on a training flight, he lost his way in the fog over England, but wanting to get back to his base, he flew until the plane was out of fuel. The forced landing in the countryside killed him. He was buried in the Catholic section of the Fakenham cemetery outside London. Over and out.

VICHY

Photograph permission of VAGA

After June 17, when Marshal Pétain asked for a stop to the fighting, the government remained in Bordeaux in total confusion. There were those who wanted to sign an armistice right away, those who wanted to keep fighting in France, and those who wanted to carry on the war in North Africa. On June 19 Bordeaux was bombed, as a reminder of the reality principle. On the morning of June 20, about fifty members of parliament gathered for a discussion held at the Lycée Anatole France. Adrien Marquet, the deputy-mayor of Bordeaux, who was horrified by the previous night's damage to his elegant seventeenth-century city, said: "We must stop this butchery! Enough! We must negotiate." "But England is our ally," the Socialist deputy André Le Troquer responded. "She is continuing the fight and we are committed not to make a separate peace." "England," replied the Radical-Socialist deputy Jean Mistler, "but England will be on her knees in two months." "How can you say that?" Le Troquer asked. "Don't we have an empire? Don't we have a fleet?" François Pietri, onetime minister of the navy, observed that "you can't win a war with the fleet." Le Troquer said: "Some of us want to continue the fight in North Africa." "The government is talking about an armistice," agreed the right-wing deputy Louis Marin. "You don't sign an armistice under the threat of enemy bayonets." These parliamentary leaders were in a state of *désarroi*, a stronger word in French than the English "disarray."

The government seemed to be splitting in three directions. A plan was formed that Pétain would remain in France to negotiate with the Germans, while the cabinet ministers and President Lebrun left for Algiers aboard a destroyer, and those members of parliament who wished to do so could board the liner *Massilia* in Bordeaux and sail for Casablanca. This plan was in fact a cunningly laid trap set by the Anglophobic head of the French Navy, Admiral Jean Darlan. It was Darlan who urged the deputies to leave and Darlan who gave the *Massilia* clearance to embark on June 21. He reasoned, and rightly so, that the anti-armistice, anti-Pétain deputies would be the ones who would want to leave, perhaps to form a government-in-exile in North Africa. At the last moment, Lebrun and the ministers were asked to stay in Bordeaux, but thirty deputies left aboard the *Massilia*—good riddance, thought the pro-armistice faction.

By the time they left, the armistice delegation, headed by Marshal Pétain and General Charles Huntziger, whose Second Army had failed to stop the Germans in the Ardennes, was already en route for an unknown destination. This turned out to be a clearing in the Forest of Compiègne, about fifty miles northeast of Paris, at a place called Rethondes. It was the exact spot where the World War I armistice had been signed, on November 11, 1918, in Marshal Foch's railroad car, underlining the cyclical nature of such events. After 1918 the car had been the main exhibit in a museum built near the railway siding. Now the car was returned to the siding for further use.

Anyone who saw the newsreel of Hitler's little jig of glee, which was not unlike the jigs of football players who have scored a touchdown, will understand the strong component of revenge in the "Hundred-Year War." To reenact as the winner the scene where twenty years earlier you were the loser was irresistible. Having been beaten in the field, France had no leverage for negotiation. Pétain had no choice but to accept the German terms, which were seen at the time as catastrophic. In retrospect, though, it wasn't such a bad deal. Hitler made some rather remarkable concessions. He did not demand the important (and intact) French fleet, which was allowed to remain in its home ports, disarmed. He left the French empire, including North Africa, unoccupied.

And he left two fifths of France unoccupied, so that the French state, and a French government, would continue to exist.

Hitler wasn't making these concessions because of a generous nature, but becaue he was hoping for a *modus vivendi* with England that would allow him to attack Russia. By letting the French govern themselves, he was saving himself the trouble and the manpower. By keeping hands off the colonies, he was averting a pro-Gaullist rebellion in North Africa. By leaving the French their fleet, he was sending England a signal that England didn't pick up. Fearful that the Germans would break their promise and seize the French fleet when they felt like it, the British on July 3 attacked French vessels that were stationed at the Mers el-Kébir naval base near Oran in Algeria, two battleships and two battle cruisers, destroying three of the four. It was a show of British resolve, but it made the French wonder who their real enemy was, for 1,297 French sailors were killed.

To the French, the armistice seemed advantageous. It meant that everyone could go home, that is, the soldiers who had not been captured and the millions of refugees. It meant a return to normality, in that the French state was in good working order, and it was important to keep it that way. In the strongly centralized French system you had about 1,600,000 civil servants who would have lost their jobs and their pensions. You had, in addition, railroad men, mailmen, schoolteachers, actors, and singers who in one way or another worked for the state. It would have been anarchy to tell the civil servants to stop serving, the railroad men to sabotage the trains, the mailmen to tear up the mail, the teachers to close the schools, the actors to stop acting, and the singers to stop singing. It wasn't a question of being pro- or anti-German, but of reaching an arrangement that allowed this splended state apparatus to maintain itself.

It all corresponded to the French love of the arrangement. Who could doubt that this was the correct way to proceed? You gave a little, you got a little. In retrospect the men of Vichy could argue that keeping North Africa free of Germans had permitted the Allies to land there in November 1942. They could argue that the equally German-free unoccupied zone of France permitted the organization of the first resistance groups. A lot of Frenchmen believed that Pétain and de Gaulle were working together, as sword and shield, that they too had an arrangement.

At the same time, critics of the Third Republic saw in the Pétain regime a counterrevolution. It was not only an arrangement, but an improvement over the discredited and defeated *République des Camarades*. Pétain's government would be honest, upright, and virtuous, like the old man himself, without finagling or intrigue. There would be a return to tradition, to family, to working the land, to the old values. In fact, the bankers and technocrats who replaced the parliamentarians in the government represented the revenge of the French business class on the social programs of the Popular Front. And the return to the land was a way of playing into the German conception of France as the Garden of the New Europe. The rhetoric was one of counterrevolution, but the methods, such as the inevitable cabinet reshufflings, remained those of the Third Republic. In a little over a year, between July 1940 and September 1941, there were five *remaniements,* four ministers of foreign affairs, and five ministers of the interior.

And as always, there was a bill to pay, in terms of having done the sensible rather than the honorable thing. When General Huntziger, after signing the armistice, ran into his friend the marquis de Moustier, the marquis told him that he has lost a son in the funny war. "Poor lad," said Huntziger, "and to say that he died for nothing." "That was why I was against Vichy," Moustier said. "Because that 'nothing' was France." The honorable thing was to say, "You've beaten us, now you take over, because we're not going to do your dirty work for you." But the Pétain regime had a political agenda, it was eager to govern, and it rationalized defeat into an opportunity for reform.

The first example of doing the Germans' dirty work was right there in the armistice, in the "surrender on demand" clause. The French, who prided themselves on their right of asylum, had to turn over to the Germans their anti-Nazi refugees, "on demand." And this was the thin end of the wedge that would lead to the deportation of the Jews. Another clause that was hard to swallow was that all French prisoners of war would remain in German hands until the conclusion of peace. This would lead to further concessions in terms of providing Germany with forced labor in exchange for prisoners.

Also, whatever was not spelled out in the armistice was up for grabs. When on June 26 Hitler visited Strasbourg, capital of Alsace, and saw the swastika flag flying from the cathedral steeple, he asked: "What do you think? Must we return this jewel to the French?" Answering his own question, he said: "No, never." In July the frontier was simply rolled back to its 1914 limits. Alsace and Lorraine were annexed, and were governed by *Gauleiters*. All France could do was to protest in vain to the Armistice Commission in Wiesbaden.

In both provinces there was a heavy-handed effort at Germanization, on the theory that people can be bent and bullied into the desired shape. To speak French was punishable by fines or worse, and people were arrested for saying *merci* instead of *danke schön*. There was a drive to eradicate all evidence of French influence, no matter how trivial. Men were arrested for wearing the *béret basque*. Street names were changed. The Place de la République in Metz became Adolf Hitler Platz. The statues of military heroes, like that of General Rapp in Colmar, were destroyed. The cult of the Führer was proclaimed. Posters in offices said: *(MORGENS GRÜSSE ICH DEM FÜHRER. UND ABENDS DANKE ICH DEM FÜHRER)* (In the morning I salute the Führer. And in the evening I thank him).

Those citizens considered difficult to assimilate, such as the French-speaking, the religious, and the Jews, were simply told to leave. An estimated half a million people were expelled from Lorraine, and 120,000 from Alsace. They arrived by the trainload in unoccupied France, having left everything behind.

Two other *départements,* Nord and Pas-de-Calais, which were on the Channel and on the Belgian border, respectively, were placed under the command of the German military authorities in Brussels. The 300,000 refugees who had fled the area were not allowed to return. Aside from Alsace and Lorraine and the two northernmost *départements,* Vichy was supposed to govern with a free hand, but in fact was subject to the whims of the occupier. The German attitude was "let the French govern themselves, but if we want something, let them be quick about it." The German appetite for goods was huge—they took the gold that had been entrusted to France by the Belgian government, they dismantled entire oil refineries and shipped them to Germany, and they made the French pay for the cost of occupation. In August 1940 Pierre

Laval, by then minister of state, was told that the French were responsible for feeding the German occupation troops. When Laval said that wouldn't leave much for the French, he was told: "You'll still have more than we did in the winter of 1917–1918." It was a German reflex to justify oppressive measures by invoking World War I hardships. There was also a healthy dose of German contempt, for at about the same time, Laval went to see Field Marshal Walther von Brauchitsch, Commander in Chief of the German Army, and to show France's goodwill, offered to go to war against England. The German general sneered: "We don't need your help, which in any case would amount to nothing."

Another form of contempt was the routine and casual breaking of French laws. In the port of Saint-Malo, the German commander made French sailors serve aboard German ships in violation of the law barring them from serving on a foreign ship. Under the terms of the armistice, France was allowed to keep an army of 100,000 men, without any tanks or artillery of greater caliber than 75mm. The farce of "French sovereignty" came out in a minor incident involving a general in the Armistice Army. On September 13, 1940, a Luftwaffe troop was crossing the town of Valence, on the Rhône River south of Lyon, when it marched past the general and failed to salute him. The general complained to Vichy, which delivered a protest to the Wiesbaden Armistice Commission, with a request for disciplinary action against the German officer leading the detachment. The reply: Only the German High Command has the right to judge the correctness of German officers.

In any case, as a result of the armistice, which was vague in the extreme except for a few broad provisions, Vichy had to improvise a style for dealing with the Germans, a style which all too often consisted of weaseling, wheedling, and whining. The master of this style was of course Pierre Laval, who finally came into the government as minister of state on June 23. Pétain said it was better to have him in than out. Once in, he plotted the demise of the Third Republic and the policy of collaboration with Germany.

Laval strikes me as the most interesting political figure of the Third Republic. He is not the villain I thought he was when I was younger and saw everything about Vichy and Gaullism in black

and white. There is even a certain stature in his wrongheaded-
ness, for which he paid the well-known forfeit. It was often said
that the man was like the name, which reads the same backward
and forward, but in fact he was consistent to the point of pighead-
edness. He was convinced that Germany would win the war long
after it became apparent that Hitler's overreaching had lost it. His
vision was blurred by his dislike of England and his belief that
Germany was Europe's only defense against Bolshevism. Again,
it was the theory of the lesser evil.

Laval's pacifism was also consistent. In World War I, the army
had put his name on the *Carnet Bille,* the list of "unreliable" politicians who were placed under surveillance. As a deputy from the
working-class suburb of Aubervilliers, he had the choice of enlist-
ing or not. He pleaded varicose veins and was nicknamed "Pierre
Loin-du-Front" (Pierre far-from-the-front) by the local paper in
his district. He had the postwar French dread of another conflict,
and his between-the-wars speeches often used the imagery of death,
of the "hundreds of thousands of wooden crosses . . . scattered
throughout the cemeteries." On the day Germany invaded Poland
he told a friend, "There will be millions of corpses."

He came from the heartland, having been born in 1883 in the
village of Châteldon near Vichy. His father was one of those village entrepreneurs who has fingers in several pies: He ran a grocery store, a café, and the one-man post office. He bought and
sold livestock. Here is Pierre Laval explaining himself: "I am the
only son of a Châteldon cattle merchant. I began as an apprentice
butcher. . . . Thanks to a priest, I ploughed my way through my
studies as one ploughs the earth. I finally became a lawyer. Ah,
those early days! Two francs per consultation, damp shoes, hunger. I entered politics. I succeeded. I invested my money wisely.
Today I am rich . . . I am a man of the soil, a member of a true
peasant family."

Laval was an ugly little man, stooped and disheveled, his fingers yellow from chain-smoking, with a swarthiness that might
have gone back to the Arab occupation of France. But he had a
lively mind and a warm and unpretentious manner. In fact, he
managed to charm the crusty Henry Stimson, who wrote in his
diary on October 23, 1931, when he was President Hoover's sec-

retary of state: "Laval stands in a class by himself for frankness and directness and simplicity, and he is different from all other Frenchmen with whom I have negotiated in those respects." That year, 1931, Lavel was *Time* magazine's Man of the Year.

He also had a remarkable generosity of spirit, and was lacking in vindictiveness and meanness. Of course, in the political climate of the Third Republic, when a small group of men took turns governing, it was smart to be on good terms with colleagues of various political persuasions and to make as few enemies as possible. But with Laval it went further than parliamentary conviviality, and to illustrate this trait I will jump ahead to August 1941. A Legion of French Volunteers (LVF) had been formed in July to fight with the Germans on the Russian front. Laval was invited to attend a parade in a barracks in Versailles on August 27, to celebrate the departure of the first volunteers. After the parade, he toured the barracks, tasting the soup in the kitchen. In the crowd there was a young man named Paul Collette who had joined the LVF in the hope of killing a leading collaborator. His moment had now come, and he fired at Laval.

Pierre Barragué was the surgeon on duty that day at the municipal hospital of Versailles, when a phone call from an intern asked him to come at once and operate on the seriously wounded Laval. One bullet had hit him in the shoulder, and another was lodged in his lung and was causing blood spurts. Expecting to die, Laval was calmly dictating his will. A German officer came up and said, "Sir, your assassin has been arrested. We shall shoot him at once." "Don't do that," Laval said, "I beg you, don't do that. It would be a great mistake. You don't understand the reaction of the French public as I do—" He started spitting blood and could not go on. The X ray showed that the bullet had stopped a fraction of an inch from his heart, practically touching the forward face of the left ventricle. Barragué decided not to remove it, because Laval was a heavy smoker and his lungs were not healthy. He succeeded in cleaning and closing the thoracic wound. There were no antibiotics then, and Laval ran a fever of 104 for a few days. When he asked to see his temperature chart, they had to forge one so as not to scare him. The pulmonary congestion that followed would have killed a weaker man, but he recovered. Dr. Barragué explained that Laval owed his life to the contraction of his heart at the moment the bullet entered his body. The bullet missed him because of that single beat, after which the heart muscle relaxed over the bullet. Laval thought that this arrangement between the bullet and his heart was somehow fitting for a man whose political life had been devoted to finding *modi vivendi*. Sentenced to death that October, Collette was reprieved when Laval petitioned Marshal Pétain for mercy.

Laval had the quality of mercy. But the same man who could forgive his assassin was also responsible for the arrest and deportation of thousands of Jews and other refugees. This was because Laval was so sure of his own cunning and shrewdness and power of persuasion that he thought he could get the better of the Germans. And in applying his cunning and shrewdness he found himself doing terrible things. This was what came of having been in and out of the government from 1914 to 1940, of swinging from left to right, of being in this cabinet and that cabinet as minister of this and minister of that, of finally becoming prime minister and running the country as he would have run his father's grocery. It gave him a low opinion of human nature and a high opinion of his abilities as a schemer.

Of course, he was doing it for France, although some of his fellow politicians said he was also helping himself. It was said that as a raiser of cattle, he had profited from the clause in the Versailles Treaty that transferred German livestock to France. Then, when a gunpowder factory in La Courneuve outside Paris exploded, land values dropped in that area and Laval bought land. Then, having found mineral properties in the water of his hometown, Châteldon, Laval had it bottled; and it was by merest chance that the state-owned railroad included on its dining-car menus this little-known bottled water. Edouard Herriot, the prototypical Third Republic politico, mayor of Lyon, twice prime minister, president of the Chamber of Deputies, with his erudition and his self-indulgence, his cultivated mind and his great paunch, said of Laval: "Laval is one of those people who buy a garage and exchange it for a building, which he exchanges for a farm, which he exchanges for a collection of paintings. And each time he keeps a car, an apartment, a cow, or a Rembrandt."

This may have been sour grapes, because Laval was a clever businessman. He had two nicknames. One was *le bougnat* (the coal merchant) because Châteldon was in the Auvergne, and he had a thick, down-home, slurred Auvergnat accent with elongated dipththongs and audible final syllables; all the Parisian coal merchants were supposed to be Auvergnats, and Laval was like one of those cheerful, soot-covered, obliging *bougnats,* ready to climb stairs day or night to make their deliveries for a small payment. The other was *maquignon* (horse trader), but the kind of horse trader who uses some shoe polish to camouflage the sores on his nags, and sells you a stallion that will die of rickets within two weeks. He sold the French into not getting involved in Ethiopia, although he had to give away a piece of the French Sahara to placate Mussolini, a rather large piece, about sixty thousand square miles. But he always had a reason, which in this case was that "Mussolini couldn't grow a dozen bananas in that African desert, and from now on Italy will have to pay for its policing instead of France."

He was capable of real brilliance and foresight, as when he sold Stalin on a policy vital to French interests. This took place in 1935, when he was foreign minister. At that time the French Communist party was following the Comintern line of voting against all defense spending. The Communists called themselves "supporters of revolutionary defeatism," and said that even if France were invaded, they would not fight. Laval was a pacifist, but knew that to keep the peace France needed a strong army. In May he went to Moscow to sign a Franco-Soviet pact, and upon meeting Stalin, proposed that the Soviet leader make a statement asking the French Communists to change their attitude. Stalin said, "It is up to your government to make them change it. You are the masters in your home. Look at Turkey: Our comrades are persecuted, sewn into bags, and thrown into the Bosporus. As sad as it makes me, I maintain good relations with Ankara."

In fact, Stalin was caught between the need to remain faithful to the Comintern line of the class struggle, and his fears concerning the rise of Hitler's Germany. So, when Laval kept urging him to say something, he agreed to think it over. The statement, drafted by Laval, said: "Stalin understands and fully approves the policy of national defense being followed by France in order to maintain its armed strength at the level required by its security."

That evening, May 15, a Kremlin official approached Laval and said: "Comrade Stalin thinks it is enough to say that he understands, because, of course, if he understands, he approves." Laval replied that he knew something about grammar too, and after some further discussion Stalin accepted the phrasing "understands and fully approves." No sooner was the statement made public than the French Communists adopted the new line. But Laval, who a month later became prime minister as well as foreign minister, foolishly did not follow up. He did not ask parliament to ratify the Franco-Soviet pact, and he did not move ahead with a military pact, both of which would have contained Hitler, for fear of provoking Hitler. The pact was ratified a year later, when he was out of office, replaced by the Popular Front government that the Stalin statement had helped create. For the new Communist line of supporting French rearmament made them acceptable to the parties of the bourgeois left. And that was the trouble with Laval, who followed a moment of brilliance with a failure of nerve. As Francis Bacon put it, "Nothing doth hurt more in a state than that cunning men pass for wise."

And yet there was nothing low about Laval's motives. He sincerely believed that he knew what was best for France. He understood the French, he knew their touchstones and talismans. In 1940 the nation was in a state of shock. He saw himself as a trustee in bankruptcy. He would do the best he could. Obviously the Germans, who had crushed France in a matter of weeks, were unbeatable. The smart thing for a horse trader to do was to put his money on the winner. And although they had the muscle, he didn't think they had the brains. He would deal with them as he had dealt with the others, with cunning and the gift of gab.

Even though he was unpopular and mistrusted, even though an assassin had tried to kill him, Laval felt that he was the only one who could handle the Germans, with the help of the old man he had propped up as a sort of useful idiot. "The French never realize that I have to compromise with the Germans and trick them," he said. "With the Germans we have to use the tactics of a carpet peddler," he said. "It is necessary that I remain in order that

France shall not be handed over to a *Gauleiter*," he said. "It is I who must always repair the damage," he said. "I'm like a down quilt," he said, "I can take blows."

The Germans, in the meantime, had mixed feelings about Laval. They wanted him in power because he was willing to work with them, he was still the *bougnat* willing to climb stairs, willing to cross Europe at a moment's notice to listen to Hitler's tirades. But at the same time he was the *maquignon,* always trying to put something over on them. As Hans Hemmen, von Ribbentrop's Paris representative for economic questions, put it at his trial in Nuremberg: "We were convinced that Laval, with his great mental superiority, his tremendous knowledge, his amazing skill, and also his ability to approach his opponent from the human side, would reduce to a fraction all the demands made upon him and would probably defer the execution of such demands."

But although the Germans complained about him, Laval's policy remained one of consorting with the enemy. He was no less a courtier for trying to dupe them. This was partly out of a need to remain in power that pushed all scruple aside. Governing was his trade. Not only did he know how to do it, he needed to do it, just as collaborationist journalists needed to see their by-lines. Political inactivity was unthinkable. And so, in the name of duping the Germans, Laval was led into shameful policies, and his message trickled down to the ranks. The policeman should have said, "I am not going to arrest people in their homes in the middle of the night because of their race." But he did not say it. The lawyer-civil servant should have said, "I am not going to draft legislation depriving people of their basic human rights because of their race." But he did not say it. The system was in place and the example came from above. It came from a man who had convinced himself that he was indispensable. But as Clémenceau once said: "The cemeteries are full of indispensable men."

By way of contrast, let us consider the destiny of Georges Mandel, whom we last saw trying to finish his cherries at the Chapon Fin in Bordeaux. Mandel's real name was Louis Rothschild, but he took his mother's name in 1902, when as a very young man he wrote for left-wing publications. You could not have a name that rang of great wealth when you wrote about the oppression of the masses. Mandel had been an odd, puny, bookish child who on his thirteenth birthday asked for a subscription to the *Journal Officiel,* the French equivalent of the *Congressional Record.* In 1917, at the age of thirty-two, he was Clémenceau's chief of cabinet, a walking "facts on file," but also disdainful and insolent; he alienated a lot of people. However, after the war, he became a deputy-mayor from Lesparre in Gironde. In the Chamber of Deputies he was abrasive, insulting the military by calling them brain-dead. He served as minister of the colonies and minister of the post office, which included overseeing the government-run radio and television networks. He was said to have files on everybody through a spy network. Cartoonists pictured him listening at doors and rummaging through wastebaskets. He was known as the "Sinister Minister."

Something of Mandel's years with Clémenceau had rubbed off, however, for he was fiercely anti-appeasement. On the day of the German invasion, he was made minister of the interior. People said, "He's a bastard, but he's an energetic bastard." The anti-Semitic right had always hated Mandel, and hated him even more when he ordered the arrests of a number of right-wing defeatists. One of those arrested was Armand Thierry de Ludre, a salon fascist. Now it happened that when de Ludre was being marched to a prison south of Orléans, he could not keep up because he had asthma, and a guard, thinking he was trying to escape, shot him. Although the troops in charge of the prisoners were under army command, the right held Mandel responsible, and considered the death of one of their own as a score to settle.

After his arrest and release in Bordeaux, Mandel was one of the thirty deputies who took the *Massilia* to Morocco. As a former minister of the colonies, it was natural for him to want to continue to fight the Germans from France's overseas empire. Perhaps he saw himself as the leader of a government-in-exile. The *Massilia* arrived in Casablanca on June 24. Mandel went to see the British consul in Rabat to explore the possibility of going to England. For this, he was placed under house arrest by the French commander in Morocco, General Auguste Noguès. As it turned out, Mandel would spend the rest of his life in captivity.

He and his companion, the buxom Mme. Béatrice Bretty, were

taken under guard to the resort of Ifrane in the Rif Mountains. When the *Massilia* returned to France with the other twenty-nine deputies, Mandel remained in Morocco to face the charge of trying to establish a government in North Africa with British help. His trial took place in Meknès, where an independent-minded judge dismissed the case for lack of evidence. He was then flown back to France and interned in various *résidences surveillées* until October 1941, when he joined other prominent Third Republic detainees—Blum, Daladier, Gamelin, and Reynaud—in a military fortress near the Spanish border, the Fort du Portalet, where for the moment we will leave him.

In the meantime, back in Bordeaux, the men of the Pétain government were looking for a home. Paris was out, the Germans did not want them in the capital, "for technical reasons." Lyon was out, because Pétain disliked its mayor, Edourd Herriot, who seemed to sum up all the flaws of the Third Republic. They decided on Clermont-Ferrand, where Laval owned a newspaper and a printing plant, and they moved there on June 28. William Bullitt came to visit, and caught the mood: "The French leaders desire to cut loose from all that France has represented during the past two generations," he reported. "Their physical and moral defeat has been so absolute that they have accepted completely for France the fate of becoming a province of Nazi Germany. Moreover, in order that they may have as many companions in misery as possible they hope that England will be rapidly and completely defeated. Their hope is that France may become Germany's favorite province."

Clermond-Ferrand, however, was inconvenient. There was no office space, and the workers in the big Michelin plant might prove to be troublesome neighbors. Because the Pétain government was a puppet government, it could not reside in a normal city with a normal cross-section of the population, some friendly, some hostile. It had to find a place that was quiet and out of the way, with plenty of hotels, without bustle, and without a working-class population.

The resort town of Vichy, where ladies with triple chins and gentlemen with cirrhotic livers came to take the waters, was a possibility. It was a town that was also a brand name, a town of twenty thousand, not even a *sous-préfecture,* though during the season it doubled in size. Built around a spacious rectangular park were many hotels, side by side like row houses, along with baths, casinos, and tearooms. There were no smokestacks, and very little public transportation. Vichy had an operetta atmosphere, with its daily band concerts, its well-dressed and well-heeled cure-seekers, and its uniformed bellhops and maids whom one expected at any moment to break out into song, in waltz time.

President Lebrun observed that "if we go to Vichy, everyone will say we're a casino government. Everyone will say, 'They are only there for the season.' " But Laval liked the idea. Vichy was only eight miles from his hometown of Châteldon. Pétain said he had always liked living in hotels, and told (at some length) the story of how he had spent quite a bit of time in a hotel in Quimper during World War I. In any case, Vichy it was, and after all their wandering, the men of the government were glad to find a home, arriving on July 1 and 2. Each ministry had its hotel. The Ministry of War was in the Thermale Palace; Education, in the Plaza; Finance, in the Carlton; Navy, in the Helder; Colonies, in the Angleterre; and Marshal Pétain, in the Hôtel du Parc, facing the bulbous Moorish cupola of the main casino and the park's tall plane trees. The rooms had wrought-iron balconies, the walls were hung with blue or pink toile de Jouy, and the tables in the lobby were lacquered white wood. Madame Pétain, a lantern-jawed, square-shouldered old lady, reminiscent of a nineteenth-century armoire, was placed in a different hotel, the Majestic.

On July 4 Léon Blum arrived in Vichy and went to the Petit Casino, where the deputies gathered to discuss events. The topic of the moment was the thirty deputies who had fled on the *Massilia* and were now back, except for Mandel. Were they traitors? Had the journey aboard a French naval vessel been arranged by the government? The next day, Blum ran into Laval. It was like the old order bumping into the new. Blum, the first Socialist prime minister in the history of France, and the first Jew, whose Popular Front government had given the working class a forty-hour week and paid vacations, and a Ministry of Leisure; who had done so much for the working man that right-wing reactionaries began to say, "Better Hitler than Blum." And Laval who, Blum was sure,

intended to make France a carbon copy of Germany, while the
nation itself was inert and taciturn, like a patient under ether. Laval
was manipulating the ambitious old man Pétain, who liked and
wanted political power.

Laval was surprised to see Blum, for the newspaper *Paris-Soir*
had announced that he had fled to New York. "What of your
friends who fled on the *Massilia*?" Laval asked. "They are the
ones who wanted war, this foolish, this criminal war." Blum was
startled by the change in Laval's manner. An unbelievable arrogance puffed up his small person, as in the La Fontaine fable "The
Frog That Wanted to Become an Ox." With great certainty Laval
flung out opinions and verdicts: "I do . . . I say . . . I refuse . . .
That's the way it is . . ." When would the Socialist newspaper
be allowed to reappear? "When I say so," Laval replied. "No
newspaper will reappear if it shows the slightest reticence about
my policies. The press must follow me absolutely, uncondition-
ally."

What struck Blum was the malice which all his words and gestures exuded. Laval's fall from power in 1936 had bred a need for
revenge and reprisals, and he could now give vent to his resentment. Blum thought of the celebrated words of Cardinal de Retz
about the king's minister Mazarin: "He is the first to have introduced dishonesty into the Ministry."

In the next few days, Laval lobbied the deputies and senators.
Blum could not explain the change he saw in these men. It was
as though they had been dipped in a toxic bath, emerging as mu-
tants. They were resigned, discouraged, fearful. Laval had not so
much convinced them as infected them. There was also a scram-
ble for spoils—an embassy, a *préfecture*. Already seeing themselves as redundant, the legislators were saying: "Yes, we'll
continue getting our salaries, but what about our pensions?"

It was clear that Laval was going to succeed in abolishing the
constitution of 1875 and substituting an authoritarian regime. The
deputies continued to meet at the Petit Casino on the Rue Foch
while the senators met in the Salle des Sociétés Médicales on the
Avenue Thermale. But not everyone was there to join in the scuttling operation. Captain Félix Grat, deputy of Mayenne, had been
killed on May 13 in a counterattack on the Moselle River. Second

Lieutenant Paul Saint-Martin, deputy of Gers, had been killed on June 15 in Toulouse when his plane crashed.

On the morning of July 9 the deputies went to the Grand Casino and voted to revise the constitutional laws, by a vote of 395 to 3. André Le Troquer, a Socialist deputy who had gone to Casablanca on the *Massilia,* said: "I didn't know there were so many cowards and traitors in my party." In the afternoon it was the senators' turn, and the vote was 229 to 1 for revision. During the deliberations, one of the senators put the time to good use by writing souvenir postcards to his constituents in Creuse. Another, the sixty-nine-year-old marquis de Chambrun, great-grandson of Lafayette, whose son René had married Laval's daughter, was the single holdout. Although Chambrun was a conservative Catholic, he believed in the Declaration of the Rights of Man, and refused to throw his shovelful of dirt on the Third Republic's coffin. Then, on July 10, both chambers convened in the Grand Casino and voted 569 to 80 to give full powers to Pétain. The Third Republic was defunct. It had lasted seventy years and had ended as it had begun, in the midst of invasion.

On July 13 President Lebrun, having become irrelevant, received a visit from Marshal Pétain, who said: "*Monsieur le président,* the painful moment has arrived. You have served the nation well, and yet the Assembly vote creates a new situation. I am not your successor because this is the start of a new regime." Lebrun did not officially resign. He simply left for his son-in-law's house at Vizille, near Grenoble, where he went for drives in the country and ruminated over whether Pétain had taken power legally.

It was a curious situation, thought Jules Jeanneney, the seventy-six-year-old president of the Senate, who went back far enough to have served in one of Clémenceau's cabinets. The two chambers of parliament had turned themselves into contemplative orders. Pétain would now govern without a legislature, which would assemble only at his request. He would of course meekly obey all German demands. Soon Vichy would be full of undesirables. All the hidden ambitions would surface. Look at the people he had already brought in—Laval, an amoral ruffian without culture or conscience, Darlan, known as *l'amiral au mouillage* (the admiral at anchor, because it was said he had never been to sea), and

Alibert, a failure at everything, who couldn't get elected dogcatcher. They were already thinking of taking action against those they held responsible for France's defeat. They were already giving speeches that began, "The demagogues who lied to you," followed by twenty minutes of full-blown demagoguery.

It did not take long, Jeanneney felt, to see what a farce Vichy was. The exorbitant occupation payment of 400 million francs a day was coughed up without a murmur. On September 3 Vichy put out a decree allowing the arrest of anyone regarded as "dangerous for national defense." Jeanneney knew what that meant: Operation Scapegoat. And that month they were arrested and soon brought to trial—Blum, Daladier, Gamelin, Mandel, and Reynaud. Jeanneney could not help admiring, by contrast, the courage of the English. When they were hit, they hit back. The London blitz made him think of Paris, where not a shot had been fired, not a bomb had been dropped.

For four years this was the government of France. In fact, it was a transition government, in that it would not outlast the occupation. Pétain and his men settled into hotels, like transients. Pétain's title was the somewhat unspecific "Chief of the French State." He was neither president nor king, neither caudillo nor duce. Laval, who was vice-premier (although there was no premier), told Pétain he had more power than Louis XIV because he governed without a meddling parliament. In fact, he was governing because the Germans let him, and because he was a tool of German repression. The Germans were shorthanded, while the French had a police force of 100,000. There was, however, a Vichy program embodying some reforms. The trade unions were dissolved in the name of the workers' interests. Soldiers in uniform could not consume alcoholic beverages in public after 4 P.M., but could buy a bottle in a store, in the name of temperance. Actually, in all fairness, some of the Vichy measures were inspired by a genuine desire for social reform. Pensions for the aged, which the Popular Front had tried many times to pass, were instituted by Vichy. Another Vichy law prohibited divorce in the first three years of marriage. Still another decree changed the inheritance laws to limit the dismemberment of family farms. Another did away completely with the traditional rights of home distillers, who had been a powerful lobby back in the days when there was a parliament to lobby. The anomaly of Vichy was that it threw itself into all sorts of reformist activities, from the regulation of abortion to the reconstruction of roads and bridges, at a time when three fifths of France was occupied by the Germans, and the other two fifths was under German control once removed. The men of Vichy were acting like the crew of a sinking ship, whose captain has told them to polish the brass and swab down the decks.

In spite of this (or perhaps because reformist zeal was a form of escape from reality), the difference between Vichy and a Quisling-type government was that Pétain had mass support, at least for the first two years. There was a complete understanding between the Marshal and the people, in that he offered a comforting explanation of events: We were betrayed by bad leaders. We were beaten. We must atone. This was called the *psychologie du rachat* (psychology of atonement). It was a form of collective masochism, the corollary of which was admiration for the victor. They beat us, so they are better than we are, better led and better trained and better armed and better organized and better-looking. You had to admire a winner.

Pétain, the atoner of choice, presided over the regression of a great nation into a kind of infantilism. He was the national scoutmaster, talking to the people as if to children, saying things a child could understand. When he received a delegation of electricians who sang him a song, he said: "I like very much music and electricity." His basic message was soothing: "We have been defeated, but we are going to use this defeat to restore the good old ways." Since this could not be done in substance, it was done through emblems, through boys in short pants singing *"Maréchal, Nous Voilà"* ("Marshal, We are Here," the sappy Vichy anthem), through the *francisque* (double-bladed battleax, another Pétainist symbol) on coins, and through quoting the words of Sully, the minister of finance to King Henri IV, on bank notes: *Labourage et pâturage sont les deux mamelles de la France* (Plowing and grazing are the two udders of France).

The motto of France was changed, from the ambitious and abstract *Liberté, Egalité, Fraternité* to the more limited and down-to-earth *Travail, Famille, Patrie*. The first was the ideological program of a victorious revolution; the second the retrenched practicality of defeat. The Vichy motto was unconsciously self-mocking because much of the *Travail* was for the German war effort, the *Patrie* was three-fifths occupied, and more than a million *Familles* were divided by the prisoner-of-war situation. But to make up for reality, every day there was a little Vichy fairy tale: Pétain had received an old peasant for a hearty man-to-man talk. Upon leaving, the man said in tears: "He's an honest peasant like myself."

The Pétain cult was a cottage industry, turning out postcards and posters, portraits and statues, and a Pétain set of Sèvres porcelain with the old man's face on dishes in the famous Sèvres blue. Pétain received fifteen hundred letters a day, two thirds of them asking for the return of the prisoners of war, about which he could do nothing. His portrait hung in every classroom. He received so many presents there was no room to store them. There were glass cabinets full of dishes, and baby lambs dressed in pink ribbons, which didn't have to be stored, since they could be eaten. As Otto Abetz, the German ambassador to Paris, explained to Hitler: "Pétain is a kind of idol, like Hindenburg." When he visited Lyon in November 1940, there had never been such a crowd in the city's history. Strong men wept, and women tried to touch the hem of his tunic. Then, when his popularity waned, there was a spate of Pétain jokes: "Have you heard? The Marshal is dead." "No, since when?" "It happened three months ago, but his entourage kept it from him." It was suggested that he should have inscribed on his tomb: *Au soldat trop connu* (To the too-well-known soldier).

In fact, according to his personal doctor, Bernard de Menetrel, the Marshal's health was good. His pulse and blood pressure were normal. His appetite, which he stimulated by walking two miles before lunch, was excellent. He would walk silently, and suddenly a remark would come from out of nowhere: "What I liked best were the infantry and making love." Once, when Pétain was brought papers to sign, there was a cross made where he should sign them, and he said with annoyance, "Do they think I'm blind, or that I'm an imbecile?"

While Pétain was out pressing the flesh, Laval stayed in his

little three-windowed corner office on the second floor of the Hôtel du Parc, and held meetings, to get a sense of the national mood.
His theme song was that he did the dirty work and no one thanked
him for it. "One day the people will see what I did for them," he
said. The trouble with Laval was that he was an expert go-be-
tween, or broker, or matchmaker, or intriguer in the wings, but
he was not a leader. Vichy was a good place for him to be, as
middle man between the Germans and the French.

In the beginning, things were fairly benign as the Germans settled in and pretty much left the French alone while deciding who
to attack next. For about a year, between the French armistice in
June 1940 and the German attack on Russia in June 1941, you
could argue that in most areas there was a return to normality,
particularly in the nonoccupied zone, where a German was rarely
to be seen. It was in the interest of the occupier to foster the
appearance of business as usual. Students that fall returned to
their studies. Farmers farmed, and railroad conductors conducted. There was as yet no organized resistance to speak of.
People went back to their activities and occupations, seeking refuge in private concerns. One of my uncles, Louis-René, whose
right hand had been rendered useless by a World War I wound,
did not let events affect him. He collected paintings and furniture,
and continuted to go to the Paris auctions, while complaining that
the Germans were driving the prices up. He was indignant when
one day at the Salle Drouot a German officer bought a Boudin.
"Look at what that oaf paid! What does he know about Boudin?"
One day after the war he took me aside and said this amazing
thing: *"La résistance, ça m'est passé complètement à côté,"*
meaning roughly, "I never knew there was any such thing as the
resistance." And this in spite of having a son Philippe, who had
died in the not-so-funny war, and a daughter, Marguerite, who
was decorated for heroism in the resistance, having made a number of trips through the Pyrénées, helping people escape into Spain.

In spite of the return to normality, however, it was clear that
Vichy was allowed to govern in the same manner that a child is
allowed to play in a garden as long as it stays inside the walls. It
had a limited scope of operation, and a limited independence. In
time, in the lingo of the occupation, the word *national* came to

mean *ersatz,* as in *café national.* And it was precisely the *ersatz* quality of Vichy that led it to adopt the theory of the lesser evil. It was better for the French police to carry out disagreeable tasks than to have the Germans do it, for they would be more ruthless and would impinge on French sovereignty. As a result, you had French police manning the demarcation line between the zones, and arresting refugees and Jews and Communists, and designating hostages. Whereas, in fact, if the French had refused and the Germans had carried out those tasks, they would have been more visible as oppressors.

In any servant-master relationship, however, the servant has cards to play. There are strategies of the weak, such as trickery and deviousness, or creating dependence, or settling for half a loaf, or promising what you cannot or will not deliver. The servant can nap on duty and pad the bills. These were the Vichy *modi operandi.* You could not have too many showdowns with the Germans, but you could circumvent them and wear them down with excuses.

One day at a cabinet meeting, the minister of agriculture, Pierre Caziot, announced that he was tendering his resignation because he refused to honor a German requisition order for 56,000 horses. At this time, in 1941, Admiral Darlan, who had succeeded Laval, said: "Of course, Caziot, I won't give the Germans a single horsehair. But if I refuse, they'll take the horses from the occupied zone. Instead, I'm going to say yes, but . . . wait until after the harvest, because if you take the horses now you'll ruin our agricultural production. And if you take horses back from our peasants, then give us back the men we need. Look at our freight cars, they say on the sides, forty men eight horses. We'll give you fifty-six thousand horses if in exchange you give us two hundred thousand prisoners." In the end Darlan made so many stipulations and conditions that he wore down the Germans, and they gave up their demand for horses.

Another time, Paul Charbin, the secretary of state for provisions, and former president of the Lyon Chamber of Commerce, expressed concern about the projected size of the wheat harvest, saying they would have to cut the daily bread ration by 250 grams a day. At this point Marshal Pétain spoke up: "You should start by taking a closer look at the coffee grinders." Everyone present thought the old man's deafness had led him astray once again, but in fact he was right on target, because for months, on thousands of French farms, housewives had been taking wheat and making their own flour in their coffee grinders, outside the rationing system. Then Caziot asked Charbin what statistics he was using to project a poor harvest. "But my dear colleague," Charbin said, "my services use the documents drawn up by your services." "In that case, rest assured," Caziot said, "for we like to be modest in our projections, which not only spares us disappointment, but protects us from the voracious appetites of others."

Such was the strategy of Vichy, a mix of subterfuge, delay, and going around in circles. Often, various ministers expressed their frustration only to be told that they were not going about things in the right way. Jérome Carcopino, the minister of education, complained that the Germans controlled the legislative process through their censorship of the *Journal Officiel,* where laws had to be published to make them operative. Thus they had their hand in every appointment, and even intruded in the world of culture, backing candidates for director of the Opéra and the Comédie Française. Carcopino was trying to get his man named rector of the University of Paris, over the objections of Abetz. After all sorts of unsuccessful maneuvers Carcopino told Darlan that he'd had enough, he was going to resign.

"How you do go on," Darlan said. "It's not a question of leaving but of succeeding. Your choice is excellent, but try this time to avoid false maneuvers, and don't take the official path, because you already know it's a dead end. Instead go straight to that old leatherneck Stülpnagel [General Otto von Stülpnagel, military commander of the occupation forces], who is the only one with the power of censure. Tell him what you want. The Rectorship of Paris is the least of his concerns. After a few objections, expressed for the mere pleasure of letting you feel his authority, he will give you his agreement."

It happened just as Darlan had said it would. Stülpnagel was tall and stooped, thin to the point of gauntness, with dark crew-cut hair, parchmentlike skin, and an ageless, expressionless face, compressed into immobility by the discipline of a hereditary vocation. He was a general of the old school who in 1949 would kill himself in his cell at Cherche-Midi Prison rather than appear before a French court as a war criminal. In any case, Stülpnagel was courteous but distant, and agreed to Carcopino's candidate.

Sometimes the strategy resembled a scene from a Feydeau farce, as when Darlan summoned Carcopino to his office and said, "You can do me a favor that may result in the liberation of several thousand prisoners. It seems that von Ribbentrop [the German foreign minister] is in love with the thighs of a naked lady he saw in the Louvre, 'La Diane au Bain' by Boucher. You know it, I'm sure." Carcopino nodded. "You don't have any objection to making Ribbentrop's dream come true by sending the painting to Berlin, do you?"

"You cannot do that, Admiral," the horrified Carcopino replied. "The domain of the state is inalienable. If I gave up the tiniest fragment I would be committing a crime." But then, to please his boss, Carcopino thought of a compromise, which was to propose an exchange between the Boucher and "L'enseigne de Gersaint" by Watteau, which was in the Potsdam Museum. Of course the Watteau was fifty times more valuable than the Boucher, but Darlan did not know enough about art to see that he was proposing to exchange an egg for an ox. When the director of the Potsdam Museum received the offer, he indignantly rejected it.

Sometimes push came to shove and strategies did no good. The University of Strasbourg, expelled from Alsace, regrouped in Clermont-Ferrand, near Lyon. The Germans asked for the return of the university library, with its extraordinary collection of German-language medieval texts and manuscripts. They threatened to confiscate the Sorbonne library in Paris if the Strasbourg library were not sent back. Laval, then vice-premier, tried at first to weasel. He agreed to return the library with the stipulation that "the books necessary for the continuation of their studies will be left to the students," which could be given a broad interpretation. When the Germans noticed the gaps between what they actually got and what was in the catalog, they sent a team to Clermont-Ferrand to pick up the rest. The rector-in-exile, Terracher, whose furniture had been expropriated from his Strasbourg apartment, removed the chairs from his office just before the German team came in and received them standing. The rector stonewalled, saying he had no instructions to give them anything. But he was only buying time, for in September 1941 the books had to be sent back to Strasbourg.

Thus, even in the early years, when things were relatively benign, they were not benign for everyone. France was full of refugees. Some tried to hang on, some tried to get out, and some gave up. Albert Einstein's nephew Carl, whose book on Negro sculpture had caused a sensation in Germany, threw himself into the Oloron River on July 14 with a stone tied around his neck. The novelist Ernst Weiss took Veronal in Paris. The playwright Walter Hasenclever opened his veins near Avignon. Willi Münzenberg, onetime propaganda head of the Comintern, hanged himself in a forest near Grenoble. Walter Benjamin, the author and critic, who was turned back at the Spanish border, also killed himself.

Yet there was no immediate danger. The "surrender on demand" clause was observed in the breach. The French had a way of doing things with a *clin d'oeil* (wink). There was a big difference between measures enacted and measures applied. The Spanish were letting those who wanted to leave through with transit visas. Marseille was packed with refugees. *Quelle pagaille,* people said, what utter confusion. But there was no panic. Every day on the terrace of the Hôtel Normandie café, you could find, taking the sun and chatting with their friends, two distinguished figures from the Weimar Republic—Rudolf Breitscheid, who had been minister of the interior, and Rudolf Hilferding, ex-minister of finance. They both had American visas, but seemed to be in no hurry about getting French exit visas. "So far," said Breitscheid, "there have been no demands for extradition, and I do not think there will be any. It is unthinkable. The inclusion of paragraph 19 [the 'surrender on demand' clause] was a mere formality." But these otherwise intelligent persons made the mistake of thinking the situation was static when in fact it was changing. On February 8, 1941, French plainclothesmen came to the Normandie and arrested the two Rudolfs. "Don't worry," they said, "it's only to check your papers." They were sent to La Santé Prison in Paris, where Hilferding committed suicide. Breitscheid was deported to Buchenwald. He died there in an Allied air raid on August 28,

1944, along with the daughter of the king of Italy and the French tire king Michelin.

There were many other opponents of the Hitler regime in Marseille—Socialists, Communists, artists, and writers—some the French arrested and sent to camps that had been built for refugees from the Spanish civil war. These camps were called *centres d'hébergement surveillés* (supervised lodging centers), another term for concentration camps. At the camp of Les Mille, outside Aix-en-Provence, many of the inmates had made visa applications and were waiting to emigrate. The camp was a huge brickyard, and the inmates were put to work moving, trundling, and stacking bricks. There were no beatings or cruelty. The French style of internment was easygoing. Arrangements could be made. One man bribed the guards to let him keep his dog. The barbed-wire enclosure was used to hang laundry. Deals were struck. Men sold their place in line at the latrine or the canteen. They sold their mailing rights (one letter every two weeks). A smuggled newspaper might be rented ten or twenty times. Life was bearable, because of the French capacity to let things take care of themselves, and because most of the inmates knew they would be released. One exception was ninety Germans who had served in the French Foreign Legion, and who were turned over to the occupier under paragraph 19. Some had served France for ten or twenty years, some had four or five citations for bravery, and this was their reward. Among the released inmates were the painter Max Ernst, the writer Lion Feuchtwanger, and a troupe of circus midgets on their way to South America.

Les Mille was one of the smaller camps, with a capacity of fifteen hundred. Among the larger establishments was Rivesaltes, north of Perpignan, a camp for families with room for eight thousand. It had a bad climate and a worse appearance. Gurs, near the Spanish border in the Pyrénées, had a capacity of eighteen thousand. Gurs was divided into sections, made up of row after row of low wooden barracks, and separated by double rows of eight-foot-high barbed wire. It was here that a group of eight thousand Jews expelled from the Palatinate area of Germany in October 1940 were interned. The Gestapo had knocked on their doors and given them an hour to leave. Among them were the inmates of an insane asylum and an old folks' home.

Although conditions were relatively tolerable in these camps, the French were seriously into the business of arresting and detaining large numbers of refugees. The fate of these people would be determined, not by them, but by the occupying power. In Marseille a five-year-old boy named Erwin Glickes saw his father repeatedly arrested and released. Glickes *père,* an Antwerp diamond merchant, had taken his family out of Holland in June 1940 in their big Buick. In Marseille there was a teeming refugee colony crowding the cafés and hotels, with news arriving by *radio trottoir* (sidewalk radio). Erwin Glickes's father acted as a broker between Jews who wanted to sell diamonds and anyone who had dollars, and he did quite well on the commissions. There were periodic sweeps of the hotels by the French police, who in Yiddish were called "grabbers." The news would go out on *radio trottoir* that "the grabbers are coming." Glickes's father was arrested and sent to Gurs, where he managed to buy his way out, but was arrested again and held on a prison boat in Marseille Harbor. He was released after the family's nineteen-year-old governess came to visit him, wearing a money belt under her dress. One day Erwin accompanied his parents to the *préfecture de police* for an identity check. As they talked to the police inspector, the boy's attention was drawn to a metal-edged ruler on the inspector's desk. Erwin was wearing a long red scarf, which he removed and placed on the desk over the ruler. When he got up to leave with his parents, he picked up the ruler as well as his scarf. Outside on the street, they came to a metal railing, and Erwin contentedly rapped the ruler along the rails. His father asked him where it came from. It was the only time in Erwin Glickes's life that his father ever slapped him, and to this day he does not know why he took the ruler. The Glickes's stayed in Marseille until June 1942, when they were at last able to leave for the United States. It shows how fluid the situation was that they could stay in Marseille for two years in spite of the sweeps and the "grabbers."

In that first year, the Vichy regime was in an odd twilight zone, finding itself, testing how it would operate with the Germans and with its own people. Thus, if you were a Jewish refugee in Marseille, you might be arrested, or you might not. And if you were arrested, you might be able to talk or buy your way out, or you might not. Vichy policy was haphazard rather than systematic. It seemed to be responding to specific German pressures rather than any thought-out plan.

The government was called by some the *régime des recalés* (regime of the flunked), that is, those who had been beaten in the legislative elections of 1936 that brought the Popular Front to power. It was also seen as the revenge of the Catholic conservatives on the free-thinking left-wingers of the Popular Front. The men of Vichy made much of their personal honesty, and it's true that no one enriched himself in office. Charbin, the minister for provisions, distributed his salary to his subordinates, not wanting to earn money from the suffering of the French people. Yves Bouthillier, the minister of finance, agonized over having to ask for an extra ration of meat to host an official lunch. But here again, what was the point of all these scruples when Vichy had fallen in with German designs?

That October Pétain agreed to meet Hitler, who was on a swing through Europe, drumming up support for his attack on England. On October 23 Hitler's private train was at the Franco-Spanish border town of Hendaye to meet with Franco. They talked for nine hours, but Franco refused to be drawn into the war. Hitler privately called him "a Jesuit swine," and told Mussolini a few days later: "Rather than go through that again, I would prefer to have three or four teeth yanked out."

On October 24 Pétain traveled to the town of Montoire, north of Tours, where Hitler's car could be quickly pulled into a tunnel in case of bombardment. Pétain was hoping to soften the armistice conditions with respect to the return of prisoners, the cost of occupation, and the restricted passage across the demarcation line. In his talk with Hitler, Pétain avoided committing France to waging war against England, but he had to sign a secret protocol of support for Germany's war plans. It was a typical Vichy gambit, giving lip service without offering anything tangible.

Pétain later told one of his aides: "I'll tell you something in confidence. I didn't hear a word he said. He screams on the radio but in private he has a very low voice. And since I'm a little deaf . . . but the interpreter, Schmidt—they are all called Schmidt—spoke in excellent French." What people remembered about Montoire, however, was the photograph of Hitler and Pétain shaking hands. The cordial handshake between the conquering Führer and the defeated Marshal spoke volumes. It was a visual expression of Pétain's willingness to collaborate, short of declaring war on England. Like Dickens's Barkis, Pétain was willin'!

And yet at the time Pétain was not criticized for traveling 150 miles or so from Vichy to Montoire, *képi* in hand, so to speak, to see Hitler. Nor was he criticized when he said in a speech on October 30: "I am entering today in the path of collaboration." People, particularly those with a son or a brother or a father still in Germany, said, "He had to do it to get the prisoners back." But Montoire was a bitter lesson, for instead of responding to French requests to free the prisoners—at the very least, those 6,300 prisoners who worked for the French ministry of finance, which would make for more efficient tax-collecting—the Germans in November expelled 70,000 inhabitants of Lorraine. The first fruit of collaboration was the sixty-three trains that arrived in Lyon between November 11 and November 21, full of families separated from their homes and their belongings and reduced to the status of refugees.

Laval was seen as the architect of collaboration. To curry favor with the Germans, he had even proposed that France should bomb Gibraltar from its air bases in Morocco. He thought he knew how to talk to Hitler. In fact, Hitler described Laval to Count Galeazzo Ciano as "a dirty, democratic, cheap-jack politician who doesn't mean what he says." Pétain began to feel that Laval had tricked him into meeting Hitler. He had never liked Laval, who blew cigarette smoke in his face at cabinet meetings, and who was spending more and more time in Paris conspiring with his German *compère* Abetz, each one seeing in the other a partner in self-advancement, and now his resentment solidified. On December 2, when the finance minister, Yves Bouthillier, came to complain that Laval had promised to turn over 220 metric tons of Belgian gold to the Germans, and that he, Bouthillier, wanted nothing more to do with Laval, Pétain's response was: "Well, you're a bit offended. . . . At your age I wasn't even a major. Am I walking out on everything?" Then, after a brief silence, he added: "Don't leave; he's the one who will leave."

Pétain became convinced that Laval was negotiating directly

with the Germans in Paris because he never reported back. "I am used to working with written reports clearly presented, as a military man," Pétain said. Finally, that December, he confronted Laval and told him he wanted written reports. Laval said, "If I give you written reports, can you guarantee they won't find their way to the British Foreign Office?" which was rather insulting to the old man. Pétain replied he would keep the reports locked in a safe in his bedroom.

Things came to a head at an 8 P.M. cabinet meeting on December 13, after several ministers had urged the Marshal to get rid of Laval. Pétain used the old gimmick of asking for the resignations of all his ministers. Laval signed his, and Pétain accepted it. Laval was flabbergasted. When he asked for an explanation, Pétain said: "You do not have the confidence of the French people, and I must tell you brutally, you do not have mine. Each time you go to Paris, I never know what kind of *tuiles* [literally, tiles, figuratively, headaches] are going to fall on my head. Your friends in the Paris press attack us. It's intolerable."

This was Pétain's finest hour, his reaction to the humiliation of Montoire. In theory, the composition of the government was entirely a French matter. In fact, the Germans at once pressured him to take back Laval, but he refused. By way of retaliation against an insubordinate vassal, they ordered a census of all men between the ages of eighteen and forty-five in the occupied zone, and made crushing economic demands—coal, wheat, butter, rolling stock, the entire French production of bauxite. There were those who said that Laval could have dealt with it. But the Marshal had brought in Pierre-Étienne Flandin, who had been prime minister in the thirties, and gave him the nominal title of Foreign Minister. Flandin was one of those weak men who seem strong because they are big and strapping—he was six feet four, which is unusual for a Frenchman. He lasted less than two months. Then the Germans wanted Admiral Darlan, and Pétain had to give in. You could refuse once, but you could not refuse twice.

So, on February 9, 1941, Darlan was brought in as vice-premier, and as minister of the navy, foreign affairs, interior, and information. This accumulation of jobs was one of the Third Republic's bad habits, now repeated by Vichy. Darlan was jovial but calculating, and found places in the various ministries for all his navy pals. It was the one time in the history of France that the country was run by sailors. It was not run any better, however, for the strategy of wheedling and conciliation continued. The men of Vichy were forever asking for high-level meetings with the Germans, and further fields of collaboration. On May 11, 1941, Darlan went to Berchtesgaden to see Hitler, and struck the following deal: The Germans would have the use of the airfields and military supplies in the French protectorate of Syria. They would also have the use of Bizerte, the French naval base in Tunisia, as a supply route for Rommel. And they could eventually build a submarine base at Dakar, in the French colony of Senegal. In exchange, the Germans would agree to release about 75,000 World War I veterans from prisoner-of-war camps, to reduce the cost of occupation, and to facilitate the passage from zone to zone.

This agreement, however, was never carried out. For one thing, Vichy lost Syria to de Gaulle and the British in July. For another, the Germans never got around to using Bizerte or Dakar because after June 22, 1941, they had other fish to fry. June 22 was the day Hitler attacked the Soviet Union with an army of more than three million men, which not only changed the course of the war, but also had a ripple effect in France.

After June 22 the situation in France . . . evolved, shall we say? The Communists, who had been pro-German in accordance with the Nazi-Soviet pact, now turned against the occupier. The yearlong period when Communists had been collaborators was rich in irony. There were cases when Communists picked up by the French police were released by order of the Germans. This happened to two editors of the Communist daily *L'Humanité* who had gone to the German offices on June 20, 1940, to ask for permission to keep publishing. The Germans told them they could as long as they agreed to be censored by the *Kommandantur,* and carried no military news or weather reports. The next day, the two editors were picked up by the French police for breaking the law banning the Communist party and its activities. Three days later, the Germans ordered their release. As it turned out, *L'Humanité* had to reappear clandestinely, but not a single anti-German word appeared in it. One paragraph in the July 4, 1940, issue remains a classic of hypocrisy: "It is particularly comforting, in these times of grief, to see many Parisian workers having amicable relations with German soldiers, either in the street or in the corner café. Bravo, comrades, continue, even if this displeases certain ill-intentioned and stupid bourgeois. The fraternity of all people will not always be a hope, it will become a living reality."

But once the German divisions invaded Russia, amicable relations turned into armed reprisal. Exactly two months later, on August 21, a German naval cadet by the name of Alphonse Moser was shot and killed in the Métro station Barbès-Rochechouart by a Communist militant, Georges Pierre, a.k.a. Fabien, a veteran of the International Brigade in the Spanish civil war. By then, other resistance groups had been formed, mainly in the unoccupied zone, but none of them adopted a policy of killing Germans. It was the Communists who chose the strategy of *à chacun son Boche* (to each his German). They deliberately launched a cycle of violence and reprisal, knowing that for every German killed, ten or twenty or fifty or a hundred hostages would be executed. This would change the nature of the occupation from benign to malignant. It would shock the population. It would introduce an element of danger for the Germans. And it would confirm the Communists as the hard-liners of the resistance. The unstated reason was that the Russians were using the French Communist party to stir things up in the hope that the Germans would have to pull some troops off the eastern front and send them to France. In any case, the invasion of Russia introduced into the German-Vichy equation a new factor, Communist militants who were organized, committed, and willing to use violence.

Another factor was the enormous demand for manpower that the war on the eastern front created. As Hitler sent millions of Germans to die or be captured in Russia, he needed to replace them in the factories, and it became one of the duties of the Vichy government to supply forced labor. This resulted in making Vichy unpopular and sending many young men into hiding.

Finally the attack on Russia led France into direct military collaboration with Germany. All the collaborators who had said they were pro-German because they were anti-Bolshevik now had a chance to take up arms against their real enemy. A Legion of

French Volunteers (LVF) was formed to fight alongside the Germans on the Russian front. The first contingent of twelve hundred men was honored in a ceremony on August 27, 1941, at the Borgnis-Desbordes barracks in Versailles (it was during this occasion that Laval was shot; although out of the government, he was invited to attend). The LVF contingent was sent to Poland for training, then took part in the stalled offensive on Moscow, fighting a battle in December on a frozen lake where a hundred men were killed and wounded. I wonder how many of them ever imagined that political opinions voiced around café tables under the chestnut trees of Parisian boulevards would take them to their death forty miles from Moscow on a slab of Russian ice, in the middle of the Russian winter. The Germans held the LVF in contempt after their poor showing, and had them do a little partisan-chasing in the rear. In all, about six thousand French volunteers served on the eastern front in the LVF. Some of them were incorporated into the SS Charlemagne Division. This division was mainly French and continued to fight the Russians as late as March 1945 in Pomerania. In my mind's eye, I can see those doomed soldiers sent to defend the eastern marches as the Ivans attack. I see them on Pomerania's wide plain while the Russians advance over poplar-lined roads. I see them at the huge steel bridge in Stettin that spans the Oder, manning the anti-aircraft guns as the Russian bombers drop their load. I see them thrown against Rokossovski's army, and I see a German general distributing the first Iron Crosses to be pinned to French chests. And I wonder what made them embark on such a quixotic adventure. I somehow doubt that they were all political fanatics. Young men choose sides for other reasons. It may have been the love of the uniform. The resistance in 1941 had no uniforms and no status. With a uniform you got respect, and you got girls. It may have been a question of manhood. You joined the LVF to prove that a French soldier was as good as a German. Or it may have been a matter of temperament. If you were energetic and pessimistic, you were drawn to history's dungheap. Or, in a few cases, it may have been the urge to do something clean and uncompromising. It was better to fight the Russians on the eastern front, if only to get away from Vichy's helot mentality.

The invasion of Russia completely changed the situation in France in that it threw the Communists into resistance, and the pro-Germans into full-fledged collaboration with the enemy. Take the case of Darnand—son of a railwayman, high-school dropout, born soldier, World War I hero. In 1918 there were three men who had citations calling them "artisans of the final victory": Georges Clémenceau, Ferdinand Foch, and Joseph Darnand. Here is what Darnand did: In July 1918 he was a twenty-year-old sergeant in the 266th Infantry Regiment, in the Champagne region. General Ludendorff was preparing an attack. Darnand took a small detachment behind the lines, and in less than forty minutes brought back twenty-seven German prisoners. From the prisoners, the French learned that Ludendorff's attack was due the next day. They immediately mounted a counterattack, which was said to be the turning point of the war.

But heroism wasn't enough to obtain a commission. The officer caste kept Darnand out. And who can doubt that this was the first crack in his patriotism? Who can doubt the depth of bitterness in this man when the army he loved rejected him? Darnand returned to civilian life to nurse his resentment. However, 1940 found him in uniform again, stockier and gray-haired at forty-two, and filled with a compulsive need to repeat his World War I feat. He asked the general in command of his division, the 29th, for permission to form a guerrilla unit, and recruited 150 volunteers. In January 1940, during that strange interlude when both sides were at a standstill, Darnand staged a raid behind German lines from Forbach, a border town in Lorraine. But this time they were spotted and had to fight their way back with heavy losses. Later, in the May–June invasion, his little band fought on the Somme. Darnand was captured. "You seem very sad," a German officer told him. "I'll be sad as long as I have to look at your ugly faces on French soil," he replied.

One of the men in Darnand's guerrilla unit was Father Raymond Bruckberger, a Dominican monk who looked more like a bouncer than a priest, and loved a fight. I got to know *le père* Bruck, as he was called, in the early sixties in Paris, for he was a friend of my uncle Gratien. By that time, he had written a best-selling book on the life of Christ, and he had a drinker's red face, a thick mop of white hair, and a brusque manner. While fighting with Darnand in 1940, *le père* Bruck was wounded outside Chantilly on June 11, and was taken prisoner. He escaped with the help of a Jesuit, who loaned him a cassock. He spent some time recovering from his wounds, and then wondered what to do next. He decided to look up Darnand, whose blunt soldierly ways and fierce anti-German views he admired, and found him in Nice, where they had lunch together in May 1941. But when *le père* Bruck spoke of joining the resistance, Darnand said, "What is this resistance shit? Shepherds to whom the archangel appeared?" When *le père* Bruck mentioned de Gaulle, Darnand dismissed him, saying: "He's surrounded by Jews and Freemasons and assorted deserters."

Darnand, it turned out, was now completely pro-Vichy. "I don't feel capable of going against the authority of the *Maréchal*," he told *le père* Bruck. "He signed my citation in the first war." Darnand could not bear to see the victory of 1918 turn into the defeat of 1940, thought *le père* Bruck. Through some psychological process he had converted shame and soured love and bitterness into collaboration, into admiration for the victor. To save ourselves we must be like them, Darnand seemed to be saying. He was ready to fight by the side of the Germans, and soon became head of the Nice office of the LVF. The astonished priest, who was wearing his white Dominican robe, rose from the table and walked away, but then returned and said: "Listen closely to what I am going to tell you. One day, you will pass before the High Court, and you will be sentenced to death, and I will be enough of a *con* [fool] to testify in your favor." So it came to pass. Father Bruckberger joined the resistance, while Darnand went on to head the Milice, an organization of thugs responsible for many crimes against the French people. When Darnand was tried in Paris in September 1945, *le père* Bruck appeared as a character witness. And when he was executed on October 10, 1945, *le père* Bruck was at his side. Darnand died bravely, he said.

In a sense, France's destiny was being played out on the Russian steppe. In the big attack on Moscow that began on December 1, Hitler's armies came within sight of the spires of the Kremlin, as the Kaiser's armies had come within sight of the Eiffel Tower in 1914. Then the Russians threw one hundred divisions equipped for winter warfare against the Germans. It was 36 degrees below zero, and the German soldiers froze, and the German tanks stalled. For the first time, the Panzers were in retreat. The myth of the invincible German Army was broken. Field Marshal von Brauchitsch, who in 1940 had disdained Laval's offer of military assistance, resigned as Commander in Chief of the Army. And on December 7 the United States entered the war. "Now that the Americans are in, it's all over," de Gaulle told an aide in London.

It was in the context of his first military reverses that Hitler vented his dissatisfaction, some of which fell on Vichy. On January 5, 1942, he told Abetz: "This collaboration is completely unilateral. The French are always asking things from us without giving us anything concrete in return." The Germans were fed up with Darlan, whom they thought of as an even worse equivocator than Laval, and began to consider the return of Laval to Vichy as a favorable alternative.

Laval's return to the government was imminent. The reason behind it was that the Germans had lost a million killed and wounded on the Russian front in the winter of 1941–1942. They needed live bodies. At first workers were sought on a volunteer basis. To work in Germany was presented as a way of reducing unemployment in France. By March 1942, 62,000 volunteers had signed up. Some were convicts who did it to get out of jail. Others were drawn by the promise of high salaries. But in March 1942 everything changed, as a result of the German losses on the eastern front. Hitler appointed a *Gauleiter* for labor, Fritz Sauckel, forty-seven, a short, hard-driving man with small piggy eyes. Darlan opposed Sauckel's demands for French labor. The principal reason why the Germans wanted Laval to return was because labor needs were urgent, and they hoped he would be more tractable.

Göring was in Paris that March, and had lunch with Laval. The Germans were particularly annoyed with Pétain and Darlan because they had refused to come to Paris to attend the funerals of civilian victims of the British bombardment of the Renault plant in Boulogne-Billancourt. So at the lunch Göring was gloomy and threatening, and warned Laval that Germany was going to get very tough with France. Laval relayed this information to Pétain, who on April 17 took him back as "Chief of Government." As a sop, Darlan was named Commander in Chief of French forces. Laval proceeded to get rid of all the ministers he suspected of having engineered his ouster in December 1940, and brought in his own men. One of these was a dubious advertisement for Vichy's return to traditional values—Abel Bonnard, the minister of education, a homosexual esthete with a fondness for handsome blond German soldiers. Pétain referred to him disdainfully as *la Gestapette,* a pun on the word *tapette,* meaning "fairy."

Always the tactician, Laval decided that since the Germans were going to take French workers anyway, he would be in a stronger position to negotiate if he took the initiative. On May 12, back in office for less than a month, Laval wrote the German foreign minister, von Ribbentrop, proposing that young Frenchmen be sent to Germany to work in factories. He said he wanted to get the dialogue going again. But he pointed out that there had to be the right psychological climate with regard to French public opinion. If the Germans agreed to release prisoners of war in exchange for workers, the French would feel they were getting something in return.

On June 16 Laval met with Sauckel to thrash out the ratio. Laval wanted one POW for two workers. Sauckel countered with one for five. They compromised on one for three. Hitler agreed to exchange 50,000 POWs for 150,000 workers. This gave Laval the leverage to take the Germans' labor demands to the French people and present them as a patriotic duty, which he called *la relève* (the relief shift). He decided to give a speech on the radio on June 22 to explain *la relève.*

On June 21 Laval was alone at his desk in his little corner room in the Hôtel du Parc, when Paul Morand, the former ambassador to London, came to see him. Laval showed him the text of the radio talk he was going to deliver the next day. Morand started reading, but stopped at the phrase "I hope for Germany's victory, for without it bolshevism will move in everywhere." When Morand objected, Laval said: "A phrase like that can bring back a hundred thousand prisoners. A little politeness on the radio and I can refuse that brute Sauckel the workers that he demands by the hundred thousand." In fact, he did not stop Sauckel, for when there were not enough volunteers for *la relève,* the Germans began to take them by force, and the French police had to round them up. In February 1943 the Laval government was forced to pass a law, *Service Obligatoire du Travail* (mandatory work service) or STO, which meant that every man between eighteen and fifty could be sent to Germany.

The trouble with Laval was that he was always trying to fool somebody—the Germans, his own people, his fellow cabinet members. Getting the prisoners back was a way of tricking the work force into going to Germany. The expression of hope for a German victory was in the same vein. Did he really still believe such a victory possible after the German defeat on the outskirts of Moscow and America's entry in the war? As he put it himself: "Me, what can I tell you? I'm playing the game as if the Germans were the winners! Will they win the war? I don't know, I'm not Madame de Thèbes [a popular clairvoyant]." On the day after his radio speech, he told Paul Creyssel, the secretary general for propaganda: "I know that what I said was shocking, but I said it on purpose because it protects me from German suspicion. . . . This sentence is worth two hundred thousand workers. It will save us from Doriot [Jacques Doriot, the ultra-collaborator] and the others. One day the French people will understand." But the Germans continued to requisition French workers, and the day when the French people would understand never came. That one little sentence remained stuck to Laval like a plaster and did him more harm than anything else he ever said. In fact, it put a noose around his neck.

From June 1940 (when the Germans entered Paris) until August 1944 (when they left), occupation was the condition of life in France, as pervasive and yet as varied as the quality of the air. Hitler had said, "I will corrupt the countries I occupy," and he was as good as his word, for occupation was a degrading experience, a form of colonization, the sort of thing so-called civilized nations had done to so-called backward nations for centuries. You could reason that the vanquished would civilize the victors, as the

Greeks had the Romans, and that did happen in a minor way, but what really happened was that the victors degraded the vanquished. The occupation brought out and encouraged what was low and dishonest in people. It changed the national character, and forty years later, the French are still recovering from the shame of that time.

For the 90 percent of the population who took the position of "life as usual," the purpose of life was to feed their families, keep warm, and avoid arrest. As belts tightened, they became absorbed in the search for food, spending inordinate amounts of time in lines, which further numbed them. "All the French think about," wrote André Gide in his diary, "is that they have less sugar in their coffee and less coffee in their cup." In a country that placed meals ahead of every other activity, food restrictions were keenly felt. "Keep the water in which you boil your noodles," a magazine recommended. "It can make an excellent soup." Such was the level of discourse under the occupation.

There was a specific form of occupation humor, much of which had to do with groceries, as in the story the comedian Noël-Noël told of running into a fellow who said he could get him some cheese, some ham, some coffee, and some Marseille soap. He required an advance of five hundred francs, and promised to deliver the goods in two days. However, he did not show up. Noël-Noël reflected that to have lived for two days in the expectation of receiving so many good things was cheap at the price.

It became routine, for those who could afford it, to deal with the black market. People learned to cheat, to blur moral values, to be dishonest. It became the norm in the name of survival. You could justify the black market on patriotic grounds, by saying, "It's that much that the Germans won't get." The occupation encouraged conniving, and the rise of the middle man, the sort who knows where to find this and that, and pays off the authorities, and sells at inflated prices. So, while Vichy preached a return to virtue, there was in fact a deterioration in day-to-day morality. People got used to cheating, to lying, to being unscrupulous, to ruses. The example came from the top, for Laval was known as "the man of a thousand ruses."

Well, that's not so bad, you might say; it's entrepreneurial at heart, there's a small supply and a large demand, and you make the most of it. Perhaps, but there was something far worse, which was that the Germans turned the French into a nation of informers. To betray trust, to become a stool pigeon, was not only debased behavior but a debasement of language. It was the lowest use to which language could be put. The Germans encouraged an already existing French tendency not to mind their own business, the so-called concierge mentality. And so one half of France informed on the other half. And even among informers there were degrees, the worst being those who sent anonymous letters. There were so many anonymous letters that the Germans could not follow them up, and wondered what kind of awful people the French were to be snitching on their neighbors and their fellow workers and their business rivals and their own relatives. Because if you were quarreling with someone, if you wanted to cause someone grief, what was easier, and less trouble, than sending a poison-pen letter to the *Kommandantur*? Some Jewish mothers told their children to take their shoes off in the apartment because there had been cases where families were turned in by their neighbors for making too much noise. This was so widespread that, in the slang of the time, the informers were called *corbeaux* (crows). A famous movie came out in 1943, produced by an up-and-coming director, Georges-Henri Clouzot, that focused on finding out who in a small town was the author of a string of poison-pen letters; the film was called *Le Corbeau*. The Propaganda Office gave movie makers plenty of rope, so actually the occupation years were a golden era for the French cinema, which brought forth such classics as Marcel Carné's *Les Enfants du Paradis,* with Jean-Louis Barrault playing the mime. A thriving film industry was solid evidence that the French were not oppressed. There were more movies produced in France than in Germany, some of them with German money. In *Le Corbeau,* everybody accuses everybody else, and all the town's skeletons come tumbling out of the closets. The message was that although denouncing one's neighbors is pretty bad, everyone has something equally awful to hide. Although he took the position that he was not a collaborator and was merely exercising his profession, Clouzot had to appear before a postwar tribunal to answer charges of having served the Germans by making a film that showed the mendacity of his countrymen.

When there is so much stored-up resentment in a society that the betrayal of others becomes routine, you begin to understand why the society crumbled. And of course the Germans played on this weakness and created the profession of paid informer, people who went around tracking Jews and members of the resistance and turning them in for a fee. And without going that far themselves, a lot of other people felt that, under the circumstances, it was better not to take sides, and that those who got involved were troublemakers. So a woman in Lyon who was helping Jews obtain ID cards was told by a neighbor: "Leave it alone or the war will end without you." The threat of being informed upon was like pollution hanging in the air.

Yet you couldn't completely leave it alone, because the occupation permeated everything. Even if you did not take a position, even if you were a child or an old man, its presence was felt. It was felt by the schoolgirl who wondered why one of the poems in her German literature textbook, *The Lorelei,* was listed as being by an *unbekannter Dichter* (unknown poet). Her mother explained that it was by the Jewish poet Heinrich Heine. It was felt in a more directly patriotic way by a thirteen-year-old schoolboy, Roger Souchal, who was attending the *lycée* in Saint-Dié in the Vosges Mountains. Near the *lycée* stood the town's *monument aux morts,* which showed a French soldier with his foot on the prostrate Kaiser's head. One afternoon, in October 1940, as Roger and some of his classmates were leaving school, they spotted a German detachment with half-tracks and winches approaching the monument. The boys formed a circle around the bronze statue to protect it, which of course they were unable to do. But it was a gesture, and that gesture was part of a cycle, and you were making that gesture because of your father and your grandfather, in an unholy repetition. Between the wars there was just enough time to become an adult, and Souchal wasn't quite there, but this was something he could do. For it was a way of becoming his ancestor's ancestor, of reversing the generational current, of paying the debt. This cycle too would close, and a few years later Roger Souchal was told this story:

At the Potsdam Conference in 1945, when General Wilhelm

Keitel, who had been Hitler's Chief of Staff, saw the French delegation, he rapped his field marshal's baton on the conference table and said with disgust: "*Ach,* the French are here!" For the French had been lackeys and now they were sitting at the table as partners with the Allies, thanks to young men like Souchal, who in 1944 had gone into the resistance and been arrested and deported. An aide to General de Lattre de Tassigny heard Keitel say those words, which seemed to him to catch the essence of the German defeat, for it was Keitel who in 1940 had dictated the terms of the armistice at Rethondes.

So you couldn't completely leave it alone, whether you were a child or an adolescent, a man or a woman. There were women who refused to sit when German soldiers offered them their seats in the Métro, and there were women who slept with Germans, for a number of reasons. Some of them fell in love. One woman volunteered to work in Germany, to be with her lover when he was sent home, and was killed when the factory where she worked was bombed. Some of them did it for advantage, or because the Germans were seen as attractive and different. They were attractive because they had won. And of course there were the professionals, one of whom protested, when she was about to have her head shaved in 1944, that she was a patriot who had put twenty-eight German soldiers *hors de combat.*

All sorts of things happened that could only happen because of the occupation. As there were occupation love affairs, and thousands of occupation babies born to German fathers, there were occupation crimes. A woman in Lyon, for example, whose husband was a prisoner of war in Germany, had a lover who was a pharmacist. The woman was notified that her husband would soon be freed. She and her lover decided that this would not do. Her lover gave her some poison, and she baked a poisoned cake and sent it to her husband. Then, stricken with remorse, she sent him a special-delivery letter in which she wrote, "Don't touch the cake." He got the letter in time and left the cake next to his bunk, where his bunkmate found it, ate some, and died.

And Petiot, a mad doctor who murdered at least twenty-four persons, could only have succeeded during the occupation, when it was normal for people to vanish without a trace. No one paid

112

any attention. People were disappearing all the time, leaving France, or being arrested by the Gestapo, or going into the Maquis. Petiot's method was to tell wealthy Jews he could get them out of the country. They then came to his office, where he led them into a small triangular room with a fake double door plastered to the wall. He rang a bell and, when the door did not open, said, "wait for me here, I'll go out and open it from the other side." Then he left the room and gassed the person, for the little cell was his private gas chamber; in one wall of the room there was a small aperture with a lens, so he could observe the demise of his victims. Sometimes he told them that he had to vaccinate them for their visas, and gave them a lethal injection. He did on a small scale what the Germans were doing in the death camps. Just as the Germans told their victims they were going to the showers, he told his that he was taking them through a secret door to an underground hideaway where they would await their departure for South America. After he killed them he dismembered the bodies and placed the parts in civil defense sandbags, emptied of sand, which he dropped into the Seine at night.

Most people did not take advantage of the occupation in quite so extreme a manner. They tried to get on with their lives, and if they didn't like the Germans, they kept it to themselves or, as in the case of certain writers, they kept diaries. Thus to the novelist Jean Guéhenno, the Germans in France didn't belong there, they were out of place. "To the German I see in the street: 'What do you think you look like, with your green uniform, in our streets? Too many buttons. Why gloves in the summer? Why boots? And on your belt, the inscription *Gott Mit Uns* . . . God is with us. Some God! Is He there when you pin a little piece of white paper over the hearts of my friends? I can't look you in the eye, because I might see the small flame that makes you do these things so well."

Actually the Germans had arrived in France hoping to give a good impression. When they came into Paris on June 14, German Winter Relief trucks were right behind the soldiers, with forty-gallon tureens, dispensing soup to hungry Parisians. It didn't take long for lines to form, and the people in line said to one another, "They told us the Germans were starving." But the giving soon turned to taking, and you knew what they were taking because you could see what was no longer in the shops. In a country that produced sugar from beets and oil from olives, there was no more sugar and no more oil. One popular definition of collaboration was "Give me your watch and I'll tell you the time."

Yet is seemed in some cases that the occupiers had been chosen because of their fondness for France. Take Gerhard Heller, who ran the *Referat Schrifttum,* or literary review section, of the Propaganda Office in Paris. If you wanted to publish a book, you needed the censor's *geprüft* certification, and Heller was the censor. But he was not the stereotypical crass censor, he was a fan, a lover of French literature. As a young man, he had studied Romance languages in Toulouse on a French government grant. He did not want to ban books, he wanted to bring out as many as possible, as long as he wasn't reprimanded by his superiors for letting subversive works slip through. His instructions were: Read everything and decide what can appear. But if he made the wrong decision he might end up on the eastern front, losing his cushy job in Paris, at the center of the literary life, with a room at the Berkeley Hotel and a nice French girlfriend. There were certain duties he had to perform. He went one day with another *Sönderführer* to the Presses Universitaires de France on Boulevard Saint-Germain to tell the director to remove Jewish authors from his list. The other *Sönderführer* laid his revolver on the director's desk, for emphasis. On the other hand, Heller made it a point to be friendly with publishers. When they called, he offered them an apéritif. He approved the publication of a novel by the Communist writer Louis Aragon, and of Albert Camus's first novel, *L'Étranger.* But then the French collaborators complained. How could the Germans allow works like this to be published?

So you had the fanatical Nazis, the ideological firebrands, and the brutal enforcers, but you also had men like Gerhard Heller who were fond of France and did no more than necessary to avoid being transferred to a less pleasant place. Sometimes the collaborators, who were more Catholic than the pope, complained. In one instance, their activities provoked a quarrel between the SS and the Wehrmacht in Paris. This came about because of Eugène Deloncle, a onetime naval officer, who in the thirties had started a not-so-secret society called the Cagoule (hood), which was violence-prone. Marx Dormoy, minister of the interior in the Popular Front, dismantled the Cagoule in 1936 and had Deloncle arrested. Then in 1941 Vichy placed Dormoy under house arrest in a hotel in Montélimar. One night, a bomb went off under his bed and killed him. It was the work of Deloncle; that was the kind of man he was. In Paris he became a favorite of the SS and was placed on their list to receive subsidies.

One day that September, Deloncle approached an SS officer, Hans Sommer, with a plan to bomb some Paris synagogues to show that the French disliked the Jews as much as the Germans. Sommer informed his superior, Helmut Knochen, who thought it was a fine idea. But they would keep it a secret operation without informing the military commander, General Otto von Stülpnagel, who was a stuffy old codger. They did, however, inform Werner Best, an SS *Brigadeführer* on Stülpnagel's staff, who coordinated all civilian matters and who backed the operation. On October 2 explosive charges damaged six synagogues. When word of the SS involvement got out, Stülpnagel was so angry that he turned the incident into a crisis of the German command—the Wehrmacht against the SS. He demanded the recall of Sommer and his boss, Knochen. The report he sent to Keitel in Berlin was marked in the margin, in red pencil in Keitel's hand: *Knochenerweichung, du Schwächling* ("Softening of the bones, you weakling"—a pun on the name Knochen, which meant bones). Sommer was transferred, but Knochen was protected by Himmler, and a few months later it was von Stülpnagel who retired, showing that the SS was not answerable to the army.

Deloncle was a wild man; he was not your garden variety collaborator, and in 1944, when the tide had turned, the Germans killed him for plotting against them. The garden variety collaborators were men motivated by ambition, men feverishly climbing ladders, men who had failed in peacetime French society and were now able to succeed only because they piggybacked on the Germans. It was the price of admission. Based in Paris, where Vichy had no control, they formed a disloyal opposition, outflanking Vichy with their intemperate views and attacks. Their foaming at the mouth made Vichy seem moderate. The Germans encouraged the rivalry, for they could threaten to unleash the extremists whenever Vichy chafed at the bit.

The foremost political collaborators always seemed to me to have no genuine existence, but to be loudspeakers in human shape, activated by the Germans. Their names sounded vaguely alike—Déat, Doriot, Henriot, and, of course, Darnand, *le père* Bruck's friend, the embittered World War I hero. Marcel Déat, a rodent-like creature with bad teeth and pouchy eyes, had always hungered for political power. In 1936 he was briefly minister of aviation in a caretaker government. After that, he became a pacifist and started a newspaper called *L'Oeuvre,* in which he wrote the "Why Die for Danzig?" editorial. He continued to publish with German funds and approval, and vented his hatred of Vichy, for once again power had eluded him. Vichy was full of Jews and Gaullists, it was nothing but rottenness and intrigue. Déat had his own political party, the Rassemblement National Populaire, and he liked nothing better than to hold rallies where he talked for two hours about how rotten everybody else was. His was the case of a man who wanted to run things, under any conditions, because he felt that his talents had not been recognized.

Jacques Doriot was a large, fleshy-faced man, the son of a blacksmith, himself a metalworker who had begun political life as a Communist from the working-class suburb of Saint-Denis. Doriot went to Moscow for a Comintern gathering in 1927 and attended a meeting with Stalin, the then thirty-four-year-old Mao Tse-tung, and a ranking Hindu Communist. Doriot understood a little Russian, and he heard Stalin tell Mao and the Hindu, as he pointed to Doriot and several other French delegates: "These over here are nothing! We Asiatics know what we want!" It was the conviction that Stalin held Europe in contempt that led Doriot to break with the party, from which he was expelled in 1934. Going from one extreme to the other, Doriot became a fascist and formed the Parti Populaire Français, which was not so popular. He liked to strut about in a German uniform. The Germans underwrote his activities, keeping him on a leash to use against Laval if needed.

Then you had Philippe Henriot, a talented speaker and an anti-Communist, who drifted into a pro-German attitude, probably having said to himself at some point: "France needs a Goebbels, why not me?'' The Germans gave him a radio program, he appealed to the French fondness for articulate rabble-rousing, and families changed their mealtimes to catch him on the air. In encouraging these men and other lesser misfits, the Germans were encouraging the French tendency to fragmentation. The more groups the better, fighting among themselves, each one claiming to be the bearer of the true cross.

These men had their moment in the sun, but there was a price to pay in terms of devil's bargains, and also in the sense that it was easy to get in but not so easy to get out. Deloncle had a change of heart and the Germans killed him. Darnand had a change of heart in mid-1942 and flirted with the idea of going over to the Gaullists. Through intermediaries, he sent word that he was ready to leave for London and could turn over some important arms depots to the resistance. When Gaston Palewski, de Gaulle's chief of cabinet, brought the general the news, he threw one of his famous fits, saying: "And tomorrow if Darquier [Darquier de Pellepoix, Vichy's commissioner for Jewish affairs] wants to get circumcised, should I take him too?" Because of course Darnand was unacceptable to the resistance in France. You couldn't change partners as in a game of bridge. You were stuck with the side you had picked.

Take the case of Pierre Pucheu, who was Vichy's minister of the interior in 1941, and who decided after the Allied landing in North Africa in November 1942 that he was on the wrong side. He made his way to Morocco via Spain, arriving in Casablanca on May 19, 1943. Wanting to fight the Germans, he volunteered for the 1st Regiment of the *Chasseurs d'Afrique,* thinking that if he joined the army in a humble rank, his political past would be overlooked. But two days later he was arrested, and in August he was put on trial for treason, accused of taking part in the choosing of hostages. Pucheu was sentenced to death and shot before a firing squad on March 20, 1944, perhaps thinking that he would have been wiser to stay put. Life was not a blackboard upon which you could erase your past. Pucheu had jumped into a no-man's-land, unwanted by either camp. His was a sobering example for any Vichy figure contemplating a change of scene.

Arrivisme (the climbing instinct) was of course a strong motive at all levels of collaboration. Professor René Labroue, having had enough of teaching history in a provincial *lycée,* sought a promotion to university professor. He wrote the minister of education, Jérome Carcopino, offering to inaugurate a chair in Jewish history at the Sorbonne, and promising to teach the course in a spirit of total objectivity. Total or totalitarian? wondered Carcopino.

But *arrivisme* was not the only motive. Hatred of the British was another, as in the case of Admiral Darlan, who tracked British naval movements in the Mediterranean from French bases in North Africa and passed the information on to the Germans through the Armistice Commission in Wiesbaden.

Then there was wanting to do what you did best. Jean Bichelonne, Vichy's minister of production, was a technocrat who wanted to exercise his organizational skills, not because he preferred the Germans to the Allies, but to shine in running his department. His ideology was to fight inefficiency. It's a mistake to assume that men are motivated by ideology. Many simply want a chance to employ their talents, even if they know they're on the wrong side.

Then you had those who wanted business as usual. In the city of Lyon, the business capital of the unoccupied zone, the captains of industry were eager to be *deutschfreundlich* (friendly to the Germans) because that way the wheels of commerce turned more smoothly. Business was humming. The silk industry was making parachutes for the Luftwaffe. The Rhône vineyards were shipping wine to Berlin. In 1941 Dr. Haitinger arrived in Lyon to open a purchasing agency, the Center of German Economic Organizations. Here is a May 3, 1942, telephone conversation, monitored by the Vichy police, between the Haitinger office and the firm of Schenker and Company, which the Germans used as dispatchers:

"Good morning, Miss Honigel. This is Mr. Doré of the Schenker Company. Did you receive the case of oranges?"

"Yes, we did. Really, that was so nice. I don't know what to say."

"Is Dr. Haitinger there?"

"No, he's not here this afternoon."

"I'd like to talk to him, we're having problems with one of our employees, a young man of nineteen, who was arrested day before yesterday, Place des Terreaux [in the May Day anti-Vichy

demonstration]. His ideas are like ours, he's *deutschfreundlich.* . . .
I'd like to have this imprudent young man released. His father is
very Germanophile."

In Lyon, there was Marius Berliet, the embodiment of the in-
flexible French *patron* (boss), who owned the biggest truck company in France and kept producing trucks for the Germans
throughout the war. After the war, when Berliet went on trial, the
judge asked him: "Don't you think it would have been preferable
to lay off your workers or put them on half pay, rather than continue to make goods that helped the enemy?"

"Those are subtleties I didn't consider," Berliet replied. "In
any case we were not at war since there was an armistice. I saw
matters only as an industrial leader." Berliet wasn't fond of the
Germans, but he was a self-made man, obstinate and willful, who
was going to do what was best for him. He hadn't forgotten the
First World War when he had wanted to help and converted his
factory to the production of tanks. And then in 1918, with victory
in sight, the government canceled its final order, leaving him stuck
with eight hundred unpaid-for tanks. So in 1940, when they asked
him to make shells, he was in no hurry to convert. The exasperated minister of armaments, Raoul Dautry, requisitioned the factory and put a general in charge. But the shell-making assembly
line, ordered from the United States, with a capacity of 200,000
shells a month, arrived in Lyon after the Germans did. So Berliet
sold it to them. He had also been ordered to make a thirty-two-
ton tank-carrying truck, but by the time it was finished, the funny
war was over, so he sold that to the Germans as well. He continued making as many trucks as the Germans gave him raw materials for. He was so helpful to the German war effort that the
Allies bombed his factory twice.

Berliet was one of the last of the iron-fisted, union-busting *pa-
trons,* who spied on his men and kept a private police force. He
collaborated by unloading workers he wanted no part of: Communists, union leaders, and men of the resistance. He got rid of
his "undesirables" by having them shipped to Germany after the
STO (forced labor) law was passed in February 1943. The way it
worked was this: Berliet, like every other Lyon employer, went
before a commission on the Avenue de Saxe: it met in a dark

room with a long table around which sat a number of German officers. The Germans had a list of Berliet workers whom they wanted for the STO. Berliet told them that he could not maintain his level of production if he lost any more workers. The Germans then went down their list one by one, and Berliet had to make a case for each one. This one had a delicate task that only he could carry out. That one was too old, since the Germans wanted only men in their early twenties. Another reason was health, because they were terrified of importing workers with contagious diseases. So Berliet would say, with an embarrassed tone, so-and-so has syphilis, and so-and-so has tuberculosis. And if there was some-one he wanted to get rid of, he said nothing, and that name was checked off for early departure. The next day the gendarmes came to the man's door with travel orders and told him: "You're leaving tomorrow. It's you or your wife. If you're not here we'll take her." There were also occasions when Berliet combined the business-as-usual policy with the informer policy, when his private police turned workers over to the Germans. They conducted periodic searches of lockers, and in the locker of a press operator named Roger Minet they found the drawing of a hand grenade. Minet was taken to the plant manager, Berliet's son Jean, who asked: "What's this?" "Nothing," Minet replied. "I was doing a bit of *perruque* [literally, wig, figuratively, private work done on company time]. It's a cigarette lighter." As a result, Minet was handed over to the Germans and deported. That was where the business-as-usual policy led you, to sending your workers into forced labor and deportation.

But in ascending order of sleaziness, there were many worse than Berliet. There was the toadying, opportunistic Fernand de Brinon, Vichy's ambassador to Paris. His credentials for the job were that he bowed and scraped before the Germans. As a journalist on the take before the war, he had once written: "I had the honor of approaching Adolf Hitler several times and each time I had the rare and wonderful feeling that one gets in contact with genius." De Brinon passed on accounts of Vichy cabinet meetings to the Gestapo. As ambassador to Paris, he was given a certain number of daily *laissez-passers* to cross into the free zone, which he sold. He also embezzled the money he received from Vichy to distribute to the victims of bombardments.

Lower even than de Brinon were the anti-Semites who crawled out of the woodwork when Vichy passed its anti-Jewish legislation. One of the new laws had to do with the takeover of Jewish property, which created a new profession: *administrateurs des biens juifs* (administrators of Jewish property). You had to ask yourself what sort of person was attracted to a line of work that consisted of finding Jews to plunder? What happened only too often was that in the name of the Aryanization of commerce, you got rid of your competition by denouncing them as Jews, and by using the good old French method of meaning the opposite of what you said, as in this letter from a company in Lyon to the commissioner for Jewish affairs in Paris: "We pray you to believe that this letter is not sent in the hidden aim of hurting a competitor, for such a procedure is frowned upon by my company, particularly during a period when no competition is possible, since we are all at the same table with regard to the rationing of raw materials. . . . Nor do we wish to harm any Jews, we simply want to avoid being their victims." The French during the occupation swam in a deep lake of hypocrisy.

The prize in low conduct, however, went to the Vichy judges who collaborated with the Germans. Starting in November 1942, French courts routinely sent copies of all verdicts and all sentences to the Gestapo. When those arrested were members of the resistance, the sovereignty of Vichy was sorely tested. Example: On January 12, 1943 (by this time the Germans had occupied all of France), Paul Gachet and André Desthieux, both twenty-two-year-old Communists, one armed with a Colt and the other with a Smith & Wesson, were riding their bicycles in the streets of Lyon, following two German soldiers, pursuing the policy of *à chacun son Boche*. They turned into the Rue Villeroy, got off their bikes, and fired at the two Germans. Private Sommeschut fell to the ground, mortally wounded. On February 19, six Communists were captured by the French police, including Gachet and Desthieux. This case came under the jurisdiction of the Vichy courts, but the Germans insisted that Gachet and Desthieux be handed over to them. And so it was done. A German court-martial sentenced them to death, and they were executed on May 26.

Also in November 1942, a Special Court was set up for resistance crimes, and heading its Lyon branch was a fifty-five-year-old collaborator by the name of Faure-Pinguely. In May 1943 a Polish Jew, Simon Fryd, was brought before the court after having been captured and wounded by the French police during an attack on a ration-card center. Faure-Pinguely sentenced him to death, and he was guillotined in November.

On December 12, at 6 A.M., four men in German uniforms rang the bell of Faure-Pinguely's home at 30 Cours Eugène. Faure-Pinguely, a tall man with gray crew-cut hair, let them in. With a convincingly heavy German accent one of the four said in French: *"Monsieur,* we need some clarification on the executions you ordered, particularly of Simon Fryd."

"How can you question my good faith?" Faure-Pinguely asked. "I can assure you that the arrogance with which Fryd spoke to me was enough." That was too much for one of the other "Germans," a childhood friend of Simon Fryd, who struck the judge in the head with his rifle butt. The judge fell, and the "German" placed the barrel of his rifle against his temple and fired once. As a result, the Special Court became more cautious in handing out death sentences. But Vichy sponsored and authorized these kangaroo courts, where men were convicted in a matter of minutes without being heard. The defendant was brought in only to hear the reading of his sentence. The Lyon court sat in Saint-Paul Prison, which was convenient, for the defendant had only to go a short distance from his cell to the improvised courtroom, and, if he was sentenced to death, from his cell to the prison yard, where he was guillotined or shot.

In contrast to active collaborators—the men of Vichy, the cliques in Paris, and the business community (although in all these groups there were anti-Germans)—who were noisy and numerous, making up, say, 10 percent of the population, the resistance was tentative and small in number. Perhaps a couple of thousand joined de Gaulle in England. In France the movement started slowly and modestly with a few people with a mimeograph machine and a letterhead who wanted to provide an alternative to the cooked news put out by Vichy.

Take Henri Frenay, a career army officer and graduate of Saint-Cyr, who had grown up in Lyon on the Rue Duhamel in a traditional Catholic conservative bourgeois family, the kind of family that had been providing magistrates and civil servants and officers to France for centuries. During the funny war, when things were at a standstill, his infantry unit was near Strasbourg, on the Rhine. On the other bank, three hundred meters from his submachine gun, he could see the Germans. One day in April, he noticed some activity, and, looking through his binoculars, saw officers with red lapels, which meant generals. He counted thirteen sets of red lapels, and asked for permission to fire, but permission was refused. The next day the German radio announced that Keitel and von Brauchitsch had visited the front near Strasbourg. When the Germans attacked in May, Frenay was on the canal linking the Marne to the Rhine. His unit was stationed near the World War I cemetery of the Alpine Light Infantry, where soldiers now dug new graves so that sons could be buried next to fathers. On June 13 came the order to retreat, which said: "Flags must not fall into enemy hands." That was the important thing. So the flags were collected, and a fire was lit, and as the name of each unit was called out, an officer stepped forward and threw the flag into the flames, smoke getting in his eyes. "The French are awfully good at rituals of defeat," thought Frenay. He escaped, walking south, and made it to his mother's home on the Riviera, in Sainte-Maxime; the Riviera, still devoted exclusively to the growing of carnations, producing no food. "How thin you are!" said his mother. "And why are you in civilian clothes? Pétain," she continued, "is a father to France." Then came Montoire, the handshake with Hitler, and the policy of collaboration, and Frenay thought "Some father." His first clandestine act was to conceal his thoughts from his mother.

And yet, even after Montoire, Frenay stayed in the army, wondering what to do next. He was posted to army intelligence in Vichy, where he saw the company of guards presenting arms as Pétain left his hotel for a daily walk, hat in hand, nodding at the crowd of onlookers, or rather pilgrims, who had come from far places as though to Lourdes, their eyes misting over, crossing themselves. "Truly, people are as complacent in defeat as they would have been in victory," thought Frenay.

In March Frenay resigned his commission and returned to his hometown of Lyon, where he set up shop with a mimeograph machine, and put out a sheet called *Les Petites Ailes de France* (The Little Wings of France). In July his mother came to visit. She disapproved of his activities. "You're trying to hurt our country," she said, "and I'm sure you're doing your utmost, just as you always do. And if you think I'm just going to keep quiet about it . . . well, you're wrong! I love you dearly, as you know— my children are my whole life—but I believe that patriotic duty comes before maternal love. I'm going to denounce you to the police! I must stop you from doing harm and, yes, from doing yourself harm as well."

"You wouldn't be telling the police anything they don't already know, dear *maman,*" Frenay replied. "They're already after me. But if you insist, don't expect to see me at your deathbed."

In December Frenay merged his sheet with another clandestine publication, *Liberté,* which was run by a professor at the Lyon law school, François de Menthon. One reason for the merger was that most of de Menthon's staff had been arrested. They had not been trained in clandestine activities, so they were easy marks. It's quite possible that the French are temperamentally unsuited for this type of work. They have a hard time taking security measures seriously because they interfere with their social habits and natural garrulousness.

The result of the merger, *Combat,* became the most important underground newspaper. Its first issues in December 1941 were rather mild. *Combat* was neutral toward Marshal Pétain and gave such bland directives as "Boycott German Movies." Nonetheless, *Combat* was read with keen interest by Vichy. The Vichy attitude toward the burgeoning resistance was ambivalent. On the one hand, the Vichy police were looking for Frenay and his friends. On the other, this was the time of the first German reverses in Russia, and Vichy leaders began to think that it might be a good idea to take out a little insurance. The day might come when it would be useful to know someone on the other side who could vouch that you weren't such a bad sort.

The minister of the interior at that time was Pierre Pucheu, whose itinerary we have already followed when he tried to switch camps. In January 1941 Pucheu arranged a meeting with Frenay in Vichy and gave him a note from the ministry to protect him from arrest.

They had a second meeting on February 6. The Vichy minister and the resistance leader discussed the political situation. Pucheu ranted about Jewish bankers and gutter democrats. Frenay saw himself as buying time. As long as he kept the channel open, Vichy would leave him alone. There were no more meetings after February 6, however, for Frenay came under a cloud with his own people for consorting with Vichy, and had to explain his actions.

The kicker to this story is that in March 1944, when Pucheu went on trial in Algiers, Frenay was there, having by that time joined de Gaulle. When Pucheu was convicted and sentenced to death, de Gaulle, who had the right of pardon, summoned Frenay to his office on or about March 15. On his desk lay Pucheu's pardon plea. "Frenay," de Gaulle said, "you met Monsieur Pucheu twice in Vichy. Tell me what happened." Frenay explained Pucheu's concept of Vichy's "double game." To temporize, to alleviate the burden of defeat, until the moment came to join the Allies.

De Gaulle listened attentively, and when Frenay had finished, there was a long silence before he spoke. "This trial," he said, "is monstrous. The man is obviously not a traitor in the ordinary sense of the word. Maybe—probably, in fact—he thought he was serving his country in Vichy, but then the whole Vichy system was founded on dereliction of duty, and could only survive through equivocation. . . . In sentencing him, the Army Tribunal has condemned that system. There was no other way. And yet—" His sentence remained unfinished, and on March 20 Pucheu was shot. De Gaulle's hands were tied. To pardon Pucheu would have been unpopular with the resistance, on whom he was counting when the Allies invaded France.

Until November 1942, however, when the Germans moved into unoccupied France, dealings between Vichy and the resistance oscillated unpredictably between belligerence and a guarded benevolence. Christian Pineau, another resistance leader, was a civil servant in the Ministry of Supplies, and in the spring of 1942 he was summoned to Vichy by his boss, who told him: "If you didn't have a wife and kids I'd dismiss you. I'm looking the other way because I'm humane, not because I approve. . . . I have an opening as inspector of supplies. You don't deserve it, so no funny

125

business, my friend. I'm not going to cover for you. Here we follow the policies of Maréchal Pétain and nobody else's—understand?"

In any case, during the first year of the occupation, resistance activity was pretty tame, limited to putting out pamphlets and newspapers. The men involved weren't even armed. There was a certain amount of *noyautage* (subversion) in government offices. A friendly policeman would let you know when there was an arrest warrant out for you. A sympathetic clerk in the *mairie* (city hall) would spend hours going through registers looking for stillborn children who could be brought back to life and given ID cards. Thanks to *noyautage,* those who worked for Vichy could also pay their dues to the resistance. Then in June 1941, there was an escalation of activities when Russia was invaded. But the killing of Germans by the resistance was limited to the occupied zone, since in the other zone there weren't any Germans. And yet in the unoccupied zone, as the resistance teams began to organize, you began to see a little sabotage. But the resistance was still in its infancy, although it seemed at times that anyone with a letterhead was starting a movement, the National Front of this or that, but what did it mean? Some of these people were mythomaniacs, thought Frenay, like the distinguished opium smoker Emmanuel d'Astier de la Vigerie, who had started an organization called Libération, which he subtitled on the stationery, *Organe du Directoire des Forces de Libération Françaises,* which made him sound much more important than he was. In fact, it was not until 1942 that the resistance began to matter, owing to the help it started getting from de Gaulle and the British, the continued German reverses in Russia, which brought people into its ranks, and the growing unpopularity of Vichy because of its handling of the Jewish question.

IV

SONDERBEHANDLUNG

Sonderbehandlung means "special treatment." It was one of the euphemisms the Germans used for the extermination of the Jews. Essential to the program of mass death was concealment, and veiled language was one of the techniques of concealment. The prize for "tall tales" must surely go to Dr. Ernst Kaltenbrunner, who in 1942 succeeded Reinhard Heydrich as head of the security police (Gestapo and SD). During his trial in Nuremberg in 1945, Kaltenbrunner was asked what was meant by "special treatment." Here is his reply: "Do you know what the Walsertraum is, in the Walsertal, or the Winzerstube, in Godesberg, and their connection with what you refer to as *Sonderbehandlung*? The Walsertraum in the most elegant and fashionable Alpine hotel in all of Germany, and the Winzerstube, in Godesberg, is the well-known hotel where many international conferences were held. In these two hotels we put political leaders and diplomats such as Mister Poncet and Mister Herriot. They were given three times the rations of a diplomat, that is to say, nine times the rations of a German in wartime. Each day they received a bottle of champagne. They corresponded freely with their families, they received packages from France. These prisoners had frequent visits and all their wishes were seen to. That is what we called special treatment."

Edouard Herriot, the mayor of Lyon, who was deported in 1943, had to laugh when he read Kaltenbrunner's testimony. He had never set foot in either of those hotels. He had never been given a bottle of champagne. His rations were often a plate of soup. Visits were forbidden, and he had never received a single letter or a single package. The most surprising thing about the Germans, he thought, even more than their cruelty, was their inability to tell the truth.

Sonderbehandlung was a term that turned up over and over again in German military reports, as in this note of October 25, 1941: "Due to the risk of epidemic, we began on October 8, 1941, the complete liquidation of the Jews of the Vitebsk ghetto. The number of Jews who received *Sonderbehandlung* was around 3,000." Which meant that three thousand Jews in the Russian city of Vitebsk had been shot or gassed and buried in a mass grave. "Risk of epidemic" was another lie to cover up state policy.

The use of this kind of flat and unspecific language was part of the conditioning to do away with any moral reaction. To say that people were "treated" or "taken care of," or that areas were "swept clean," made mass murder impersonal and bureaucratic. It was a way of sidestepping all moral questions by focusing on logistics. The only conceivable way to implement the Final Solution was to convert it into a set of logistical problems, such as crowd control and railroad timetables. It was one thing to kill large numbers of civilians who were on the army's invasion route in Russia. The problems there were how to kill them and how to bury them, and the morale of the troops who did the killing. But when you began deporting people from occupied nations like France, the problems were compounded. You had to identify and arrest those you wanted to deport. You had to transport them over long distances. You had to build and staff camps to receive them. You had to devise stratagems for killing them without alarming them beforehand. You had to dispose of the bodies. You had to negotiate with the government of the occupied country, if it had one. You had to deal with public opinion in that country. At each step of the way, there were practical problems to be solved. The men who were carrying out the Final Solution did not stop to consider what they were doing, so intent were they on how to do it. Their moral sense, already dulled by their conditioning, was further diminished by the mechanics of the task at hand.

When Reinhard Heydrich, whom Göring had placed in charge of implementing the Final Solution, convened the Wannsee Conference in January 1942, veiled language was used. The words "death" and "killing" were never uttered. "Treated appropriately" was the euphemism used for slaughter. The Jews would be brought to the east for labor utilization. "Within the framework of the Final Solution," Heydrich said, "the Jews must be transported under appropriate guard and there assigned to appropriate work service. . . . It goes without saying that a large number of them will be eliminated by natural decrease. The final residue will have to be treated appropriately."

Heydrich listed the countries from which Jews would be removed. In occupied and unoccupied France, he said, the seizure of Jews for evacuation should in all probability proceed without major difficulty. In saying this, Heydrich did not fully understand France or the Vichy government, for there was a period when Vichy actively helped the Germans deport Jews, and another period when they dragged their feet.

The basic Vichy policy, always in the line of give and take, was to protect French Jews by delivering foreign Jews to the Germans. It was "our" Jews against "your" Jews. Aside from its squalid aspects, this transaction was only partly successful. There were roughly 320,000 Jews in France in 1940, about half of them foreign. Approximately 75,000 Jews were deported to death camps, primarily to Auschwitz, of which roughly 50,000 were foreign and 25,000 French. Vichy, in spite of the bargain struck, was unable to prevent the deportation of a large number of French Jews. In Holland, however, which was under a German military government, 110,000 of the 140,000 Jews were deported, almost 80 percent of the total Dutch Jewish population, as compared to less than 25 percent of the total Jewish population of France. Thus, Vichy could argue that it had successfully protected three fourths of the Jewish population, while critics of Vichy could point out that it had aided and abetted in the deportation of 75,000 Jews, of whom about 2,000 returned, according to a train-by-train compilation by the historian Serge Klarsfeld.

When Vichy took power in July 1940, there was not a great deal of sympathy in France for the Jews. In the thirties, a time of depression and high unemployment, France had been swamped with Jewish refugees from Germany and Central Europe. This put a strain on the goodwill of a people known for their leniency in offering asylum to political refugees. In fact, the refugee problem in France was more Spanish than Jewish, since there were 400,000 Spanish refugees as against 160,000 Jews. However, the Jewish refugees seemed more visible, they filled up entire neighborhoods of Paris, and this was at a time when there was an increasingly unpopular Jewish prime minister, Léon Blum. So there was an obsession in France with the refugee question—"Save us from the immigrants, the outsiders, the alien menace"—and much of this obsession was converted into anti-Semitism.

There were various forms of French anti-Semitism. For the neofascist right, as exemplified by a writer like Robert Brasillach, it was a feeling that with the Popular Front government of Léon Blum, the Jews were taking over and were leading the state to ruin. The anti-Semitic newspaper *Gringoire* published a list of all the Jews in the cabinet—ministers, chiefs of cabinet, and attachés—and the list was long. It was pointed out that Jean Zay, the Jewish minister of education, had once published a poem that insulted the French flag. It was noted that Georges Mandel, the Jewish minister of the interior, had been connected with a newspaper backed by the corrupt financier Stavisky, a foreign Jew. As for the old Catholic right, it connected Jews with radicals and Communists, and somehow the Jews were blamed for events in Spain, where the anticlerical government was killing priests and burning churches. In a man like Pierre, Cardinal Gerlier, the archbishop of Lyon, there was a latent anti-Semitism based on the conviction that the collapse of the Catholic banking house where his family had invested its money, the Union Générale, had been caused by the Jews.

All these anti-Semitic strands became interwoven in times of crisis such as the Dreyfus case or the approach of war. Even a staunch Third Republic moderate like Jules Jeanneney, the elderly president of the senate, could write in his diary on June 11, 1942: "Jews in the occupied zone must from now on wear the yellow star. This is shameful for us. But in truth the Jews don't have the habit of solidarity. Those most apt to resistance only bothered with their own personal case and all their efforts were to settle it at X%. They have not finished their expiation." Nor was there a great deal of sympathy for the Jews on the part of some prefects who were privately anti-Vichy, such as Pierre Trouille, prefect of Corrèze, a *département* to the west of Lyon, who wrote in his diary: "The Jewish colony of Corrèze is numerous, too numerous in truth, for this concentration of unfortunates will sooner or later bring down the German thunder."

In such a climate of opinion, it was not surprising that Vichy wasted no time in passing anti-Jewish measures. Vichy came to power on July 10, and on July 22 a commission was formed to investigate recently naturalized Jews. On August 27 a 1939 law forbidding anti-Semitic propaganda was revoked. This was a signal for the anti-Semitic sheets in Paris to vilify at will.

Raphaël Alibert, the minister of justice, drew up a so-called Jewish statue. On September 30 Paul Baudouin, the minister of foreign affairs, noted in his journal: "It is now clear that the only way to prevent the application by the Germans of harsh anti-Jewish measures is to draw up more moderate measures for all of France." (This was the theory of the lesser evil in full bloom.) "The statute prepared by Alibert is severe, much too severe. My point of view is that the Jewish problem should be treated as a problem of foreigners . . ."

Baudouin's entry for the following day, October 1, noted that "for two hours the statute of the Jews was discussed. The *Maréchal* was the most severe. He insisted in particular that there be no Jews in the departments of Justice and Education." This last should be taken with a grain of salt. For Pétain had no consistent view on the matter, but was swayed by people in his entourage like his doctor, Bernard Menetrel, who resented what he considered the takeover of the French medical profession by Jews. Pétain often adopted the opinion of the last person he had spoken to. Georges Villiers, the Lyon businessman whom we last saw with an escaped convict, cleaning up a building to house refugees, had become mayor of Lyon in June 1941 and was invited to Vichy to lunch with Pétain at the Hôtel du Parc. "Well," the *Maréchal* said in greeting, "what is happening in our good city of Lyon? It can't be easy." Villiers at that point had hired the celebrated flutist Moïse for the Lyon Philharmonic, but was told by Vichy that he would have to fire him because he was Jewish. "He's Jewish," Villiers told Pétain, "but he's the best flutist in France, and since we're trying to improve the orchestra I'd like to keep him." "You're right," Pétain said. "I'd do the same." Turning to an aide, he said, "give instructions that Villiers can keep his Moïse."

But in the fall of 1940, as part of the preemptive strategy, a vast body of anti-Jewish legislation started appearing, in keeping with the French mania for codifying everything to the nth degree. It started in a way that did not seem threatening. What could be more harmless than a census? On September 27 foreign Jews were asked to come by a police station and give their name, address, profession, and nationality. And they did, by the tens of thousands, wanting to be law-abiding and thereby sealing their fate. For when the Germans went looking for these Poles, Greeks, Russians, and all the others, they knew exactly who they were and where to find them. And the census could not have been taken without the help of the French police, who did the paperwork and kept the files, and who used an ingenious mechanical filing system devised by the police inspector André Tullard, who was proud of its effectiveness, not realizing that it was an instrument of the Final Solution.

Nor did it seem threatening to define who was a Jew, in the law of October 3: "Will be considered Jewish any person with three grandparents of this race, or two grandparents if his or her spouse is also Jewish." But in the law of October 4 there seemed to be a bit of an escalation: "Foreigners of the Jewish race may be interned in special camps, or be placed in forced residence, by a decision of the prefect in the *département* of their residence." And then, on October 18, an ordinance was passed that Jewish businesses would have to declare their net worth. This was handled by the *préfectures,* and French banks cooperated when the Germans asked them to block Jewish bank accounts.

Over the next months, in 1940 and 1941, the *Journal Officiel* churned out this great miasma of legalistic nonsense, the result of which was to turn Jews into second-class citizens, to humiliate them, to set them apart from the normal life of the country. Aside from Germany, France became the only nation to proclaim a state anti-Semitism, buttressed by such innumerable and incredibly petty laws as these: a law limiting the number of Jewish trial lawyers. A Jew could not hold a job where he was in contact with the public. He could not run a restaurant or sell lottery tickets. A Jew could only shop for two hours in the afternoon, by which time food stores had run out of supplies. Jews were banned from concerts, theaters, museums, libraries, parks, public gardens, and the châteaux of the Loire.

The French measures bore more than a passing likeness to those enacted in Germany a few years before. Let us refer to a cabinet meeting of November 12, 1938, held in Berlin, in which the leaders of the Reich displayed just the same kind of pettifoggery. The question was, should there be a special section for Jews on trains, or should there be compartments that they could use only once Germans were seated?

GORING: I find it more sensible to give them a special section.

GOEBBELS: Not when the train is crowded.

GORING: Just a minute. There will be only one Jewish car. If it is full, the other Jews must stay home.

GOEBBELS: . . . Let's take the Munich Express. . . . Suppose there are two Jews on the train, and the other cars are crowded. These two Jews, then, have a car to themselves.

GORING: If the train is really full, as you say, believe me, I don't need a law. The Jew will be thrown out, even if he has to sit by himself in the toilet for the whole trip.

GOEBBELS: . . . Another ordinance should forbid Jews to visit German spas, beaches, and summer resorts. . . . I wonder if it isn't necessary to keep Jews out of German parks. Nowadays, packs of Jews stroll through the Grunewald. It is a constant provocation; we constantly have incidents. What the Jews do is so exasperating that there are constant brawls.

GORING: Well, we'll set aside a certain part of the park for the Jews. Alpers will take care of putting animals there that look like Jews; the stag has just the hooked nose for it.

GOEBBELS: Next, Jews must not sit around in German gardens. . . . There are Jews who don't look much like Jews. They sit down next to German mothers and German children and begin to gripe and stink up the air.

In enacting their own anti-Jewish measures, the French were doing exactly what the Germans wanted them to do. As Kurt Lischka, the number two SS officer in Paris at the time, put it on January 30, 1941: "It is better to let the French do these things, so as to avoid the reaction of the French people against anything coming from Germany. The German services will hold themselves to making suggestions." Lischka, the Breslau-born son of a bank employee, was part of a small but growing SS office in Paris. After going to law school, he had joined the Gestapo at the age of twenty-six, in 1935. Lischka was eventually sent back to Berlin under a cloud after being charged with corruption in the theft of watches from people he arrested.

Lischka's boss was Helmut Knochen, who was thirty years old in 1940. The word *Knochen* means "bones," but this Knochen was a cultivated and worldly man. He had a doctorate in English literature from the University of Magdeburg, his hometown, and had written his thesis on Coleridge. He joined the SD in 1936 as part of its so-called intellectual wing, and in less than two years was promoted to major. In November 1939 he captured two British agents on the Dutch border in a daring raid and received the Iron Cross from the hands of Hitler himself. As we have seen, General Stülpnagel asked for his recall in October 1941 after the attacks on the synagogues, but he was protected by Himmler.

Rounding out the initial SS trio was Theo Dannecker, who in 1941 was twenty-eight years old. He had joined the SS at the age of nineteen and had gravitated to Eichmann's Jewish Affairs Section in Vienna in 1938, where some of Eichmann's obsession with the Jewish problem rubbed off on him. When he arrived in Paris in the summer of 1940, he was asked to go to the Ministry of Colonies and look into Madagascar as a possible Jewish homeland. Dannecker was a vain and self-important young man who needed someone to open the car door for him and carry his things.

In keeping with its policy of making suggestions, the Paris SS office urged Vichy to set up a commissariat for Jewish affairs. In March 1941 Xavier Vallat was named to head up the commissariat. He was an odd choice, for he had already annoyed the Germans in his previous post in charge of veterans' affairs, for his curmudgeonly attitude and defense of Jewish veterans. Nonetheless, the Germans accepted Vallat. Since their policy was to let the French handle Jewish matters, it would have been inconsistent to quarrel with Vichy's choice.

Vallat, the tenth child of a teacher, came from the region of Vienne, south of Lyon. His was a family of the old Catholic right, with its nostalgia for the monarchy and a Joan of Arc-like mingling of religion and nationalism. When Vallat's father was informed that one of his sons had been killed in the Argonne in 1915, he said: "God gave him to us, God took him back." Vallat's anti-Semitism was part of his general xenophobia. He was anti-Jewish, he said, in the same way that he was anti-German and anti-Russian. He didn't mind Jews in homeopathic doses, he said, but there were too many of them, and they had taken over medicine and the law and the banks and the department stores and the grain business.

Vallat had the distinction of being the only member of the National Assembly who made an anti-Semitic remark when Léon Blum came to power on June 6, 1936. "When the average Frenchman sees," he said, "that the decisions of Monsieur Léon Blum are taken in a group that includes his secretary, Monsieur Blumel, his secretary general, Monsieur Moch, his confidants, Monsieur Cain and Monsieur Levy, and his penholder, Monsieur Rosenfeld, he will be apprehensive."

And yet, in his compartmentalized way of thinking, Vallat exempted from his prejudice old French Jewish families and Jews who had fought for France. To understand this double standard you had to go back to 1917, to a military hospital at Estrée-Saint-Denis in the north of France, which was being evacuated. A young *Chasseur Alpin* was about to be left for dead on a blood-soaked stretcher. The last remaining surgeon decided that it was worth trying to save him, and amputated his crushed left leg above the knee. A Jewish stretcher-bearer helped carry him back to the French lines, where a Jewish nurse helped him back to health. The young man survived, although he was missing a leg and blind in one eye. A few weeks later Vallat's parents were looking out the window of their house near Vienne when they saw someone hobbling down the path on crutches—Xavier Vallat had come home.

In his new job, Vallat soon had the Germans grumbling that he was blocking their every initiative. At that point they wanted to start interning foreign Jews in camps around Paris. Vallat went to see General von Stülpnagel on April 4 to tell him that he was against internments. What, the general asked, did he propose to do? "Will you send your foreign Jews back to their countries of origin?"

"Most of them came from the Reich," Vallat replied, "or countries occupied by the Reich. Do you want them back?"

"You could send them to Spain," the general said.

"Spain is not going to create a Jewish problem on its own territory after having settled it four centuries ago," Vallat rejoined.

On the same day, Vallat had a talk with Theo Dannecker, whom he detested on sight for his fanaticism and posturing. When Dannecker said that Jews should be separated from non-Jews, Vallat replied: "The ghetto is a ridiculous and stupid old-fashioned idea of no interest in the modern world."

"Vichy is full of Jews," Dannecker angrily replied. "Pétain is friends with the Grand Rabbi, and nothing is done about it."

Reporting to Otto Abetz on June 25, 1941, on his talks with Vallat, Dannecker said: "Vallat wandered round and round on the subject and showed no understanding."

In spite of Vallat, however, the Germans went ahead with their plans. On May 14, about 6,400 foreign Jews in Paris, who were listed on the census roll, were summoned to police stations to have their papers checked. The 3,400 who showed up were arrested and sent to camps in Pithiviers and Beaune-la-Rolande, about fifty miles south of Paris, and in Compiègne, north of Paris, where the armistice had been signed. Then, in August 4,230 Parisian Jews were arrested in reprisal for Communist agitation and sent to the newly opened camp of Drancy, three miles outside Paris. Drancy was an unfinished housing project, high-rise and low-rent, with apartment buildings on three sides of a rectangular court. These camps were administered by the French police, who had also arrested and processed the interned Jews.

In the meantime, Vallat was drafting more anti-Jewish legislation: a law banning Jews from the universities, and a law for the Aryanization of Jewish property. In September Cardinal Gerlier came to see Vallat and told him: "No one knows better than I do the terrible harm the Jews have done to France. It was the crash of the Union Générale, sought by the Jews, that ruined my family. Your law is not unjust, but it is lacking in charity in its application."

The Germans, however, were increasingly unhappy with Vallat. They complained about the light penalties administered to those who violated the anti-Jewish laws. In Lyon the Jew Marc Hazan had refused several summonses to fill out the census form and was fined one hundred francs, which was not even a slap on the wrist. Lischka complained in a letter that Jewish painters were still allowed to show their works at the Salon d'Automne. Vallat's method of dealing with such letters was not to reply. Dr. Werner Best, the top civilian assistant to General Stülpnagel, said that "Vallat ought to be called 'the Commissioner for the Protection of the Jews.' "

Then, on December 12, 1941, 743 French Jews, many of them veterans, were arrested in Paris in reprisal for attacks on German soldiers. Vallat, a stubby, stocky, multiple-chinned man with an opaque monocle covering his blind eye, went over to the Germany military headquarters at the Hôtel Majestic and asked that the veterans be freed at once. Werner Best told him that they could not be freed collectively. "I would prefer that you give me a list of individual cases," he said. Vallat drew up a list of sixty, but when he brought it to Best he lost his temper. "Not only are there in this group three hundred and fifty veterans," he said, "sixty of whose war records I personally salute, there is even an Alsatian who won the Iron Cross for courage in the ranks of the German Army." Vallat's intervention did no good. On December 15 fifty-three of those arrested were shot as hostages.

It was Vallat, again with the aim of preempting German policy, who created the UGIF (Union Générale des Israélites de France) on November 29, 1941, whose purpose was to let the Jews manage their own affairs. But in fact the UGIF became an instrument of German policy, just as Vichy was. Its first task was to collect a billion-franc fine levied by the Germans on the Jewish community. Vallat helped the UGIF obtain bank loans by using the blocked accounts of rich Jews as collateral. Another UGIF task was to provide shoes and blankets when Jews interned in French camps began to be deported in 1942. The UGIF thus became part of the deportation process, while promoting the idea that Jews would benefit from Vichy's "protection."

The UGIF had offices, employees, a budget. It did a certain amount of social and relief work, and it conducted a voluminous correspondence with members of the Jewish community. It became a clearinghouse for information concerning the anti-Jewish measures. On who was Jewish and who was not, on exceptions and special cases, on Jews married to Aryans, on nationalities thought to be protected. Families of those who had been arrested wrote the organization to inquire where their relatives were. The UGIF was allowed to operate in Drancy and had lists of internees there, but could do little to help them. It was successful in appealing a small number of cases, like that of a woman who had gone out for an hour without her yellow star and was arrested, and of a woman arrested in the street who had left a three-month-old baby that she was breast-feeding at home. Jews sent to Drancy had their apartments placed under seal by a police commissioner. Then a social worker from the UGIF would ask to have the seals lifted so that she could bring the prisoners things from the apartments.

To counter the charge that they were collaborators, the UGIF people could point to their clandestine work in the unoccupied zone, helping Jews cross into Switzerland and Italy, and using double-entry bookkeeping and coded entries to cover their underground activities. "In very difficult conditions" meant that someone had escaped arrest. "Needs food" meant that someone needed a false ration card. The UGIF produced false documents and funds for those trying to escape France, and it placed Jewish children with Aryan families. But in the end, it had the same ambivalence vis-à-vis the Germans that Vichy had. It might be able to get around them here and there, but at the price of cooperating with them on a day-to-day basis.

Jacques Helbronner, the president of the Jewish Consistory in France, and a personal friend of Pétain, who saw him twenty-seven times in 1941, protested to the Marshal about the creation of the UGIF at a meeting on March 7, 1942. "I spent an hour and a half with the *Maréchal*," he reported. "He is kept in ignorance of what is going on. He knew nothing about the UGIF. . . . When I told him about [the camps in] Compiègne and Drancy, he replied, 'It's terrible.' I was not expecting such forthright ignorance. I told him that Aryanization was an economic blunder, and he asked me, 'What does that mean, Aryanization? . . . Does it mean that the Jew who loses his business is ruined?' He indicated that he felt the Commission for Jewish Affairs should be a protector of Jews." But this was partly Pétain's "senility defense," pretending not to know what was going on when much of the time he knew very well. A year and a half later, on October 23, 1943, when the seventy-year-old Jacques Helbronner and his wife were arrested in Lyon and deported to Auschwitz, Pétain did nothing to help his old friend.

At about the same time that the first hostages were being rounded up in Paris to be shot or deported, there was a shooting party at Schonof, von Ribbentrop's hunting lodge, on October 26, 1941. Count Galeazzo Ciano, Mussolini's foreign minister, was having fantastic luck. Himmler, there with his personal doctor, Felix Kersten, said with a snarl: "Look what good luck that Ciano has. I wish the Italians in Africa had been such good shots. In Albania they scattered like sheep. But here Ciano does fine! When there's no danger, the Italians are heroes."

"Don't begrudge him the pheasants," Kersten said.

"Of course I don't begrudge him the pheasants. Personally I find no pleasure in blowing the poor creatures to bits. Defenseless birds. I would never have come to this shooting party if the Führer had not expressly asked me to do so."

More pheasants flew by, and most of them went straight over Ciano's head. "It's just as if they were bewitched," Himmler said. "They all fly to Ciano."

Nearby, von Ribbentrop said: "Isn't this shoot symbolic? As we combine to shoot down the pheasants, so we'll also combine to down the enemies of Germany!"

Kersten told Himmler he liked deer-stalking, to which Himmler replied: "How can you find any pleasure in shooting from behind cover at poor creatures browsing on the edge of a wood, innocent, defenseless, and unsuspecting? Properly considered, it's pure murder. I've often bagged a deer, but I must tell you that I've had a bad conscience each time I've looked into its dead eyes."

Kersten went over to Ciano, who said, "Wonderful this shoot. Fantastic beaters. Lots of pheasant. But women not pretty in Germany. Comic hens but no golden pheasant. No grace. And these *Tedeschi* always look so angry. Why not laugh a bit?"

As the year ended, the Germans had lost patience with Xavier Vallat. An SS report dated December 11 said: "Vallat has proved in numerous ways that he has no serious intention of accomplishing a real and efficient Aryanization. It was hardly to be expected in view of his anti-German sentiments." Vallat and the Germans had different agendas. To Vallat and the men of Vichy, anti-Semitism meant limiting the economic and political influence of the Jews, while to the Germans it meant the destruction of the Jews.

Finally there was a showdown. A meeting between Dannecker and Vallat on February 20, 1942, turned into a violent argument, which was not without its droll side, since each was claiming to be a better anti-Semite than the other. According to Dannecker's account, he told Vallat: "With your delaying tactics, you have proved once more that you did not really want the separation of Jews from non-Jews."

Vallat replied "in an unheard-of tone": "I have been an anti-Semite a lot longer than you have. And what's more I'm old enough to be your father."

This was no way for one of the conquered to talk to his conqueror. "This is an official conversation," Dannecker reminded him. "You cannot talk to me this way."

"Yes," replied Vallat, "but I cannot tolerate a man half my age treating me like a subordinate."

"And I can't tolerate your language," replied Dannecker, "the more so since your statement is without any foundation. I deem this reproach to be a piece of incredible impertinence and I consider this meeting over."

Vallat's goose was cooked. He was not only fired, he was forbidden to enter the occupied zone. His replacement was the fawning Darquier de Pellepoix, a mediocrity and failure, whose only notable trait was his militant anti-Semitism. In 1938, when the assassinated attaché vom Rath was lying in state at the German embassy in Paris, and when even French anti-Semites were saying, "He may have been killed by a Jew, but it's still one German less," Darquier de Pellepoix had laid a wreath at the foot of vom Rath's coffin.

The replacement of Vallat was one of several events at the start of 1942 that completely changed the way Jews in France were treated. Up till then, there were divergences between the German Army and the SS, and within the army itself. Hitler, in September 1941, had demanded that for every German soldier killed in occupied countries, fifty or one hundred hostages be shot. This order was issued by Field Marshal Keitel via the OKW (Armed Forces High Command) on September 16. Then, on December 7 and 12, Keitel signed the *Nacht und Nebel* decrees, which were specifically directed at France, where sabotage and attacks on soldiers were on the increase. Lieutenant Colonel Hotz, the popular military commandant of Nantes, had recently been killed. Hitler argued that death sentences only created martyrs and should be meted out sparingly (except to hostages). All suspects whose cases could not be cleared up at once were to be transferred to Germany after a court-martial "under cover of darkness" *(bei Nacht und Nebel)*. The suspects would vanish without a trace. Not even their next of kin would know where they were. Keitel and the head of his legal department both objected to this, but Keitel finally issued the order with a preamble that it was "the carefully weighed and considered will of the Führer that . . ." a phrase to distance himself from the decree.

So now the Wehrmacht, with its traditions of honor and legality, was immersed through these orders in the machinery of repression, in the barbarous methods of killing and deporting suspects without a trial. For in practice, the SS used the N&N decree to get rid of whomever they wanted by sending them directly to concentration camps.

On January 15, 1942, General Otto von Stülpnagel wrote Keitel to object to the reprisal order, which he said was in violation of military tradition, international law, and human practice. Stülpnagel's objection amounted to a letter of resignation, and in February he was replaced by his cousin, General Karl Heinrich von Stülpnagel.

With the arrival of the second Stülpnagel, there would be no more quarreling between the army and the SS, which now had a free hand to deport the Jews. In addition, the Wannsee conference that January spelled out the program of the Final Solution. So the stage was set, and needed only the overzealous Theo Dannecker to put matters in motion in France. That February Dannecker went to Vichy to see the German consul general, Krug von Nidda, who told him that he believed the French were finally ready to do something about the Jewish question. Von Nidda suggested deportations of one thousand to five thousand a month. There were also the thousand hostages who had been arrested in December. Some had been shot and the rest were being held in Compiègne while awaiting deportation.

On March 4 Dannecker was in Berlin, telling Eichmann that the French should do "something really positive, like the deportation of several thousand Jews." Eichmann agreed. They might as well ask for five thousand. He wanted to ask the French for a service charge. After all, he was doing them a favor. Thus, the initiative for the deportation of French Jews came from Dannecker rather than Eichmann. Some of the men in the field were more active than their bosses.

With the green light from Eichmann, Dannecker went to Compiègne on March 12 to designate who should be deported. On March 20 the police commissioner of Compiègne reported to the prefect of the Oise *département* in Beauvais that on March 19, 178 Jews, guarded by gendarmes, were transferred from Royal-Lieu in Compiègne to the camp of Drancy, the point of departure for deportations: "These 178 Jews were chained two by two. Many wore the Legion of Honor and military decorations. One of them asked me the name of the chief judge in Compiègne. Why did he want to know? I asked. He said, 'Because I am a judge myself, I am Monsieur Laemle, judge at the court in Paris.' Pointing to his handcuffed wrist, he said, 'And in spite of everything, we remain French.' Someone handed the judge some chocolate, which the man he was handcuffed to grabbed, saying, 'It's for me, it's for me.' "

Dannecker had one last obstacle to overcome, and that was to find a train. The whole scheme of deportation depended on trains, at a time when they were urgently needed for troop transports on the eastern front. That is why the Final Solution began with Polish and German Jews, who were closer to the death camps. The priorities of the Final Solution were in conflict with military priorities. Eichmann had to build up his authority slowly so that his needs were met over other freight movements. At this point, however, Eichmann told Dannecker that it was up to him to find a train.

Dannecker found a passenger train, and 1,112 Jews, about one half foreign and one half French, arrested as hostages in December 1941, were deported on March 27. It was the first and next-to-last time a passenger train was used, because these trains required guards between each car. Subsequently, freight trains with locked cars became the transport of choice. Dannecker himself made this inaugural trip from France to Auschwitz, to see that everything went without a hitch. One of the deportees, however, escaped. Of the other 1,111, twenty survived.

It was a three-day trip eastward across France, then across all of Germany and two thirds of southern Poland, then onto the main Katowice–Auschwitz–Krakow line. A spur track went right up to the camp, a marshy tract of land between two rivers, at the entrance of which there was a wooden ramp five hundred meters long (replaced in 1943 with a cement ramp). As the train chugged up to the ramp, the deportees saw watchtowers and barbed-wire fences; they caught their first glimpse of the *rayés* (striped ones), as well as SS officers and men assigned to the arrival. At the ramp itself, there was an immediate selection between the fit and the unfit. The latter were driven away in trucks to the "showers," passing signposts that said: *Toward the baths* and *Toward the disinfection.*

Outside the "showers," SS officers reassured the new arrivals: "You will now be bathed and disinfected so we don't get any epidemics in the camp. Then you will be taken to your barracks where you will get some warm soup, and you will be put to work utilizing your skills. Get undressed here in the yard and put your clothing down in front of you on the ground." As the new arrivals undressed, the officers continued to give instructions and answer questions. "Put your shoes next to your clothes so you can find them again after the bath." "Is the water warm? Of course. Warm shower." "What is your trade? Shoemaker? We need them urgently. Report to me right away afterward."

Once the victims were inside, the door with the rubber seals and iron locks was closed and they could hear the bolts being fastened. On the ceiling, the seals of six apertures were removed. A head wearing a gas mask could be partly glimpsed at the vent—a "disinfector." Containers of small blue pellets dropped through the vents, which were then quickly shut. As Rudolf Hoess, the camp commandant, explained it at his Nuremberg trial: "It took us from three to fifteen minutes to kill the victims in the gas chambers, the time varying according to weather conditions. We knew they were dead when they stopped screaming. Usually, we waited half an hour before opening the door and removing the bodies, which our special commandos went over to remove rings and gold teeth." When the bodies were removed, the women's hair was cut off and the gold teeth were pulled out and they were taken to the ovens, tended by another special commando. The fires had to be stoked, the fat had to be drained off, the mountain of burning corpses had to be turned over so the draft could fan the flames. It was all done on the day of arrival. This group never even went inside the camp, which the other group, the fit, was led into to be registered and shaved and tattooed and uniformed and to begin camp life.

After the first train on March 27, the deportations stopped temporarily in April and May because there were no more available trains. During those two months, three important political events took place: the return of Laval in April, the arrival of an SS general to run the Paris office (a sign of the expanded SS role), and the visit to Paris of Himmler's chief aid, Reinhard Heydrich.

One of Laval's first decisions was to appoint a new chief of police, thirty-three-year-old René Bousquet. In Bousquet you had the perfect civil servant, who believes above all else in the institution he is serving. He had gone into the prefectoral branch, where he had risen as quickly as his colleague Jean Moulin. He was decorated for organizing rescue operations when the Garonne River flooded. In 1940, as prefect of the Marne *département,* he took a clear anti-German stance. When two Communists were shot by the Germans, he put on his prefect's uniform and placed wreaths with tricolor sashes on their graves. As a result, the Germans wanted to bring him before a court-martial. But Bousquet, as Laval's chief of police, developed the River Kwai syndrome. He was so proud of his police that he was ready to strike a devil's bargain: If his men were given better weapons, if they increased in number, if he could establish a police school and keep independent of German supervision, he would cooperate on the deportations.

Bousquet became friends with Karl Oberg, a paunchy, bald, round-faced, bespectacled SS general who arrived in Paris that May. Fernand de Brinon, the obsequious Vichy ambassador, wrote that "General Oberg was a fat Prussian with a shaven head who knew nothing about France or French ways of thought, could not speak our language, was not very intelligent, and was completely dominated by a young SS officer, Major Hagen, who had the advantage of speaking French well, but the dreadful disadvantage of hating us and of nursing his resentment of us."

Still in his twenties, Herbert Hagen owed his rapid advancement in the SS to his friendship with Eichmann, with whom he had gone to Palestine in 1937. Hagen wrote in his report on the trip, dated November 27, 1937: "The way the Jews have of distrusting one another is apparently not the determining factor in Palestine's economic chaos . . . the Jews' complete inability to manage their country's economy is demonstrated by the existence in Jerusalem alone of some forty banks that thrive on swindling their own people." Such was the youthful, efficient bureaucrat and dedicated anti-Semite who, from his sunny office on the Avenue Foch, overlooking the Bois de Boulogne, would be advising Oberg on the deportations to Auschwitz.

Reinhard Heydrich arrived in Paris on May 5 and stayed for a week, to get the Final Solution moving. He was an excellent example of the harebrained types that could rise within the Nazi hierarchy. The son of a music teacher and an actress, he joined the navy but was dismissed for getting a girl pregnant, and then joined the SS. It was Heydrich who had the idea of starting a party intelligence service, the *Sicherheitdienst* (SD), which he headed and which in 1939 merged with the Gestapo as the Office of Reich Security, or RSHA. He soon became Himmler's favorite, not only because he combined ruthlessness with an inventive mind, but because Himmler felt he could control him. For Himmler had convinced himself, even though there was no proof, that Heydrich was of "mixed race." This, Himmler thought, was the secret to Heydrich's character. He was compensating for his Jewish side by excelling in sports, by being a champion fencer, the best shot, the best rider, and by piloting his own plane. He was pitiless with Jews for the same reason, so Himmler believed, even though in appearance he was the prototypical blond brute.

Heydrich saw Bousquet on May 6, because he wanted to enlist the cooperation of the French police in exchange for promises of autonomy. At his collaboration trial after the war, Bousquet testified that he had resisted Heydrich's demands and said to him: "Let me tell you that you are making it impossible for us to stay in our jobs. Why are you asking us to do things you would not do yourselves?" Heydrich, again according to Bousquet, rose, stood at attention, and said: "This is the language of a man, which I can understand."

According to German documents, however, a gentleman's agreement was struck between Heydrich and Bousquet that the French police would retain a large measure of autonomy and would in exchange help with the deportations. In addition, Bousquet proposed that the foreign Jews in the camps in the unoccupied zone be deported. Not realizing that deportation meant almost certain death, Bousquet saw this as a way of getting rid of undesirable foreigners.

The Germans were doing a good job of keeping the true nature of the deportations a secret. On May 16 Dannecker received a report about a certain Armand Taub, who had been mistakenly sent to Auschwitz since he was in an "exempt" category, being married to a non-Jew. Should Taub be repatriated? Dannecker added this note to the report: "It is out of the question to repatriate anyone from the concentration camp." Because of course, someone repatriated from Auschwitz would reveal the camp's true purpose.

After his talk with Bousquet, Heydrich gave the go-ahead for the deportation of six thousand Jews, and went back to Prague where about two weeks later, on May 27, he was mortally wounded by two Czech resistance fighters. But, as we know, the cemeteries are full of indispensable men, and the carrying out of the Final Solution went on without him.

In France the way was clear for further deportations, with the French police making no objections to rounding up Jews and putting them in camps. But a major obstacle remained—the availability of trains. This was where Dannecker the eager beaver took another initiative. On May 13 at 11 A.M., he went to see General Kohl, chief of the department of rail transportation for France. They talked for over an hour, and Dannecker found the general receptive and willing to help. As he put it in his report, "I gave the general an overlook of the Jewish question and the policy concerning the Jews in France. I was able to see his uncompromising anti-Semitism and his 100 percent approval of the Final Solution of the Jewish question, which has as its goal the total extermination of the adversary [*mit dem Ziel Restlöser Vernichtung des Gegners*]." In his zeal, Dannecker neglected to use the usual veiled language and openly mentioned extermination. As we will see, this was not the only time he got carried away.

Kohl told Dannecker: "If you wish to evacuate ten thousand or twenty thousand Jews eastward, you can count on me to give you the necessary rolling stock." Kohl added that "he considered the solution of the Jewish problem in France as a vital necessity for the occupation troops. That is why, at the risk of being taken for a brute by certain people, he always adopted a radical attitude toward this question."

With Kohl's promise to provide trains, the deportations resumed on a regular basis. In 1942, there were forty-three trains from France to Auschwitz, each carrying about a thousand Jews: one in March, four in June, eight in July, thirteen in August, thirteen in September, and four in November. Of the 75,000 Jews deported from France to Auschwitz during World War II, about

40,000 were sent in 1942, the peak year, when the system was running at maximum efficiency.

The story of each of these trains is depressingly similar. People were herded in and herded out, and most were gassed on arrival. They were gulled, lulled, dulled, and pulled into the gas chambers. There were very few escape attempts. On the list for train number five, which left Beaune-la-Rolande on June 28, the following notation appeared next to the name of Adolf Ziffer: *Tot bei fluchtversuch* (Killed during an escape attempt). The circumstances that removed these people from a normal life into the cycle of deportation were heartrending: On train number three, which left Drancy on June 22, there was a twenty-year-old girl, Annette Zelman, who had been arrested on May 23. The reason for her arrest was that she was planning to marry an Aryan, an infraction known in Germany as "racial soiling." The young man's father, a Paris doctor named Henri Jausion, complained to the police, and Annette was sent to Drancy and deported a little more than a month later. Dr. Jausion said that he had merely wanted her returned to her family.

Train number three is worth examining for another reason: of its 1000 passengers, 435 were French Jews. Laval's agreement with the Germans to abet the deportation of foreign Jews in exchange for protecting French Jews had not yet been made. In addition, 150 of those French Jews were World War I veterans. Gendarmes were assisting in the deportation of compatriots who had fought for their country. If Xavier Vallat had still been commissioner for Jewish affairs, he would have acted to protect his beloved *anciens combattants,* but he had been replaced by the flunky Darquier de Pellepoix.

Here is a June 26 report from Guibert, the French commander of Drancy, to the Paris police *préfecture*: ". . . Captain Dannecker arrived on Saturday June 20 at 8:45 A.M. and said he must have 930 internees ready within the hour and prepared for the Monday departure on the 22nd. I told him that this was impossible, since the doctor was absent. I asked him to trust me, that I would have the 930 ready on Monday morning at 6 A.M. There was only one way to reach this figure, and that was to include French Jews, notably veterans. . . . I had to add 150 veterans to reach the figure of 930. . . . I even had a small reserve of 15 in case of last-minute changes. . . . Saturday and Sunday were devoted to rounding up the designated 930 and searching their baggage. I must tell you that this operation was carried out in a way that gave me full satisfaction. . . . On Monday morning the 930 were in the courtyard at 5:45 A.M. . . . I was asked by the Commissariat for Jewish Questions to release two or three, drawing replacements from my reserve. . . . Dr. René Bloch, surgeon at the Hospital for Sick Children, and holder of the Legion of Honor for his conduct in the 1914–1918 war, was imperatively designated by Captain Dannecker. . . . Three or four internees in poor health had to helped aboard the bus. One of them had to be carried aboard on a stretcher, and after a medical examination, Captain Dannecker ordered that he leave with the others.'' This June 22 train consisted of 934 men and 66 women. There were twenty-four survivors.

In carrying out the deportation program, the mainspring was Captain Dannecker, who took on an importance that was completely disproportionate to his rank. Dannecker's superiors in Paris, General Oberg and Major Knochen, did not know what to make of his zeal and ambition. He was always writing notes, reports, and telegrams, in which he used their names without their knowledge. He knew he was protected by Eichmann, to whom he reported directly as head of the anti-Jewish section in the Paris office of the SS. Dannecker saw that it was to his advantage to take a vigorous position on the Jewish question to which both Hitler and Himmler attached so much importance. It was a way of shining and currying favor, of earning favorable fitness reports. It was also a way to compensate for his private life, a topic of some concern, for he was a great habitué of nightclubs and brothels, and had on several occasions created scandals that had to be hushed up. Knochen felt that the more Dannecker got into the nightlife, the more he tried to make up for it with anti-Jewish activity, multiplying notes and telegrams. It was Dannecker who went to Drancy to supervise the departure of every train. He was known in the camp as Captain *Verboten*: *verboten* to smoke, *verboten* to look out the window during inspection, *verboten* to walk in the courtyard.

Dannecker finally went too far, making Oberg and Knochen realize that they had to get rid of him. On June 11 he met with Eichmann in Berlin and proposed to deport 100,000 Jews in one hundred trains. He did this on his own authority without consulting with his superiors, who observed that he must have been crazy to propose such huge figures that had nothing to do with reality. He told Eichmann that he could expedite three trains a week. Each train would have one locomotive, three passenger cars for the guards, and twenty freight cars containing about one thousand Jews.

Upon his return from Berlin, bad news awaited Dannecker. On June 16 General Kohl had been ordered to send to Germany, for the spring offensive on the eastern front, 37,000 freight cars, 800 passenger cars, and 1,000 locomotives. This would seriously cut into Dannecker's needs, but he decided to go ahead anyway, for Kohl said he would have some trains for him at the end of June.

The next step was to work out a plan with the French police, but in the meantime the yellow star ordinance had come out, which had an unanticipated result. The ordinance required all French Jews in the occupied zone over the age of six to wear a yellow star sewn on their garments over the heart. Every Jew had to go to the nearest police station and collect three stars, which would be charged against his textile rations. Again, as in the case of the census, most Jews were law-abiding and went to get their stars. But this effort to isolate them had the opposite effect by making them visible. It was shocking to see a man walking down the Champs-Élysées wearing his *Croix de Guerre* next to a yellow star. It was heartbreaking to see a group of little girls playing in the street, stars pinned to their dresses. The star brought persecution out into the open for everyone to see. Knochen wrote in a note on June 16: "A large majority of the population does not understand this measure. There are continuous complaints about 'poor Jews,' particularly Jewish children. It is not seen as a matter of race, but religion. . . . But the yellow star has been well received among anti-Semites. . . . With these measures, there are many persons reappearing as Jews who were previously hidden. The population of Paris does not hide its surprise at such a large number of Jews."

Dannecker had now scaled down his deportation plan from 100,000 to 40,000 Jews, and badly needed the French police to make mass arrests. On June 26 he went to see Jean Leguay, Bousquet's assistant. Dannecker was afraid he would not be able to meet his quotas if he was limited to foreign Jews, and told Leguay that he wanted a concrete proposal for the arrests of 22,000 Jews in the Paris area, 40 percent of whom should be French nationals. Leguay said he would have to report to Laval. Laval, informed of Dannecker's demand, said at a cabinet meeting on the same day, June 26, "I will give a reply to this myself. It will be negative."

Armed with Laval's refusal, Leguay on June 29 told Dannecker "very clearly that the French government is not disposed to arrest, between now and July 15, the number of Jews in Paris that you had demanded." Vichy was strenuously resisting the German demands, and Dannecker saw his plan collapsing. He was so angry with the French position that once again he overstepped his authority, and told Leguay that he, Dannecker, was going to arrest 22,000 Parisian Jews and would require the assistance of 2,500 French policemen to do so. "You must get in touch with the Paris police chief," he said, "for it is probable that I will from now on take direct charge of this action and for a time of about two weeks, I will need, each day, at least twenty-five hundred men of the French police in uniform, in addition to some plainclothesmen." Knowing he had Eichmann's support, Dannecker was trying to force the hands of Oberg and Knochen by presenting them with a *fait accompli.*

The next day, June 30, Eichmann arrived in Paris and backed up his man. Eichmann also established a plan for trains that would leave from cities other than Paris—two from Bordeaux, one from Angers, one from Rouen, one from Chalon, and one from Orléans. Knochen resented Eichmann, who had once been his aide and was now a lieutenant colonel while he was still a major. He also thoroughly disliked Dannecker, but had to remain on good terms with him, for he was having an affair with Dannecker's secretary, Marianne Birreshorn, whom he would soon marry.

To show Dannecker that he was under a cloud, he was omitted from the crucial meeting on July 2 attended by Oberg, Knochen, and Bousquet when Bousquet caved in and agreed to use French police to arrest foreign Jews in both zones. Bousquet started by taking the position Laval had instructed him to take. When the Germans asked, "What about our plan to deport 10,000 Jews from the unoccupied zone and 22,000 from the Paris region?" he replied: "Following a comment of the *Maréchal,* Laval proposed that the French police should not make the arrests in the occupied zone. This should be left to the occupying forces. For the unoccupied zone, Laval proposed, with the backing of the *Maréchal,* to arrest and transfer for the moment only the foreign Jews."

Thus Bousquet conveyed the Vichy position: Let the Germans make the arrests themselves in the occupied zone. In the unoccupied zone, the French would arrest only foreign Jews.

This would never do, thought Knochen. It would be a disaster to have German troops round up Jews in the Paris region. Public reaction would be terrible. To give in to the French position would be to lose credibility, to lose prestige, while to try to force the French police to make the arrests would invite a political crisis with Vichy. Knochen worried about losing his pleasant Paris assignment, now that with Heydrich's death he had lost his mentor. In his report, Knochen wrote that "on the French side they had nothing against the arrests themselves. Only having the French police carry them out was embarrassing. This was the personal wish of the *Maréchal.* " Thus, Knochen, like Bousquet, was hiding behind Pétain.

Then an annoyed General Oberg intervened, saying: "I am forced to see that even though the French have allowed the yellow star in the occupied zone, they have not yet attained a sufficient understanding of the Jewish question to proceed in the arrests of Jews without hesitation. The only conclusion is that Vichy does not yet understand this problem."

Bousquet replied that the French had nothing against Jews being arrested, but did not want it done by the French police, which would be troublesome. This was the Marshal's main concern.

Oberg said that if the French government was opposed to arresting Jews, it should not count on the understanding of the Führer. This was the "Führer" or "bogeyman" argument. Once Hitler was apprised of this obstinacy, he would unleash his fury on the

French people. Bousquet was warned by both Oberg and Knochen that if he did not develop a more positive attitude it would be seen as a direct flouting of Hitler's will.

Bousquet was so shaken by what sounded like an ultimatum that he went beyond his instructions and arrived at a compromise with the Germans. The French police would arrest foreign Jews in both zones, but not French Jews. Supposedly spared, French Jews were nonetheless deported by the thousands—6,500 in 1942. But Bousquet and Laval considered it damage control. By insisting on the distinction between French and foreign Jews, they pointed out later, they saved more than 80 percent of the former.

At a cabinet meeting the next day, July 3, Pétain and Laval agreed to the compromise reached by Bousquet. Pétain said the distinction between French and foreign Jews would be understood by the public. Laval said it was a distinction between "French Jews and the refuse sent to us by the Germans themselves." "The intention of the German state," he went on, "is to create a Jewish state in the east of Europe. It would not be dishonorable if I expedited one day toward this Jewish state the innumerable foreign Jews who are in France."

There is every indication that Laval genuinely believed the German cover story about a Jewish state in Eastern Europe. How could he have known about the death camps when even people who were sent there did not know? Ignorance made them submissive and they went meekly to their deaths. Jewish women in Drancy insisted on taking their children with them.

This is why when Dannecker arrived in Vichy on July 4 to brief him on the forthcoming deportations, Laval told him: "You should be ashamed of yourself to separate the parents from their young children." Having no suspicion of their true fate, he thought it was cruel not to deport children with their parents. Laval did not like to discuss these matters with Dannecker, whom he thought was a madman, and also he told Bousquet to deal only with Oberg, whom Bousquet was cultivating, inviting him to lunch at home to meet his wife.

On July 6 Dannecker reported to Eichmann: "To this day, we've only been able to raise the question of foreign Jews, to at least start things going. In a second phase, we will proceed to Jews naturalized after 1919 or 1927. . . . On July 4 Laval proposed that at the time of the evacuation of Jewish families from the nonoccupied zone, children under sixteen should be taken too. As for the Jewish children who remain in the occupied zone, the matter does not interest him.'' After the war, Laval would be accused of callousness in sending children to their deaths, whereas in fact he believed he was acting in a humanitarian way by keeping families together.

According to the minutes of the July 10 cabinet meeting: "In a humane intention, the chief of the government obtained—contrarily to the initial German proposals—that children under sixteen be allowed to accompany their parents." The Germans, knowing what their fate would be, did not want to take the children, while Laval, not knowing, insisted until they consented.

Initially the Germans had wanted to clear out the provinces first, but their compromise with the French made them concentrate on Paris, where the bulk of foreign Jews lived. Dannecker was preparing what he called his "great Parisian action," where he hoped to catch 22,000 in the net. At the same time, most of the trains ordered by Eichmann from the five provincial cities could not be filled because there were not enough foreign Jews in those areas. Only one, from the western city of Angers, was able to leave, thanks to the activity of the SS captain there, Hans-Dietrich Ernst, who succeeded in rounding up 824 Jews, 201 of them French. The train left for Auschwitz on July 20.

But not every SS officer was an Ernst or a Dannecker. In Bordeaux, for instance, the SS officer in charge was a man named Luther, who conducted no operations against the Jews. The head of the anti-Jewish section was Hans Bordes, who did not make a single arrest. When he got letters of denunciation, he threw them away. He was reprimanded for his passive attitude, but no action was taken against him. Thus, it was not surprising that the Bordeaux train, due to leave on July 15, had to be canceled. When Heinz Roethke, Dannecker's assistant, told Eichmann this on July 14 by telephone, Eichmann threw a fit. To him, the Jews were a transportation problem and nothing else. He, Eichmann, had pledged that this train would leave Bordeaux filled with Jews, so the cancellation was a loss of face, a blow to his professional pride.

"Why was that train canceled?" Eichmann demanded in fury.

"Because the bearers of yellow stars [French Jews] could not be included," Roethke explained. "In Bordeaux there are only one hundred and fifty foreign Jews."

"Don't you realize it's a matter of prestige?" Eichmann asked. "I have had long conversations with the Ministry of Transport to obtain these trains. I finally succeeded in obtaining them, and now Paris is canceling a train. This is the first time I have seen such a thing. It is the sort of thing that will make a very bad impression. I don't even want to inform Mueller about it [Heinrich Mueller, the head of the Gestapo], for if I did I would look ridiculous. I am going to think things over. I wonder if it is not better purely and simply to cross France off the list of countries from where Jews can be evacuated." Thus, the French would be punished for their unwillingness to comply with the Eichmann timetable by being deprived of a deportation program.

In Paris, however, a Commission for the Organization of the *Rafles* (roundups), consisting of Knochen, Lischka, Dannecker, Bousquet, Darquier de Pellepoix, and others, met on July 8 to decide how to carry out the "great Parisian action." Here is how it would be done: Police inspectors would sort out the census files of foreign Jews and group them by *arrondissement* (district). The police commissioner in each of the twenty *arrondissements* would then get his district's files. Armed with names and addresses, which the Jews themselves had provided, the police would have no trouble arresting them. The prisoners would then be assembled in the *mairies* (city halls) of each *arrondissement* and divided into two groups: adults with no children, who would be sent directly to Drancy, and families, who would go by bus to a way station, the Vélodrome d'Hiver, or Vél d'Hiv, a huge indoor sports arena for winter bicycle races. From there, they would be sent to the four camps near Paris. The plan called for arresting an estimated twenty-two thousand Jews: six thousand (the childless adults) to Drancy, six thousand to Compiègne, five thousand to Pithiviers, and five thousand to Beaune-la-Rolande. From each of these camps, one thousand Jews would be deported weekly. To carry out the operation, a task force of nine thousand policemen would be deployed. The students in the police academy had to be recruited to make up the manpower. There were 1,632 arrest teams, carrying 23,926 index cards, who would start out at 4 A.M. to catch people still asleep.

A second meeting of the Commission for the Organization of the *Rafles* took place on July 10, when it was decided to establish the age limit at fifty-five for women and sixty for men. The date of the action, set for the thirteenth, was moved up to the sixteenth, after the French national holiday of Quatorze Juillet. Various deportation details were attended to, such as the number of buckets (in lieu of toilets) assigned each train. There would have to be forty buckets per train, which would add up to eight hundred buckets for twenty trains.

On July 10 Dannecker cabled Eichmann: "French police will carry out the arrest of stateless Jews during July 16–18. It is expected that after the arrests about 4,000 Jew-children will remain behind. . . . I request an urgent decision by letter as to whether the children of the stateless Jews about to be deported may be removed also."

Unknown to Dannecker, Major Knochen had already filed a report about his subordinate's nocturnal activities, in which in several instances he had gone to brothels and administered severe beatings to the girls of his choice. He was an embarrassment to the service, Knochen said and asked for his transfer to the eastern front. Another way of cutting Dannecker down to size was to arrange for him to miss the *rafle* that he had inspired and organized, and whose leader he claimed to be. Only July 11 he was sent on the weeklong tour he had asked to take of the internment camps in the unoccupied zone.

On July 15, the eve of the roundup, workers in the Paris office of the UGIF, on the Rue de la Bienfaisance (Charity Street), were preparing nametags with little strings from lists provided by the Paris police. The UGIF leaders clearly knew what was coming, and there was some discreet leakage. There were also leaks from various police commissariats, and in some cases money changed hands. In other cases, the arrest team said: "We'll be back in half an hour when the family's ready," thus giving them a chance to escape.

On the morning of July 16, on the Rue des Thermopyles in the

14th *arrondissement,* two gendarmes knocked on an apartment door. Nine-year-old Annette Muller awoke and heard them say, "Hurry up, get dressed." And heard her mother reply, "Take me, but don't take my children." "Now, now, *madame,* don't complicate things and everything will be fine," one of the policemen said. Her mother pulled a sheet off the bed, spread it out on the floor, and began throwing belongings on it. But then she stopped and said, "I must comb Annette. She can't leave looking like that." She hunted around for the comb. It was nowhere to be found. One of the policemen took the little girl aside, looked her in the eye, and said: "Go and buy a comb at the notions shop and come back right away, hear?" The woman in the shop told her: "Run away, don't go back." Run where? Annette wondered. She paid for the comb and returned to the apartment. As they left, she and her brother Manuel and her mother, she picked up her doll, but the gendarme who had told her to go buy the comb pulled the doll out of her arms and threw it on the bed.

Now they were herded into the Vél d'Hiv through the tunnel by which the bicycle racers came onto the track, and they found room in the bleachers. Big ceiling lamps shone down on them. Families huddling together, surrounded by their belongings. Suitcases wrapped in eiderdowns, tied with string. A Red Cross ambulance, removing people on stretchers. No bathrooms, no water, no food, no place to sleep. People weeping, people spitting blood, people sitting there shaking with their faces in their hands. A Red Cross worker gave Annette a cookie and a sardine. There seemed to be a great many children. Some were playing on the Vélodrome track. Scratchy loudspeakers announced: "It is forbidden to run on the track."

Several days later they boarded trucks for the camp of Beaune-la-Rolande. The order had not yet arrived from Eichmann whether children should be deported with their parents, so the ones under sixteen were held temporarily at the camp while their parents were deported. At Beaune-la-Rolande, Annette and her brother were saved by nuns, who placed them in a French family in the unoccupied zone. Annette's mother was sent to Auschwitz, where she died.

On the morning of July 16, on the Rue de la Convention in the

159

15th *arrondissement,* fourteen-year-old Lazare Pitkowicz, his younger brother, and his parents were arrested and taken to the Vél d'Hiv. Lazare volunteered to fetch water for women and the elderly, and, using money people gave him, was allowed to go and buy bottled water in a grocery store in the Rue Nelaton. He noticed when he returned that one of the exits was not guarded. Lazare told his mother that he wanted to make a run for it. "What is a fourteen-year-old boy alone in Paris going to do?" she asked. He went to his father, who thought for a long while and then nodded. Lazare kissed his parents for what would be the last time and walked out through the unguarded exit. He had a school chum whose parents put him up, which was a brave thing to do, for those who harbored Jews were severely punished. Then he went to an UGIF children's home on the Rue des Rosiers, but sensing that there was something wrong with it, went back to his chum's. A few days later the UGIF home was raided.

Lazare Pitkowicz left for Lyon with false papers and became a courier for the resistance, delivering messages on his bike all over the city. In 1943, by which time the Germans had reoccupied the unoccupied zone, he was bicycling across the Place Antonin Poncet one afternoon when a *traction avant* (a black Citroën used by the Gestapo) cut him off. He was arrested with his messages and taken to the École de Santé (Gestapo headquarters) and questioned. Who did he know? He was shown photographs to identify. He was stripped, and struck, and whipped. They used their fists and their feet. An officer came in and said in French with a German accent: "I'll show you how to make a child talk." "He hit me in the *parties sensibles* [sensitive parts, a euphemism for genitals] with a *nerf de boeuf* [swagger stick]," Lazare recalled. "I had the good sense to faint." As a way of gaining time, and looking for a chance to escape, he decided to tell the Gestapo about some fictitious meeting places he could lead them to. He told them that every evening a car came to the Place des Cordeliers in central Lyon to pick up his messages. Two Gestapo men followed him as he rode to the Place des Cordeliers on his bike. When one of them went into a café, he threw his bike at the other one and ran off on his fifteen-year-old legs. In 1945 Lazare Pitkowicz, by then seventeen, became the youngest *Compagnon de la Libéra-*

tion, the highest Free French honor. He received the decoration from the hands of General de Gaulle. Perhaps he and others like him redeemed the conduct of those nine thousand French policemen involved in the *rafle* on July 16 and 17 who were just doing their jobs. Many said they were disgusted by what they had to do . . . but they did it.

The results of the big *rafle* were disappointing. They had collected 4,051 children, 5,802 women, and 3,031 men—far more women and children than men. Certain police inspectors had advised certain rich Jews not to be at home. A note from the director of the Paris police said: "It should be noted that in some cases, when they refused to open the door, the inspectors had to force them. There were five suicides and three attempted suicides."

On July 20 Dannecker was back from his trip to the unoccupied zone, where he had visited the camps of Les Mille, Rivesaltes, and Gurs. In a conversation with the director of the camp at Les Mille outside Aix-en-Provence, Dannecker was told that Jews were still fleeing France. Ten thousand had left in 1941, and were continuing to leave in 1942, though it was more difficult since Lisbon was now barred to them, and the only route was via Casablanca. According to Dannecker's report: "The chief of the camp at Les Mille . . . remarked that the Jewish emigration organization HICEM paid any price for passage on ships to permit Jews to emigrate. This is a proof that the world Jewish community knows that the Jews in territories under German sovereignty are headed for their total destruction." Once again, Dannecker's vehemence had caused him to express himself without the usual circumlocutions. And if Dannecker knew what was going on, then his superior, Knochen, had to know. Knochen, at his trial in Paris after the war, said under oath: "I did not know the real fate of the Jews who were sent to Germany. From what Eichmann told me, I thought they were being concentrated so that they could be sent to Palestine and Madagascar once peace was established."

When Dannecker got back to Paris, he saw at once that the deportation program was in big trouble. The Paris *rafle* had netted only about twelve thousand, while trains were scheduled to deport forty thousand. These trains had been arranged for in advance on the basis of projected results, and there was a large deficit to make up. There could be no more cancellations because they would make Eichmann look bad and threaten the credibility of the entire program. Thus, Dannecker reported, "a new action against the Jews must be launched IMMEDIATELY. We must expect that the category of non-French Jews will be insufficient, and that the French will have no other solution but to include the Jews naturalized in France since 1927 and even since 1919. On several occasions the undersigned has explained to Bousquet's representative, Leguay, that for our part, we have the firm intention of evacuating, from August first, ten thousand Jews—for the moment—coming from the nonoccupied zone. My recent trip to that zone has allowed me to ascertain that the police officials there have not yet been informed of any projected action. We must thus insist on the necessity for an action as swiftly as possible. . . ."

The problem of the four thousand children under sixteen was cleared up on July 20 in a telephone call to Eichmann, who gave the go-ahead as soon as trains became available. As it happened, it was only in mid-August that the deportation of children began. Since their parents had been sent away earlier, these children were orphaned in the camps for three weeks while their fate was being decided by the Nazi bureaucracy.

On July 27 Leguay told Roethke that the French were ready to deliver three thousand to four thousand foreign Jews from the camps in the unoccupied zone. Roethke replied that these Jews "could only be considered a small down payment." Leguay said that Vichy estimated a total of only twelve thousand Jews in that area. Roethke replied that on the basis of Dannecker's tour, there were three times that number. The French must make every effort to find "deportable elements." If need be, they should intern all the foreign Jews in the unoccupied zone.

While these discussions were taking place, Jews caught in the Paris *rafle* were being processed and deported. The buses started arriving in Drancy on July 16 and 17, and the passengers waited for hours in the camp courtyard under a hot sun to be registered. Categories of exemption were established: Pregnant. Married to a non-Jew. Employed by a German office or agency. Member of an exempt nationality.

The first train carrying those captured in the *rafle* left Drancy on July 19 with an escort of forty gendarmes as far as the German border at Neuburg, where German guards took over for the rest of the trip to Auschwitz. Four more trains left Drancy, each with about one thousand passengers, on July 22, 24, 27, and 29. By then Drancy was pretty much emptied out.

On July 28 Roethke recapitulated: The plan now was for thirteen trains to leave in August and thirteen in September. He was worried about a "loss of inventory." He was counting on five trains of Parisian Jews from July 28 to August 7; then four trains from August 7 to 17 with Jews from the unoccupied zone; then, four more trains from August 19 to 26 with children from the Paris *rafle;* then two more on August 28 and 31 with more Jews from the unoccupied zone. As for the thirteen trains in September, he had not yet determined where the "inventory" would come from.

On July 31 a train left the Pithiviers camp with 1,049 passengers. Some of these were mothers who were forcibly separated from their children before embarking. It was the duty of the gendarmes to push them into the cattle cars, prodding them with their gun butts. On August 3 another train left Pithiviers with 1,034 passengers, most of them women, and the same scenes were repeated.

On August 3 Dannecker briefed General Oberg on points to raise at a dinner at the Paris-Paris Club, where he would be joining Laval, who had been complaining about the "demential" number of Jews coming into the unoccupied zone. He could now be told that when the police started arresting Jews in that zone as well, the Jews would no longer be so eager to move there. This was Dannecker's last report in the Paris SS office, for at about that time he was transferred to Bulgaria, where he devoted his energies to deporting twenty thousand Jews from Bulgarian-occupied Thrace and Macedonia.* His place was taken by Roethke, who, although less flamboyant, was no less a frenzied bureaucrat. A born inquisitor, Roethke had studied theology in Berlin before joining the Nazi party. An idea of his mentality can be gleaned from the handwritten comments he wrote in the margin of an August 4 memo from the Italian consul general in Paris, Gustave

*Dannecker hanged himself on December 10, 1945, in the American-controlled prison of Bade-Tolz, in Germany.

Orlandini, who insisted that no anti-Jewish measures should be taken against Italian Jews without the specific agreement of the appropriate Italian consulate. "This is not true at all!" wrote Roethke in the margin. "Absurdity! Insolence! This was not approved by me!"

On August 5 a train carrying 1,014 passengers left Beaune-la-Rolande, and on August 7 the resources of Pithiviers and Beaune-la-Rolande were combined to fill a train—647 Jews from the former and 426 from the latter. That about exhausted the "inventory" from the Paris *rafle,* with the exception of the four thousand children under sixteen remaining in the camps.

While all this was going on, two American Quakers, Mr. Noble and Mr. MacClelland, reported after seeing Laval on August 6: "It is not easy to find an explanation for these deportations. Up to a certain point it may be an urgent German need for labor. . . . But seeing that children, old people, and the sick have been deported (we know cases of epileptics, of the paralyzed, of madmen and the senile regrouped in a camp to be deported), and seeing that their destination . . . is the Jewish reserve in Poland, the need for labor does not completely explain these measures. . . . The best explanation we can find is that the German plan for a new Europe calls for a purge of undesirable elements. While other aspects of the plan have been delayed, for example the Russian campaign, this part, in the hands of fanatics, is pitilessly pursued in keeping with the original plan. . . . [The Jews] have no illusions concerning the fate that awaits them in Poland."

By August 10 the four thousand Jews promised by the French had been shipped to Drancy and Beaune-la-Rolande and were ready to be deported. A train left Drancy on August 10, carrying one thousand German Jews from Gurs in the Pyrénées. These were the same people who had been sent to France from Baden and the Palatinate in October 1940, and had been interned by the French. Some of them were quite affluent, arriving at the camp well dressed, their wives in furs. They tried to make camp life as civilized as possible; Gurs, for example, had a Beethoven club, English classes, and a library. And now, after almost two years, these Jews, who had been expelled from Germany, were being sent back there and to points east, shuttled from internment camp to death camp. From this particular August 10 train, there was one survivor. On August 12 another one thousand left Drancy, coming originally from the camps of Les Mille, Gurs, Noé, Récébédou, and Vernet.

On August 13 an order from Eichmann arrived from Berlin: "In no case should there be convoys made up only of children." The children had to accompany the adults, so that the adults could look after them. This was the signal for the first deportation of children. Since there was a train leaving Beaune-la-Rolande the next day, August 14, it was decided to add about one hundred children to the list. In the regulation order made out in triplicate before each deportation (the bill of lading, one might say, one copy to Berlin, one to Paris, and one for the officer in charge of the train), this indication appeared: *Darunter erstmalig Kinder* (For the first time including children).

So then came the Children's Hour. It was decided in the next few days to transfer three thousand, ranging in age from two to twelve (older ones had already been deported) from Pithiviers and Beaune-la-Rolande to Drancy. (On August 29 the personnel in those two camps shared a bonus of twenty thousand francs for a job well done.) The buses began arriving at Drancy on August 15, their engines grinding, raising clouds of dust in the courtyard. The children got off the buses and stood there, bewildered. They looked around and saw barbed wire and uniformed guards. They were hostages to the gods of darkness, but where was the God of children? He was not in strict attendance.

In the courtyard, silent and confused, children four and five years old picked through the rows of bags, looking for their *baluchon* (bundle). The youngest ones did not know their names. One of them said: "I am Pierre's little brother." Some of them had cardboard name tags around their necks, but more often they had lost their tags, or the rain had washed out the names. Many were barefoot. Physically, they were in a pitiful state, undernourished and covered with vermin and open sores. Mentally, they were in a state for which childhood does not prepare one. What does a child, who feels life in every limb and breath, know of death?

Drancy was not equipped to receive large numbers of children.

Teams of women inmates were given armbands that read: SOCIAL SERVICES and permission to move about in the children's part of the camp. They were kept in what was called the *escalier de départ* (departure stairway), where they slept in large barrackslike rooms, one hundred to a room, on straw mattresses on the floor. Many got diarrhea from the cabbage soup that was served at every meal. It was useless to wash their clothes or their mattresses, for a few hours later they would be soiled again. There were pails on the landing, as there would be pails in the cattle cars.

And they waited. And they wept at night. And during the day they played "search games." Some of them had franc notes that their mothers had sewn into the lining of their clothes. A six-year-old boy to another boy: "You be the gendarme and see if you can find my money." It was the children in their games who made up the term *Pitchipoi,* to designate the unknown and mysterious place where they were bound, and this invented word was adopted all over the camp: *Pitchipoi,* the unnameable. A little girl to her doll: "We're going to *Pitchipoi.*"

On the day of departure, the children were awakened at five and dressed in the semidarkness. Some refused to move. They lay on the damp straw crying. The gendarmes, who had to carry them downstairs past the overflowing pails, were unnerved. They heard a four-year-old boy addressing his absent mother, repeating, *"Maman, je vais avoir peur"* ("Mommy, I am going to be afraid"). The children lined up in the courtyard, where bus engines were already running. It was still dark enough that the camp searchlights were on. Some children were pulling suitcases that seemed bigger than they were, and some were carrying bags made from bedsheets, and some were holding dolls and teddy bears, and it took two and a half hours to process them on to the buses. Their names were called out, and if there was no answer, they wrote down *enfant sans identité,* and went on to the next name.

Seven trains with children together with adults left Drancy on August 17, 19, 21, 24, 26, 28, and 31. Their progress from then on is painful to record. These words spring to mind: the Swiss Guards' song, *"Notre vie est un voyage dans l'hiver et dans la nuit. Nous cherchons notre passage dans un ciel ou rien ne luit"* ("Our life is a journey into the winter and the night. We search for our passage in a sky where no star shines"). Children in the freight cars—like the subway at rush hour—for three days, in a closed and windowless car in the heat of August, with the stink, the lack of air, and the difficulty of relieving oneself. Those who survived the trip arrived ill and dehydrated at Auschwitz and were taken at once to the gas chambers. Not one survived. And some of those children were two years old. And they had been escorted to the border by French police, in the land of Voltaire and the Rights of Man.

And in his office at the Hôtel du Parc, Laval, whose naïve insistence that children be deported with their parents had led to just that, was governing France. And in the hotel dining room, Pétain was reminiscing about Verdun over lunch. And in his Paris office on the Rue Monceau, René Bousquet was wondering about promotion to a ministerial post in recognition of a job well done. And in Auschwitz, the SS doctor Johann Kremer made this diary entry for September 2, 1944: "At three this morning I attended for the first time a special action. It made Dante's hell look like a quasi-comedy. It is not without reason that Auschwitz is called an extermination camp."

It was when the Jews were taken from the camps in the unoccupied zone in August that two distinguished cardinals, men who had the authority to act as spokesmen for the overwhelmingly Catholic French population, men whose measured opinions carried enormous weight, decided to speak up. The persecution of the Jews caused the pro-Pétain Church to challenge the Vichy regime. Opposition developed into a passionate struggle for basic human values, led by Church elders.

Sixty-two-year-old Pierre, Cardinal Gerlier, archbishop of Lyon and Primate of the Gauls, on August 19, 1942 wrote a personal letter to Pétain that was still rather mild in tone: "We have learned that the very painful measures taken in the occupied zone against the Jews have begun to be applied on this side of the line. We cannot consider without pangs of the heart a treatment which violates the essential rights of all human beings and the basic rules of charity." This was a man who had said, of the anti-Jewish legislation: "We do not forget that the French authorities have a problem to solve."

Seventy-two-year-old Jules-Géraud, Cardinal Saliège of Toulouse, the capital of the Languedoc in southwestern France where courtly love was born, had been there since 1928, and was known to be energetic and authoritarian. But in 1932, during a visit to Rome, he took a fall in a corridor of the French embassy that left him partly paralyzed and gave him a serious speech impediment. Confined to his office, unable to speak in the pulpit, understandable only to a few familiars, the cardinal nonetheless continued to administer his archdiocese.

Now it happened that near Toulouse there were two camps that had been built for Spanish refugees, Noé and Récébédou, which became internment camps for Jews. On August 3 and August 8, 450 Jews were evacuated from these two camps, and on August 20 Cardinal Saliège received a visit from a Catholic social worker, Mlle. Dauty, who had witnessed their departure. "They had to go on foot from the camps to the railroad station," she told him. "It was a terrible spectacle, the elderly and the infirm stumbling as they walked. . . . Old women, weeping, were obliged to stop every few steps. At the station there were heartrending scenes, people fainting, attempted suicides, screaming fits."

So impressed was Cardinal Saliège by her account that he went at once into his study and wrote, in his barely decipherable hand, a pastoral letter to be read that Sunday, August 23, from the pulpit of every church in his archdiocese. The letter was typed, mimeographed, and distributed by bicycle, and a copy somehow reached M. Chenaut de Layritz, the prefect of the Haute-Garonne *département* of which Toulouse is the *préfecture*. De Layritz summoned the cardinal's vicar, Monsignor Louis de Courrèges, telling an aide: "Get Courrèges over here. Saliège is practically senile."

"I must say," the prefect told the vicar, "that I deplore that the points of view of the Church and of the state should be so far apart. I ask you to prevail on the cardinal not to have this letter read." Saliège refused, although he did agree to tone down the wording, changing *scènes d'épouvante* (scenes of horror) to *scènes émouvantes* (poignant scenes).

The prefect banned the letter, and ordered every mayor in his *département* to see that it not be read in the parish churches, as it was "hostile to the government." Most of the parish priests defied the prefect's order, in the first open conflict between the

Catholic Church and Vichy. They climbed up in their pulpits and expressed by proxy the true outrage of a good soul:

"That children, that women, that men, that fathers and mothers should be treated like a vile herd [vil troupeau], that members of the same family should be separated from one another and sent to an unknown destination—this sad spectacle it was reserved for our times to see. . . . You cannot do whatever you wish against these men, against these women, against these fathers and mothers. They are part of humankind. They are our brothers."

Saliège's pastoral letter had tremendous impact. For the first time, someone had spoken out and said: "You cannot do these things." Excerpts soon appeared on posters printed by the Communist resistance, and the text of the letter was transmitted by diplomats to their governments. The public was now informed about matters that were not mentioned in the censored press, making apparent the rift between the real France and the phantom France of Vichy. On August 26 Laval summoned Monsignor Rocco, the secretary of the Vichy nuncio, Valerio Valeri, who was out of town. "The Holy See should be informed," Laval said, "that the eventual retirement of Cardinal Saliège would be welcomed by Vichy, a government to which he is obviously unfriendly." The pastoral letter would sow discord in an already divided population, he said. The British would see to it that it was spread all over the world. "Personally," Laval added, "I do not want the police to search the archbishopric, where the Gaullist sheet *Combat* is prepared." Laval expressed his "unshakable resolution" to send back to Germany all non-French Jews. "Even those who are given sanctuary in religious establishments," he warned, "will be taken out and turned over to the Germans, who will deport them to a sort of home in Poland."

On August 26, the same day that Laval saw Monsignor Rocco, there were further roundups all over the unoccupied zone, and these Jews began to leave for Drancy in groups of one thousand. On August 28 Hauptsturmführer Geissler, a Gestapo officer, was in Bousquet's Vichy office and overheard a telephone conversation between Bousquet and a Swiss police official who was complaining that because of the French sweeps, the Swiss border was overrun with fleeing Jews.

"Yes, you know," Bousquet said, "I'm ready to turn over the

Jews to anyone who wants to rid France of them. If you want them, you can have them all!'' Then: "Yes, I understand you very well, but for a long time, our line of conduct was influenced by the same considerations, and then we were forced to realize that we were wrong. These persons were not grateful, and that is the reason why we must rid our country of them.'' And finally: "All right, I'll think about it some more, and we'll talk again.''

Among the Jews rounded up on August 26 in the unoccupied zone, 550 were from Lyon who were taken to an empty factory in the suburb of Vénissieux while awaiting transfer to Drancy. A Catholic group called Amitié Chrétienne, recently formed by the Jesuit priest Pierre Chaillet to assist refugees and Jews, sent a team to Vénissieux led by Georges Garel, an electrical engineer, and a Jewish-born priest, Father Glasberg. They arrived at night to a scene of indescribable confusion. The electricity was out, and there were only a few candles available. Families sat huddled in the dark, trying to grasp what was happening. Garel and Glasberg decided to persuade families to give up their children. This was a very strange job of salesmanship. They had to talk to people they didn't know, who often spoke little or no French, and convince them to leave their children behind in the hands of complete strangers.

"You can imagine what it was like,'' recalled Garel, "going up to people and saying, 'Give us your children.' You couldn't tell them, 'You are doomed, let the children survive.' We had to say as little as possible. And in the dark it was hard to find the families with children. So we decided to give orders rather than to plead. We said, 'We came for the children.' Sometimes we used physical force to pull them away. '' Sometimes the parents agreed, putting on a cheerful face for the sake of their children and promising that they would be back to get them soon.

Garel and Glasberg rounded up eighty-four children, who were taken to a safe house at 10 Montée des Carmélites. On August 29 General Robert de Saint-Vincent, commander of the 14th military region in Lyon, received the following request from the chief of police, Marchais: "Lend us several squadrons from your garrison, to keep order during the embarcation of 550 Jews that we are sending to the occupied zone.'' The general replied: "I will never lend my troops for this type of operation." Forty-eight hours later he was asked to resign his commission within the fortnight. He wrote the minister of war, General Bridoux: "You would give your cook a week's notice, and you're giving me two."

When the 550 Jews from Lyon left for Drancy on August 31, the prefect, Alexandre Angeli, noted that 84 children had been removed from the group and taken in charge by Father Chaillet, who was acting with the support of Cardinal Gerlier. On September 2 Angeli called the cardinal and told him: "Tonight, there is a train coming from Les Mille camp with Jews that we are turning over to the Germans. We will add a car so that you can put the children that you have on board. I ask you to bring these children to the station."

"Monsieur le préfet," Gerlier replied, "their families have entrusted these children to me. You are not going to ask a father to deliver his children to the police, I hope."

Angeli said that he was forced to insist, and that he was coming in person to the archbishopric to talk to him.

"In that case," said Cardinal Gerlier, "if you want to come to the archevêché, come to the archevêché! But I can tell you, you're not getting the children." And he hung up.

Father Chaillet and several of his associates were in the room when the cardinal took the prefect's call. "Now get out of here," Cardinal Gerlier told them. "I don't want to see you. The prefect is coming to ask me to give up the children, and I don't want to know where they are. Take care of it!" But as they left, the cardinal asked where the children were hidden. Father Chaillet, knowing that Gerlier was capable of changing his mind under pressure, gave him a false address. Soon homes were found for the children with Catholic families in the Lyon area.

On September 3 Father Chaillet was arrested and placed in a résidence surveillée. Cardinal Gerlier wrote a pastoral letter to be read on September 6: "The new measures of deportation taking place against the Jews are leading to such painful scenes that we have the imperious and painful duty of protesting. We are seeing a cruel dispersion of families where nothing is spared, not age, not weakness, not illness. The heart is wrenched at the thought of the treatment received by thousands of human beings and even

171

more at the thought of what we cannot foresee.''

The results of the August 26 *rafles* were disappointing. The Germans had been hoping for fifteen thousand Jews, but the French rounded up only seven thousand. Roethke was furious. He knew there were still tens of thousands of foreign Jews in the unoccupied zone, in cities like Marseille and Nice and the Riviera, but the French were dragging their feet. Every other European country was showing better results than France with regard to the Final Solution. Now he wondered how he was going to fill the trains he had ordered for September and October. Something had to be done.

On September 2 there was a high-level meeting between Laval and General Oberg, during which it became clear that Laval was very much disturbed by the dissension in the ranks. Generals were disobeying orders. Priests were becoming anti-Vichy militants. Always sensitive to changes in public opinion, Laval was now much more hesitant to comply with German demands. There had been, he explained, an unprecedented resistance on the part of the clergy, led by Cardinal Gerlier. "Since I can't arrest the cardinal," Laval said, "I arrested his right arm. And that's saying a great deal in a state governed by Marshal Pétain.''

Laval went on. "Please believe in my complete honesty when I promise to settle the Jewish question, but remember that the delivery of Jews is not like the delivery of merchandise in a Prisunic [five-and-ten] store, where you can buy all the goods you want and always at the same price. . . . We will deliver to you the Jews from Germany, Austria, Poland, Hungary, and Czechoslovakia. After that, we will deliver the Jews who were naturalized after 1933. Do you have any other demands?'' Oberg answered that he did not. "Then please don't press me further in the light of my present difficulties,'' Laval said.

Laval then raised the question of the destination of the transports. "Foreign diplomats,'' he said, "have asked me more than once what the destination was for the Jewish transports turned over to the occupation authorities. I reply that in principle they are sent to the southern part of Poland. But I'd like to know the best way to reply, to avoid any divergence with the information you give out.'' Since Oberg was not about to tell him that the

Jews were being sent to the extermination camp at Auschwitz, it was agreed that Laval would say they were being sent to Poland for employment. This was a pretty flimsy explanation, for why would they take small children, the elderly, and the ill as a labor force?

The meeting between Oberg and Laval provided no relief for Roethke, who saw his ambitious program crumbling. He had thirteen trains to fill for the month of September. He had not forgotten Eichmann's wrath when he had reported the cancellation of a single train, and did not want to inform him that seven more were being canceled. So on September 8 Roethke called in Leguay, who told him that the poor showing on August 26 had been due to "leaks which sent many Jews to the border regions, where the French police got tired of chasing them in the mountains."

"Well," Roethke asked, "where did the Jews of Nice, Cannes, Lyon, and Marseille all go?" Dannecker had told him there were eight thousand Jews in Nice alone.

"They fled to the villages," Leguay answered. "As a result, there are no more Jews available. We will have to suspend actions until October."

"But that's out of the question," Roethke said. "The plan for the September transports was fixed by Berlin in July and you have known about it since August. It must be respected."

"But how?" Leguay asked.

"How, I can't say. Empty the camps. Make new sweeps in the occupied zone. This is not my problem."

Suddenly Leguay had a bright idea: "Why can't we arrest right away all the Lithuanian, Estonian, Latvian, Yugoslavian, and Bulgarian Jews is Paris?"

"Good idea," Roethke said. "Do it immediately."

Roethke was like a factory supervisor worrying about production figures. You could replace the word "Jew" with the words "roller bearing." He was disgusted with French half-measures. They had done nothing about the Dutch and Belgian Jews. They had done nothing about denaturalized Jews. They were lying when they said there were no more Jews in the camps. He had to stick to the schedule for September and October, since the winter offensive of the eastern front meant there would be no trains available between November and February. On September 9, the day after his disappointing meeting with Leguay, Roethke wrote his superior, Knochen: "I think that the French government must be shown in a drastic/ manner that the Jewish problem must be solved in any case."

By September 14 Roethke had been able to fill six trains with a combination of people taken in the August 26 *rafle* and people from the camps in the unoccupied zone. These trains left for Auschwitz on September 2, 4, 7, 9, and 14. But there were seven more trains due to leave in September, and he desperately needed to find seven thousand more Jews. Thus, on September 14, there was a roundup of Lithuanian, Estonian, Latvian, Yugoslavian, and Bulgarian Jews, as Leguay had proposed. Two days after their arrest, about four hundred from this group were deported with six hundred from the unoccupied zone, reaching Auschwitz on September 18, where most of them were gassed. The time that elapsed between the proposal to arrest them and their deaths at Auschwitz was ten days. On September 18 there was an emptying out of Drancy and Pithiviers. On September 21 and 23, trains left with half foreign and half French Jews, the latter making up the shortage of the former.

On September 22, Roethke proposed arresting 5,129 influential Jewish doctors, lawyers, and businessmen in Paris. But now there was dissension in the SS ranks. Although Roethke was Eichmann's special envoy, Oberg and Knochen opposed this action. The time was not right. The French police could not be trusted. Knochen, exasperated with Roethke's enterprising spirit, wrote Eichmann that "attempts have been made to obtain the arrests of French Jewish nationals. . . . It is impossible at present to go after this category without taking into account the risk and the consequences." Oberg wired Himmler to back up Knochen, and Himmler agreed for the moment to leave French Jews alone. So it was good-bye to arresting French Jews, good-bye to Roethke's ambition, good-bye to Vichy's complete servility. In the struggle between the realists and the extremists, the realists had won. The German occupiers, like Vichy, had to be responsive to French public opinion.

Deprived of French Jews, Roethke on September 23 rounded

up 1,594 Roumanians. Although an ally of Germany, Roumania was not expressing any interest in its expatriate Jews, and this indicated they could be arrested. Two days later, on September 25, a train left Drancy containing 729 Roumanian Jews; on September 28 another train left with 594 Roumanians.

There was one more train scheduled for September, and Roethke was determined not to cancel it, but he had to send it off one fifth full, because even by scraping the bottom of the barrel, he could only round up a mixed bag of nationalities. These included 55 Dutch, 38 Belgians, 23 French, 22 Poles, 19 Roumanians, 17 Bulgarians, 7 Luxembourgers, and 30 others, a total of 211. The Belgians had been arrested in their homes on the day before the train's departure on September 30. One of the Dutch passengers was eighty-seven-year-old Samuel Slipper, sent as part of a "Jewish labor force" to Poland. The order preceding the arrival of the nearly empty transport explained that "this train was sent off even though it carried only 211 Jews. This was absolutely necessary for reasons of politics and prestige, for several French services tried to prevent this last departure scheduled for September." This was Roethke's way of covering himself for not meeting the quota. The result of Vichy's changed attitude and Oberg and Knochen's refusal to arrest French Jews was that the entire October program was compromised. No trains left that month, and no Jews were deported.

During October, however, Greek Jews were arrested in Paris, and there were 1,745 arrests in the unoccupied zone, which provided enough people for four additional trains in November. Each time the SS went after a new nationality, it had to obtain the approval of the Foreign Ministry in Berlin. The SS was told in October that it was all right to arrest Greek Jews. Roethke noted that according to the census lists there were 1,416 of these in Paris. The date for the *rafle* was set for November 5. The French police conducted the operation, made 1,060 arrests and organized the transfer to Drancy. Pleased with the results, Roethke sent a memo to Knochen: "We have the impression that this time, the French police really kept the action secret until the last moment, conforming to instructions."

All these new arrests would help make up the October deficit.

A November 4 train from Drancy contained one thousand Jews, with more women than men. A November 6 train of 1,000 included 617 who had been arrested in the Poitiers area. The trains of November 9 and 11 contained mostly Greeks, many of them Sephardic Jews from Salonika, one of the oldest Jewish communities in Europe. However, the November 11 train, the last of 1942, was short, with 745 passengers. To help fill it, the SS raided the Rothschild nursing home and removed thirty-five elderly patients, six of them over eighty and twenty of them over seventy.

According to Jacques Lévy, a survivor of the November 11 transport, when the train left, the gendarmes gave them words of hope and encouragement: "You'll see, everything will be all right." There were about seventy to a car (while the normal complement was forty men or eight horses), with two buckets of water per car to be used as toilets when the buckets were empty. The car was sealed and barricaded from the outside, and a sharp whistle announced the departure. On the second day a man in Lévy's car, went mad and had to be bound and gagged. Lévy had never before seen the complete moral and psychological disintegration of a human being.

The grand total for 1942, starting on March 27 and ending on November 11, was 43 trains carrying 41,951 Jews, including about 7,000 children under seventeen. On December 19 Eichmann cabled Paris: "What are the plans for 1943? I must inform the *Reichsbahn* [railroad]. The possibilities of welcome exist." Knochen replied that deportations would resume in February 1943.

But by February 1943 the war had taken a change in direction, which had a bearing on the implementation of the Final Solution. For on the previous November 7 and 8, 1942, a British-U.S. force of 400,000 men, under the command of General Dwight D. Eisenhower, had landed at Casablanca, Oran, and Algiers. It was a surprise to Hitler, who had thought the armada of five hundred was headed to reinforce General Montgomery's battle against Rommel at El Alamein. After some brief fighting between Vichy troops and the Allies, an armistice was arranged by Admiral Darlan, who happened to be in Algiers visiting his polio-stricken son. Darlan thus had the distinction of being regarded as a traitor by both Pétain and de Gaulle. As he had collaborated with the Germans, so was he now collaborating with the Americans. Darlan saw wartime events as a speculator might—German shares were dropping, Allied shares were rising, it was time to sell short. He made what Alfred Fabre-Luce called the "*Benito Cereno* leap," after Melville's story in which a captain, taken prisoner by his cargo of slaves, pretends when another ship's officer comes aboard, to be still in command, then leaps into the officer's skiff. But in Darlan's case the leap was fatal, for he was assassinated on December 24 by a young French monarchist who had been put up to it by the British and the Gaullists, thereby relieving the Allies of the embarrassment of having to work with him.

On November 10, right after the Allied landing in North Africa, Laval was in Berchtesgaden conferring with Hitler. He felt flattered that Hitler held his hand at length and that there was a tricolor bouquet of flowers in his room. In the next room orders were being given to occupy the whole of France, in violation of the armistice agreement. This action was called Operation Attila, and on November 11, German troops crossed the demarcation line and invested the unoccupied zone. The myth that there was a part of France that Vichy governed could now be laid to rest. Pétain was powerless to protect the French people and could not even protect his own minister of war, General Weygand, who was arrested by the Germans. Weygand was beside himself at this German invasion, and told Admiral Platon, when the latter said it was useless to protest: "You are worse than a dog rolling in shit."

After Darlan's defection to the Allies, the Germans were afraid that the French fleet in Toulon might also defect to North Africa and decided to stage a preventive raid. The raid took place on November 27, but the commander, Admiral de Laborde, had time to give the order to scuttle ship. The crews drew up the gangplanks and began the long and arduous procedure of sinking their ships. On the battleship *Strasbourg,* they blew up the boilers with explosive charges and spiked the cannons. On the dock the Germans brought up a tank, which started firing its 88mm cannon, hitting the *Strasbourg*'s bridge and killing a naval officer. The *Strasbourg* fired back with heavy machine guns, hitting several Germans. It was the only Vichy-German engagement of the war. Under a smoke-filled sky, ships were on fire, listing and sinking, leaning into one another, soon to provide the background for snapshots of German soldiers. Sixty vessels went down, while two submarines took off for Algeria. It was a stalemate. Nobody captured the French fleet, which was undefeated because it had never fought, and whose only role was to self-destruct. When the captains said they were going down with their ships, they didn't have far to go—a few feet of water in the harbor.

For the Germans there was worse news than the landings in North Africa in the loss of two decisive battles, one in the 120-degree North African desert heat, the other in the subzero Russian winter. And the reason both battles were so decisively lost was that Hitler insisted on commanding his armies, even though his one notion of strategy was to "stand and fight." All those around Hitler saw that he was losing his grip. Dr. Ferdinand Sauerbruch, Germany's most famous surgeon, who had supported him since 1933, saw Hitler in November 1942 and found him muttering disjointed phrases, such as "I must go to India," and "for every German killed ten of the enemy must die." Sauerbruch told friends that Hitler was unquestionably out of his mind. Some officers were still saying, "our Führer has more strategical ability in his little finger than all the generals together," but those who met with him regularly, like Keitel, knew better. Hitler lived in a dream world, to which the real world was supposed to conform and fall in with his crazy demands. One day he asked Keitel: "How many light field howitzers are we producing monthly?" "About one hundred sixty probably," Keitel replied. "I demand nine hundred," Hitler said. "How many eighty-eight-millimeter anti-aircraft shells are being turned out monthly?" "About two hundred thousand," Keitel answered. "I demand two million," Hitler said. "How on earth can we do that?" Keitel asked. "Every single round has a clockwork time fuse, and we don't have enough of those. We only have a few factories turning them out." "You fail to understand me," Hitler said. "I will talk it over with Speer, and then we will build the factories and within six months we will HAVE the fuses." "Dream on," thought the servile Keitel, but kept his mouth shut.

Hitler's "I want it and I want it now" thinking led to disastrous results at Stalingrad, where he would not let General von Paulus escape encirclement when he could still break out. Twenty German divisions were trapped there. The end came in January 1943. In the cellar of Stalingrad's Univermag department store, von Paulus sat on his camp bed in a state of collapse, wondering what to do next. On the last day of the month he and twenty-four other generals surrendered. One hundred and fifty thousand German corpses lay frozen on the ground. The line of prisoners stretched out endlessly, and included Bismarck's grandson. It began to dawn on the French that the Russians would beat the Germans, and they said: 'Don't fight too long with the same enemy, he begins to catch on.''

In Egypt Rommel seemed on the verge of defeating the British, but was stopped at El Alamein, sixty-five miles from Alexandria and the Nile Delta. Here, as at Stalingrad, victory was turned into a rout. General Montgomery was supplied with troops from Malta. In October 1942, the pyramids almost in sight, Rommel was thrown back. The men of Vichy started saying, "It's time to start putting water in the wine," or, in Count Ciano's words: "The God of war has now turned from Germany and gone over to the other camp."

In France in 1943 the SS continued to chart its deportation schedules. Now in most major cities of the formerly unoccupied zone there were SS and SD offices, one of whose jobs it was to round up foreign Jews. In Marseille on January 22, 23, and 24, a three-day *rafle* called "Action Tiger," netted about one thousand Jews. As the train left Marseille for Compiègne, some of the passengers asked for food. A German officer replied: "Our soldiers are starving in Stalingrad. These Jews don't need to eat."

All during 1943, however, the struggle with Vichy continued over the deportation of French Jews. On January 21 Knochen cabled Eichmann to tell him that there were still 3,811 Jews in Drancy, including 2,159 French ones. Could the French Jews be deported? Eichmann replied that he had no objections. In the meantime, two trains of foreign Jews left Drancy for Auschwitz on February 9 and 11.

Roethke, who was planning to deport a trainload of French Jews on February 13, held a meeting with French police officials on February 10. The officials told Roethke that the question of the deportation of French Jews had not been settled and that the French police would not take part in any such action. In a report to his superiors, Roethke wrote: "I replied to these gentlemen that their point of view surprised me, since in 1942 we had already deported French Jews who had broken the law." Roethke told Vichy that the February 13 train would leave with or without its help. The stiffening of the French position came ten days after the German surrender at Stalingrad. In the light of the German defeat, Vichy was exercising caution in its anti-Jewish collaboration. If there was an Allied victory, which seemed increasingly likely, the many surviving French Jews would tell what had been done to the others. Thus, the Vichy attitude became: If you want to deport French Jews, don't involve us. On February 13 a train carrying one thousand French Jews left for Auschwitz with a German escort.

Also on February 13, two Luftwaffe officers, Colonel Winkler and Major Nussbaum, were working late at headquarters on the Place de la Concorde. At 9 P.M. they left their office and were walking along the Right Bank *quais* of the Seine on their way to the Hôtel du Louvre when they were shot by a resistance team, and died during the night. In reprisal, the arrests of two thousand Jews was immediately ordered all over French.

When the Germans had gone into the unoccupied zone on November 11, 1942, their Italian allies had taken over eight *départements* on the French-Italian border, including the Riviera with the cities of Nice and Cannes, Savoie with Chambéry, Haute-Savoie with Annecy, and Isère with Grenoble. Many Jews had fled in 1940 to the Riviera because there were so many hotels, and because the winter season that used to bring English and American visitors had been canceled by the war. From 1940 to November 1942, when the Riviera was unoccupied, if you were a Jew and could prove you had enough money, the authorities looked the other way. Hotel managers wanting to maintain their occupancy rate evaded the Vichy antihousing laws. The word spread that in Nice and Cannes and Antibes and Juan-les-Pins, the living was easy. Tristan Bernard, the great Surrealist poet, and a Jew, was in Cannes, making bon mots: "What do you call the inhabitants of Cahors? The Cadurciens. The inhabitants of Pont-à-Mousson? The Mussipontins. The inhabitants of Juan-les-Pins? The Is-ra-é-lites." There were of course incidents where Jews were chased

from the beaches, but generally a spirit of Mediterranean toler-
ance prevailed. In Nice you could see rabbis in traditional garb
walking the streets. The Hôtel Roosevelt served as a synagogue.

When the Italians occupied the Riviera after the North African
landings, Jewish residents wondered what the change would mean.
The answer was not long in coming. Germany's only major European ally was divided on the Jewish question, but in France,
the Italians protected the Jews under their control. When, on December 20, 1942, the prefect of the Alpes-Maritimes (the Riviera
and its hinterland) decreed that all foreign Jews should be sent
inland to the *départements* of Drôme and Ardèche, the Italians
opposed the move. When Marcel Ribyère, the police prefect in
Nice, wanted to stamp JUIF on the Jews' ID cards, the Italian
consul general informed him that only the Italians could deal with
Jewish questions in their zone of occupation. Captain Salvi of the
carabinieri told Ribyère that any French policeman who detained
a Jew would be arrested. In addition, the Italians put a guard around
the Nice synagogue on the Boulevard Dubouchage, to protect it
from anti-Semitic demonstrations.

On February 24, 1943, Roethke was informed by the French
that the roundup of two thousand Jews in reprisal for the killing
of Winkler and Nussbaum had already begun, but that there had
been three separate incidents in the Italian zone where attempts
to arrest Jews had been rebuffed. South of Lyon, in the Isère
département, the Italians had prevented the arrests of two to three
hundred Jews, as they did in Grenoble with one hundred Jews. In
Annecy, gendarmes arrested some Jews and held them in the gen-
darmerie barracks. When the Italians demanded their release, which
was refused, they surrounded the barracks with heavily armed
carabinieri, and the gendarmes gave in.

These incidents had three important results. First, they frustrated the Germans, who could not understand the Italian attitude, because none of the arrested Jews were Italian. How could
they, the Germans, carry out efficient anti-Jewish measures when
their allies were sabotaging their efforts? Second, the Italian attitude put some starch into Vichy's efforts not to hand over French
Jews. Laval could point to the differences in the treatment of Jews
by the Italians and by the Germans. Third, Jews began to flock to

the Italian-occupied section of France. The SS chief in Limoges reported to Paris on March 2, 1943, that a great many Jews were leaving his area, since it was notorious that the Italians did nothing against the Jews and also kept the French from doing anything to them. The Italians had placed all Jews under their protection. In a telex to Berlin on March 15, Kurt Lischka reported: "The Jews there feel in perfect security and freely go about their dirty business, notably black market. The rich Jews have a great influence not only on the French population but on the Italian military." Thus the 1943 deportations from France took place in the context of a turn in the fortunes of war and of an Italian refusal to have anything to do with the Final Solution.

The two thousand hostages for the February 13 action were however rounded up and deported on March 4 and March 6. But there was a showdown with the French when, later in March, Knochen announced that he intended to deport fifteen hundred French Jews still in Drancy. Leguay and Bousquet, who until then had been downright obsequious in their willingness to comply with German requests, were changed men. On March 22 when Leguay went to see Oberg's deputy, Herbert Hagen, he told Hagen flatly that the French police would not take part in the deportation of French nationals. Hagen trotted out the old "Führer" argument. "When I objected," he reported, "that his attitude was stupefying, since we were talking about Jews, Leguay declared that the *Maréchal,* as well as Laval, although they did not intend to express a pro-Jewish attitude, did not want for humanitarian reasons to assume the responsibility of a transfer of Jews to the Reich. For my part, I drew his attention to the fact that this attitude was all the more strange because the Führer in all his speeches . . . had placed the accent on the need for a radical solution of the Jewish question."

An annoyed Hagen told Leguay's superior, René Bousquet, on March 25 that "General Oberg feels obliged to express his great surprise that the French government has not yet abandoned its 'sentimental' point of view, in spite of the Führer's declarations regarding the Jewish question. General Oberg will thus be obliged to carry out these transports himself." Two trains left on March 23 and 25, each one carrying about one thousand foreign Jews, but after that there was a three-month interruption in departures, which showed that the French strategy of saying *non* seemed to be working.

The Germans then tried another tack, which was to force Vichy to repeal the naturalization of some French Jews, which would make them stateless and deportable. On March 6 Roethke had proposed "to demand of the French government . . . the publication of a law removing the French nationality to Jews naturalized after 1927." Laval was too canny to say no to this proposal, but made effective use of delaying tactics. The Germans had chosen 1927 as the cutoff date because that was the year the French had relaxed their residence requirement from ten to three years, which had led to a massive post-1927 immigration of Jews. The Germans estimated that fifty thousand Jews had entered France between 1927 and 1932, the year that the French were proposing as the cutoff date.

There may have been another factor involved in Laval's change of heart. In 1943 rumors began to circulate about the true nature of the camps where the Jews were being deported. Two men sent to Auschwitz in 1942, Honig and Haim Salomon, succeeded in escaping and making their way to Nice in the beginning of 1943. But when they told their story to Jewish leaders in Nice, no one believed them. The Nice rabbis tapped their foreheads with their index fingers. In May 1943, however, Félix Olivier-Martin, Vichy's assistant secretary for youth, went to Laval and asked him about what policy to adopt toward young Jews who were in the various Vichy youth movements. This is what Laval told him: "There is a political problem. On one side there is Germany, which wants to exterminate them, on the other side there is Italy and the Vatican, who are in agreement to protect them. . . . It is as important for me to get along with Italy and the Vatican as it is for me to get along with Germany. In playing this game I can save many people on the rebound. . . . In any case, I ask you to stifle any anti-Jewish initiatives among your subordinates." Laval had stopped believing in the Jewish home in Poland, or in work camps. Somehow, he knew that the true purpose of deportation was "extermination."

And he continued to play cat and mouse with the Germans over the denaturalization law, whose passage would have permitted many thousands of French Jews to be deported. This law was now at a complete standstill. Vichy's evasions so infuriated Himmler that he personally came to Paris on June 8 to spur matters on. He insisted that the law must be passed at once. A plan was drawn up to arrest the estimated number of Jews that the law would affect on June 24. But June 24 came and went, and the law was not signed.

In June there was one train, which left on the twenty-third. It was so hot that the guards had to open the cars, providing the prisoners with a chance to escape. A penciled note thrown from the train said: "We are 50 in this cattle car, sitting on the floor or on our bags. Impossible to move. Three jumped from the train, which was going 50 to 60 kms. We don't know if they're all right. They say we're going to Metz where there will be a triage. I'm keeping my spirits up in spite of the terrible heat and no water."

On the same day, June 23, Roethke was informed that the denaturalization decree had been signed and that the cutoff date was 1927. The Germans planned new sweeps, but the law did not appear in the *Journal Officiel*. Why, no one knew, for Darquier de Pellepoix wrote Roethke on July 17 that "Laval and Gabolde [the minister of justice] have signed law number 361 removing French nationality from Jews naturalized after August 10, 1927."

It was a "the check is in the mail" situation. When August came and still no denaturalization law had appeared, Hagen asked to see Leguay on the fifth. What was going on here? he wanted to know. It was incomprehensible that the new law had not been posted. Leguay said he was baffled. He didn't know what the reason was. Apparently the situation was confused because there were two laws. Nine days later, on August 14, Laval told Roethke flatly: "I cannot open myself to the reproach of publishing laws that will deliver French Jews." Such a measure had to be approved by the Marshal and would be discussed at the August 17 cabinet meeting. The law, if approved, must be worded in such a way as to give the Jews a three-month delay to apply for exceptions. On Roethke's August 15 report of his meeting with Laval, General Oberg wrote this in the margin: "Insolence becomes a method!" Roethke concluded: "It must be stated that the French government no longer wishes to follow us in the Jewish question. . . . It is handy for Laval to hide behind Pétain, although he declared during our conversation that while he was not anti-Semitic, he was not pro-Semitic either. . . . It is no longer possible to count on any large-scale help from the French police for the arrest of Jews, unless, a few days or weeks from now, the military situation in Germany changes radically in our favor.''

The Germans were practically admitting failure. Stretched as thin as they were all over France, they could not carry out the necessary *rafles* without the help of the French police. On August 14 Roethke, making one final effort to salvage the law, came to Vichy, where Laval told him that Pétain was shocked that even women and children would be denaturalized. The law would be discussed at the August 17 cabinet meeting, but given its importance, it could only be signed by Pétain himself. Vichy announced on August 24 that Pétain had decided that he could not sign the law because of its collective character, which was deeply offensive to the French people. Denaturalization, if done at all, should be done on a case-by-case basis. Because of Vichy's waffling, the German plan for a massive deportation of French Jews failed.

The key to the turnabout was the military situation, which was increasingly gloomy for Germany. The Allies had invaded Sicily on July 9 and 10. Mussolini had resigned under pressure on July 25, and seventy-two-year-old Marshal Badoglio took over. On September 3 Montgomery slipped two divisions across the Straits of Messina and invaded the toe of the Italian boot. It was in this context that the Vichy cabinet found the courage to kill the denaturalization law. With the Allies on the continent of Europe, and with the Wehrmacht taking a beating in Russia, Laval had stopped saying that he believed in a German victory.

Only one deportation train left France in July, on the eighteenth. A survivor, Henri Bulawko, recalled: "The train stops, the doors slide open, and strange creatures in striped clothing jump onto the car, like horrible gnomes escaped from hell. Behind them, SS shouting, '*Los, raus, alles raus* (Quick, out, all out).' " No trains left in August, and there was only one in September, on the second. A survivor, Robert Lévy, recalled: "We were expecting to work hard in factories, in coal mines, in stone quarries, but we did not think our destruction had been cold-bloodedly planned.''

The conduct of the war, which had been favorable to foreign Jews in France by providing a haven in the Italian zone, now turned against them. Secret negotiations were going on between Eisenhower and Badoglio for a separate Italian armistice. In the meantime, there were thirty thousand Jews on the Riviera. Angelo Donati, an influential Jewish-Italian banker in Nice, went to Rome to negotiate an agreement that would allow those thirty thousand Jews to go to Italy until they could find passage to Tunisia. He also negotiated with shipping firms for their passage and for trucks to pick them up in Nice. But as Donati's talks were going on, so were the armistice discussions. On September 8 Eisenhower announced the conclusion of the armistice from his headquarters in Carthage, to force the indecisive Badoglio's hand. Badoglio had to go along, the Italians pulled out of France, and the Germans immediately sent troops into Italy and the Italian-occupied zone in France, trapping the Jews waiting to be evacuated. In Nice, where twenty thousand Jews were waiting for the green light to go to Italy, panic struck when teams of SS moved in for the great *rafle* they had so long been denied. André Chennault, the new prefect of police, refused to turn over the census list of Jews to the SS, saying that the Italians had taken it with them. Since there were no lists, the SS resorted to "physical examinations" in the street, ordering male suspects to drop their trousers and show whether they were circumcised. The going rate for informants was two thousand francs per head. In the month-long sweep, thousands were caught. It was the worst manhunt of the occupation.

Among the refugees trapped in Nice in those September days was a family of Roumanian Jews called Klarsfeld. Arno and Raissa Klarsfeld had met when they were both students at the Sorbonne. They married and remained in Paris and raised two children, Serge and Tanya. In 1939 Arno joined the French Foreign Legion, was captured in one of the June 1940 battles, and escaped from prison camp. He took his family to Nice, where he had an engineer friend. They found a small apartment, and the engineer offered to build them a hiding place in the back of a closet. Nice seemed safe for the time being, but you never knew. So a false wall was installed in the closet and painted white. On the upper part of the wall some shelves were built, which Raissa stacked with linen. Below the shelves was a long rod to hang clothes on. There was a low door that you had to crawl through into a small triangular hiding space.

Then came September 1943 and the SS manhunt. At first, they raided hotels and rooming houses. Then they began stopping people in the street. Then, acting on tips, they started coming to apartment buildings. On September 30 at midnight, a time when there was absolutely no traffic, Raissa Klarsfeld heard a truck stop in front of the building. She woke her husband. Knowing what it meant, they grabbed the children and crawled into the hiding space.

The area was so cramped that they had to remain standing. Serge Klarsfeld, then eight, and holding on tightly to his mother in the dark, could hear the Germans burst into the apartment next door, and the sounds they made as they struck someone, and the cries of a little girl, and a man's voice saying, *"Au secours police française"* ("Help French police"). These words did not seem ironic to the boy, for he knew nothing of Vichy's doings, and he really believed that the French police would arrive, just as troops had arrived to save the settlers from the Indians in the illustrated books he read.

Then his father, thinking things over, decided that when the Germans came into their apartment, it would look suspicious if no one was home. The Germans would search each room all the more carefully and discover the hiding place and they would all be caught. So Arno decided to go out in his pajamas and greet the SS. He had spent six years in a Jesuit school in Bucharest and had learned to speak German fluently. He told his wife and children: "If I am deported I will survive because I can work, but you will die."

A few minutes later the Germans came in and asked him were his family was. He told them they had gone to the country while the apartment was being disinfected. The SS then began to search. One of them opened the closet and pushed the clothes aside; behind the false wall the eight-year-old boy could hear the rustle of dresses and thought, "All he has to do is knock on the back wall to see that it's hollow." But the German did not knock. His sister Tanya who had bronchitis and was coughing a lot, stuffed her pajama sleeve into her mouth to keep quiet.

The Germans told Arno Klarsfeld to get dressed, then they waited outside. "If I don't have the keys and I leave the front door un-locked behind me when I go," he thought, "it won't look right." But his wife had the keys. So he went back to the closet, tapped on the hollow wall, and said two words in Roumanian: the keys. The little door opened and his wife's hand emerged with the keys, and he kissed her hand and took the keys and left. Those were the last words Serge Klarsfeld ever heard his father say. To this day, he cannot bear to hear the sound of coathangers being moved in a closet.

Raissa, Serge, and Tanya stayed in the hiding place until 6 A.M., and crept out when the children could no longer stand it. Raissa looked out the window and saw no one, and got the children's clothes. She opened the front door. A man passing by told her the Germans were gone. She and the children went to the engineer friend who had made the compartment, and he took them in.

The Jews caught in Nice were deported in the last five trains of 1943, on October 7 and 28, November 20, December 7, and December 17. Aboard the October 28 train was Arno Klarsfeld. According to a survivor, he was selected for work duty upon arrival at Auschwitz, being a healthy and robust thirty-eight, but displayed a rebellious spirit almost at once. He did something which caused the Polish block chief to strike him, and, to everyone's amazement, he struck back, which entitled the small group of deportees from France in the mainly Polish block to a measure of respect. But he was punished by being sent to the *Fürstengrube* (Mine of Princes), a work detail from which he returned so weakened that he died in March 1944.

One of the consequences of that day in Nice was that in later years Serge Klarsfeld devoted his life to hunting down Nazi war criminals. He found a partner in this activity. In 1963 he married Berlin-born Beate Kunzel, whose father had served in the Wehrmacht but who shared her husband's determination that the men who were responsible for the Final Solution should not be allowed to go free because of the apathy of governments. In 1967 the Klarsfelds embarked on a life of militant Nazi-hunting, with Serge doing the archival and legal work, and Beate doing the legwork. Their first target was Kurt-Georg Kiesinger, who had been elected chancellor of West Germany despite his record of having orchestrated Nazi propaganda for the state radio during the war. In November 1968 Beate Klarsfeld attended a political meeting in Berlin as a member of the press and managed to get close enough to Kiesinger to slap him soundly across the face. She was sentenced to a year in prison, which was later suspended, but her action drew attention to Kiesinger's past, and in the 1969 election he was defeated by Willy Brandt.

The Klarsfelds then turned their attention on two of the SS officers who in Paris had been responsible for deportations: Kurt Lischka, the number two man in the pre-Oberg days, and Herbert Hagen, Oberg's deputy. It was Lischka who on April 2, 1942, had turned down a request from the German embassy to free an arrested Jew who was the friend of a German diplomat, saying that no exceptions should be made or "the French will think there are no German anti-Semites except the Führer himself."

After the war Lischka and Hagen vanished. They were tried in absentia in France and sentenced to life imprisonment. But by 1971 when the Klarsfelds started looking for them, they were both living openly in Germany—Lischka in Cologne and Hagen in Warstein—and were listed in their respective phone books. Hagen had been back to France twenty times on business trips and had once gone to Israel as a tourist. It took years for the Klarsfelds to whip up German public opinion concerning the two former SS officers, and at one point they tried to kidnap Lischka in front of his home to publicize the case. Finally, in October 1979, Lischka and Hagen were put on trial in Cologne. Lischka was sentenced to ten years and Hagen to twelve. The prosecutor stressed that they had "completely and fully understood" that they were sending Jews to their deaths at Auschwitz.

In the meantime, the Klarsfelds had picked up the trail of Klaus Barbie, thanks to a secret report that the German embassy in La Paz had sent to Bonn saying that Barbie was living there as a Bolivian citizen under the name of Klaus Altmann. Armed with this information, the Klarsfelds urged the reopening of the Barbie case. Beate Klarsfeld went La Paz in January 1972, where she gave her story to the Bolivian press. This created a furor and led to the French asking for Barbie's extradition. Eventually Barbie was brought back to France in 1983 and put on trial in 1987. By his persistence in reviving dormant cases, Serge Klarsfeld was able to play a part in the tragedy of his time and of his people, and to repay his father for his sacrifice.

The total number of trains for 1943, seventeen, was less than half the previous year's total of forty-one. The Vichy government drew the line at using French police to arrest French Jews and at tampering with the naturalization laws. In the land of Cartesian thinking, where the rule of law is society's anchor, to change a law arbitrarily and retroactively so that one group of people would lose the protection of the state was repugnant to the men of Vichy.

Of course there was a price to pay. The Germans were looking for a way to clamp down on Vichy and found one that November. Pétain was planning to give a talk on the radio on the thirteenth in which he would announce that in case of his death, political power should return to the National Assembly. This was a blow to Laval, who was supposed to be his successor. It was also a form of self-repudiation, since Pétain had come to power as an alternative to the detested and corrupt parliamentary government. Pétain was saying in effect: "I have failed. Let us go back to the previous system." The move could also be seen as a farsighted way of blocking General de Gaulle's eventual path to power. But the Germans embargoed the speech, and a stiff reprimand arrived on November 29 in the form of thirteen-page letter from Foreign Minister Joachim von Ribbentrop, acting as Hitler's mouthpiece. In this letter Pétain was accused of a "constant struggle against all positive actions," and of making "constant difficulties to the application of a policy of real collaboration." And the chief complaint was the nondelivery of French Jews, which was thwarting the final solution.

At this point, at the end of 1943, when they had obviously lost the war, and the actions of the resistance were multiplying, the Germans took the gloves off. There was no more pretense at negotiation. There was no more reliance on the goodwill of Vichy. Now there were German demands of do this or else. And what they wanted first was to bring into the government three leading collaborationist leaders, two of whom, in the pay of the Germans, had been trashing Vichy for years. The three were Joseph Darnand, the head of the Milice, Philippe Henriot, the radio orator, and Marcel Déat, the editor of the virulently anti-Vichy newspaper *L'Oeuvre*. Darnand would replace René Bousquet as head of the police. General Oberg, under pressure from Himmler, had to ask for the departure of his friend Bousquet, who was going after the Milice, which he saw as a threat to his own department. Laval had to give in to the German demands, saying, "Better Darnand than a *Gauleiter*." Darnand was named secretary general for the Maintien de l'Ordre (Maintenance of Order). The Milice became a sort of French SS, doing the dirty work of the Germans which the French police now declined to do.

Henriot the nihilist, who knew he was on the wrong side but who was going to take it all the way, was made secretary of state of information and propaganda. It was said of Henriot on the French program of the BBC: "There are French victims in the Allied bombardments, alas, but one can sense in Henriot a feeling of regret that there are not more of them." Déat the rabblerouser was made secretary of state for labor and national solidarity. The Déat style is displayed in his choice of language in this diary entry about his imminent appointment: "Not only the pig has been slaughtered, but the blood sausage [*boudin*] is ready. There remains only the *Maréchal* to taste it." Pétain detested Déat but had to swallow the *boudin*.

And so the power-hungry Paris collaborators, whose obedience to the Germans had been tested and paid for, finally came into the government. Pétain became a prisoner in his own office while Laval continued to maneuver, but in a much more restricted field of action. As for the deportation program, it continued to operate through August 1944, thanks to SS squads all over France, who continued to arrest Jews with the help of the Milice. In 1944 there were thirteen trains. One of the fifteen hundred Jews on the April 13 train was sixteen-year-old Simone Jacob, the second youngest survivor of deportation in France, who as Simone Weil later became a cabinet minister in the Mitterand government. Even after the invasion of France the Germans were still at it, although many railroad tracks had been sabotaged and they were busy fighting the Allies on French soil. There were shortages of and delays in the arrival of Jews at Drancy, which was under new management—the SS officer Alois Brunner had taken it over from the French in June 1943. Between July 20 and July 24, 1944, more than a month after D Day, Alois Brunner, needing to fill a train, raided six children's homes managed by the UGIF on the outskirts of Paris, including one in Neuilly for babies still at the breast. He brought back five hundred children aged one to fifteen; three hundred of them left Drancy on the July 31 train.

I have provided this blow-by-blow and almost train-by-train description of the deportation program in France to show exactly how mass murder was accomplished. By adopting the corporate model, in which production goals must be met, the Nazis created a new kind of criminal behavior, acting in a set of circumstances that erased all awareness of a moral dimension. The value of human life, the injustice being done, the cruelty of the method, and the horror of the goal did not matter. What mattered was the success of the corporate endeavor.

This was done be converting a human tragedy into a series of logistical problems. No one ever said, "We are arresting people without legal basis and taking them against their will to another country where they will be hideously murdered." They talked about trains, they talked about timetables, they talked about buckets. The official correspondence resembles that of a multi-national corporation concerned about the timely shipment of goods. The language of commerce was often used. Thus Roethke talks about "inventory" and says to Leguay about a shipment of Jews: "This is only a small down payment." Thus Laval can tell Oberg: "Do not think you are in a Prisunic where you can always buy the same goods at the same price."

A second corporate technique was the fragmentation of tasks. The people involved in each step in the deportations saw only that step. One set of policemen arrested the Jews. A second set guarded them in Drancy. A third set escorted them on the trains to the French border, where the Germans took over. Limited knowledge and involvement further blunted the moral dimension and reduced responsibility.

A third corporate technique was the encouragement of individual enterprise. It is striking to see to what extent the deportation program in France was launched thanks to the efforts of one overzealous officer, Theo Dannecker, who seemed more prodding than prodded by Eichmann. It was Dannecker who took the initiative to go to General Kohl and ask for the indispensable trains. It was Dannecker who visited the camps in the unoccupied zone so as to see for himself how many Jews were held there. It was Dannecker who attended every single departure at Drancy. Dannecker was the pace-setting regional manager who wants to outperform his colleagues and keynote the sales meeting. Eventually, his superiors, Oberg and Knochen, were placed in the position of having to rein in the irrepressible Dannecker and his successor, Roethke.

A fourth corporate technique was to employ secrecy. Very few men, even in the SS, knew what was really going on. This had the initial benefit of keeping the victims pliable. An April 29, 1943, telegram from Berlin to Paris emphasized that nothing should be told the Jews about conditions at Auschwitz. There should be "no anxiety-producing revelations on the nature of what was awaiting them." By trickery, or, one might say, misleading advertising, the victims were led unsuspecting to their deaths. The stereotype of the Jew—the subject of a Vichy-sponsored exhibit, "Le Juif et la France," that opened at the Palais Berlitz in September 1941—as crafty, cunning, and unscrupulous was totally contradicted in practice when roughly seventy thousand Jews meekly let themselves be arrested, deported, and gassed, thanks to the use of obvious tricks and transparent lies. How easy it was to encourage them with false hopes at the point of departure by telling them they needed work boots and giving them a few zlotys (Polish currency), how easy to fool them at the end of the journey with bath towels and dummy shower heads. The Jews were ingenuous. They believed what they were told. There were very few escape attempts. Not a single attempt was made by the resistance to sabotage a deportation train, for interfering with the movement of civilians to a work camp was not a high priority.

This secrecy allowed the French (both Vichy and the resistance) to buy the convenient explanation of the Jewish home in Poland. Even if they suspected it was not true, it absolved them of responsibility. In the case of Laval, it was not in his nature to insist that children be deported with their parents for any but humanitarian reasons. If Laval had had any suspicions in 1942, which indeed he did have a year later, he would have kept his mouth shut.

The Germans felt frustrated by Vichy on this topic. Eichmann, when he was hiding in Argentina after the war, was interviewed by the Dutch journalist Wilhelm Sassen, who asked him why the Final Solution had failed in France. Eichmann replied: "First, Dannecker's lack of greatness, and Knochen's lack of focus. Second, the resistance of the Laval government, which after a good start became immobilized, and perhaps, made more prudent by the lack of success of our armies, acted more discreetly.

"Rarely," Eichmann went on, "did a country fight so hard for the Jews of its own nationality than did France. . . . Whatever results we had in Paris were due to my own energetic intervention, because I knew that Dannecker had a liaison with a young person in his office and wanted very much to stay in Paris. I threatened him several times with immediate recall if he did not act fast. . . . I had to struggle in France with a superbureaucracy, and if I told you that I had to write one hundred paragraphs and make one hundred *démarches* to get one Jew out, you can imagine how bad the situation was. . . . I always said so, France was a rotten egg."

This was the way matters looked from Berlin, but in France at the end of the war they looked rather different. For Laval had been ready to turn over thousands of foreign Jews who had taken refuge there. In his view, they were not France's responsibility. No one had asked them to come; they had simply arrived and been let in. They were not French citizens, so he did not feel under any obligation to protect them. Indeed they were useful as a form of exchange through which the French Jews could be saved. This attitude he expressed quite openly, as in a conversation with the Protestant pastor Marc Boegner in September 1942: "The invasion of Poland sent tens of thousands of Jews into France," he said, "which upset the demographic balance of entire regions. Depressed and deracinated, these foreigners formed a dangerous element. They were marginal people, living expediently, accessible to hostile propaganda, an element of demoralization and discord, a threat to public order. To get rid of these too numerous immigrants was a form of national prophylaxis."

There is something really unpleasant in the callousness of these remarks. Because in spite of Eichmann's frustration, more than seventy thousand Jews were deported from France and gassed at Auschwitz. For Laval and others to say they didn't know the true fate of the Jews is not enough. When people are so obviously being mistreated—like a vile herd, in the words of Cardinal Saliège—you don't want to be involved in it *de près ou de loin* (from near or from afar). Proximity brings contamination. Laval's crime has nothing to do with what he knew or didn't know; it was that he consented to govern when criminal measures were carried out by his government and his police against innocent people. There was something basically wrong, something low and dishonorable, in wanting to govern under those conditions. He was a real collaborator. He believed in the German New Europe and, until 1943, in a German victory. He weaseled back and forth, so as to get crumbs from the master's table. His obsession with scoring small tactical points made him immune to feelings of disgust.

Laval genuinely believed that he had saved France from bloodshed and economic ruin, and he said, with his accountant's mentality: "The four years of occupation cost us less than three months of war." He had no illusion about his fate, for as he put it; "I didn't have a microphone in my hand, I had the frying pan."

Laval was tried in October 1945 and found guilty and sentenced to death. The execution was set for Monday, October 15. For a long time he had kept a vial of cyanide stitched inside the lining of his jacket, and he took the poison on that morning to cheat the firing squad. But the cyanide was so old it didn't work and his stomach had to be pumped out. He was half dragged and half carried to the execution stake in a courtyard of Fresnes Prison and shot at 12:23 P.M.

V

LYON '43

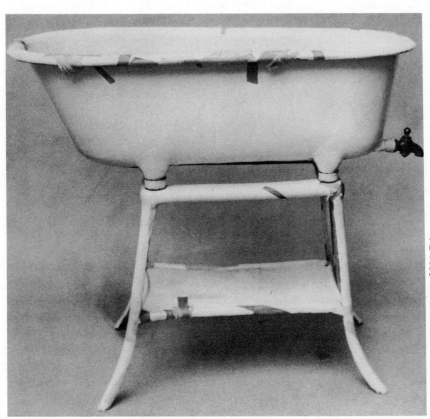

H itler signed the Operation Attila order for the reoccupation of the south of France on November 10: "If revolts take place in parts of the French colonial empire, preparations must be made for a swift occupation of the unoccupied territories of France." On November 11 German troops crossed the demarcation line at dawn, and by 9:40 A.M. they were moving into the great and ancient city of Lyon, which had witnessed and survived the world's conflicts ever since the early Christians had been thrown to the lions in its Roman arenas.

The heart of this city of seven hundred thousand was a peninsula washed by two rivers, the Rhône and the Saône. Wars had come and gone, but the rivers had not ceased to flow, and the inhabitants had not changed their eating habits or been evicted from their homes. At the tip of the peninsula were the Perrache railroad station and the adjacent Hôtel Terminus. At the upper end was the Place des Terreaux, with a seventeenth-century city hall, and behind that, the hill of the Croix-Rousse and *vieux* Lyon with a network of *traboules* (connecting passages through buildings and between streets), like an aboveground sewer system, and almost as dirty and evil-smelling. Between Perrache and Terreaux stood the vast Place Bellecour with an equestrian statue of Louis XIV. A familiar meeting place was "under the tail of the bronze horse."

The riverbanks were lined with solid six-story houses, as alike as the kernels on an ear of corn, side by side, block by block, a first line of defense against threats to such bourgeois value as thrift and lack of ostentation, houses that attested to the French saying "There is no such thing as a small profit." In the courtyards, looking like miniature houses, were rows of mahogany letter boxes with brass plates. Behind the identical façades of its houses, Lyon was a city of undercurrents, its twisting stairways with their dark banisters seeming to be made for clandestine meetings and conspiracies.

The sky was usually gray, making everything look faded, like living in a room with dirty windowpanes. The little red streetcars and the florists' carts provided some color, as did occasionally the setting sun behind Fourvière hill. In 1840 mudslides had sent houses on the side of Fourvière tumbling down. The leading citizens made a pilgrimage up the hill and vowed to replace the chapel there with a cathedral, to appease the gods. When war with the Prussians was declared in 1870, they walked up the hill again and vowed to replace the cathedral with a basilica if Lyon was spared from invasion.

The invasion was postponed, and now, on November 11, 1942, there were German tanks on the Place des Terreaux, and a swastika flag was draped above the city hall entrance. A helmeted sentry sat behind a machine gun on the sinister-sounding Guillotière bridge, a half-filled bottle of Beaujolais by his side. The Germans occupied Montluc Prison, Grange-Blanche Hospital, and the Part-Dieu barracks. It had all been done quietly. People living next door to the barracks woke up the next morning, opened their shutters, and saw that the sentry at the entrance had changed uniform.

On December 17 General Niehoff arrived as commander of the France-Sud military region. Lyon became a training center for young Wehrmacht recruits. They had their own movie houses and restaurants and brothels. For the officers, there were Chez Francine and Chez Blanchette. The girls were required to have three medical inspections per week. The young recruits ate rich food and drank local wine and congratulated themselves on being on the banks of the Rhône rather than the Neva. Oh, what a lovely war!

For in November 1942, the Germans were still considered the victors. All of Europe was German, from the Normandy beaches to Stalingrad. But that was about to change, and as the war went badly, and the territory occupied by Germany shrank, the resistance became more active and the occupiers found themselves in an increasingly hostile environment. Shortly after their arrival, on November 28, two young men on bicycles fired at a German soldier on the Place Bellecour, wounding him and inaugurating the cycle of attack and reprisal.

To deal with such disturbers of the peace, a special police unit was installed in Lyon, as well as in twelve other cities in the unoccupied zone. The KDS *(Kommando der SIPO und SD)*, generally called *Einsatzkommando,* like the killer units on the eastern front, came with its own staff of interpreters, secretaries, drivers, cooks, cleaning women, and, of course, highly motivated SD officers as well as regular police (SIPO). The KDS was divided into six sections: (1) Administrative; (2) Judicial Matters; (3) Economic and Black Market Reports; (4) Repression of Political Crimes; (5) Repression of Nonpolitical Crimes: and (6) Intelligence. These sections were not of equal importance. The economic section, for instance, had a staff of two, while Section Four (Repression of Political Crimes) had a staff or more than fifty, not counting the French agents and informers working under contract or free-lancing. It was Section Four that did the dirty work—that is, it fought the resistance and rounded up the Jews.

In terms of arrests, interrogations, and paramilitary operations, Section Four was more important than the other five sections put together, and it was known as the Gestapo, since its agents were more visible and brutal (in fact, the SD had been merged with the Gestapo, but the name stuck). Section Four itself was divided into five subsections, the names of which give some idea as to the extent of its police work: (4a) Anti-Communism and Countersabotage; (4b) Anti-Jewish; (4c) Escaped Workers and Bearers of False Papers; (4d) Counterespionage; and (4e) Archives.

In order to dismantle resistance networks, find foreign Jews for the deportation trains, and track down deserters from the forced labor squads, Section Four depended on the recruitment of informants and double agents. Section Four had to infiltrate the resistance. It had to develop a network of agents who would scour neighborhoods for Jews. It had agents working full and part time, like the barman at Le Perroquet, who was on a retainer to pay close attention to the conversations of his customers and to call the office when someone suspicious turned up. Or like the woman who was sent to Montluc Prison as a *mouton* (prison spy). Or like any street adventurer or neighborhood führer wanting to make himself look important. Thanks to Section Four, a Lyonnais maxim was being observed in the breach: It is better to stick your nose in a jug of Beaujolais than in other people's business.

Suspects were taken to KDS headquarters at the Hôtel Terminus, where they were subjected to what the Germans called a "reinforced interrogation." This was done according to an SD regulation from Berlin dated June 12, 1942: "Reinforced interrogations can only be applied if in the course of preceding interrogations it becomes clear that the person under arrest has important information concerning the enemy, or concerning plans that he refuses to communicate. . . . Such reinforced interrogations can only be applied against Communists, Marxists, Bible students (Jehovah's Witnesses), saboteurs, terrorists, resistance agents, or Polish or Russian vagabonds."

Thus, torture was condoned, and once condoned, became routine. The hotel *baignoires* (bathtubs) became the most common and convenient devices of torture—immersion, oddly enough, is a method that German nannies, or *Schwesters,* have been known to use as punishment on their small charges.

Commanding the Lyon KDS was Lieutenant Colonel Werner Knab. A tall, thin man of about forty with a military bearing, angular features, and light brown hair parted in the middle and almost shaved on the sides, Knab had had a checkered career in the SS. He had gotten into some trouble during the 1940 Norway expedition, which had landed him in one of the four *Einsatzgruppen* on the Russian front in 1941, whose single mission was mass murder. To have gone through such an experience left its mark, and Knab saw the Lyon assignment as a rest cure by comparison. He had a fine apartment on the best street in Lyon, the Boulevard des Belges, overlooking the Parc de la Tête d'Or. He had a cook and a butler and a mistress. He delegated most of the work and handled relations with the French. For Knab, who had done his duty on the Russian front, the war was as good as over.

In any case, the real hands-on police work was not done by the head of the KDS, but by the head of Section Four, which dealt with so-called political crimes. The head of Section Four had to be an energetic and ruthless person, the same type as Theo Dannecker in Paris, the sort who was hungry for promotion and would not only follow orders to the letter, but would take the initiative. The head of Section Four was of medium height, more Latin-looking than Aryan, with brown eyes, brown hair, and ferretlike features, and his name was Klaus Barbie.

Barbie could have passed for a typical middle-class Frenchman, the one named Durand, and in fact the Barbies were descended from a French Huguenot family named Barbier which had fled to Germany in the seventeenth century when Louis XIV was persecuting Protestants. Klaus Barbie was born on October 25, 1914, but his parents, Anna and Nicholas, did not marry until January 30, 1915. They were both teachers in the elementary school in the village of Udler outside Eifel in the Saarland, and in that place and time, a birth out of wedlock was something of a scandal.

For Klaus Barbie, being born a bastard was a terrible stigma. In German law, the principle "once a bastard, always a bastard" still held sway. A child born out of wedlock could not be legitimized by his parents' marriage, nor could he inherit their estate. Knowing himself to be outside the normal line of parental succession, Barbie felt that he had no place in the world. He was a misfit—someone who wanted to take his rightful place in society but was not entitled to it. Having been denied a conventional birth, he was an untouchable.

This was a topic that came up again and again in his talks with three French psychiatrists while he was awaiting trial in Lyon in 1985 and 1986. He railed against Willy Brandt, also a bastard. How could a man like this, he asked, have been allowed to become chancellor of West Germany? How could a bastard like Willy Brandt have won the Nobel Peace Prize? Willy Brandt was just scum, he should never have been allowed to rise in German politics. Barbie also made a point of saying that he had been born on the same day as the Kaiser Wilhelm II, as if that coincidence would somehow help legitimize him. Such was the accident of birth that gave Klaus Barbie feelings of personal worthlessness. There was in him a need for legitimacy and validation. He was a man in search of something to erase his original flaw.

Along with that, there was the example of Barbie's father, who had gone to war shortly after his birth and had come home in 1918, when Klaus was not yet four, with severe wounds, including a piece of shrapnel in his neck that doctors could not remove. And then, in 1923, when Klaus was nine, the French occupied the small coal-rich Saarland area where the family lived, and a German *Freikorps* leader was captured and shot. So Klaus Barbie went through the experience of being occupied, and of seeing his father deteriorate and take to drink as the result of his wounds.

Also in 1923, Barbie left home to attend the Frederick Wilhelm grammar school in Trier, a pleasant university town on the Moselle River, a few miles from the Luxembourg border. In school he studied the classics, learning to translate Latin and Greek. In 1933 he graduated with his *Abitur* (degree). But graduation was also a time of personal tragedy, for in 1933 both his father and his brother died—the former of a neck tumor connected with his wound, and the latter, who was two years younger than Klaus, of heart failure. The death of the legitimate brother and true son and legal heir perhaps gave rise to mixed feelings of sorrow and relief that could not be acknowledged.

Barbie wanted to go on to the university and study law or archeology, but his grandfather refused to give him any share of his father's inheritance, which would have paid his tuition and expenses. Nineteen thirty-three was also the first year that Hitler was in power, and various party organizations were springing up. Not knowing what else to do, Barbie enlisted for a six-month work detail in the *Arbeitsdienst* (compulsory labor service) and was sent to Schleswig-Holstein, on the North Sea. After that, he joined the Hitler Youth, becoming a *Fahnenführer* (patrol chief) in charge of 120 boys. There he met a man who urged him to join the SS. Barbie was the ideal recruit, for his need to belong made him pliant, eager to do the right thing, to become what the nation required, to conform and gain approval.

At the same time, joining the SS was a form of social promotion in the New Order. The alternative was to look for a job in the middle of a depression. Klaus Barbie joined the SS, on September

26, 1935, for the same reason that Julien Sorel, the hero of Stendhal's novel *The Red and the Black*, joined the seminary—to improve his lot in life. In Hitler's Germany, when your parents didn't have the money to send you to the university, joining the SS was one of the better ways of getting ahead.

The brain of Klaus Barbie was waiting to be washed, and washed it was during a year of training at the SS school in Bernau, near Berlin. At Bernau hard physical training alternated with inspiring lectures on the life of the Führer and the doctrine of racial selection. There was the instilling of automatic obedience—*Befehl ist Befehl*—an order is an order. There were military exercises with real weapons under combat conditions. Recruits had to dig a hole as a tank approached, and were given just enough time to jump into the hole as the tank treads passed within an inch of their heads. Games were played with live grenades, and casualties were suffered.

Special attention was paid to the Jewish question. Experts, including Eichmann, came to lecture. On several occasions, during the period when the SS and Zionist leaders were collaborating on the migration of Jews to Palestine, noted Zionists came to talk on the future of the Jewish state. Recruits were instructed on the role of the SD in the solution of the Jewish problem. They learned such maxims as "We must have the will to kill coldly and tranquilly."

The main thrust of the indoctrination was to instill in the recruits that they were fortunate indeed to be joining a racial and biological elite, a new ruling class chosen from the best Aryan stock. They were a brotherhood, a group of superior beings above the law, as they could only be tried by SS courts. The feeling of a secret brotherhood was developed through slogans such as *Blut und Boden* (Blood and Soil), and through a great deal of ceremonial rigmarole. You got your lightning-bolt double-S collar patches on Hitler's birthday, April 20, and you recited the loyalty oath, which could be summed up in two words: blind obedience. You got your dagger, another visible sign of belonging. The SS motto was etched on your belt buckle: *Our Honor Is Our Loyalty.*

When Klaus Barbie graduated from Bernau in 1937, he was a fairly representative example of the New Man, merciless and packed with purpose. He believed in the crusade against Jews and Bolsheviks. He believed that his mission in life was to serve the goals of his Führer. He was ready to do the bidding of his superiors. There had once been a concept of honor in war. You didn't kill civilians, or torture suspects, or take hostages in reprisal. But that concept was not taught at Bernau.

Barbie was assigned to an SD unit in Düsseldorf, where he joined the Nazi party. In 1938 he did three months' military service in the infantry, and then it was back to Düsseldorf. In April 1940 he was married—by his unit commander, in keeping with SS usage—to Regina Willms, a lively young woman who played the piano and worked in a Nazi-sponsored children's nursery in Düsseldorf. A daugher, Uta, was born in 1941.

By the time of his marriage, the war was on. Barbie, by now an SS *Untersturmführer* (second lieutenant), followed his SD unit, which was posted to the army invading the Low Countries. He was sent to Amsterdam, where he was involved in the deportation of Jews, and where he was promoted to *Obersturmführer* (first lieutenant). After Amsterdam, he had a couple of other assignments before being sent to Lyon as head of Section Four.

Once in Lyon, Barbie settled into his offices at the Hôtel Terminus and began developing his informant network. One the SD priorities at the end of 1942 was the continued deportation of Jews. There had been no trains since November 1942, and in Berlin, Eichmann was concerned about the prospects for 1943. On December 31 Knochen had cabled from Paris that the trains would resume in mid-February. He cabled again on January 21, saying there were 3,811 Jews in Drancy, but 2,159 were French. Because of Vichy's obstructive attitude, more foreign Jews had to be found in a hurry, and on January 26, 1943, Knochen cabled the regional SD offices, ordering them to arrest all deportable Jews and send them to Drancy. Over the next couple of weeks, Jews started coming in from Bordeaux, Orléans, Poitiers, Angers, and Dijon.

In Lyon, in response to Knochen's request, Barbie was taking a close look at the operations of the UGIF, which had several offices in the city. Lyon being a center for refugees, the UGIF was particularly active. It had five directorates, divided into sections. Before the Germans arrived that November, the UGIF had been getting on well with the Vichy authorities. A report covering the period from June 1 to June 25, 1942, said: "We are finding understanding and even cordiality from most of the authorities. This goes for most civil servants and employers. . . . But often employers refuse to hire Jews, stating that their position is too uncertain given the new laws, and also because of fear of the Labor Department inspectors. But rarely do we have the feeling that such refusals stem from anti-Semitism."

More Jewish refugees were arriving daily, crowding the small UGIF offices. In the words of the report, there was "a pathetic stream of isolated members of dispersed families. People in misery, without belongings, finding it almost impossible to find a place to stay, are the prey of anguish, and often someone in their family has been arrested or deported." The UGIF tried to get rich Jewish families in Lyon to help. "Alas! The results have been so disappointing that we don't even dare quote the number of replies."

After the arrival of the Germans, the UGIF continued to provide a variety of services to Jewish refugees. It sent some Jews into the Italian zone. It distributed money to the needy. To a man looking for work. To a woman trying to get her son out of the Gurs camp. It provided doctors and lawyers. Its activities were numerous, and some of them were secret. For under cover of its health and welfare operations, a team of UGIF volunteers was engaged in smuggling Jews into Switzerland, the border being a mere eighty miles away. A method had been found to cross it; thereafter a Jewish agency in Geneva took the refugees in hand. This underground railroad was being run out of the UGIF office of the Fifth Directorate—Aid to Refugees—in a two-room apartment on the second floor of a dingy building in *vieux* Lyon, at 12 Rue Sainte-Catherine. Here false papers were prepared, funds were collected, and the refugees gathered before their excursion to the Swiss border.

These activities came to the attention of Section Four through an informant at about the same time that in Paris Knochen was clamoring for more Jews. It was decided to spring a trap. Half-a-dozen armed Section Four men in civilian clothes would arrive at the Rue Sainte-Catherine office in the morning when it opened and would arrest whoever came in. It was what the French call a *souricière* (mousetrap). The *souricière* was set for Monday, February 9, because Monday was when a doctor and a nurse were in attendance and when money was distributed to the needy. It was the busiest day of the week.

On Monday Lyon had on its February face. It was a bitingly cold winter morning, with a wind from the north blowing snow flurries through the street. In the bedroom of their small apartment, the Goldbergs, a recently arrived Polish couple, looked out the window at the falling snow. Their four-year-old son Michel was asleep on the living-room couch. Michel's first memory of his new home was his mother telling him, "Don't run in the apartment." His father was off to the UGIF office, where he did volunteer work, and asked him to come along. But Michel's winter boots were being resoled, and his mother said, "No, it's snowing and he doesn't have his boots."

André Deutsch, a Roumanian-born UGIF accountant, was bringing thirty thousand francs in bank notes because this was the day when the refugees came in for their weekly handouts. It was his last day on the job. He was all set to leave for Savoie, in the Italian zone. The Germans had assured him that he was safe as long as he worked for the UGIF, but he had his doubts.

Chana Grinzspan's eight-month-old son René had a cold. She was taking him to the Rue Sainte-Catherine to see the doctor. She had been in Lyon since October 1942. She and her husband were Polish refugees who had been living in Paris, and been rounded up in the July '42 *rafle* of the Vél d'Hiv. Chana's husband was deported, but she was released because she was nursing her baby, who was then barely a month old. Some people in the Lyon suburb of Caluire gave her a room. She was afraid to go to the city hall for her ration card, so she asked the UGIF social worker to do it. She had been going to the UGIF office regularly since then. In addition to the services provided, it was a place where you could meet friends and find out what was going on.

Victor Szulkapler and his family had been in Lyon about eight months. They were living six in a room at 20 Rue du Docteur Zola in the suburb of Villeurbanne. He and his older brother, Rachmil, were Polish-born, but he could pass for French and had an ID card in the name of Victor Sorbier, while Rachmil had an accent and his card bore his real name. The brothers were the leaders of the smuggling operation and went to the Rue Sainte-Catherine every day.

André Deutsch arrived at the office shortly after nine and found himself greeted by an armed man wearing a leather trench coat and a felt hat who announced, "German police." Deutsch was searched, divested of the money he was carrying, and told to take a seat in the far room.

Mrs. Grinzspan arrived in midmorning, holding her baby in her arms. She saw nothing suspicious, no Germans at the entrance or on the stairs. But as soon as she touched the handle, the door opened by itself, and a man put his hand on her shoulder and told her she was under arrest.

Twenty-year-old Victor Szulkapler sized up the situation the moment he walked in. Those who had Jewish ID cards, including his brother Rachmil, were on one side of the room, and those with French cards were on the other. One of the Gestapo men was saying to the switchboard operator: "When they call, tell them to come as usual." Szulkapler realized that he had a chance because he had a French ID card. But he and his brother wore identical rings. So he asked to go to the bathroom, where he removed his ring and put it in his pocket. When he came out, he gave his brother a signal that said, "We don't know each other." He showed a Gestapo man his card and told him he had come there to meet a friend. "What a country," the Gestapo man said, "where you can't tell a Jew from a Gentile." Victor Szulkapler was detained for two very long hours, during which he made a point of not communicating with his brother. When he was released, he went to the post office off the Place des Terreaux and sent a telegram to the Jewish Consistory in Nice reading: MISTER SCHORBAN ARRIVED AT THE UGIF IN LYON. *Schorban* is the Yiddish word for grief. Then he went home and announced: "I'm here, but Rach is gone." And he thought, "The funny thing is, I don't look that different from my brother."

As the day advanced, more unsuspecting refugees, looking forward to their weekly stipend or a doctor's care, stepped into the *souricière,* were arrested, and searched, and registered. One amazing thing happened. Two young women, having been caught, managed to talk their way out. Twenty-year-old Eva Gottlieb, one of the team that was getting Jews out of France, arrived at the Rue Sainte-Catherine early in the afternoon with her mother. She had a French ID card, but her mother did not, and the two women were separated at the entrance and sent to different sides of the room. Eva happened to be carrying the sheet music of a Beethoven symphony, having just come from her piano class. As she waited, one of the SD men picked the sheet music off her lap and began to leaf through it. He could read music and—standing there in his felt hat and long trench coat—started humming the familiar melody. Eva Gottlieb reminded him that she was French. The SS man told her she could go, and she did, leaving her mother behind. Her life had been saved, she later reflected, because she had awakened a Gestapo man's musical instincts.

When Leah Katz, a pretty sixteen-year-old with curly red hair, walked in the door, the SD man who opened it said in German: "Here's another Jewish kitten." Pretending not to understand, and seeing at once that she had made a big mistake, she said; "I must have the wrong office. I'm looking for a doctor for my sick mother." They detained her, however, and after she had been there a few hours, and seen people weeping and praying and imploring, Leah decided she had to do something. What did she have to lose? They would either release her or deport her. So she went up to the SD man who had called her a Jewish kitten and speaking in German said that her mother was sick. *"Das freches dings vas du bist,"* he responded angrily. "You little insolent thing. When you came in, you said you did not speak German, but you speak it well enough when you want to beg." And he slapped her hard across the face. Then, in a complete change of manner, he told Leah she could go, but kept her bag, saying that she had to come for it the next day at the Hôtel Terminus, and handed her a couple of stamps from her change purse. She ran to catch the Number 7 streetcar where someone paid her fare in exchange for the stamps. The next day she went to her family doctor, and asked him to take a medical certificate to the Hôtel Terminus, to explain why she couldn't go. "I'm not going there," the doctor said. She thought: "He's French and Catholic, and if he's not going, I'm not going." Instead she went to the hairdresser and dyed her hair black.

One other person was released that afternoon. As the hours dragged on, and the room filled up, Chana Grinzspan's eight-month-old son began to cry from hunger and could not be silenced. She told an SD man that she had to feed him, and he let her go, say-ing, *"Qu'est-ce qu'il a, le gosse? Allez lui donner du chaud"* ("What's wrong with the kid? Get him some hot food"). Between life and death there hung a thread—a missing pair of boots, a sheet of music, a crying baby.

At around 6 P.M., the SD started calling the men by groups of twelve. Then it was the women's turn. They were eighty-six in all, including twenty-one employees of the UGIF. Montluc Prison was full, so they were taken to Fort Lamothe, an old military fort outside Lyon garrisoned by the Wehrmacht. Those who called the UGIF office after six were told: *"Es ist fertig mit diesen Leuten"* ("It's all over with those people").

Most of the eighty-six men and women who spent the night of September 9 at Fort Lamothe were too overcome with shock and grief to think clearly. But David Luxenburg, a thirty-six-year-old Polish-born Jew who had come to the Rue Sainte-Catherine that morning to inquire about the possibilities of flight to Switzerland, thought of escape as he looked out of the foot-square window of the cell he shared with other victims of the *souricière*. It was a question of seizing the opportunity. The next morning before dawn, a guard opened the door of the cell and told them all to go to the toilet. It was still dark, and instead of following the others, David Luxenburg made his way to the roadway circling the fort, beyond which stood a six-foot-high fence topped by barbed wire. There was a sentry some distance away, but he was looking in the other direction. Taking off his coat and throwing it on top of the barbed wire, David jumped up and over the fence, using his scarf to pro-tect his hands, and found himself in the street, trembling with fear and cold, for he had to leave his coat behind. He walked away, and soon came upon a woman, who told him where he was. Yes, there was a streetcar back to Lyon a few blocks away. But he had no money, he explained. She fished into her purse and pulled out two francs. David Luxenburg took the streetcar and stayed with his brother Aaron, who was a naturalized French citizen, and helped him get away. When going over the fence, he had barely noticed in the dark that another man from his cell had fol-lowed him from the prison, but he had not waited to find out what happened to the man.

In a telegram to the Paris office that Barbie drafted and signed on September 11, he reported two escapees—David Luxenburg and Siegfried Driller. Sloppy work, to say the least, his superiors were sure to say. The eighty-four remaining Jews were moved to the prison at Chalon, north of Lyon. The operation had been carried out, Barbie noted, upon learning that the UGIF office was helping Jews to cross the border into Switzerland illegally. This enterprise was partly financed by a Jewish committee in Geneva.

On February 12 the eighty-four were transferred to Drancy. Gilberte Lévy, one of the UGIF social workers, a thin, sparrowlike woman, had never in her life seen a place as filthy as Drancy. It was swarming with vermin. She woke up at night picking bedbugs out of her ears. There were even bedbugs in the soup. The Lyon group stayed together, and waited. Train departures took place on February 13, and on March 2, 4, 6, and 23, but they were still there. Then on March 25, twenty-two of the eighty-four were taken away. One of the deportees that day was twenty-two-year-old Juliette Weill, whose letter to her family shows that the prisoners had no idea where they were headed. Any destination might have been imagined as an improvement over Drancy. "Dear ones," she wrote, "here we are at Drancy on the morning of the great departure, an event we have so often discussed. . . . For the moment, we do not need you, but when we return, we are counting on finding you all in good condition, and we must feel that you are as strong as we are. This is not farewell, it is only an au revoir."

But Gilberte Lévy was not in the initial group of twenty-two. Nor was she on the trains that carried the remaining fifty-six to Auschwitz, of whom three survived, one being Rachmil Szulkapler. Gilberte was one of six who slipped through the cracks of the system. She was pulled from the Lyon group and put on a vegetable-peeling detail. Then, because she was a trained social worker, she was assigned to help take care of the children who were still coming through the camp. It was depressing work, because once they were cleaned up and comforted, they were adorable, but just as you were getting to know them, they were gone. By this time Drancy had refined the handling of children, and there was a playroom with scenes from the fables of La Fontaine painted on the walls. The contrast between the enchanted world of the playroom and the reality of what was in store for the children weighed heavily on Gilberte Lévy. So she was relieved when in August 1943 she was transferred to a warehouse outside Paris that stored property stolen from Jews. She was part of a work detail that tagged and crated these articles before they were sent to Germany. The warehouse was like a department store. It had a furniture department, a silver department, and an art department. She received an occasional letter. In one she learned that her sister had been deported to Auschwitz. In July 1944 Gilberte was deported to the huge, crowded camp of Bergen-Belsen, which was in the midst of a typhus epidemic. There, she worked in a Kommando that made plastic devices for the Luftwaffe. At first the inmates had a little bread to eat, but then the bread ran out. In the end, their only food was a raw rutabaga every two days. Bergen-Belsen was not a death camp, there were no gas chambers, but the inmates were dying so fast the crematoria were working full time. In April 1945, with the Allies closing in, the SS evacuated the camp and put the survivors on a ghost train that wandered aimlessly eastward. When the train stopped, they got off and picked thistles and made thistle soup. One day the train arrived at a village on the Elbe and Gilberte Lévy saw a Russian officer on his horse. A month later she was back home in Paris.

Michel Goldberg was another survivor; at least that was how he saw it. His father had been sent from Drancy to Beaune-la-Rolande. His mother found out where her husband was and went to the camp in the Loiret *département,* south of Paris. She started chatting with one of the gendarmes, to whom she gave a bolt of cloth, asking him to help her get her husband out. The gendarme replied that he would see what he could do, but it came to nothing, and her husband was deported. She did not ask for the cloth back, not being in a favorable negotiating position.

After the war Michel Goldberg learned that his father had died at Auschwitz. In his dreams he began to see six blue-black digits on his forearm getting bigger because he was growing. Later, when he had a family of his own, his daughter asked, "Why don't we visit your father's grave?" He had to tell her that there was no grave. His father was a small pile of ashes mixed in with others.

Because of his daughter's question, he understood at last that when there was no grave, there was no mourning, and when there was no mourning, you never stopped mourning.

In 1979, thirty-six years after that February day in Lyon, Michel Goldberg, now forty years old and a company director, with a wife and three children, decided that there was only one way he could bury his father. The man who had ordered the *rafle* of the Rue Sainte-Catherine, Klaus Barbie, was alive and well in Bolivia, which had refused a French request for extradition. Goldberg decided that he would fly to Bolivia, buy a gun, pretend to be a reporter, confront Barbie, and shoot him.

Michel did manage to meet Barbie and spent an hour talking to him and one of his friends at a café table in La Paz. It was clear that Barbie was a local notable. People came up to his table and said, "*¿Hola, Klaus, como estás?*" Barbie's friend said to him: "But Klaus, why are you in demand? You were only an *Obersturmführer* in Lyon."

"That may be," said Barbie, "but I had more power than a general, and I was in the capital of the resistance! I changed the course of history in arresting Jean Moulin."

"How so?" Goldberg asked.

"Jean Moulin was so intelligent that if he had lived it's him and not de Gaulle who would have taken over in France. The French would probably have gone Communist."

Goldberg felt the gun in his pocket. This was the moment. He would have to do it out here in the open. He would have to shoot this contemptible braggart who was sitting two feet away from him, the only identifiable link in his father's death. That this man lived was an insult to the victims. Goldberg, who had not accompanied his father to the Rue Sainte-Catherine on that morning long ago, still felt the guilt of the survivor. But it wasn't enough. He didn't feel the necessary rush of hatred and rage that would have made him empty his gun into Barbie. He was incapable of firing, being brought to reason by more practical considerations—thoughts of his wife and family, of the time he might have to spend in a Bolivian jail, of the chance that he would be shot by Barbie's bodyguard. It was all a fantasy, really, that he had followed as far as he was able.

It took almost a month for the Vichy government to respond to the action against the UGIF office. On March 6, 1943, Marshal Pétain wrote Fernand de Brinon, his ambassador in Paris, asking him to lodge a protest with the Germans, since the UGIF was an official organism created by the French government, and it was up to the French authorities to take sanctions against the organization if any were required. The Germans replied on March 20 that their action was justified because the UGIF officials were conducting "reprehensible and detrimental acts."

After the *rafle,* the UGIF started right up again, even though it had lost the office, the furniture, the files, and the employees. The directorate moved to a new office around the corner, at 9 Rue de l'Hôtel de Ville, and by mid-February was delivering services, distributing soup tickets, sending packages to Jews in hospitals and prisons, and providing health and welfare help. Jews at first were afraid to come to the new quarters, but after a few weeks things were back to normal. In April, the Lyon UGIF was upgraded to regional delegation for the southern zone, under a new director, Raymond Geissmann. There were no more illegal activities. Geissmann, who worked with Barbie and the head of Section Four's anti-Jewish subsection, Wenzel, reported on May 19: "I congratulate myself that I have very courteous relations with the *Einsatzkommando* of Lyon."

Judging by Geissmann's reports, his principal concern in the fall of 1943 was not the Germans but finances. His office was so broke that it could not pay the board for children that it had placed with French families. Geissmann's October 1943 report said: "It is sad to say that often people with big fortunes continue to amass their wealth instead of thinking of their fellow Jews in misery. . . . We have come to the conclusion that, just like all the other things they say about Jews, the reproach that we are 'always supporting each other' is as false as the rest."

Geissmann was all too conscious of the limits of the UGIF's activities. It could only play a health-and-welfare role, and could do nothing about the deportations. The UGIF's transactional policy—if it maintained good relations with the Germans, it would in return obtain leniency for the Jews within its orbit—was constantly exploding in its face.

Thus, in August 1943, the UGIF's Paris office was raided and forty-six employees were arrested. As the Rue Sainte-Catherine incidents had shown, there was no safety in working for the UGIF. Also in August, Raymond-Raoul Lambert, a well-connected leader in the southern zone, was arrested after being seen by Roethke coming out of Laval's office just as Roethke was going in. The spectacle of a Jewish leader lobbying the Vichy premier was one the Germans found intolerable.

The greatest blow to Raymond Geissmann came in October, when Jacques Helbronner, the head of the Jewish Consistory, was arrested in Lyon. Helbronner was seventy, and had just had his prostate removed, but Geissmann could do nothing for him in spite of his courteous relations with *Einsatzkommando* of Lyon. At that moment Geissmann wanted to dissolve the UGIF, which was absolutely powerless to protect even the old and the infirm, but Paris prevailed, and the organization lumbered on into 1944, although by the time of the Allied landing, Geissmann was the only senior official left in the southern zone, and Lyon the only regional office still operating. In Paris the leadership was collapsing, which resulted in the organization's most egregious mistake—a failure to disperse the children in the homes it ran in the Paris area. Those homes were raided in July, and 233 children were taken to Drancy, and more than 200 were deported on July 31, 1944. After all, the UGIF was a relief organization. Its mission was not to hide children. And as more of its leaders were arrested, the more cautious the men who replaced them became, refusing to do anything that might provoke the Gestapo's anger. So the smuggling operation that had been carried on from the Rue Sainte-Catherine office, for which the UGIF and its clients paid dearly, could in retrospect be viewed as one of the more heroic episodes in that group's history.

André Devigny, the infantry lieutenant whom we last saw being hit in the buttocks by friendly fire in June 1940 as he and his men were fording a river, had been treated for his wounds in Bordeaux and sent on convalescent leave to his home in Savoie. There in 1942, in the city of Annemasse, he met Edmée Deletraz, a tall brunette in her thirties with a lively, intelligent face who had grown up in Brussels, where her father was director of the Philharmonic. Edmée was in the resistance, helping people cross into Switzerland and working with the so-called Réseau Gilbert. This was an intelligence network of former French officers run by Colonel Georges Groussard, the onetime commander of the French military academy, Saint-Cyr. His allegiance was to Charles de Gaulle and he operated out of Geneva. Through Edmée, Colonel Groussard recruited Devigny, who agreed to get in touch with his officer friends in various parts of the unoccupied zone and extend the network.

By 1943 Devigny had enlisted half a dozen officers including Lieutenant Hitter in Marseille and Lieutenant Nollet in Lyon. In March 1943 Hitter arrived in Lyon with a promising new recruit, the foreman of a gunpowder factory in Toulouse. He was Robert Moog, a blond, blue-eyed Alsatian with a low brow, a sincere smile, a hearty manner, and a German accent. He hated Germans, he said, for having expelled him from his home.

Hitter introduced Moog to Nollet and Devigny. The Alsatian had brought with him samples of different kinds of gunpowder the factory where he worked was producing, and said that six wagonloads a day were being sent to Germany.

"We have to stop this," Nollet said.

"A bombing would do it," Hitter said.

"A bombing?" Moog said. "What about the civilian population? The factory is right in the city."

"Then what?"

"Sabotage."

"Bombing or sabotage, we'll need the blueprints," Devigny said.

"I may be able to borrow them," Moog said, "but I'll have to get them back fairly fast."

"We'll make a copy," Devigny said.

They then had a congenial lunch, during which Moog said he was glad to have found some kindred spirits and asked them to call him Bobby. Two weeks later, Moog arrived with the blueprints, copies of which were taken to Colonel Groussard in Geneva, who decided to carry out a sabotage operation with the help of the British Buckmaster network. Moog became a trusted agent who had brought Groussard his biggest operation, and he met many of the men involved. He took part in hiding explosives in a veterinary school in Toulouse. He met Perkins, the British officer who ran the Buckmaster operation in the area, and learned the location of the castle where the Buckmaster radio transmitter was kept.

On April 12 Moog told Hitter about an even bigger operation in Paris, and they left by train for the capital. When they emerged from the Gare de Lyon, they were both arrested.

In the meantime, Colonel Groussard had asked Devigny to carry out an "action mission" against an Italian counterespionage agent in Nice by the name of Oswald Angrisani who was working for the Germans. Devigny and another man arrived in Nice on April 14, having been briefed on their target. Angrisani was making the most of his Riviera assignment, going to the casino every night with a different girl on his arm and then hitting the nightclubs. He drove a Lancia and had a villa in the hills called L'Éolienne, and he usually got home between midnight and one. Devigny and his partner located the villa and waited in the shadows on the night of April 14 for Angrisani to arrive. At about one o'clock, the Lancia arrived. Angrisani got out and opened the garage door, then got back in the car and drove it into the garage, Devigny and his partner following. When Angrisani got out of the car again, Devigny clubbed him with his blackjack, but it was a glancing blow and Angrisani made a bull-like rush for him. Devigny's partner fired and Angrisani dropped; Devigny gave him a bullet in the head to finish him off. The two men separated and Devigny hid out with friends in Nice for a day before going back to Annemasse.

On April 17 Devigny went to the Annemasse station to meet the train on which Edmée Deletraz usually returned from making a weekly visit to her sick sister in Lyon. He spotted her as she got off the train and walked in her direction, but she pretended not to know him, staring straight ahead and whispering as she passed, "We are all very sick." Devigny thought that she must have heard about the action in Nice and was upset because he had killed a civilian. Then he turned around and spotted Robert Moog at the back of the station platform, and wondered what he was doing there. He had never come to Annemasse before.

Outside the station, Devigny was grabbed by three men who threw him into a car. In the front seat sat Robert Moog, who said two words: "German police."

In the meantime, as Devigny later learned, his friend Hitter, arrested in Paris, had been deported to Buchenwald. Moog had then headed south to direct the arrests of all the others he had met—the British officer, Perkins, the director of the veterinary school where the explosives had been stored, the owners of the castle, Lieutenant Nollet in Lyon—about thirty persons in all.

Edmée Deletraz left Annemasse on April 16 to see her sister, Yvonne Charlaix, who was in Lyon's Clinique du Parc being treated for cancer. Upon leaving the clinic, she went to her usual mail drop, the Nony laundry on the Rue Bechelevin. The laundress told her: "The man who brought the mail from Toulouse is not the one who usually comes. He is waiting for you in the Grand Café." She decided not to go to the café. Instead, she took the valise with the mail back to the Clinique du Parc and left it under her sister's bed.

Then she went back to the laundry, where the men in the long trench coats were waiting, among them Klaus Barbie. Robert Moog was there in handcuffs, repeating the scenario of his fake arrest in Paris. Edmée was taken to the Hôtel Terminus for questioning. She said she came each week to see her sister, and was in fact on her way to a lab to pick up some test results. Barbie drove her there and took the results back to the Hôtel Terminus where he had them dipped in a solution to detect invisible ink, believing they were resistance reports. Nothing showed up, so Edmée was released and told to check with Section Four whenever she came to Lyon. The Germans let her go in the hope that she would lead them to other members of the network, and on April 17 she did indeed lead them to Devigny in the Annemasse train station.

In the car from Annemasse to Lyon, Devigny thought: "I'm leaving behind three children. Three orphans." The Germans had searched his room and found 25,000 francs. They took a road along the Swiss border, where they saw a gray-uniformed Swiss soldier on patrol. "Take a good look," Moog said. Devigny was brought to Lyon's Montluc Prison and placed in a cell on death row.

When we last saw Jean Moulin, prefect of Eure-et-Loire, he was in Chartres after a run-in with the occupation troops. Dismissed by Vichy in November 1940, he left for Marseille, grew a moustache, and changed his name to Jean Mercier. Through the American consul, Hugh Fullerton, Moulin obtained an American visa, and on September 9, 1941, he left Marseille, went to Spain, then Portugal, and took a flight from Lisbon to London on October 19, his prefect's card hidden in the handle of his suitcase.

From London, after seeing de Gaulle, he was sent to the training school at Ringway, Lord Beaverbrook's property in Suffolk, where he learned coding and made the required seven jumps. Then it was waiting, and more waiting, until December 31, 1941, when a four-engine Armstrong-Whitley took him, his radio operator, and an aide across the Channel. The new year was rung in while they were in the air—with tea and sandwiches, no champagne. Moulin had made a drawing for the pilot of the spot where they were to be dropped, just south of Avignon, at the juncture of the Rhône and Durance rivers.

Then a dark line appeared, the French coast, and soon Major Benham, the dispatcher, told him they were over the drop zone. "It's exactly the point." He raised his thumb and said, "Go," and Moulin and his radio operator, Hervé Monjaret, and his aide, Raymond Fassin, leaped into the night, landing in a swamp. With the parachute restricting his movements, it took Moulin an hour to extricate himself. Then he went looking for the others, whistling to establish location. The radio was lost in the muck, as were his compass and his Colt automatic, but he had the 500,000 francs and a matchbox with a microfilm order from de Gaulle hidden in its false bottom.

A month later, in Marseille, Moulin met the founder of the underground newspaper *Combat,* Henri Frenay, and gave him 250,000 francs. Moulin's mission was to fuse the various resistance movements already operating in France and place them under Gaullist control. The incentive was money and arms from London, but it was uphill work. Each group, proud of its autonomy, was quarreling with the other groups. They saw in Moulin's endeavor an attempt to inhibit the resistance for fear it would develop leaders who could challenge de Gaulle in popularity and accomplishments. They saw the London people as dilettantes trying to tell them, the seasoned veterans, how to do their jobs.

Moulin needed patience to convince these men, who spent much of their time and energy squabbling. Each group claimed to be more important than it was, and made bloated claims of membership. Frenay claimed 33,000 members for his underground group, also called *Combat,* and flirted with Allen Dulles and the OSS for an alternate source of financing. He did not like Moulin and told him that he knew nothing about underground work. *Libération,* the union-backed Socialist movement run by the quixotic d'Astier de la Vigerie, claimed seventeen thousand members. In 1941 d'Astier had admitted to the union leader Léon Jouhaux: "Our action is limited to verbal expression." He was, however, pro-Gaullist and in 1942, along with Frenay, began to receive weapons dropped by parachute in 300-pound containers. Terrains had to be found for drops and landings, the locations of which the BBC announced in codes. The nature of the resistance changed from distributing newspapers to carrying out sabotage and military actions.

Moulin was based in Lyon, but was constantly on the move. In May 1942 he was summoned to Vichy by the director of personnel, Georges Hilaire. Laval wanted to bring back into the government a few left-wing prefects with anti-German records to give him credibility. Was Moulin prepared to accept another assignment? Moulin said he was not prepared to collaborate with the Germans. "It's not collaboration that matters," Hilaire said, "it's what you put into it." Almost with a wink. The old trickster policy.

Jean Moulin spent the rest of 1942 trying to bring together various resistance factions. It was finally agreed that there would be a single military unit, called the "Secret Army," under a single military leader. In August Frenay recruited a general named Charles Delestraint, a short, dapper man who in 1940 had been de Gaulle's superior when he was commanding an armored division. Delestraint agreed to head the Secret Army. Frenay soon began to wonder whether he had done the right thing, for Delestraint was not at home in underground work, where there was no clear line of command, and you never knew who was giving the orders, and where every decision was subject to endless debate. Delestraint wanted to write proclamations to the troops, which Frenay thought was absurd, and he was obsessed with the prerogatives of command.

In September Frenay and d'Astier were sent to London to meet de Gaulle, and spent much of their time disparaging Jean Moulin.

D'Astier referred to him as "that little appointed clerk." When they got back to France, Jean Moulin set up a coordinating committee, which met for the first time on November 27 in a suburb of Lyon. Frenay criticized General Delestraint, saying he had no experience in clandestine work. There were such scenes that Delestraint said he would attend no more meetings. Jean Moulin tried to smooth things over by giving them all titles. Frenay became "Commissioner for Military Affairs," and d'Astier, "Commissioner for Political Affairs." In January 1943 Moulin announced that he wanted to create a national council of the resistance, representing all the different factions, which Frenay objected to on the grounds that it would be a return to the old political parties. At another meeting, on February 21, 1943, there were bitter arguments over Frenay's "redoubt" plan: He wanted to encourage and support free zones in the Alps and the Jura Mountains, made up of groups of deserters from the forced labor (STO) program who were fleeing into the *maquis* (wilderness). Moulin said this would be premature, and he reduced Frenay's budget for *Combat*. Frenay was sure that Moulin was trying to weaken his movement by tightening the pursestrings. Then in March Moulin and Delestraint went off to London for a month.

In the meantime, the Germans having moved into the unoccupied zone in November 1942, the resistance groups were hunted with far greater purpose than they had been by Vichy. Now there were SD offices in all the major cities whose main assignment was to go after the "terrorists," and who began having some success. The resistance groups were lax when it came to security. All too often, correspondence was transmitted *en clair* (uncoded). German agents were easily able to infiltrate resistance units, as Robert Moog infiltrated the Groussard network. When suspects were questioned, they often talked, so that from a single arrest an entire group could be dismantled. As 1942 had been the year of attempted unification of the resistance, 1943 was the year of its undoing. Like a mortar bracketing its rounds until it hits the target, the SD was closing in on Jean Moulin from several directions. From one came Robert Moog, who had arrested André Devigny and was keeping Edmée Deletraz under surveillance, and who, in May 1943, was transferred to Lyon to assist Klaus Barbie in his operations.

Another pressure point was Marseille, where the local head of *Combat,* a thick-necked, broad-shouldered former infantry lieutenant named Maurice Chevance, active and energetic, had done a lot of recruiting. One of his recruits was another young officer on "armistice leave," Henri Aubry. Another was a meaty-faced, bespectacled refugee from the north called Lunel, also known as Multon.

On April 28, 1943, the Marseille Gestapo arrested Chevance and Lunel. Three days later, Lunel agreed to work for the Germans and started giving them names. His information was so useful that in May he was moved to Lyon, where the top resistance leaders were based. Henri Aubry had not been arrested in Marseille, having also moved to Lyon to serve as Chief of Staff to General Delestraint, who shuttled between Lyon and Paris.

With his staff-officer mentality, General Delestraint was drawing up plans for resistance activities once the Allied landing came. One plan he particularly wanted was for rail sabotage, which would hamper German troop movements. Inside the government-run French railway system, there was a large and active resistance organization run by thirty-one-year-old René Hardy, a gaunt, red-haired man who was a railroad inspector. Hardy was an authentic resistance hero who had built up from scratch an extensive team of *cheminots* (railwaymen). In the repair shops at the Lyon depots of Perrache and Les Brotteaux, courses on sabotage were given. You could, at little risk, change the destination labels on cars. You could mix abrasive powder into the oil reservoirs of locomotives. You could derail trains without using explosives, by cutting the tracks, which did not require complicated tools or a large number of people, and although the tracks would be repaired, at least you had derailed the locomotive.

But Hardy was also a born liar and fabulist. He mixed fact and fiction, saying that he had graduated from Saint-Cyr at the top of his class, that he was head of sabotage for all of France, and that he was an engineer for the railroad. He was often in Lyon, not only on resistance business, but because he was in love with a young woman named Lydie Bastien, a femme fatale type, leggy and languid. She was described as "too beautiful," presumably meaning a certain kind of flaunting seductiveness. In any case, General Delestraint met Hardy in Lyon in May and asked him to draft a railway sabotage scheme, which would be called the "Green Plan." Hardy holed up in a farmhouse and drew up a 150-page plan that consisted of a series of maps marking the spots where German reserve divisions were stationed and the railway lines that would have to be knocked out to slow their movement. In general, the idea was that more sabotage and less Allied bombing would save civilian lives.

Delestraint went to Paris, but continued to communicate with Hardy through his new Chief of Staff, Henri Aubry. Messages from the general were placed by Aubry in a mail drop at 14 Rue Bouteille, in the name of Mme. Dumoulin, where Hardy could pick them up. It was this mail drop that Lunel learned about on May 24 from another resistance agent who did not know Lunel had been turned by the Gestapo. And it was this mail drop that the Gestapo had under observation of May 27 when Henri Aubry's secretary left a message that René Hardy must come to Paris on June 9 for a meeting with General Delestraint at 9 A.M. at the Metro station La Muette. Aubry was the sort of person who when he goes shopping notices at the cash register that he's forgotten his wallet, and he did not bother to code the message. He did not, however, use René Hardy's real name, but his resistance name, Didot.

Didot was a name well known to Klaus Barbie, who saw it often in reports on the actions of *résistance fer* (rail resistance). Paris was urging him to do something about the Didot network, which was sabotaging trains daily. He had just received a report that a leave train had been derailed south of Mâcon, leaving five soldiers dead and twenty severely injured.

Naturally Barbie was elated to learn about the message mentioning Didot. This single message, which the Gestapo allowed Hardy to pick up, gave them the means to arrest both Hardy and Delestraint. Barbie ordered Moog and Lunel to conduct a surveillance of the Lyon–Paris express from June 1 on. The two had met Didot in Marseille and knew what he looked like.

Hardy returned to Lyon with the Green Plan on June 4, later claiming that he had not seen the message about the June 9 meeting. However, he had to go to Paris for a different meeting, he said, and asked Lydie Bastien to reserve a *couchette* (berth) on the June 7 Lyon–Paris express. Lunel and Moog were at the station, where Lunel spotted Hardy. The two men got on the train, arranging for Hardy to be arrested when it stopped at Chalon. Lunel and Moog continued on to Paris, where on June 9 they arrested General Delestraint, who turned up punctually at the La Muette Métro station, wearing the Legion of Honor in the lapel of his overcoat. The general later asked to have a mirror and an armchair in his cell, in accordance with his rank.

In what happened next, I have relied partly on Barbie's own account. In 1947, when Barbie, a wanted war criminal, was hiding out near Munich, he applied for an intelligence job with the U.S. Army Counter-Intelligence Corps under an assumed name. To establish his bona fide as a trained intelligence man, he wrote an account of his capture of Jean Moulin for Special Agent Robert S. Taylor, who would be hiring him. Mr. Taylor, now living in Syracuse with the German woman he married on his tour of duty in the forties, has kindly translated the document Barbie gave him, which had lain undisturbed in his files over the years.

It might be objected that a convicted war criminal, sentenced to life imprisonment, a man known to lie whenever it served his purpose, should not be taken seriously in telling his version of the events. But in this case Barbie was not disclaiming responsibility for his wartime actions, he was claiming it, because he wanted to make a good impression on his prospective employer. He was not saying, "I didn't sign this" or "I never saw this person before," as he did so often during his trial, he was admitting his role in a major antiresistance action. Thus, on the one hand, there was no reason for him to lie, and on the other, his version is corroborated in other German documents.

"Shortly after midnight [on June 7]," Barbie wrote, "the *Kommando* in Chalon reported to me that René Hardy had been arrested. The next day [June 8] I went to Chalon in my car to pick him up. A cell door opened and before me stood a slender, somewhat pale man in middle age. His hair shone a light red. I approached him with the words: 'Good morning, Mr. Hardy, your game is up.' . . . A small incident brought us, as humans, somewhat closer together. Hardy had his glasses on. I knew that he carried them merely as camouflage. I asked him to lend them to

225

me for a moment, as I had forgotten mine. He looked at me with astonishment and mistrust, but handed them to me. I took out my handkerchief and wiped the glasses off with exaggerated gestures. Hardy laughed with embarrassment as I returned the glasses and said: 'Hardy, your eyes this time were just as bad as your glasses, otherwise I would not have caught you.' "

" 'You are quite right,' he replied, 'the next time I will be fitted with better glasses.' I am not sure if it was this incident that caused Hardy to confide in me, but he suddenly stretched out his hand and assured me that he had no fears about his future. . . . I decided at that moment to win Hardy over in order to penetrate the leading circles of the resistance, but for the time being I kept these plans to myself."

Instead of sending Hardy to prison, Barbie gave him favored treatment, kept him under house arrest, gave him food and newspapers, spent hours in conversation with him, and listened to him talk at length about his fiancée Lydie Bastien. And lo and behold, over the next few days, according to Barbie, René Hardy began to talk without any pressure having been applied. "In easy conversation, with liquor and wine, Hardy related almost everything to me, everything he knew. However, the names of the leading figures in the resistance he withheld. At best I could keep his arrest secret only two days, then he would be 'burned,' as the technical expression went. I put my cards on the table and asked him if he was willing to work with me. At first he refused, but only for appearances. I put the situation before him: Here his activities, there the judgment. Then he agreed. Because of his prominence in the resistance movement, I had to obtain permission for my plan from Berlin, which I soon received."

Why had Hardy so readily agreed to cooperate with the Gestapo? To escape torture and imprisonment was the obvious reason. Also, Barbie may have threatened to arrest Lydie Bastien. And third, it was in Hardy's nature to connive, to play cat and mouse, to think that he was outsmarting the other fellow when he was in fact being outsmarted.

Barbie told Hardy that he was letting him go, and that he should meet his contacts in Lyon and tell them the following story: He had jumped from the train in Mâcon, having spotted Lunel, and figured that he might be arrested. He should send this same story by courier to Paris, to excuse his absence at the meeting there. "I left Hardy the fullest freedom of movement," Barbie went on, "though I admit that on the first day I had qualms that I would never see him again. But he came to me every evening, gave me reports, and slept in my office."

Meanwhile, Jean Moulin was back in Lyon after a detour on the Riviera to open an art gallery as a cover. He was an art collector who, on his modest prefect's salary, had managed to acquire an Utrillo, a Soutine, a Rouault, and a Chirico. In February he opened the Galerie Romanin in Nice, with the backing of the Paris art dealer Paul Petrides, who loaned him four Utrillos and two Vlamincks for his *vernissage* on February 9. There was a portrait of the *Maréchal* hanging in the foyer, and Moulin invited all the local Vichy authorities. Mounting art exhibits was a good excuse to travel.

Moulin was informed on June 15 of General Delestraint's arrest. His most urgent task was to find a replacement for the general, and he thought of Colonel Schwarzfeld, an army officer of suitable rank who belonged to a small resistance movement. Moulin set about organizing a summit meeting of the different branches of the resistance, which Schwarzfeld would also attend. He asked André Lassagne, a Lyon high-school teacher and resistance leader, to find an appropriate place to meet. Lassagne had a childhood friend by the name of Dugoujon who was a doctor in the suburb of Caluire, and who agreed to let them use a room in the house on the Place Castellane that served as both his home and his office. They would pose as patients in his waiting room. The day of the meeting was June 21.

"In the middle of June," Barbie's account continued, "Hardy received word from Paris by courier that there would be a meeting of the resistance in Lyon in the near future. The meeting was to choose a new chief of the resistance, since General Delestraint had been arrested. Hardy came to me immediately with the message and laid the original text before me. It was clear to me that here was the chance to come to grips with the leading figures of the resistance."

Barbie formed a plan to arrest all those attending the meeting in a surprise raid. To do this, Hardy would have to attend the meeting and be arrested along with the others to allay suspicions.

But he would be allowed to escape. He would be loosely tied up, and would attack his guard, who would have been briefed beforehand. When Hardy made a run for it, the guard would fire at him but miss.

Although Hardy knew about the meeting, he was not invited to attend. But on Sunday, June 20, he arranged to see Henri Aubry, who was back in Lyon. Aubry came by the Pont Morand, where Hardy was sitting on a bench next to a man reading a newspaper. The man was Barbie. Aubry took Hardy to lunch at a restaurant called Le Pélican and explained the situation. The meeting the next day would be attended by leaders of the different resistance factions, and he, Aubry, would represent *Combat*. Henri Frenay had been kicked upstairs by de Gaulle. To get Frenay out of France, where he was constantly quarreling with Jean Moulin, de Gaulle had brought him to Algiers, where he had formed a government, and made him minister for prisoners of war. Aubry felt that René Hardy, who was also affiliated with *Combat,* should come to the meeting and bolster his position. Hardy readily agreed and may indeed have volunteered. Where and when would the meeting be held? he asked. "I don't know," Aubry replied, "but come to the bistro across from the Caluire *ficelle* [literally, string, actually, a funicular going from the Croix-Rousse to Caluire, which was on a plateau above Lyon] at 1:45 P.M."

"Hardy spent the evening of the 20th with me," Barbie went on. "I went over all the details of the raid with him, in particular assuring him again that he would be given his freedom. One technical difficulty existed, as to how the meeting place should be determined without mistake. I assumed that the meeting, because of its importance, would last two or three hours. Thus I would have time. Hardy suggested to me that he be followed in a sort of echelon, with men posted at various corners. . . . In order to be wholly certain, I gave Hardy a piece of yellow chalk. With this he was to mark the steps and doors which led to the meeting place."

On the evening of June 20, Jean Moulin had dinner with the man who had been appointed to take his place in case of arrest, Claude Serreules. He had been dropped by parachute on June 16 and had served as de Gaulle's chief of cabinet. One more meeting, Moulin may have thought as he proceeded to his rendezvous with

Serreules. There have been so many meetings, in museums, in theaters, on the banks of the Rhône. One of the advantages of Lyon was more letter boxes and fewer concierges. Cordier, when he came to tell me about Delestraint, said he always carried his toothbrush. "If they arrest me I can at least brush my teeth." A mist over the stone *quais*. In Lyon things are what they seem. Widows wear black and lovers hold hands. But are they? The Rue de l'Abondance, a good joke with its windowless walls. They're always eating or hoarding their money. It's the last place on earth for a beggar. And Vichy. As soon as the old fellow says, "Frenchmen," he conveys a sense of catastrophe. And the other one, saying, "Why are you taking so little, please take a bit more." You can see it changing, first they arrested people for tearing down Laval posters in factories, but just the other day, in a movie house on the Place des Terreaux, a man who cheered Laval on the newsreel was attacked by the others. Thus, perhaps, did Moulin's mind ramble as Serreules saw him arrive in his gray overcoat, with his tired adolescent's face, the black scarf concealing a scar on his throat. Moulin told him he was expected at the meeting the next day.

In the meantime, after Devigny's arrest, Edmée Deletraz had gone to Geneva to report to Colonel Groussard. He had told her to go along with the Gestapo and check in with them whenever she went to Lyon. She did so, her contact being Captain Fritz Hollert. Toward the end of May, Moog asked Edmée to come with him to the Rue Bouteille. The Gestapo had arrested Mme. Dumoulin—the mail drop was in her name—and were occupying her apartment. Moog wanted Edmée to answer the door in case anyone from the resistance came by, but no one did.

Then, on Monday, June 21, Edmée went to the Hôtel Terminus. Moog told her, "Come with me, I'll show you a Frenchman who's understood [meaning Didot/Hardy]." He led her to a room where three Section Four men, Hollert and Barbie and Paul Heimann, were sitting at a table with a French civilian who was introduced as Didot. She had never seen him before; he had reddish hair and a lean face. "Some resistance men are holding an important meeting," Moog told Edmée. "The delegate of General de Gaulle will be there. Didot will be there. The rendezvous is at two o'clock at the Croix-Rousse funicular. From there, he doesn't know. You will follow him and come back and tell us where he went.''

"If the meeting is in an apartment building," Didot said, "this woman will not be able to tell at what floor and in what apartment I've gone." There was a moment of silence, than Didot said: "Give me a pack of cigarettes. I'll empty it and leave the pack on the doormat." The Germans laughed, and one of them threw Didot a pack of cigarettes. Edmée was then told to go and wait at the École de Santé, the new and more spacious SD headquarters on the Avenue Berthelot across the Rhône. It was 11 A.M. and Edmée thought, "I've got to warn these people." She went to the butcher on the Avenue de Saxe, another mail drop, and left a message for one of her contacts, Jean Cambus. She proceeded to the French Red Cross, where another contact, Colonel de la Brosse, told her, "Don't worry, we'll take care of it." She visited a third contact, then she went to the École de Santé, where the Germans came to take her to the *ficelle*.

Only André Lassagne and Jean Moulin knew where the meeting place was. The others had to be led there by either of the two. This was a good method but, still, the whole operation was amateurish. No security had been arranged at Doctor Dugoujon's office, which was on a big open square. There was no protection, no one at a window to spot untoward arrivals, no emergency exit in case the meeting was interrupted. It was all arranged with Gallic offhandedness.

Nor was there any punctuality. Different people arrived at different times. André Lassagne got to the *ficelle* at 1:45 P.M. on his bicycle, where Aubry and René Hardy were waiting. Surprised to see Hardy, Lassagne pointed out that he had not been invited. Hardy replied that he did not want to attend the entire meeting, but only to talk briefly with Max (Moulin) about a pressing matter. They got on the funicular, and at the top Hardy and Aubry took the Number 33 streetcar, while Lassagne followed on his bike.

Tailing René Hardy were Moog and Edmée. "See them over there with Didot," Moog told her, "the two others? Follow them and come back with your report." The *ficelle* was about to leave, and she hopped on. At the top of the hill she took the streetcar, and when Hardy and Aubry got off at the Place Catellane and turned left, she walked straight ahead, wondering what to do. "By this time," she thought, "the resistance people have been warned, they know they've been betrayed." So she took the *ficelle* back down to Croix-Rousse, where she found the Germans waiting, annoyed. Barbie was there too. He told her to get into his car and said, "We've already lost half an hour. Show us the way." So, once again, Edmée took the funicular and when they reached the top, she said, "They got off here." "And then?" Barbie asked. "And then I lost them," she answered. Barbie told her to go home.

In the meantime, Jean Moulin was due to meet Raymond Aubrac (of *Libération*) at 2:15 at the funicular. Claude Serreules and Colonel Schwarzfeld were supposed to join them, but Serreules got his instructions mixed up and missed the meeting entirely, thereby escaping arrest. The result was that Moulin and Aubrac waited for them, and when Schwarzfeld finally showed up and they took the *ficelle,* they were forty-five minutes late.

According to Barbie, "On the day of the meeting, Hardy kept his rendezvous at the appointed place. They greeted him and took a road which led to the city's edge [Barbie apparently left out the funicular, to simplify the story]. As agreed, I had them followed through my agents, done by echelons, whereby Hardy and the other two men were given over to the next agent and the report was brought back to me, as to where they were. In this manner, it was quite easy to find the meeting place. After about an hour, it was reported to me that Hardy, who had been joined by a fourth person, had entered the lonely villa of a doctor. I must admit that the choice of this place was excellent. No one would suspect that among the patients who went in and out were the leading figures of the French resistance."

It was nearly 3 P.M. by the time Moulin, Aubrac, and Schwarzfeld arrived at Dr. Dugoujon's house. The housekeeper, not knowing they were supposed to join the other gentlemen who had been shown to a room on the second floor, led them into the waiting room, thinking they were patients. Actually Moulin had a note from his doctor referring him to Dr. Dugoujon for his rheumatism.

"As soon as possible," Barbie's account goes on, "I drove to the villa with my men. The drive was through the city and into a suburb. A few hundred meters from the doctor's residence, I climbed out and in a few minutes the house was surrounded. I noticed immediately on the house the chalk marks that Hardy had made. I followed the marks, which pointed to the second story, and then saw a mark on a door. I kicked it open—and stood opposite a group of men. At the same moment I fired a shot into the ceiling, since I had reckoned with armed resistance. There was absolute quiet after the shot. A number of those present had thrown themselves on the floor, the others raised their hands. Hardy also fell on the floor, according to plan. The surprise was complete. They were searched quickly and several revolvers were found. Everything had gone as fast as lightning. I didn't look at Hardy. I noticed merely that he played his role excellently and acted superbly. One by one, the men were brought before me. They all gave me false names, which I expected. It made no difference to me, for Hardy had told me of their various personalities and descriptions. The whole questioning was only a matter of appearance.''

Barbie said to Aubry, whose code name was Thomas, ''Well, Thomas, you don't look well. You were more cheerful yesterday on the Morand bridge. I was reading my paper, and it was such a fine day, I thought, we'll leave you alone one more day.'' A strange thing happened. The men all had handcuffs put on them except for René Hardy. Why this most favored treatment? Barbie covered himself by having his bodyguard, Steingritt, say, ''We're out of handcuffs. '' Hardy's hands were tied with a rope. Then they were put up against the wall and searched, but Hardy's pistol was not found. He said later he had hidden it in a special pocket of his sleeve.

''To my alarm,'' Barbie's account goes on, ''I noticed that the leaders who were to head the discussion were missing. I was afraid they had been warned shortly before the raid. Then the waiting room occurred to me. I looked into it and saw a row of supposed patients. Every person there was brought unobtrusively before Hardy, who gave me a sign as soon as he recognized one. To be sure, I found the missing ones among this group.

''I observed the removal of the prisoners from the window,'' Barbie's account continued. ''Calm, somewhat pale, Hardy allowed himself to be led away by my man. Nothing in his manner betrayed what was to come. Suddenly, as he started to climb into the car, he tore himself loose, jumped on the man, dealt him what seemed like a light blow, and ran away. At the same moment the shooting began. Shot after shot rang out, all missing Hardy, who ran as hard as he could.

"Then suddenly something happened, something which had not been planned. One of my men had forgotten his instructions in the excitement of the moment. He rushed after Hardy and shot at him. I saw him take aim and stand over Hardy, who had thrown himself into a ditch. At the last second I called the man and distracted his aim. Then another man forgot himself. It was too late to stop his shot, but it only wounded Hardy in the lower arm."

Thanks to the two soldiers who got carried away, it was a pretty convincing escape. Hardy found refuge in a nearby house, but was soon picked up by the French police who were investigating the Caluire shootout. He was taken to the Antiquaille Hospital to have his wound treated. By this time the word was out that Hardy had betrayed the others, who were locked up in Montluc Prison. Raymond Aubrac's wife, Lucie, sent Hardy a food package with some cyanide-laced jam, but Hardy was suspicious and did not eat it. He was able to let Barbie know where he was, and on June 28 he was transferred to the German-run Croix-Rousse Hospital. When Hardy was well enough to be discharged, Barbie arranged another escape. He gave Hardy the necessary papers under an alias. Hardy dyed his hair black and left the hospital during the night. Barbie made arrangements for their next meeting, and Hardy behaved as though everything was fine, but Barbie never saw him again. Hardy fled Lyon with Lydie Bastien, spent some time in Paris, and in 1944 reached Algiers, where he joined Henri Frenay's cabinet, having convinced Frenay that he was not responsible for the Caluire episode.

There are two documents that corroborate Barbie's account. The first is a letter from Ernst Kaltenbrunner, Heydrich's replacement as head of the SD, to Foreign Minister von Ribbentrop, on June 29, 1943, completing his May 27 report on the resistance in France. The letter said: "Questioned after his arrest, Hardy, alias Didot, chief of railroad sabotage, made a full confession. . . . Since Hardy gave us detailed information and was willing to collaborate with us, we used him several times with success to arrange meetings. He reconstituted for our services the plan to sabotage the railroads. Thanks to a plan Hardy lent himself to, the SD of Lyon, in collaboration with special units, succeeded in surprising in Lyon a meeting of the leaders of the Secret Army, which led to a number of arrests."

The second document is a report found in the SS archives in Lyon after the Germans fled in August 1944. The arrest of the resistance leaders was code-named "Flora." "Thanks to the surveillance of the mail drop of the railway sabotage section," said the Flora report, "Multon [Lunel] learned of a planned meeting on June 9 in Paris. Thus Multon made possible Didot's arrest on the train and turned him over to the Lyon section, where he was subsequently used as a counteragent. This led to the arrest in Lyon of Moulin, Jean, personal delegate of General de Gaulle. . . . In addition, on June 9, 1943, our agent was able to arrest in Paris, Vidal, or Charles Delestraint, chief of the Secret Army for all of France."

In December 1945, the French secret service (DST) came across the Flora report and arrested Hardy. This was the start of the "Hardy affair," which went on for years and was never resolved. Hardy spent two years in prison awaiting the outcome of the pretrial instruction, or judicial inquiry. He finally came to trial in January 1947. His old friends from *Combat,* like Henri Frenay, testified in his favor. There was no corroboration of the Gestapo report. Hardy had a hotshot lawyer named Maurice Garçon who made a clever defense plea along the lines of "this great resistance hero should be decorated, not jailed." Hardy was acquitted on January 24, 1947.

Two months later to the day, Hardy was rearrested. In the archives of the *couchette* division of the national railroad, a report dated June 8, 1943, had been found. Filed by the conductor of the Paris–Lyon express, it stated that a passenger by the name of René Hardy (he had used his real name on the *couchette* reservation) had been arrested on June 7 by the Germans at Chalon-sur-Saône and taken off the train. Once again, there was a prolonged judicial inquiry, and Hardy spent three years and two months in prison. The second trial got under way in May 1950. This time Henri Frenay was a witness for the prosecution. This time Hardy could not deny having been arrested on the train. This time Dr. Dugoujon testified that when Hardy was hiding in a ditch, "children playing hide-and-seek could have found him." This time Edmée Deletraz testified that she had seen Hardy at the Hôtel Terminus on June 21. But Hardy's friend and liaison agent, Roger Bosse, testified that Hardy had been with him at that time, and the persuasive Maurice Garçon got Hardy off again. Many years later, Hardy admitted in a film interview that Roger Bosse had committed perjury to get him off the hook. All the years of his life, Hardy remained an enigma, for although the evidence against him was overwhelming, he had twice been acquitted by the courts. He died in 1987, at the age of seventy-six.

In the meantime, Barbie did not know which of the resistance leaders Jean Moulin was. His first guess was André Lassagne, whom he put through a simulated firing squad to make him talk. On June 22 Jean Moulin was removed from Montluc Prison and returned in the evening, unable to walk and with a bandage around his head. On June 23 he was tortured again. On Thursday, June 24, Raymond Aubrac saw him being half carried, half dragged by two German soldiers. Dr. Dugoujon, who had been arrested with his "patients," overhead two German guards talking. "It's really a shame," said one. "But he's a dangerous man," said the other.

Christian Pineau, the Vichy civil servant who had been reprimanded by his boss in 1942 for resistance activities, was also in Montluc, where he passed the time listening to trains. He knew them all by now. The Savoie express, taking women and children to the mountains. The Lyon–Marseille, taking them to the shore. He had learned to appreciate the magic word *Pakete,* and the pleasures of a hard-boiled egg. He volunteered for the razor detail in the prison. It gave him a chance to talk with new arrivals. For ten minutes each morning, he cut hair with his old razor.

At 6 P.M. on June 24, the good-natured guard, the one who had given him a light for his cigarette, opened his cell and took him out to the courtyard, where a man was lying on a bench. Pineau recognized Jean Moulin, although he was unconscious, swollen-lipped, and sunken-eyed, with an ugly bruise at the temple. The guard gave Pineau some soap and water and told him to shave Moulin. Why do they want him shaved? Pineau wondered. The dull blade scratched along his cheeks. Moulin opened his eyes and said: *"Boire"* ("Drink"). Pineau turned toward the guard and said,

"*Ein wenig Wasser*" ("a little water"). The guard brought the water, which Pineau gave him drop by drop. He remained at Moulin's side as the light failed. At nine o'clock the guard returned and said, "You still here? Late. You go back."

One June 25 the resistance leaders arrested in Caluire were transferred by train to Fresnes Prison in Paris, where they joined General Delestraint. Jean Moulin, however, was in such bad shape that Barbie drove him to the Neuilly villa of Colonel Boemelberg, Paris head of the Gestapo, at 40 Avenue Victor Hugo. André Lassagne, brought to the villa, was confronted with Moulin there and said he was more dead than alive, hardly breathing. After that, Moulin vanished.

Moulin's sister Laure tried to find out what had happened to him, and went to the *Registratur* of the Gestapo on the Avenue Foch. She was taken to see an officer, Heinrich Meiners, who told her: "I have the dossier in my office. I know everything. I conducted the investigation, but I can tell you nothing." She insisted, and Meiners told her that her brother had died on the way to a hospital. Where was he buried? she asked. "Not buried, cremated," Meiners said. "The ashes will be given to the family. "Your brother did his duty." Meiners went on, "but you understand he was working against us." He promised to send her a death certificate, and did. The certificate stated that Jean Moulin had died in Metz on July 8, 1943. The cause of death was given as *Herzlähmung* (cardiac arrest).

Why would her brother have died in Metz, in eastern France, practically on the German border? Laure wondered. Continuing her inquiry, she learned that he had been so badly beaten by Barbie and his gang in Lyon that when he arrived at Colonel Boemelberg's Neuilly villa, the male nurse attending him recommended that he be moved to a hospital in Germany because it would be awkward for him to die in France. He was taken to the Gare de l'Est by ambulance and placed in a compartment on the Paris–Berlin train. He died on the way, near Frankfurt, and his body was taken off the train to the police post inside the railroad station. The police officer on duty there, incredibly, was Johann Meiners, father of Heinrich Meiners, the Gestapo officer at the Paris *Registratur*. In his report Johann Meiners said, "The corpse was that of someone who has suffered greatly. It was in a state of complete physical deterioration." Metz was shown on the death certificate to cover up the fact that Moulin had been taken to Germany. His body was cremated, and the urn was brought back to Paris and deposited in Père Lachaise cemetery, where it was registered as "X . . . coming from Germany, July 12, 1943." It seemed clear that Jean Moulin, who had cut his throat the first time he was arrested because he was afraid of giving in, had not done so the second time either, and, as a result, had been beaten to death. As for the German agent Moog and the traitor Lunel, the former was killed in a plane crash in 1944, while the latter was shot by the resistance when France was liberated.

Gertrude Stein and Alice B. Toklas had decided to stay in France for the duration of the war rather than return to the United States. In 1940 Miss Stein was sixty-six, settled in her ways and in no mood for an ocean voyage. She and Miss Toklas found a nice house in Aix-les-Bains, in the unoccupied zone, a house alone against a mountain with a big garden full of bushes and trees, and two sisters, Clothilde and Olympe, one a cook and the other a maid, and a goat named Bizerte. The reason for the goat was that milk was hard to find. Miss Stein walked the goat and the goat ate flowers.

The women's main activity was the hunt for food, thinking about eating, everyone with a pack of their back or a basket in their hand or a big bundle on the bicycle—hoping for provisions. You did not buy nowadays only with money, you bought with your personality. The buyer had to make the sales pitch. You might hear a little boy saying to a lady with three apples on her hat, "I would like to have three apples like that," even though they were small apples. The farmers were beating their wheat with flails because that way they were allowed to keep it, whereas if they used machines the government took it. And the wild ducks in the marshes of the Rhône's headwaters were happy about the war because all the shotguns had been confiscated, and they sat peacefully in the ferns. They returned to the ancient condition of never having been shot at.

What Miss Stein missed the most was dental floss. What Miss

Toklas missed the most was tobacco. When the ration cards came in for tobacco they were for men only, but Miss Toklas put her name down at the tobacconist's using only her initials. The next year they changed the cards, and initials would not do, which did not seem fair, since boys of eighteen were young enough for chocolate rations and old enough for tobacco rations. She had to rely on friends bringing in cigarettes from Switzerland. Then she found a French Army sergeant who sold her some of his army ration. Came November 1942 and the Armistice Army was disbanded, but the Italians arrived and had plenty of smokes.

Their house in Aix-les-Bains belonged to a captain in the Armistice Army, and now that he was on indefinite leave he wanted it back, so they moved to a modern villa in the village of Culoz, on the other bank of the Rhône near the *sous-préfecture* of Belley. Miss Stein often had to go into Belley to fill out this form or that form. There were more government employees than ever, and more regulations, and more avoidance of the law. The saddest thing, said Miss Stein's friend M. Gallais, was that in World War I the French were a united people, whereas now there were the denouncers and the denounced. And now in 1943 there was the feeling that one or the other had been or will be a traitor. And now little coffins began to arrive with a note inside or a rope telling the recipient to go hang himself. The owner of the local pharmacy was a *collabo* (collaborator), and had already been sent a coffin and other attentions, and recently the Germans had come to search his house. Someone had sent them a list of the explosives he had supposedly stockpiled in his basement. Everyone thought it was a very good joke.

A German in 1942 had told Miss Stein that the French were a pleasant people, and he liked them, but none of them had three qualities, only two: They were either honest and intelligent, or *collabo* and intelligent, or *collabo* and honest. But he had never met one who was *collabo*, intelligent, and honest.

And now in June 1943 two young men came by, who were twenty-one and were leaving for the STO (forced labor). They would have gone into hiding, they said, were it not for the winter, for would the war be over before next winter? Miss Stein told them to pretend they were travelers to Germany and to learn the language and read the literature and contemplate the landscape as though they were travelers, and still know the Germans to be their enemies. They could have done the *maquis,* which translated meant "taking the heather." And people in 1943 were saying, *"Ma foi, c'est long"* ("By my faith, it's taking a long time"), a nice medieval expression. They were also saying, "Of course, Germany cannot win, and France, which seems to be beaten, really is a country that can see and shut one eye and then shut the other eye, opening the first eye." And when the *vignerons* (wine growers) harvested the grapes that year, they all said it would be a victory wine. "It's going to be over soon," said one. "How do you know?" asked the other. "It's very simple," said the first. "My wife has had enough of it."

The fact that Miss Stein and Miss Toklas were Jewish did not concern them unduly, for the Italians were not arresting Jews. However, when Miss Stein went into Belley that June to see her lawyer, he told her that he had a message from the *sous-préfet,* Maurice Sivain, who had always been so helpful. The message was: "Tell these ladies that they must leave at once for Switzerland, tomorrow if possible, or they will be sent to a concentration camp." For the Gestapo in Lyon, which claimed a zone of operations that extended into Savoie, was going after Jews in the Italian zone, and there was reason to believe that they were about to stage a raid in the Belley area. The Lyon Gestapo, or Section Four, was headed of course by Klaus Barbie, although Miss Stein did not know his name.

"How can we go," Miss Stein asked, "since the frontier is closed?"

"That could be arranged," her lawyer said.

"You mean pass by fraud?" Miss Stein asked.

"Yes," he said, "it could be arranged."

She went home and talked it over with Miss Toklas, and they decided that no, they were not going, it was better to go regularly wherever they were sent than to go irregularly where nobody could help them if they were in trouble. Here they were and here they would stay. As it happened, the warning about a raid in Belley was a false alarm.

* * *

It was a busy year for Barbie, for after the Caluire arrests he began ranging far and wide in the area under the Lyon Gestapo's jurisdiction. Ignoring the Italians, his Section Four teams conducted various operations in their zone, the most sensational of which was the abduction of two leading Third Republic figures, President Albert Lebrun and André François-Poncet, the distinguished French ambassador to Berlin in the thirties. The Germans, aware of the recent flight of Chambéry to Algiers by General Alphonse Georges (Gamelin's second-in-command in 1940), apparently feared that Lebrun and François-Poncet would also join de Gaulle, although nothing was further from their thoughts. They were each living quietly in the Italian zone near Grenoble. Lebrun was in his son-in-law's villa in Vizille, while François-Poncet was in a villa called La Condaime near the village of La Tronche; both men were under the rather debonair guard of Italian troops.

The Italians were in fact rather sweet, thought Lebrun. When he told the officer in charge of his guards, "I am nothing, why bother with me?" the officer replied, "You are not in office but your people still love you." But in June a new group of guards arrived, fifteen in all, who were slovenly and undisciplined. Their uniforms were dirty and they didn't march in step, and took long naps. On August 13 Lebrun was told that he would be transferred to Florence. He said: "You will have to take me by force." "I must tell you," the officer replied, "that if the Italians leave Isère, they will be replaced by Germans." This sounded like a warning, and Lebrun told his wife that something was up. As for François-Poncet, the captain commanding his guards, Mascheroni, told him that the Germans did not have the right to arrest anyone in the Italian zone, but they did it anyway.

In August Barbie was ordered to arrest the two for deportation to Germany while avoiding an incident with the Italians. He organized his unit—eight well-armed men and two Citroëns with false license plates. They left Lyon on the morning of August 27, but one of the cars blew a tire. It was missing a spare, so they had to stop another Citroën and confiscate its tires. In Grenoble Barbie presented himself before the Italian military command, but did not disclose his true mission. He said he needed to speak to Lebrun in the name of General Niehoff, commander of the German Army in southern France. He was given permission to proceed, but had to go the rest of the way with an Italian escort of an officer and four men. This was a setback, for the Italians now saw that Barbie was not alone but had two carloads of men, a tipoff that he was planning to carry out some kind of action.

They headed south toward Vizille, and when they got to Lebrun's villa, Barbie told his men to cut the telephone line. Accompanied by the Italian officer, he went into Lebrun's office, where the French president (who had never formally resigned) was writing letters in the company of his wife. Barbie wondered what to do next, for he was sure the Italians would try to prevent Lebrun's removal. The nervous Lebrun was already making a scene, shouting that he wanted nothing to do with the Germans and was under the protection of the Italians. Barbie quietly gave one of his men the order to disarm the four Italians outside. Lebrun picked up the telephone to call the command post of his absent guards, but the line was dead. Barbie's man returned and said in German that his order had been carried out. Barbie then went up to the sofa where the Italian officer was sitting with Lebrun and demanded his gun. When the Italian protested, Barbie's man grabbed the gun. Showing Barbie a key, the German told him the Italians were disarmed and locked in a room.

"You are under arrest," Barbie told Lebrun.

"What is all this?" Lebrun asked.

"No speeches," Barbie said. "You have two minutes to get your things."

"It is shameful to treat a former chief of state this way," Lebrun said.

"You are nothing anymore," Barbie said.

Barbie told Mme. Lebrun to prepare a small suitcase for her husband, as shouting and profanity came from the room where the Italians were locked up.

Barbie, in the lead Citroën, crossed Vizille with Lebrun in the backseat, his men covering the French president's head with his jacket so that he would not be recognized, but Lebrun angrily pulled it off. When the car crossed the Isère River and turned right, Lebrun realized they were going to La Tronche to pick up François-Poncet.

François-Poncet was having lunch with his family when a German soldier with a submachine gun appeared at the window. Barbie had gone in through the garden with two men, and when he came into the dining room, François-Poncet did not seem surprised, although his wife and two sons were terrified. "You are the ambassador Poncet?" Barbie asked. "I have orders to arrest you. You have five minutes to get your things."

"I knew you'd come for me one day." François-Poncet said. "I'm ready to go. My suitcase is packed." Barbie wondered whether the suitcase was packed because he was planning to flee to Algeria. François-Poncet spoke fluent German and called Barbie by his rank, which surprised him, for very few people knew the SS ranks, which were different from those in the regular army.

When François-Poncet saw Lebrun in the car, he expressed surprise for the first time, saying, "What, you too?" They shook hands, even though they had not always seen eye to eye. On the drive back to Lyon, the Germans went at high speed, worried that the Italians might be in pursuit. When they came to a railroad crossing, the gate was down, but one of Barbie's men jumped out and told the gatekeeper at gun point to raise it. Once Barbie and his men were out of the Italian zone, they relaxed and lit cigarettes, and laughed, and joked about kidnaping the two Frenchies under the nose of the Italians. Barbie seemed mightily pleased with himself, thought François-Poncet.

They arrived in Lyon at about 4 P.M. and spent the night at the École de Santé. It was a bad night, with the heat, and the mosquitoes, and the guard smoking cheap cigars. While they were waiting to be questioned, François-Poncet overheard a conversation between Barbie and the Lyon police chief, Marchais. The police chief was saying that he had discovered an arms depot that he wanted to show him, and Barbie thanked him warmly, and congratulated him, and François-Poncet thought, "So this is what it has come to, a French policeman is helping the Gestapo. Fine thing!" The next day they were on the train to Paris and then they were deported to the castle of Kufstein in the Austrian Tyrol.

After the war, André François-Poncet was made high commissioner of the French occupation zone in Germany, where Barbie was in hiding. One day in 1947 in the town of Augsburg, Barbie heard police sirens. A big car stopped ten yards from where he was standing, and who should get out but François-Poncet. How the situation had changed, Barbie thought. Now they were in his country, and he was the fugitive, while François-Poncet was the man in charge.

As I said, it was a busy year for Klaus Barbie, and things didn't always go his way. There were some setbacks, one of which occurred three days before the abduction of Lebrun and François-Poncet. André Devigny had been arrested on April 17 in Annemasse and was on death row in Montluc Prison. In mid-August, Devigny's father, a Savoyard farmer wearing studded boots, faded corduroys, and a black hat, came to the École de Santé (the first time he'd been in Lyon in ten years) to inquire about his son, and was taken to Barbie's fourth-floor office. "My son has been imprisoned in Montluc for four months," the old man said. "He's done nothing, I have come to ask when you propose to release him." Barbie gazed at the old farmer, his blue eyes, his furrowed face, his bristly white moustache. "Sit down, please," he said. "Were you in the last war?" "I did my duty," Devigny's father replied. "In what branch?" "An infantry regiment. I rescued two wounded German soldiers in 1914."

Barbie sent for Devigny's file, read it, and frowned. "Your son is a terrorist," he said. "He was working for the British." "No, not my son," said the old man. "I brought him up. I can answer for him." "We have proof of his activities in this file," Barbie said. "I don't believe it," the old man said. "I raised seven children. I taught them to behave decently." "Children can be brought up the right way and still go bad," Barbie said. "If you write to him now and tell him to confess, he'll be released." The old man stretched out a crippled right hand, saying, "Gervillier, 1914. My wife's written the letters in our house for the last thirty years." "Then I can't help you." Barbie said.

On August 20 Devigny was brought in to see Barbie, who told him: "The investigation of your case is complete. The espionage and assassination you are accused of are punishable by death. Consequently you will be shot."

After spending four months handcuffed in his cell, Devigny nonetheless felt morally and physically strong. In May he had been taken for questioning to the École de Santé in a car without door handles. He had been tortured for two weeks and had not talked. A hot iron on the soles of his feet. Ten times, the *baignoire*. Each time he did not talk, he felt better. The depth of his contempt for the SD increased. Barbie did not take part in the torture; he came and went, he said a few words, he supervised. Devigny saw torture as an aspect of combat. He was defending not land, but the freedom of his friends, which he refused to surrender.

Devigny was in cell 107, ten square feet. That summer there were about four hundred prisoners in Montluc. They spent an hour a day in the courtyard. From the tiny window of his cell, he could see the tobacco factory and a railroad bridge. He could hear Franzel, the warden, run his ring of keys along the railing as he came by.

One day Devigny noticed that the three vertical wooden slats in the lower panel of his cell door were of slightly different colors. Examining them more closely, he saw that the slats were not fitted on the sides with mortise joints. The gaps between them were patched up with pieces of a different wood. Devigny had learned to remove his handcuffs with a safety pin. Using a soup spoon that he had ground down to a point on the concrete floor of his cell, he was able to loosen the slats and remove them so that he could squeeze through his cell door at night and wander up and down the hall, for the guards did not do rounds after lights out. It was considered impossible to escape because of the prison's double walls and the guards in the courtyard.

At first, Devigny did it as a game, leaving his cell to chat with the other prisoners. On one of his nighttime sorties, he erased the chalked instructions on a cell door—*Kein Essen, Kein Ausgang* (No Food, No Going Out)—and the following day the man in that cell was fed and aired. Devigny got so he could remove or replace the slats in less than two minutes.

If he could get out of his cell, perhaps he could get out of Montluc. To each problem, there was a solution. He fashioned a rope from his blanket and mattress cover. He made a grappling hook from the frame of an old lantern in the hall. As the weeks passed, Devigny became possessed by the demon of escape. In June Jean Moulin had come and gone. On August 6 Captain Jean Gatard, one of his death-row comrades, had gone before the Montluc firing squad. Deportations to various camps became more frequent. Then on August 20 he heard his own death sentence from the lips of a man who seemed to enjoy imparting that type of information.

When Devigny was returned to his cell that day, he found that he had a cellmate, an eighteen-year-old deserter from the Milice. Devigny had to include him in the planned escape, which was now urgent. They decided on August 24. It was a moonless night. Devigny waited until the clock at the tobacco factory across the street struck ten before dismantling the door. Once in the hall, he shimmied up the heavy metal rod that opened and closed the transoms in the skylight, reaching for the edge of the big open transom, and followed by the Milice deserter. They crawled through the transom and found themselves on a gravel-covered terrace. A little higher, and they were on the prison's flat roof. They could see the perimeter wall flanking the Rue du Dauphiné, the inner wall, the sentries on their rounds, the tips of their cigarettes glowing in the dark, the cell windows like black squares in a crossword puzzle.

Midnight struck and the guard was changed. Devigny hooked his homemade grappling iron on the inside of the parapet that went around the roof and lowered himself down the rope. On the ground lay a parcel he had thrown down earlier, containing a second grappling iron and a second rope. The Milice deserter followed him down the first rope. They stood in the prison courtyard catching their breath.

A sentry approached. Devigny and his accomplice pulled back into the shadows, but the sentry came right at them, as if he knew they were there. Devigny jumped out and strangled him from behind until the man fell on the ground on his stomach, his steel helmet concealing his face. Devigny drew the guard's bayonet from its scabbard and plunged it into his back.

The two men crossed the courtyard to reach the low inner wall that separated it from the infirmary. Devigny fixed the grappling iron to the top of the inner wall, and they went up and over the wall and jumped onto a covered gallery at the top of the infirmary. From the gallery they climbed up to the building's sloping tiled roof. Two tiles knocked against each another, and the two escapees remained motionless for a long time, with Devigny thinking of the dead sentry, of the rope he had left hanging from the wall, and expecting at any moment to hear cries of *Achtung!*

Taking stock, Devigny judged that there were about fifteen feet from the infirmary roof to the perimeter wall. They were five yards from freedom. The roadway inside the perimeter was brightly lit, with one guard who rode around and around on a bicycle. Devigny timed him once around. At 3 A.M. he tied one end of the rope to the infirmary chimney and threw the grappling iron over the top of the perimeter wall. It caught. The rope now stretched above the roadway, from the infirmary roof to the perimeter wall. Gripping the rope, Devigny swung into space, hand over hand, his back over the void, cursing the bright light. Then they reached the perimeter wall, jumped down—and were free. Devigny headed toward the center of Lyon in his socks and shirt-sleeves because the Milice deserter had forgotten the package with their shoes and jackets on the infirmary roof. They went their separate ways. Devigny had a doctor friend at 92 Boulevard des Belges who gave him clothes and found him papers and showed him how to get to Switzerland. From Switzerland he went to Algiers, where he joined de Gaulle.

For the two who escaped from Montluc, there were hundreds who died there. At about the same time that André Devigny escaped, there arrived at Montluc a thirty-eight-year-old former naval officer named André Frossard who had been operating a business in Lyon that clandestinely bought military matériel for the resistance. He was caught and sent to Montluc's *Baraque aux Juifs* (Jew Hut), a long wooden shed built in the prison courtyard to house Jewish inmates—Frossard was one-fourth Jewish, which, as it turned out, was not lethal. The *Baraque aux Juifs* was used as a warehouse for hostages, at a time when the pricetag for killing one German soldier was forty to fifty hostages. In fact, almost all the Jews there were sentenced to death, with only a momentary permission to go on living.

The long, narrow shed, with most of the windows covered over with yellow paint, reminded Frossard of the old Salvation Army barge moored on the Seine River in Paris. There were two rows of beds, with 150 inmates for sixty beds. Soon clothing took on the smell of crushed bedbugs. Frossard was taken to the École de

Santé for questioning. He was strung up by the hands and feet, then suspended by a pole and immersed in cold water. And the strange thing was that everything else was normal. Here you were hanging naked over a bathtub while a secretary typed, and people told jokes, and someone smoked, and someone munched on a sandwich, and someone else looked out the window. Barbie sometimes came in to supervise. Frossard saw him as a mediocrity who had sold his conscience to the party, which in exchange had given him the power of life and death over others. That was the transaction—to obtain power you would not otherwise have had. Barbie felt no remorse because he had long ago sold his conscience. There was nothing interesting or special about him. He was a henchman who seemed to enjoy his work and wanted to do it well.

The world in Montluc Prison, according to Frossard, was like the world outside—it was divided between those who were and those who were not Jews. Those who were, were not treated as enemies. They were not even treated as an inferior race. They were treated as a completely different species. They were not even given the respect one gives an enemy. One day he saw a Jewish family crossing the courtyard, the grandfather, the father, the children, and the mother with a baby in her arms. They were being led by an SS guard, who threw up his arms and said, "*Ach,* it's all of Israel."

There was an SS guard called Witmayer who liked to play a cruel game with an old Polish Jew by the name of Dominitz. Witmayer made Dominitz learn a phrase in German, made him repeat it word by word, and over and over, every day. The phrase was: "The Jew is a parasite who lives off the Aryan people." Dominitz learned the phrase so well that he began to recite it by reflex, even when he wasn't asked. As soon as the door of the *Baraque* opened, he would start. It was as though the phrase had magic properties to protect him. It didn't, though; and the day came when he was picked as a hostage for the firing squad. As Dominitz left, Witmayer made him say it one last time. But it was obvious that Witmayer was in the grip of something he scarcely understood. He was still a Jew-baiting, racist SS, but there was an undertone of affection for the man he had so often humiliated and was humiliating for the last time. When Witmayer asked Dominitz to repeat the phrase, there was something almost like fondness in his voice, as if a shaft of humanity had pushed through the veneer of his conditioning. Not that it did Dominitz any good, for he was taken off to be shot.

Then one day Marcel Gompel arrived in the *Baraque aux Juifs.* His family, one of the two hundred richest in France, owned the Trois Quartiers department store. Gompel was a distinguished physiologist at the prestigious Collège de France. He had wanted to be a surgeon, but during World War I he had received a bullet in his head that miraculously did not touch his brain, and he lost an index finger—you couldn't be a nine-fingered surgeon. Gompel was a collector of books and paintings, and a collector of people, with many friends in the arts and sciences, among them Einstein, who remarked: "Gompel is one of the two men in France capable of understanding my work."

Gompel eventually moved to Lyon to join the resistance group *Combat,* even though he was frail and white-haired and over sixty. He collected stamps, and every Sunday on the Place Bellecour there was an open-air *bourse aux timbres* (stamp show), and he couldn't resist browsing there. One Sunday the Germans surrounded the Place Bellecour—then it was the Jews on one side, everyone else on the other side. Gompel had always refused to carry false papers and went along with the Jews. He was taken to the École de Santé for questioning, where an address book was found on him containing codes and abbreviations. The Section Four team gave him the *baignoire,* and as he was being removed from the icy cold water, they threw boiling water over his back. He arrived at Montluc Prison covered with third-degree burns.

There was very little that Frossard could do for Gompel. There was no medical care. Whatever you came in with, you could die of. He had seen a schoolboy with a hole in his head big enough to put your fist into, if you wanted to put it there, from being struck repeatedly in the same place, who was accused of distributing leaflets. Under torture the boy was asked for names, so he gave those of two of his classmates who were sympathetic to Vichy. A third-degree burn victim like Gompel should have been given intravenous liquids to keep his body from dehydrating. He lay on his stomach unable to move, for the muscle tissue under the skin was burned, and he could not drink because the water burned his throat, and he could barely breathe because his lungs were dehydrated, and he could not urinate because his kidneys and bladder were dehydrated. Two days after his arrival, Gompel tried to rise, fell forward into Frossard's arms, and died. He had not told the Germans what the code numbers and abbreviations in his address book meant. He had not given them any names. For two days his body remained in the *Baraque aux Juifs*. Finally it was removed and thrown in the courtyard, over a pile of coal.

It was a strange and cloistered life that Barbie and his men led in Lyon, a life so far removed from normal activities that it can scarcely be imagined. They went out in their black Citroëns and arrested people, then they tortured them in the École de Santé, then they jailed them in Montluc Prison, then they had them shot or deported. They became accustomed to their daily routine, which did not prevent them from carousing during off hours in bars and restaurants, or from availing themselves of the pool of young women willing to sleep with Germans. Barbie in fact contracted a venereal disease in the fall of 1943. He was out of commission for two months, being treated in Germany, where he had left a wife and a daughter.

Most incidents in which Section Four was involved fell into clear and discernible categories, but once in a while there was one that was baffling enough to illustrate the irrationality that took over in wartime. Things happened, and you didn't know why. On August 18, 1943, a police inspector, Albert Taborin, was ordered to go to Montluc Prison at 10 A.M. because a German-speaking inspector was wanted. When he arrived he saw in the prison entrance a little *gazogène* (wood burning) funeral van with a few soldiers standing around, and a shortish man in civilian clothes, who by his air of authority seemed to be in charge and introduced himself as Lieutenant Barbie.

Barbie told Inspector Taborin that an inmate had died from a contagious disease and had to be cremated at once. Taborin had been asked to come along to facilitate things with the people at the cemetery. (This was one of many instances in which the German occupiers were dependent on the French police's cooperation.) The soldiers then brought out a coffin, the lid of which was not nailed down but was kept on with a wire. This coffin was then loaded into the van.

"I will drive to the cemetery in my own car and meet you there," Taborin said. "No" replied Barbie, "you're coming with me." He had two pillows placed on the coffin, sat on one, and gestured to Taborin to sit on the other, while two German soldiers, acting as escort, sat behind the coffin on the floor of the van. Taborin thought it was a funny way of dealing with a corpse that was supposed to be contagious.

When the van arrived at Guillotière cemetery on the Avenue de Berthelot, Taborin explained to the cemetery director, M. Paulaud, whom he knew very well, that the Germans wanted to cremate a body. "That's a good one," Paulaud said. "I haven't had any coal for the oven since the war started." Barbie made a call, a coal truck arrived in half an hour, and the oven was stoked. The coffin was placed on the oven ramp. At that moment one of the cemetery employees wanted to cut the wire that held down the lid. Barbie jumped up to stop him, and the man explained that you could not put any metal into the crematorium. Those were the rules. "I make the rules," Barbie replied.

The coffin was pushed into the oven. Taborin, looking through the crematorium's little window, saw that the corpse was wearing a German uniform. When the cremation was over, Barbie told Taborin he could leave. Taborin said he needed to know the identity of the deceased for his cremation report. Barbie told him to come by the office the next day and he would have it for him.

On August 19 Taborin went to the École de Santé and was led into Barbie's office. Barbie did not seem to recognize the inspector. Taborin said he had come for the identity card of the man who had been cremated. There were about ten ID cards on Barbie's desk, and he riffled through them, pulled one out, apparently at random, and said "It's this one." The inspector took down the name Simonet, Henri, then asked him what should be done with the ashes. "Throw them out," Barbie said. The inspector pointed out that under French law this would constitute *viol de sépulture* (violation of burial place). "Do what you want," Barbie said.

To this day, more than forty years later, Inspector Taborin has no idea what happened to that German soldier and why his burial was handled in such a peculiar way.

VI

LYON '44

Photograph permission of Hirschl & Adler Gallery

A cornered animal is at its most dangerous, and in 1944 Germany was cornered. On January 22, Allied troops landed at Anzio, and started inching their way up to Rome, thirty-three miles or so to the north. In June the Allies would land in Normandy. On the eastern front, the Russians reached the prewar border of Poland in February, and were clearing the Crimea and the Ukraine. Between 60,000 and 100,000 Germans, trapped in Sevastopol on the tip of the Crimean peninsula, were massacred. The Germans were getting back some of their own. They were also fighting on two fronts.

In Germany people were being arrested and sentenced to death on charges of defeatism—Otto Kiep, former German consul general in New York from 1931 to 1934, and Elizabeth von Thadden, headmistress of a girls' school in Schwetzingen, near Heidelberg, to name two. On the eastern front, something happened that had no precedent in German military history. In February three German generals captured at Stalingrad sent an appeal over the Soviet radio urging German troops, encircled at Cherkassy, to surrender. The three generals were Daniels, Schimatis, and von Seydlitz; and there could be no doubt as to the authenticity of the broadcast, for General Daniels addressed a personal appeal to a captain in his old battalion.

In France, just as 1942 had seen massive deportations, and 1943 had seen the arrest of the resistance leaders, 1944 saw the rise of the Maquis. The forced labor (STO) law had been passed in Feb-

ruary 1943. At first, the young men went off to Germany obedi-
ently, but with every month the number of no-shows increased,
particularly those from mountainous areas where it was easy to
hide, like Isère and Savoie. The Maquisards were forming, but it
took money to feed and equip them. However, they were organizing too early for London, for they couldn't be used effectively
until the Allies landed in France. Henri Frenay was furious
with Jean Moulin for reducing his budget just when he needed it
for the *réfractaires* (draft dodgers). When Moulin returned from
London in 1943, he brought with him a paltry thirty-six forged
ration cards.

As for the forced-labor situation, Gauleiter Fritz Sauckel had
gone from frustration to frustration with Laval, who kept blowing
smoke, but when the smoke lifted, nothing had been gained. At
first Sauckel had tried to get workers on a voluntary basis. In the
fall of 1942, he desperately needed 700,000 foreigners to go to
Germany to free up 700,000 German workers who could then be
sent to the eastern front. But the French, as usual, were dragging
their feet, whereas the German armaments workers had stayed on
the job through the Christmas holidays, round the clock, to turn
7.5mm war-booty cannons into anti-aircraft guns.

At a meeting in March 1943 at the Paris headquarters of the
OKW (military command), Sauckel said: "The French government is made up of specialists in delay only. If the first 250,000
workers had arrived on time, that is to say in the fall of 1942, we
might have been able to mobilize our workers earlier and form
the new divisions and we would not have had the encirclement of
Stalingrad."

In Sauckel's mind, the defeat at Stalingrad, the turning point of
the war, was attributable to French bad faith. The screws had to
be tightened. Forced labor had to be mandatory. But that didn't
work either, since young men by the thousands ran for the hills.
On August 6 Sauckel had a six-hour showdown with Laval. He
demanded 300,000 men and 200,000 women. But Laval held his
ground, saying: "Don't you see that the demand for three hundred
thousand men will provoke a massive departure to the Maquis,
and that the demand for two hundred thousand women will launch
an open revolt across France? Is that what you want? Are you
sent by General de Gaulle?"

A dejected Sauckel wrote Hitler a few days later: "I have completely lost faith in the honest goodwill of Premier Laval. His refusal constitutes pure and simple sabotage of the German struggle against bolshevism."

The program, however, sputtered along, and the walls of French cities were covered with posters showing a smiling mother and daughter with the caption: FINISHED THE RAINY DAYS. PAPA IS MAKING MONEY IN GERMANY. Marshal Pétain paid lip service to the STO in his 1943 Christmas message: "Workers, my friends! Know that far from your homes you are still working for France."

Sauckel's efforts were hardly a total flop, for by the start of 1944, there were 439,000 French nationals working in Germany. They were part of a massive foreign-labor force of four million busily turning out planes, guns, and munitions. In some German factories, nine out of ten workers were foreign. In one that made airplane engines, the assembly line was 88 percent Russian.

In France, however, the mood changed in 1944. The number of *réfractaires* increased. The Allied landing was in the air. The French were not only escaping the recruiters, they were attacking STO offices and destroying files. In Marseille the STO director, Kupfer, was assassinated on January 19.

It was not only Laval, thought Sauckel, it was his own ambassador in Paris, Otto Abetz, who was sabotaging his efforts. Sauckel was a man for confrontations, and he had it out with Abetz in early 1944, saying: "You, Abetz, you have organized the resistance of German offices against the mobilization of workers. Today, I am in Paris with an order from the Führer, and in this matter, some heads are going to roll."

"My name starts with the first letter of the alphabet," Abetz replied, "so I assume that mine will be the first to roll . . . but let me say this: If ever the Maquis puts up statues in France, you will deserve the finest, with this inscription: 'To our number one recruitment agent, Gauleiter Sauckel, from a grateful Maquis.'"
Sauckel stormed out, slamming the door.

So in 1944, everyone could tell that the Germans were on their way out. The resistance became much more boldly combative, and the Germans responded with the rage of the about-to-be-defeated. Nowhere was this tragedy played out with greater barbaric intensity than in Lyon, that city of shadow zones, where the walls were said to be the "color of sorrow." The back rooms of cafés still smelled of *pot-au-feu* and waxed linoleum, but down the street, a murder was taking place. The cycle of attack and reprisal accelerated like a tape on fast forward.

On January 10 Lorenz Neumann and Albert Donisch, two German policemen belonging to the *Todt* Regiment, were bicycling down the Quai Saint-Clair at 2:15 P.M., drowsy with rich food and good wine, after a copious lunch in the celebrated Mère Brazier restaurant, when they were shot and killed by some young resistance fighters. The German reaction was immediate. Werner Knab, Barbie's superior, ordered the SD to round up hostages at random in the vicinity of the shooting. Obviously the ones who had committed the *attentat* had fled, and the sixteen hostages who were picked up had nothing to do with it, including a postman who had been delivering mail on the Place Tolozan. Six more hostages were drawn from Montluc Prison, to make the ratio eleven to one.

These twenty-two hostages were taken to the basement of the École de Santé, which had been renovated with cells and implements of torture, and were machine-gunned to death that same evening. Then Barbie, who was in charge of the executions, notified the French police to pick up the bodies of twenty-two prisoners who had tried to mutiny. According to one of his Section Four men, Ernst Floreck, who was questioned after the war, Barbie drew up a report and told Floreck that he was citing him as a witness to the mutiny. When Floreck protested that he did not want to be implicated in a false report, Barbie replied: "Someone had to be there and it might as well be you." (When Barbie was returned to France in 1983 after spending thirty-two years in hiding in Bolivia, he still stuck to his story, telling the judge who questioned him: "As for the deaths of the twenty-two persons in the cellars of the Gestapo, as far as I can remember, it was an attempted escape. Those people of the resistance tried to escape during an air raid alert when there was a blackout. They were killed by guards during an escape attempt. It was my duty to alert the French authorities, who came to get the bodies.")

When Commissioner Adrien Richard arrived with his men to take delivery of the bodies, he noted first the smell of blood. Then he saw that all the bodies, including that of the postman with his bag full of mail still suspended from his neck, were piled in one cell. They had been shot in the head at close range and had fallen backward. Commissioner Richard counted 180 submachine-gun cartridges on the cellar floor.

A few days later, a retired Paris policeman named Denis Jacquesson was summoned to Lyon to identify the body of his twenty-year-old son André, which had been taken to the Institut Médico-Légal (the morgue) and cleaned. Denis Jacquesson looked at the body on the stone slab and recognized his son, although the boy's eyes had been gouged out and his fingernails ripped from his hands. Just to make sure, he asked the attendant to pull down the young's man's trousers, and he saw the scar, the result of a hernia operation. Then Jacquesson pushed the hair off the young man's brow and said *"C'est bien mon Dédé"* ("That's my Dédé"), Dédé being the diminutive for André.

This was the kind of routine daily work the SD and Section Four were now engaged in, sometimes with the help of the French Milice, which gave the events of 1944 a civil-war aspect. The Miliciens went after their traditional enemies, the left-wingers and the Jews, in what they called *réglements de comptes* (settlement of accounts).

The head of the Milice in Lyon was a former naval officer named Jean Lécussan who, like his German counterparts, had a genuine fondness for violence. On January 11, the day after the shooting of the twenty-two hostages, Lécussan and August Moritz, the head of Section Six, went after eighty-year-old Victor Basch and his seventy-five-year-old wife. Born in Budapest, Victor Basch had come to France as a young man and had a distinguished career as a Sorbonne professor and a social activist. He had been involved in a number of important causes, starting with the Dreyfus case, and had been elected president of the League of the Rights of Man. His whole life had been devoted to correcting injustice. At the age of seventy-five, he had flown into embattled Madrid to see for himself what the outcome of the civil war would be, and came home convinced that France would be next.

And now on this winter evening, at 8 P.M., came a knock on the door of his home at 116 Grand Rue de Saint-Clair, in the neighborhood where the two German policemen had been shot.

The old man and his wife were prodded with gun butts into the black Citroën. Moritz had planned to take them to the École de Santé for questioning, but told Lécussan they were too old to arrest. So they were taken down to the banks of the Rhône, about fifteen minutes from their home, led down a path, shot in the head, and left there. Because Victor Basch was a Jew. Because his wife had refused to be separated from her husband.

Now the Milice and the SD were working in complete harmony, often in mixed teams. This was the period of summary executions, of massacres and mass graves, as if the Gestapo were compensating for the Allied advance with a reign of terror. They paid no attention to the laws of war, or humane standards, but became a killing machine, which was after all what the *Einsatzgruppe* was originally intended to be. People were killed for insignificant reasons, such as distributing pamphlets. There was also a plan to get rid of all the prisoners in Montluc, so as to leave no trace of arbitrary imprisonment. And at the same time, the hunt for Jews continued and the deportations were speeded up. It was an end-of-the-world atmosphere.

Above all, the Germans were determined to destroy the Maquis before the Allies landed because a strong Maquis coming down from the mountains armed to the teeth would form a veritable second front. The mountains where the Maquisards were hiding, however, had a dual character. They were a refuge, but they could also be a trap. One of the largest such groups was on the Plateau des Glières, a tableland in Haute Savoie between Annecy and the Swiss border, twelve miles long and seven miles wide. At an altitude of 4,500 feet, it seemed to offer good protection, particularly in the winter when it was snowed in.

To Glières came not only the STO *réfractaires,* but some regular army men, some local Savoyards, and some veterans of the Spanish civil war who had been hiding out since 1939. In early 1944 the total fighting force consisted of 450 men, large enough to draw attention, but too small to sustain a determined onslaught.

These were men who wanted to fight, who wanted to show London that the Maquis wasn't just a sender of radio messages. They had been up there for months, and they were organized up to a point, living in some empty cabins. Food was a problem, most of it coming from the nearest town, Petit-Bornand.

Weapons were a greater problem, and Théodose "Tom" Morel, the career officer in charge of the Glières Maquis, kept asking London for arms drops. But the French in London were of two minds. They told the Maquisards to emulate the Yugoslavs—disperse and reform, choose your moment, harass the enemy, don't stay in one place like sitting ducks. But, attracted also by the propaganda value of Glières as a sliver of Free France, they launched a slogan: "Three countries are resisting in Europe: Greece, Yugoslavia, and Haute Savoie."

Morel knew he needed at least three times as many men to hold the plateau. In the meantime, the Maquisards prepared a drop zone with bonfires at the four corners, and on February 14, fifty-four containers floated down. Of course, they missed the drop zone and had to be dug out of the snow. Now the Maquisards had machine guns, rifles, hand grenades, and blue uniforms, which made them look vaguely military. There was another drop on March 4, and Morel had enough weapons to arm five thousand men. The drops meant that London was taking them seriously, but also that the Germans knew they were there. The enemy had heard the passage of the planes, they had listened in to such messages as "The little man likes Byrrh [a popular apéritif]," which announced another drop.

There were no Germans on this desolate, roadless, snowbound, cliff-surrounded land mass, but there was a unit of French gendarmes in Petit-Bornand which reached an agreement with the Maquisards, an agreement that was almost still-born because of one of those disputes over protocol of which the French are so fond.

On February 18 a detachment of gendarmes, led by the highest-ranking officer in Petit-Bornand, Major Raulet, went up to the plateau and met with Morel, who greeted them wearing a less-than-regulation uniform consisting of a leather jacket, ski pants, and the floppy beret of a *Chasseur Alpin*.

"Good morning, *monsieur*," Morel said.

Annoyed at not being addressed by his rank, Raulet said: "I'm in uniform. You can see I'm a major."

"But you don't know my rank in the resistance," Morel replied.

"You're right," Raulet said, "but you will call me *mon com-*

259

mandant [major], or I am sorry to tell you that this meeting will be over."

As the conversation continued, they became less formal and worked out a system in which the Maquis and the gendarmes would avoid each other. They would take different paths at different hours, and when the Maquis went to Petit-Bornand for supplies, the gendarmes would look the other way. The point Morel made was: "We are fighting the Germans, so leave us alone."

Later, when it was all over, Werner Knab, chief of the Lyon *Einsatzgruppe,* and commander of the SS and SD troops that attacked the plateau, along with regular army and Milice units, sent the following report to General Oberg, his boss in Paris: "Concerning the attitude of the gendarmes who tolerated the supply of terrorists, I have asked that they be arrested and brought before a court-martial."

The agreement between the gendarmes and the Maquis, however, was imperfectly observed. On March 1 a medical student named Michel Fournier, who was working in the Glières infirmary, went into Petit-Bornand for medicine and was arrested. On March 9 Morel took one hundred of his men to the village of Entremont, where sixty gendarmes were garrisoned, to collect some hostages he could exchange for Fournier. He surrounded the Hôtel de France, where the gendarmes were headquartered, and they compliantly allowed themselves to be disarmed; all except their commander, Captain Lefèvre, who refused to be taken prisoner. He and Morel got into a shouting match, until finally Morel said: "So this means war." "Yes, this means war," replied Lefèvre, pulling a hidden revolver from his pocket and firing it point-blank at Morel, killing him. Lefèvre was also killed by a submachine gun burst from one of Morel's men.

On March 11 there was a huge drop, 680 containers. On the same day, Morel was buried on the plateau with full military honors, his coffin draped with the red, white, and blue parachutes from the drop. But his men were demoralized. The next day, March 12, the Glières plateau was bombed for the first time by planes coming from Dijon. The fifty-pound bombs didn't do much damage, but it was a shot across the bow. Some thought Glières should be evacuated. But when they radioed London this message came back: "We consider Glières a bridgehead. We will parachute a battalion. If operation succeeds, massive drops." At this point the Allied policy was to have the Maquis create what the French called *abscès de fixation* (local problem spots to hold down German troops), and the men on the Glières plateau, with enough weapons for five thousand men, firmly believed that reinforcements would follow. In a sense they were the dupes of those weapons, and of the promises made by London.

Captain Maurice Anjot, like Tom Morel a career army officer, took command. He was soon to be attacked by General Karl Pflaum's 157th Alpine Division of about seven thousand men, assisted by SS units and one thousand men of the Milice. They were armed with mountain artillery and heavy mortars and had air support. On March 23 General Pflaum visited the approaches to the plateau and announced himself satisfied with the preparations.

On March 26 the attack up the plateau began. The German Alpine troops in their white winter uniforms maneuvered through the trees, blending in with the snow. Anjot's men covered the paths with machine guns, but the Germans got through at Monthievret and poured through the breach, a tide of men in white climbing up the plateau. They took some losses, and the Maquisards could hear the German wounded calling out, *"Muti,"* the diminutive for mother.

It was a hopeless situation. The Maquis lost forty-three dead in the first day of fighting. As night fell, Captain Anjot ordered a retreat in the thigh-deep snow. Some got through the mountain passes. Some fell into German ambushes. Captain Anjot was killed in a skirmish with a German patrol. The Germans took 180 prisoners. There was a custody battle for the prisoners between the SS and the Milice. Knab wrote Oberg that he did not want to turn them over to French courts, which would be too lenient. He wanted them all shot as terrorists. Darnand, the head of the Milice, ordered a commission to go to Annecy and question the prisoners. The Germans protested that this was in flagrant contradiction to Oberg's orders that all prisoners be brought before court-martials. Finally, in a compromise, eleven prisoners appeared before a court-martial on May 4. Five were shot and the others were deported.

* * *

In July 1987 I visited the village of Izieu, which is about twenty miles south of the *sous-préfecture* of Belley, where Gertrude Stein had gone to fill out forms and see her lawyer. I had a hard time finding the village because it is not only off the main road (*Nationale*), and off a secondary road (*Départementale*), it is up a steep hill, hidden from view by a bigger village that serves as a screen.

And once you find Izieu, there's only a cramped cluster of low stone houses with old tiles, built around a church and the inevitable *monument aux morts,* with streets barely wide enough to let a car through, and 136 inhabitants, almost all of them farmers, men of the earth, close to the seasons. As Henri Perret, the mayor of Izieu, explained, every French regime, from the monarchy to the Republics, has governed the village with a light hand, because it is so remote. Perret, who is spry at seventy-three in spite of his rheumatism, and has a sharp-featured, lively face, pointed out that even a village the size of Izieu has a history. In the small city hall, there is a birth registry that has been kept without interruption since 1652.

Some years ago, Perret was digging in his backyard, planting trees, when his shovel hit something solid—it was an old Roman tile. Digging further, he found pieces of an amphora, and a skeleton. The wooden coffin had crumbled into dust, but the coffin nails remained evenly arranged around the skeleton in an oblong pattern. This proved to Perret that Izieu had existed since the conquest of Gaul by the Romans. In fact, he said, the Romans had occupied the village with Egyptian conscripts who practiced the cult of Isis and Osiris, hence the name Izieu.

In his view, Izieu had been a fortified town, strategically located at a high point at the corner of three provinces, Savoie, Dauphiné, and Bourgogne. In 1814, during the Napoleonic wars, an Austrian detachment had come through the Pierrechatel pass and bivouacked outside the village. The Austrians demanded two hundredweight of wheat, which the mayor collected, but the soldiers never came to pick it up, and it was auctioned off. The mayor was always chosen from one of the half dozen landowning families in the village, for until the revolution of 1848, France did not have universal suffrage—only landowners could vote. These landed families got rich through the quality of their durum wheat and vineyards. In 1914 the village had a population of three hundred, but World War I losses cut that by half.

Perret took me for a stroll down the main street, where we ran into an affable couple who invited us to taste the wine from their harvest. We stepped down into their cellar and started sipping the slightly acidic but wonderfully fresh Savoie white with its sugges-tion of woods and berries, and Perret reminisced about World War II, when he had been a teacher in a Lyon suburb. When the Ger-mans came in November 1942, they were short of space and a garrison was moved into the school. Perret told himself that he must remain cold and unfriendly, but on the third day he began saying hello to the soldiers.

"Of course," said the wife of the man who had invited us to taste his wine. "You can't remain like cats and dogs." "The German Army was always correct," agreed her husband. "It was the SS."

"They had their chuck wagon in the courtyard," Perret said, "and you could see them line up for their meals, for lunch, sau-sage, Swiss cheese, and bread. And I noticed that some of our schoolchildren, who had nothing to eat, were being fed by the soldiers. They seemed to be good fellows, glad to be in France and not on the eastern front. They liked to laugh, and there was one who could imitate the sound of a bicycle tire bursting, and when he saw a girl go by on a bicycle he'd make that noise at the window and when the girl got off her bike to inspect the damage they all laughed uproariously."

Downhill from the village, perhaps a mile away, was the hamlet of Lelinaz. In this hamlet there was a large manor house with a splendid terrace overlooking the valley, the Poncet, a tributary of the Rhône running through the valley, and the mountains in the distance. Facing this fine, green-shuttered stone building was a farmhouse which, Perret explained, had formerly been used to grow silkworms fed on mulberry leaves, and silk merchants from Lyon used to come to buy the cocoons. The manor was the house Mme. Zlatin had rented at the end of 1942, he said. "You can imagine. Izieu was a place where nothing ever happened, but Ma-dame Zlatin's arrival was like a rocket falling from the sky."

Sabina Zlatin and her husband, Miron, had met in France when

263

they were young, both fleeing the anti-Semitism of their native Poland. Her face was strong and leonine, and she had thick chestnut hair and clear blue eyes. Miron was an agronomist. The Zlatins settled in the northeast, near Nancy, where they operated a model farm. At the Agricultural Fair of 1939, the minister of agriculture was so impressed with Mme. Zlatin's exhibit that he asked her what he could do for her, and she told him that she and her husband would like to obtain French nationality.

Sabina Zlatin was also a licensed military nurse, and after the 1940 armistice, she and her husband moved to Montpellier in the unoccupied zone, where she worked in the military hospital. But then she was told that would no longer be possible, in view of the anti-Jewish statutes. So she volunteered to work in the two camps south of Montpellier, Agde and Rivesaltes, where Jews were being interned. Mme. Zlatin rode to the camps on her bicycle wearing a billowing blue cape. One day a Gypsy woman thrust a baby in her arms with an address tag around its neck like a parcel. Mme. Zlatin left the camp on her bicycle with the baby concealed under her cape and delivered it to the address. It was a small victory, she thought later, upon learning that 400,000 Gypsies had been sent to the ovens.

She started taking Jewish children into her home. The Vichy authorities did not bother her. The prefect of Hérault was actually helpful in small ways. But when the Germans returned in November 1942, the situation became unsafe, and he told her: "*Madame,* I advise you to leave the region." He suggested she go to the Italian-occupied zone. By this time, there were seventeen children in her care. She and her husband took the children to Chambéry, capital of Savoie. There, the prefect told her: "*Madame,* the only place you will be safe is the *département* of Ain. Why don't you go see the *sous-préfet* in Belley?"

She learned that the attitudes of individual Frenchmen in positions of power differed widely, and that they had less to do with government policy, which could be interpreted in a variety of ways, than with qualities of heart and a lack of prejudice. For instance, Marcel Wiltzer, the *sous-préfet* in Belley, was a warm and sympathetic man who went out of his way to be helpful. He drove her around the countryside to look at houses. He had heard of a big house, a onetime Catholic summer camp, for rent in Izieu, and they went to see it. It seemed perfect, being spacious with lots of big rooms that could be turned into dormitories, a garden for a playground, and it was in a rural area where food could be obtained. Better than that, it was so far off the beaten track that they would be practically invisible. Standing on the terrace and looking out at the sweeping panorama before them, the curve of the river below, and the fir-covered mountains beyond, Marcel Wiltzer turned to Sabina Zlatin and remarked: "Here, you will be tranquil." No German had ever come to Izieu, and, for that matter, no Jew.

Sabina and Miron Zlatin moved the seventeen children into the big house, and Marcel Wiltzer sent them a truckload of furniture. One of the first things she did was pay a courtesy call on the then mayor of Izieu, Henri Tissot. He received her gruffly, asking; "What do you want?" She explained that she had rented the big house to use as a *colonie d'enfants* (children's home), and asked if he could sell her some potatoes. "Give her a kilo of flour," Tissot said to his wife, to get rid of her.

Tissot then wrote a letter to Marcel Wiltzer in Belley, saying, "I felt that I should let you know that this children's home is Jewish in composition." Wiltzer tore up the letter. According to Henri Perret, the present Izieu mayor, who knew him, Tissot was not a bad fellow. He was brusque by nature, and he was worried about more mouths to feed in a time of hardship. The letter to Wiltzer, Perret said, was just to cover himself in case there were inquiries.

But all through 1943, while the Italians occupied Savoie, there were no inquiries, and the children's home prospered, until at one point there were eighty children there, and Mme. Zlatin had to turn the barn into a dormitory. Friends arrived to help her manage the place. One was Léon Reifman, a Roumanian-born medical student in Clermont-Ferrand until the anti-Jewish statutes had forced him to give up his studies. He helped run the infirmary on the top floor, with his parents, his twenty-seven-year-old sister Sarah, a doctor, and her ten-year-old son Claude. Another friend was Leah Feldblum, twenty-six years old, who had left Antwerp with her parents in 1940, and who took care of the smaller children. In 1943 she twice refused a chance to cross into Switzerland in order to remain with them.

One drawback of Izieu was that the village had no school. Some of the older boys in Mme. Zlatin's care, those over fourteen, could attend the *lycée* in Belley as boarders, but what about the others? The problem was solved by Marcel Wiltzer and his successor, Maurice Sivain, who arranged for a government-paid school-teacher to live at the children's home, where she would run a one-room school. Twenty-one-year-old Gabrielle Perrier, whose first teaching job this was, arrived in September 1943, and Mme. Zlatin was glad to see her because they had been improvising classes up until then. Mlle. Perrier borrowed materials from schools in Belley, blackboards and desks with tops that opened, on the backs of which the children could tack their classroom schedules. There were classes for children from five to fourteen, utilizing the same curriculum as other schoolchildren all over France. Gabrielle Perrier liked the work because the youngsters wanted to learn. Some were quite gifted at drawing or writing, and she told several of them that they would have a brilliant future. Mme. Zlatin urged her to give the children timely essay topics, one of which was: "One of your relatives is a prisoner. You sense his homesickness for his native land in his letters. Write to him about France, about his city or town, and pick words that will bring him comfort and joy." The oddest thing about this arrangement was that by delegating a teacher to Izieu who was a government employee, Vichy was helping to operate a home for Jewish children.

In this forgotten corner of France, the children led a life in which the war intruded only over the radio, and they rejoiced over such Allied actions as the bombing of Hamburg. Otherwise, they lived in the home, which was officially called the "Settlement for Refugee Children from Hérault," very much as they would have in any boarding school. For breakfast, they had cocoa with bread and jam; for lunch, soup and cheese; and for dinner, noodles and vegetables and, occasionally, meat. At Christmastime, there were gingerbread and quince jam. Miron Zlatin covered the countryside, pulling a small trailer on his bicycle, buying whatever was available from the farmers.

The children rose at seven, went to class, and took afternoon naps. Depending on the season, they went swimming in the Poncet, or tobogganing in the snow. On Thursdays and Sundays, they went on hikes and picked mulberries and blackberries. On April Fool's Day the children played a traditional French prank of pinning paper fish surreptitiously on each other's backs. When the weather was good they would spend evenings on the terrace with its spectacular view.

Friendships were formed. German-born Paul Niederman, who as a small boy had been chased down the street by members of the Hitler Youth, spent most evenings talking to his friend Theo Reis. He and Reis wondered where their parents were, when the war would be over, and what they would do when it was over. Theo Reis said: "Promise me that whatever happens we will meet after the war." Early in 1944 Paul Niederman turned sixteen, and because he was tall for his age, Mme. Zlatin smuggled him to Switzerland when the chance arose. Theo Reis, who was the same age but considerably shorter, stayed behind.

In 1944 there were forty-four children at the home, twenty-one of them French, the rest Austrian, German, Dutch, and Polish, for the most part. The situation in France was changing. The Italians had left Savoie in September 1943, and the Germans were now occupying it. Some were garrisoned in nearby Belley and scoured the countryside for Jews, paying informants so much per head. When a Jewish doctor in a neighboring village was deported, Mme. Zlatin knew they were no longer safe. She began to arrange for the dispersal of the children, and sent Léon Reifman to Chambéry to see the Catholic bishop Costa de Beauregard. When Reifman explained to the bishop that he was looking for Catholic homes to place the children, the bishop gave a little start and said, "Can you for one minute imagine that we would mix Jewish and non-Jewish children?" He did, however, say he would think the matter over. Several days later, Reifman received a calling card from the bishop with his message written under the engraved name: "Regrets that he is unable to give a favorable reply to your request."

In the meantime, there were two incidents that Mme. Zlatin, had she been blessed with a more suspicious nature, might have wondered at. The first was that Antoine Wucher, a mechanic who sometimes fixed things at the home, asked if his eight-year-old son René could stay with them for a while. Wucher had four children from a first marriage and two with his present wife, the mother of René. His wife was now sick in the hospital, Wucher said, and since he worked all day, he had to find a place to put the boy. Mme. Zlatin took René in, the only non-Jewish boy in the home.

The other incident involved a farmer named Lucien Bourdon, who lived in Brens, halfway between Izieu and Belley. Bourdon was not a native of the area; he had been born in Metz, capital of Lorraine, in 1906, and was one of thousands who had been ejected from that area in 1940. Somehow he had landed near Izieu with his wife, and had rented land from another farmer. The main thing to remember about Bourdon is that he was born German, during the period between 1870 and 1918 when Lorraine was annexed by Germany. He spoke German as if it were his native tongue, and went to German schools until he was twelve. Bourdon was one of those whose nationality had been imposed upon them by war.

Bourdon's neighbors knew that he was friendly with the Germans in Belley. He had been seen drinking with them on occasion at the Café Nevy on the Place des Terreaux. Marcel Bouvier, who owned the Chantemerle farm, later recalled that after a few drinks, Bourdon said the French were not up to the Germans. In addition, Bourdon's closest friend was Antoine Wucher, whom the local resistance suspected of *collabo* activities, such as driving trucks for the Germans on anti-Maquis operations.

But the Zlatins didn't know any of this. In fact, Miron Zlatin was on cordial terms with Bourdon, who had offered to sell him vegetables. One day in March 1944, Bourdon asked Miron: "Do you have a big boy who can give me a hand with my crops?" The Zlatins sent over fifteen-year-old Fritz Loebmann, who had an ID card in the name of François Loban, and who spent several weeks on Bourdon's farm. Bourdon quizzed him about the children's home, and the boy admitted that all the children, including himself were Jewish. Bourdon made the boy go to Mass on Sunday, saying, "It will do you good. People will think you're Catholic." Then, at the end of March, Bourdon sent the boy back to Izieu, explaining that it was now the off-season.

The Easter holidays were coming up in the first week of April, which meant that the older boys would be home from the Belley *lycée*. Mme. Zlatin left for a five-day visit to Montpellier on April 3. She had been working on getting the children dispersed and had found a priest who agreed to take fifteen of them on April 12.

Léon Reifman had been away too, but returned on the morning of Thursday, April 6, on the Belley bus with a couple of the *lycée* boys. He reached the house at about 8:45, and went upstairs to the infirmary to say hello to his sister Sarah. Shortly after that, two trucks, followed by an open convertible, drove up the road from the valley and into the courtyard of the children's home.

Earlier that morning, Lucien Favet had gone to work in the fields of his employer, Eusèbe Perdicoz, whose farmhouse—the building that had once been used for raising silkworms—was across the road from the children's home. Someone from the farmhouse always brought Favet a *casse-croûte* (snack) at 8:30, but on this day there was no *casse-croûte,* so he walked over to the farmhouse to see what was going on. He saw two trucks in the courtyard and thought it was customers come to buy wood. Then he saw a German officer and some soldiers wearing only caps, no helmets. Lucien Favet walked behind the stone fountain in front of the children's home, where three men were leaning against the ledge surrounding the fountain. Two of the men were wearing gabardine trench coats. The third man was Lucien Bourdon. From inside the farmhouse, Eusèbe Perdicoz looked out the window and also recognized Bourdon with the two SS men.

Léon Reifman heard the dining-room bell ring at nine for breakfast. He started walking down the stairs when he saw three men in civilian clothes in the foyer downstairs with his sister. One of the men spotted him, and called out, "*Monsieur,* come down, we would like to talk to you." His sister signaled him not to. Reifman went back upstairs to the infirmary and opened the window that gave onto the terrace, but saw a German soldier below. Going into another room, he jumped out the window into the garden and hid in some thick bushes at the garden's edge. German soldiers came into the garden to search it, and one came so close to Reifman that he actually thought that they had made eye contact. But the soldier walked on, as though he had not seen him. From his hiding place, Reifman could hear soldiers yelling "*schnell, schnell,*" as they herded children into the trucks—like bundles, thought Perdicoz, still watching from his window. They were thrown into the trucks like bundles. Reifman remained in hiding until nightfall, then made his way to the Perdicoz farmhouse. The farmer told him that some of the soldiers had said they were disgusted at having to do this kind of work. Perhaps that was why the soldier had pretended not to see him, thought Reifman.

The next day, Perdicoz's son Aimé took Reifman to Marcel Bouvier's farm, Chantemerle, about ten miles away, where he could remain in hiding for a while. Aimé's wife, Juliette, had been in the vegetable garden of the children's home picking leeks when the trucks wound up the road. She too recognized Lucien Bourdon. When the Germans took the children, she went into the empty dining room and started crying, because the bowls on the table were filled with cocoa. The children had gone without having their breakfast.

The trucks carrying the children and the staff were headed for Lyon, a couple of hours away. They traveled down the Izieu road, and at the first crossroads, a hamlet called La Bruyère, one of the trucks stalled. It was a *gazogène* vehicle, and it needed more wood. It had stalled right in front of the Confiserie Bilbor, a small candy factory operated by Henri Borgel, whom the Germans asked for wood. It happened that one of the workers in that factory was nineteen-year-old Geneviève Pichon, whose sister Marcelle was the common-law wife of Antoine Wucher, and the mother of René Wucher, who had been picked up with the other children. And it also happened that the boy was sitting in the very back of the truck, where he could be easily spotted.

While Henri Borgel went to get wood, the two trucks rolled into the courtyard. According to Geneviève Pichon, she was at the *confiserie* dipping chocolates when one of her fellow workers said, "The *Boches* are there with the Izieu kids." She went out to have a look and noticed her nephew René, who called out *"Tatan"* ("Auntie"). Then the Germans let the boy off the truck for a kiss, and the next thing René Wucher knew, he was under a table, eating candy, surrounded by women's skirts.

That evening at 8:10 P.M. in Lyon, a telex signed by Klaus Barbie was sent to SD headquarters in Paris. The message read: "This morning, the Jewish children's home 'Colonie d'Enfants' in Izieu (Ain) was seized. Forty-one children in all, aged from three to thirteen, were captured. In addition, there took place the arrest of all the Jewish personnel, that is to say, ten persons, including five women. We were not able to find any money or other valuables. The transport to Drancy will take place on April 7, 1944."

The telex established the Izieu *rafle* as a Section Four operation under the command of Barbie, although his presence at Izieu cannot be ascertained. In fact, there was a mistake in the message, which possibly would not have been made had he been in Izieu himself. There were actually forty-four children, but three of them were older boys who were mistaken for personnel. Thus, there were seven rather than ten adults: Miron Zlatin, then forty years old; Sarah Reifman and her parents, Moses and Eva Reifman; Leah Feldblum, twenty-six, the teacher-counselor; Mina Friedler, thirty-two, born in Turkey, who lived with her daughter Lucienne at the home; and Lucie Feiger, sixty, a camp counselor. The government-appointed teacher, Gabrielle Perrier, was away for the Easter holiday.

The telex, which of course was in German, revealed a use of language meant to demean. The word translated as "seized" was *ausgehoben,* which actually means "pulled from the nest." Thus, the first sentence said literally: "This morning, the children in the Jewish home 'Colonie d'Enfants' in Izieu (Ain) were pulled from their nest." Instead of ten "persons," the German word used was ten *köpfe,* or heads as in "heads of cattle." So the sentence actually read: "In addition, there took place the arrest of all the Jewish personnel, that is to say, ten heads, including five women . . ." The task was facilitated by denigrating the victims through language.

When the telex reached the SD office for Jewish Affairs in Paris, it provoked a discussion that was referred to in a handwritten note added at the bottom of the telex: "This affair was discussed in the presence of Dr. v. B. and Hauptsturmführer Brunner." (Dr. v.B. was Baron Kurt von Behr, the monocled director of the Einsatzstab Rosenberg, a looting agency that confiscated the furniture and valuables of deported Jews. He committed suicide in 1945. Alois Brunner was the Gestapo officer in charge of deportation.)

"Dr. v.B. stated that, in cases of this kind, special measures regarding the lodging of children had been provided for by Obersturmführer Roethke. Haupsturmführer Brunner replied that he had no knowledge of such instructions or such plans, and that as a matter of principle he would not consent to such special measures. In these cases, also, he would proceed in the normal manner as regards deportation."

Edgar Faure, one of the French prosecutors at Nuremberg, used the Izieu telex as an example of Nazi war crimes, and brought it before the court on February 5, 1946. Here is part of his statement to the court: "One can say that there is something even more striking and more horrible than the concrete fact of the abduction of these children, and that is the bureaucratic tone of the report, and the conference where several officials are tranquilly discussing it, as one of the normal procedures of their department. All the machinery of the state, that is, the Nazi state, was activated on such an occasion and for such a goal. It is a true illustration of the phrase we have seen in Dannecker's report: 'A cold demeanor.' "

In the meantime, Mme. Zlatin was in Montpellier, where on the afternoon of April 6 she received a telegram that read: FAMILY SICK. SICKNESS CONTAGIOUS. Dressed in her nurse's uniform, she left at once for Vichy, where she was received on April 7 by a high official at the Hôtel du Parc. When she asked what could be done about the children, he replied: "Why are you concerning yourself with those dirty kikes?" When she insisted, he said: "Find them yourself." It was too late because they were gone, and so was her husband. Mme. Zlatin then went to Paris and joined the resistance.

On April 8 Lucien Bourdon's neighbors saw a truck with German soldiers in it pull up to his house. They loaded his furniture into the truck; then Bourdon and his wife climbed in and they drove away and were never seen again in the area. It was learned later that Bourdon's wife had been allowed to return to their home in Lorraine, but he had been taken to Saarbrücken to be a guard in a German transit camp. On August 2 the resistance caught up with Antoine Wucher. They took him to the mountain village of Ambléon, about five miles north of Izieu, stood him up in front of the cemetery wall, and shot him.

When Mme. Zlatin learned the details of what had happened at Izieu, and how Lucien Bourdon and Antoine Wucher were involved, she began to see things more clearly. It was obvious that both Bourdon and Wucher had made a deal with the Germans—Wucher for cash and Bourdon so he could go home to his native Lorraine. Wucher had actually sent his eight-year-old son René to spy on them, although the boy was surely not conscious of having done so, and then the truck had conveniently stalled in front of the *confiserie* where René's aunt worked and where the Germans had released him. Bourdon had taken in Fritz Loebmann in order to quiz him, and had then informed the Germans in Belley that there was a house full of Jewish children who were ripe for the picking, and from there the matter had been referred to Section Four in Lyon. It was a tale of two informers, who had betrayed and sent to their deaths forty-four children for personal gain.

In 1947 Lucien Bourdon was arrested near his home in Metz and brought to Lyon to stand trial that June. There was a strong suspicion that he had turned in the Izieu children. But he said in his defense that he too had been arrested by the Germans and had been forced to go with them to Izieu. Testifying at the trial, Eusèbe Perdicoz said he had seen Bourdon with the Germans, and that he had looked much more like an interpreter and accomplice than a prisoner, coming and going and involving himself in the proceedings. But in 1947 much of the evidence concerning Izieu was still missing, so Bourdon got off with a sentence of "national degradation for life," which meant that he could not vote or enjoy other benefits of citizenship.

As for the children, they spent the night of April 6 in Montluc Prison. The next day they were put on a passenger train to Drancy, with the older boys in manacles. Leah Feldblum had an ID card in the name of Marie Louise Decoste, but when the Drancy authorities sought to separate her from the children on the grounds that she was French, she revealed her true identity.

On April 13 Feldblum, the Reifman family, and thirty-four of the forty-four children were deported to Auschwitz on the seventy-first deportation train to leave France. Of the 1,500 people on the train, 300 were under the age of nineteen. Upon arrival two days later at the Auschwitz ramp, the children were lined up in rows of five with Leah Feldblum at their head. An officer came

up and asked, *"Sind diese deine Kinder?"* ("Are these your children?"). She replied *"Dieses ist ein Kinderheim"* ("This is a children's home"). She was holding on to six-year-old Émile
Zuckerberg, a fetching little boy with blond bangs whom she had
comforted during the trip, but the officer pulled her violently away,
and the children were led in another direction.

That was the last time she saw them, for they were gassed that
very day, while she survived to tell the tale. For the rest of her
life she would see the children as they were herded away from
the Auschwitz ramp: Émile Zuckerberg, who had been pulled from
her arms—to the ovens. Thirteen-year-old Raoul Bentitou, who
was always singing—to the ovens. Theo Reis, whom she would
remember feeding the chickens and pitching hay—to the ovens.
Nina Aronowicz, so pretty when she wore a big bow in her hair,
who had an uncle and aunt in America—to the ovens. George
Halpern, so good-natured that everone spoiled him, everyone's
little friend, dear Georgy—to the ovens. Lilian Gerenstein, the
eleven-year-old who had written a letter to God: "God? It is thanks
to You that I enjoyed a wonderful life before, that I was spoiled,
that I had lovely things, things that others do not have. God? As
a result I ask just one thing of You: BRING BACK MY PAR-
ENTS. HAVE THEM COME BACK ONE MORE TIME." Lil-
ian Gerenstein—to the ovens. The Krochmal sisters, Liane, seven,
and Renata, nine, whose family had been refused an entry visa to
the United States by the State Department on July 1942: "The
conclusion has been reached that a favorable recommendation for
the issuance of a visa may not be sent to the appropriate consular
officer." Liane and Renata—to the ovens. Henri Goldberg and his
brother Joseph, who used to help Eusèbe Perdicoz with the
chores—to the ovens. Eleven-year-old Alice Luzgart, with her shy
smile and her ribbed sandals, who five days before the *rafle* had
written her sister Fanny that she and her friends were discussing
what they would be when they grew up: "I chose accountant, but
you know, my girlfriend chose a nicer profession that I did. She
wants to be a student midwife in the maternity ward when she
grows up. She told me she'd like to operate on the mothers to
bring little children into the world because she likes little babies.
Don't you think that's a fine profession? Maybe I'll change my

mind and copy her." Alice Luzgart—to the ovens.

Miron Zlatin was deported with several of the older boys on the all-male train of eight hundred seventy-eight that left on May 15, the seventy-third deportation train. This was one of the few trains that did not go to Auschwitz. Instead it made two stops. The first was in Kaunas, Lithuania, where about four hundred of the deportees were let off and sent to the Projanowska camp, where they were put to work in a peat bog; the rest continued to Tallinn, Estonia, where they were interned in the fortress of Reval. Zlatin was in this latter group. His wife did get one letter in which he said that he was in a castle on the Baltic, working in a mill, and that each night he returned with his pockets filled with flour for his cell mates. Then she heard no more.

In 1945 the newly formed de Gaulle government requisitioned the Hôtel Lutetia in Paris as a center to welcome returning deportees, and Mme. Zlatin was put in charge of the welcoming committee. One day a man wearing a Russian greatcoat came up to her and showed her a photograph, asking, "Do you know this man?" She said it was her husband. The man in the greatcoat said: "Then I'm sorry to tell you that he was shot on July 31, 1944." It was a double blow. First, because she had not been certain that her husband was dead. And second, because July 31 was the date of their wedding in Nancy.

Early on the morning of April 7, 1944, Henri-Gaston Meyer, a forty-two-year-old teacher in Saint-Claude, a town of artisans and light industry in the Jura Mountains, about seventy miles northeast of Lyon, left on his bicycle for the town of Chassal to pick up a chicken he had won in a school lottery. Returning to Saint-Claude later that morning with the chicken in his basket, he found that he had an escort—two long lines of German soldiers marching into the town.

The German action in the Jura, where the Maquis was scattered in dozens of mountain villages, was called Operation *Frühling* (spring). After crushing the Maquis on the Plateau des Glières in March, General Pflaum's 157th Alpine Division had been ordered to the Jura with elements of the Lyon SD under the command of Klaus Barbie. As we know, Barbie had to be in Lyon on the evening of April 6 to send the Izieu telex, and so he and his men must have left in the early morning in order to be in Saint-Claude on April 7—a man with too many appointments, rushing to stay on schedule. He said later there were two Holy Fridays in his life that were important to him. The first was in 1939, when he announced his engagement, the second on April 7, 1944, when he was ambushed by the Maquis coming into Saint-Claude and was slightly wounded in the knee.

The plan for Operation *Frühling* was that the Alpine Division would surround the Saint-Claude region and four commando units would sweep through. The troops were assembled in Annecy from March 31 to April 4. Between April 4 and 7, the area was surrounded. One commando unit headed for the mountain village of Vulvoz, five miles south of Saint-Claude, through forested ravines with poor visibility. The unit came under heavy fire from well-camouflaged Maquis positions on the heights above the road, and suffered five dead and thirteen wounded. It could not disengage until nightfall, when reinforcements arrived from Saint-Claude. The next day the main operations focused on this region, and the outnumbered Maquisards fled in all directions.

Operation *Frühling* lasted from April 7 to 19. Barbie's mission was to set up headquarters in Saint-Claude and pick out the Maquisards among the population. He took over the Hôtel de France and barred the roads leaving town. On April 8 several inhabitants noticed a truck speeding through town, with boots sticking out the back—the bodies of German soldiers.

On the morning of April 9, Easter Sunday, the *garde-champêtre* (rural policeman) went through town with his drum rolling, announcing that all men between the ages of eighteen and forty-five were invited to go at once to the Place du Pré, the main square, and have their papers checked by the Germans.

Henri-Gaston Meyer, the man who had won the chicken, was awakened by the drum roll that morning, and got dressed and climbed up into the attic of his house, thinking he would jump out a back window and make a run for it across the field and into the woods. But he could see from the window that the Germans had set up a machine-gun post at the edge of the field. So he went to the Place du Pré, where men were already standing in two lines waiting their turn to come before two SD officers in gray-green uniforms sitting behind desks. One of the officers, wearing a white scarf made from parachute silk, was Barbie, and when Gaston-Meyer's turn came, it was Barbie who questioned him.

Gaston-Meyer was amazed to see that the Gestapo had a file on him, which Barbie opened and from it read aloud that his grandfather had been a prisoner of war in the 1870 war. Barbie raised his head and said, "Grandfather Joseph Meyer, prisoner in Reichshoffen. Worked well for us in Saxony. Good grandfather. You will sleep in your own bed tonight."

Gervais Millet, one of the Maquisards who had fled the fighting around Vulvoz, was now hiding in Saint-Claude. The *garde-champêtre* announced that the Germans would conduct house-by-house searches for those who did not come to the Place du Pré. Seeing no way out, Millet went. Soldiers surrounded the square. Every ten meters there was a machine gun. There were two groups, he saw. Some were being led into a girls' school and would obviously be deported. The others, mostly older men, would presumably be released. Millet had a beard and wore a sheepskin coat, which to the Germans meant Maquisard, so when he gave his name and profession, he was directed to the group headed for deportation. But he protested that he was a *pupille de la nation* (ward of the state, meaning that his father had been killed in World War I), and a *père de famille nombreuse* (father of more than three children), and did this not merit some consideration? *"Ja, Ja, gut,"* muttered the German officer, and Millet was transferred to the group that was sent home. The next day, he was shocked to see his chief in the Maquis, Kemmler, in a German combat car with the German officer who had let him go, standing with his foot on Kemmler's chest, as if coming back from the hunt with a a trophy.

René Chambard, the technical director of the Daloz factory, makers of wood products, also heard the drum roll that morning. The German officer who questioned him was wearing a cap with a death's head and crossed bones on it. He was obviously the man in charge, an arrogant little fellow who did not stand up to salute a passing Wehrmacht general, and who sat astride his chair, wearing a white scarf. When Chambard saw that some of his factory workers had been detained, he went up to the man in the white scarf and said he had no right to arrest his workers because his factory had been classified *Betrieb,* that is to say, it had a factory exemption from the STO. Barbie lost his temper and shouted *"Raus"* ("Get away"). Chambard retorted that he had proof, and Barbie said, "Go and get it." So Chambard went to his office, took a Daloz letterhead and stamped *Betrieb* on it. He took the letterhead to Barbie, who gave him permission to remove all his arrested workers from the ranks.

Henri Troussier, twenty-two years old, tall and thin, with a long mournful face and a beard, was a radio repairman in the Maquis. When Troussier's turn came on the Place du Pré, Barbie went through his wallet and found a list of radio frequencies. With his fingers Barbie mimed the tapping of a radio operator, and went *ti ti ti ti ti.* Troussier was led into a classroom of the girls' school with three other men, who were then called one by one. Troussier realized that they were being taken out to be shot. He hid under a bench. At one point, Barbie came in and asked where the fourth one was. He spotted Troussier under the bench and said, "I haven't forgotten you. I'm going to take care of you." But he became busy with other matters. Then twenty new prisoners were brought in. One was a doctor named Bourrud, an elderly bachelor, who was weeping because Barbie had set fire to his house after finding a World War I rifle in his study. All his life, Dr. Bourrud had collected rare books, and his entire library had been burned to ashes. He was like someone mourning the loss of his family.

When René Chambard went home after managing to get his workers released, his father told him that their family doctor and friend, Dr. Bourrud, had been arrested. "He's an old soldier," the father said. "You're president of the Legion of Honor Association. You've got to get him out." René Chambard went to the Hôtel de France and was led to a room behind the bar where Barbie was sitting alone at a table, eating mushrooms with cream. Chambard mentioned the doctor, and Barbie said: "I've already talked to the medical association and to the Legion of Honor Association and I'm sick of hearing about it." "I represent Marshal Pétain in Saint-Claude," said Chambard, "and you don't have the right not to listen to me." Barbie did not object when Chambard sat down. Chambard suggested that to clear his conscience as an officer, it was enough to make an arrest in principle, since Bourrud had been punished enough by losing his house and his book collection. "I promise to think about it," Barbie said, and two days later Dr. Bourrud was released.

The troops used in Saint-Claude belonged to the 99th Alpine regiment based in Briançon. Alfons Glas, a corporal, was one of the guards at the SD command post in the Hôtel de France. In the late afternoon of April 10, five Maquisards in civilian clothes were brought in and were lined up against the wall of the dining room with their hands up. One of them was their leader, Kemmler, an Alsatian. Alfons Glas watched as Barbie asked Kemmler a question in French. Kemmler replied *"Jamais"* ("Never"). Barbie, who had gloves on, struck him in the face with his closed fist and repeated the question, Kemmler again said, *"Jamais,"* and Barbie struck him again. Kemmler was now bleeding from the nose and mouth, and Barbie had blood on his gloves. There was a piano in the dining room, and Barbie sat down and without removing his gloves played the first bars of "Parlez-moi d'Amour" ("Speak to Me of Love"). Then he went back to Kemmler and hit him some more. Night fell, and the next day Barbie and the others continued questioning Kemmler while Alfons Glas watched. When Kemmler passed out, Barbie and his men left the room. Glas approached the Maquis leader. He was sitting in a wicker armchair. His body and head did not move, only his eyes. After about half an hour, his eyes blinked, then shut, and his head moved forward slightly. Five minutes later a pool of urine had collected under the chair. Barbie and his men came back later and removed the body.

The Jura operation that concluded on April 19 was particularly violent. Maquisards were shot out of hand whenever they were found. Farms suspected of supplying the Maquis were set on fire. Two hundred and four enemy hiding places were discovered and destroyed. There wee 923 arrests, including the 302 men arrested on the Place du Pré on April 9, out of 1,400 who had their papers inspected. There were 148 French dead and six German dead. It was a major operation on a divisional scale.

The Germans explained their savagery as a response to the actions of the Maquis. Alfred Bohnke, who was in the Lyon SD but in a different section than Barbie, testified after the war that Barbie "was known for his rather radical position toward resistance movements." But this, said Bohnke, could be explained by "the terrible acts of the Maquis. German soldiers were tied up with barbed wire, and were then doused with gasoline and set afire. Others were castrated, and swastikas were burned on their bodies with hot wires. The SIPO [regular police] in Lyon had photographs of the victims."

As for the radio repairman Henri Troussier, he was taken to Montluc Prison, where Barbie questioned him saying, *"Toi, tu as une tête de Juif"* ("You look like a Jew"). Troussier said it must be the beard, for his family had been Catholic as far back as it could be traced. Barbie must have believed him, because instead of being sent to Auschwitz, Troussier was sent to Buchenwald, which was not a death camp, for it had no gas chambers; it was, rather, a slow-death camp through disease and malnutrition.

Buchenwald (the name means beech forest) was one of the first concentration camps, built in 1937 in a grove of beech trees on Ettersberg hill about seven miles from Weimar, a capital of German culture, where Goethe had lived. Arriving in Weimar station in June 1944, Troussier's first greeting was schoolchildren making faces at him. He and his fellow passengers walked the seven miles to the camp, which was the size of a city and at that point had twenty thousand inmates. The sign at the gate said: RECHT ODER UNRECHT MEIN VATERLAND (My Country Right or Wrong).

The prisoners were showered and shaved, and went naked to the *Effektkammer* (clothing room), where they were all out of striped uniforms, so that they had to grab what they could, a shirt and a pair of pants, no two alike. Then they spent a month and a half in the quarantine camp before being moved to the big camp with its fifty blocks. In this camp there were three-tiered bunks with straw mattresses, and the food consisted of a pound of bread a day, sometimes sausage, a little margarine, and *ersatz* coffee. Everything was *ersatz;* the cheese was made from charcoal.

The social composition of the camp was intricate, Troussier found, and amounted to a stratified class system. The first inmates had been ordinary criminals, who wore green triangles; these were followed by political inmates, who wore red triangles with an initial indicating their nation of origin. Troussier, for instance, wore a red triangle with an *F* on it. These were the two important groups, the others were marginal—the asocials with black triangles, the homosexuals with pink triangles, and the Jehovah's Witnesses with purple triangles. An intense struggle for control of the camp went on between the green and red triangles.

At first the greens were in control, but as more politicals arrived from outside Germany, many of whom were Communists, the reds won out because the Communists were better organized and more motivated. They took over the key camp jobs, such as the canteen with its cash flow and barter possibilities, and the Statistics Bureau, which made up the work assignments. You could help your friends by putting them on *Holzhof* (light work) and getting them classified DAKAK *(Darf auf Keinen Fall aud Aussenkommando)* (Must not in any case be sent to an external *Kommando*). Because everyone knew that being sent to the "external *Kommandos*" in satellite camps amounted to a death warrant. One desirable assignment was the pig detail, for Buchenwald had its own pig farm, with nine hundred pigs which were fed with potato peels, and those who were on the pig detail were given potatoes and carrots and onions by the cooks. It was a gift of life, particularly in 1945, when rations were severely reduced. The downside was that in the winter you could get frostbite from handling the frozen potato peels.

The French inmates arrived with a bad reputation. The French had given in to Hitler and were collaborating with the Nazis. They were thought of as easygoing and self-indulgent. The oldtimers in the camp, the German Communists, felt that the French had to prove themselves. They had to show that they could obey the regulations and not get the rest of the block in trouble. And when one of the French inmates in Troussier's block urinated outside the door to save himself a trip to the toilet, the German block leader gave them a little lecture: "We, the German antifascists, who have been here for seven or eight years, did not get ourselves killed so that you French newcomers could take advantage of our sacrifices. If you want to leave here alive, you'd better change your ways."

Troussier and his fellow Frenchmen adjusted to the rhythm of the camp, learning to be up at four for the roll call and then off to their work details. Troussier worked in an underground factory that made V-1 buzz bombs. There was talk about sabotage, but it was risky, because at every step there were controls, and if you were caught you were hanged. It didn't take much to end up at the end of a rope. Look at the Russian who pissed in the tails of the torpedoes to short-circuit them, Troussier thought. When you worked in this great cavern with thousands of others, you realized how the pyramids had been built—like anthills.

When he returned from work in the evening, Troussier would head for his favorite spot, a magnificent, high-trunked oak tree with hugh spreading branches. A plaque at the base said that Goethe used to come and meditate under its foliage. Troussier would sit under the oak and think about his girlfriend in the Maquis and about his family. He met a German inmate, an oldtimer, who told him there was a legend connected with the tree, which was that if it ever caught fire, Germany would be destroyed.

On August 24 the Allies carpet-bombed the V-1 plant next to the camp. The bombs rained down, and there were so many explosions you could barely see the sun through the smoke. Some of the bombs hit the camp and the adjacent houses, killing the wife and children of the camp commandant, Pister. It was on this day that the inmates recovered quite a few weapons from the bodies of dead guards, which they concealed inside the camp. But even better, an incendiary bomb hit the fabled oak tree and split it in a hundred pieces, and there was a near riot as the inmates fought over the remains as if over a religious relic.

After that, no more German planes were seen, just Allied aircraft. The Germans knew they were beaten, and conditions worsened. In 1945 the rations were down to half a pound of bread a day and a raw rutabaga. The camp experience taught Troussier that severe hardship does not develop one's better instincts. He had seen inmates attack children—for there were children in the camp—for their bread ration. He had seen inmates remove clothes from a dying man. He had seen them risk death by slipping through the barbed wire in March 1945 to grab some Brussels sprouts that had survived the winter. He had seen corpses being pulled by their feet through the mud. In Buchenwald, everything had a name, and these men were called the *Leichenträgers* (carriers of corpses). You could see men start to decline, and you knew that the descent was irreversible. Fifty-three thousand died in Buchenwald, the first cause of death being tuberculosis. It didn't take long. You began to spit and sneeze, and soon you were in the custody of the *Leichenträgers*.

In 1945, with the war almost over, came the worst suffering. The camp population had doubled to forty thousand, and so had the number of deaths—in February more than five thousand, in March the same number. There were too many dead for the ovens. They were piled up in the courtyard, wait-listed for the crematorium. When guards tore down the map of Germany in Troussier's block, he knew that the Allies had invaded Germany. In February, thousands of planes few overhead on their way to bomb Dresden. There was a new work detail—loading the furniture of the SS officers into trucks.

The SS were evacuating as many inmates as possible. They had a plan to destroy the camp, but in the confusion were unable to carry it out. The 6th Armored Division of General Patton's Third Army was reported to be fifty miles away. On April 11 a tank group, commanded by Captain Robert J. Bennett, sent a patrol into Buchenwald and found the camp unguarded. The remaining twenty thousand inmates had taken it over. And soon the living skeletons were chewing gum and eating Spam. After the Americans had arrived, inmates continued to die at the rate of forty per day for the next two weeks. And on April 16 General Patton issued the following order to the city of Weimar: That at least one thousand inhabitants of the city, half of them women, must visit the camp, arriving there on foot as the inmates had. So no one could say that nothing had gone on there, and that the concentration camps had never existed.

Henri Troussier, who had ended up in Buchenwald because he had carelessly carried radio frequencies in his wallet, survived, made his way back to Lyon, and eventually entered the family business. One memory came back to haunt him, the thirst he had suffered in the sealed cattle car that had transported him and the others to Buchenwald, when for three days they were given no water. It was an unbearable experience. And to this day, forty-four years later, wherever he is, Troussier carries a flask of water.

On May 2, when Robert Nathan, a twelve-year-old boy living in the Croix-Rousse section of Lyon with his parents, went to school, the teacher made an announcement: "I have received a letter from the Germans asking me to give the name of all my Jewish students. Tell your parents not to send you to school anymore, so I don't have to give your names." Robert Nathan stopped attending school. He stayed home or played the game of the *traboules,* those narrow, street-level tunnels that run through the buildings of old Lyon. The game consisted of seeing how far he could go by using only the *traboules.*

At home, he heard his parents discussing the disappearance of his uncle Isaac, his father's brother. Isaac had been arrested by the 2d Section of the Milice, run by Paul Touvier, who was operating a protection racket with wealthy Jews. Touvier saw the Milice as a way to get rich. Physically, he was more Germanic than many of the Gestapo officers he often dined with, having wavy blond hair, aquiline features, and deep-set, intense blue eyes.

One of Touvier's men got in touch with Robert Nathan's father, André, and told him: "We've got your brother, but it will cost you fifty thousand francs to get him back. We'll meet at the café near your apartment, and we'll bring your brother. And then get out of Lyon. I don't want to see you again." The meeting was set for May 9 at the café. No sooner was his father out the door than Robert's mother said: "You'd better follow him and watch what goes on." So Robert followed his father and positioned himself at the entrance of a *traboule* across from the café. A little while later, two black cars drove up and he saw his father come out of the café, flanked by two men. One of the men was blond and blue-eyed. Robert Nathan thought he must be German. He never saw his father again. Years later, he learned that on the day his father had gone to the café, his uncle Isaac had already been deported and killed in a camp. Paul Touvier, whom he identified as the blond man with his father, didn't even have the criminal's integrity of carrying out his end of the bargain.

In every mountainous region of France, the Maquis was stepping up its activity. Who would have thought the Massif Central would become a battleground, wondered Pierre Trouille, prefect of Corrèze, a mountainous *département* to the west of Lyon. He felt caught between a rock and a hard place, having to remain on good terms with both the Germans and the Maquis. New conditions had to be taken into account. The Maquis was evaluating the behavior of Vichy officials and saying, "We'll talk when the Germans are gone." On the other hand, the Milice was making more noise than the Germans. Its attitude was "we know what to do with these lukewarm prefects—throw them in jail."

There was a good deal of fighting in Corrèze in April 1944, and the prefect had to remain neutral. The Germans were infuriated by their losses. In Tulle, the *préfecture,* the *Kommandant,* wanted fifty hostages because his favorite *aide-de-camp* had been killed. Trouille went to see him and said, "This repression cannot be taken against an innocent population; don't forget that the hostage system always goes against its intended aim." Finally, the Germans settled for four "terrorists." Trouille wrote in his diary: "The dignity of the government is long since gone in a *département* where the prefect exists only because he is tolerated by the Maquis and the Germans."

On April 8 Trouille went to Vichy to report to Laval, who was wearing his customary white tie and chain-smoking Balto cigarettes, which he threw away after two puffs. He seemed crushed by the burdens of his office. They had lunch with Pétain in the dining room of the Hôtel du Parc, which was lined with glass cases filled with the gifts of the faithful. The Marshal would be eighty-eight in a few days, and as Trouille looked at him, still pink-cheeked and clear-eyed, he thought that one could say of him what was said of the dying Victor Hugo: "Near him, one breathed an odor of majesty and death."

Trouille told how the Germans had burned houses and taken hostages in the first week of April. Mme. Pétain exclaimed: "And to think that they try to tell us they've changed since 1914."

"My dear prefect," Pétain said, "I am willing to admit that there are sincere patriots in the Maquis, but there are also Communists and terrorists."

"The immense majority are good people," Trouille said, "fighting for their ideals."

"Very good," responded Pétain's doctor, Ménetrel, "just like

Vichy," and everyone laughed, including Pétain, who said: "I'll come and see you one of these days. Corrèze is the *département* of France where I was most warmly welcomed. . . . but not right away. When things have calmed down." Turning to his wife, he said, "In any case my dear, if we are stopped by the Maquis, try and be nice to them." Then he closed his eyes and fell asleep at the table. The others coughed to wake him up, his eyes opened and he said: "You see, the *Boche* will always be the *Boche,* as I knew him in 1914 and as he is today; but he understands firmness. . . . As for the Maquis, I dealt with the mutineers of 1917, and that was far worse. The Frenchman is mercurial, but he can be brought to reason." And then Trouille realized that the *Maréchal* believed only in his own prestige and authority, outside of and removed from events. As long as there were two gendarmes at the entrance of the Hôtel du Parc to present arms when he came in or went out, he would remain.

The Germans, expecting an Allied landing in May, decided to move Pétain closer to Paris. On May 7, he left Vichy for Voisins, in Seine-et-Oise, after a final lunch at the Hôtel du Parc. As they got into the big American car, Mme. Pétain remarked to her husband: "You're not going to sleep in the car, I hope." Pétain snorted. "Three hundred forty-six kilometers after lunch without my nap, you must be joking! I'll wear your hat, and you wear mine, and you can do the saluting!"

At Voisins Pétain's role was purely ceremonial, illustrating the irrelevance of Vichy. He visited the National School of Shepherds to watch the shearing competition, and went to Versailles to see Queen Amelia of Portugal. Then at the end of May, under German guard, Pétain was moved to the Gothic castle of Lonzat, ten miles from Vichy, where the German troops chopped down magnificent old trees that were older than he was, for their fields of fire.

On May 26, eight hundred American bombers took off from Italy and headed for the Lyon area. They divided into three groups—two hundred to Chambéry, two hundred to Saint-Étienne, and four hundred to Lyon. At 10:40 A.M., the Lyon sirens sounded as from twenty thousand feet the planes dropped several thousand incendiary bombs over the city, randomly hitting civilian and military targets. It was a devastating bombardment, a cyclone of steel and fire, razing entire city blocks, killing 700 civilians, more than had been killed up until then by the Germans in all the hostage-taking and reprisals, and wounding 1,129. One of the doctors who studied the casualties said that half had died of curiosity. Wanting to see what was going on, they had stayed in the street until it was too late. Among the buildings destroyed was the SD head-quarters in the École de Santé, and about a half dozen SD men were killed, including Fritz Hollert, who had served briefly as the chief of the *Einsatzgruppe,* which found new offices on the Place Bellecour. A few days before the bombing, Mireille Guille, a secretary at the École de Santé, saw Barbie and his men torturing an eighteen-year-old boy. She was so revolted that she went to get Hollert, who told them to stop, gave the young man something to drink, and took him to the infirmary. Hollert then reprimanded Barbie on his methods. The bombardment was a blessing for a number of those arrested by the SD, for it destroyed the Gestapo archives and Barbie's men no longer knew who had been charged with what. But for the city of Lyon, it was the worst disaster of the war, and the resistance leader, Alban Vistel, cabled Algiers: LYON BOMBARDMENT, MORAL RESULT CALAMITOUS, POPULATION PAINFULLY INDIGNANT. REPEAT, ENORMOUS SACRIFICES FOR IN-SIGNIFICANT RESULTS.

After the bombing, Pétain was invited to Lyon to visit the wounded and buck up the city's morale. On the drive from Vichy to Lyon on June 5, Pétain wondered, How had it come to this? The reports he was getting told of reprisals all over France, the Germans killing hundreds. And to top it off, they wanted him to give speeches on the radio. However, he was in a relatively cheerful mood, having heard of the capture of Rome, and that a landing in Normandy would take place any day. He began to hum "Tipperary."

Coming in to Lyon, he saw that the walls were still covered with posters showing an Allied snail crawling up the Italian boot. "All propaganda is absurd," Pétain remarked, to no one in particular. "Germany was never able to conduct a two-front war—and today less than ever." There was a reception in the Salon Rouge of the Hôtel de Ville, followed by a speech from the balcony. A meager crowd had gathered to listen to the old man with the seven stars on his *képi,* who told them: "I saw your bombed neighborhood. I saw the abominable destruction. I deplored the attitude of my former Allies. They are conducting themselves like the enemies of a defenseless France. They can crush the nation, but they will never crush the soul of France." In the afternoon, Pétain visited the wounded in the Grange-Blanche Hospital, and had a comforting word for each. He spent the night in the home of friends outside Lyon, and awoke the next morning to hear the news of D Day.

Back in the castle of Lonzat, Pétain did not have much to do. Each morning, the Prussian general von Neubronn, an old duffer close to his age and a veteran of World War I, arrived with maps and different-colored crayons to explain the military situation in Normandy. On July 10 he said that Hitler had fired von Rundstedt, his Commander in Chief in France. "Our generals have a harder time in this war than the last," he said. "There were so many Allied planes in the air that the new Commander in Chief, von Kluge, had to move on foot in the ditches along the hedges."

Vichy now had no bearing on events, on the conduct of the war, or on the excesses of the Milice, which was taking advantage of the general confusion to settle its own scores. The Germans gave the Miliciens a license to kill, and Darnand's men combined with the SD in gangsterlike operations. At the top of their hit list was Jean Zay, who had been minister of education in the Popular Front. Zay had a Jewish father and a Protestant mother, and had been raised a Protestant. But it was not only Zay's partial Jewishness that made him a target. It was an act of youthful rebelliousness, for as a student he had been a pacifist and had written these lines about the French flag, which the right had never let him forget: "I hate your filthy colors. . . . And don't forget that despite your generals and your victories, for me you're just something I wipe my ass with."

Zay had been arrested by Vichy on trumped-up charges in 1940 and was imprisoned in Riom, a town in southwest France where the trials of the Third Republic leaders had been held. The technique for assassinating a man who was in the relative safety of a prison was to arrange for his transfer to another prison for security reasons. The Milice, with the blessing of the Germans, took care of the transfer. But instead of assuring the safety of the prisoner, it carried out his liquidation. On June 20 a black Citroën, with three Miliciens, arrived in Riom to take custody of Jean Zay and supposedly drive him to a prison in Melun, south of Paris. They drove him up a mountain road and shot him. Darnand's cover story was that the car had been attacked by the Maquis.

The reply was not long in coming, and its target was the silver-tongued Philippe Henriot. The popular orator was credited with having singlehandedly limited pro-Gaullist enthusiasm in France. In early June he had spent six days in Germany visiting the destroyed residential areas of Leipzig and Frankfurt. In Berlin he met a fellow demagogue, Joseph Goebbels, who had a bust of Napoleon in his antechamber. Henriot gave a morale-boosting speech to French factory workers, and talked to Sauckel about improving their food rations.

Back in Paris, he went to the Gare de l'Est on June 27 to see his son off to Germany as part of the foreign labor force. Then he went to the movies on the Champs-Élysées with his wife, and then home to the Ministry of Information on the Rue de Solférino, where he dismissed his Corsican bodyguard, who offered to sleep in a cot in the hall. At dawn on June 28, three cars pulled up in front of the ministry, and the men of the resistance *groupe franc,* dressed in Milice uniforms, tricked the concierge into letting them in. They found Henriot in his bedroom and killed him in front of his wife.

Henriot was given a state funeral. There were discussions among the men of Vichy on whether his coffin should be placed in the courtyard of the Hôtel de Ville (Paris city hall), or, more grandly and visibly, on the square in front. The latter location was selected, and 400,000 Parisians, about one fifth of the city's population, filed past his coffin. In her village retreat in Savoie, Gertrude Stein wrote: "The death of Henriot has been an immense excitement. . . . Henriot did perhaps more than anybody to turn Frenchman against Frenchman, he was a very able propagandist, he used the method not of a politician but of a churchman, he had that education . . . and he held the middle classes."

There was bound to be a reprisal for killing Henriot, and it came ten days later. When we last saw Georges Mandel, he had been arrested in Morocco and brought back to France, and interned in the Fort du Portalet in the Pyrénées with Blum, Daladier, Gamelin, and Reynaud, the supposed villains of the Third Republic and the 1940 debacle. "So long as I am in power," Laval vowed, "the prisoners will not be handed over to the Germans." But in November 1942, when the Germans occupied the free zone, Helmut Knochen of the Paris SS personally came to the fort and seized Mandel and Reynaud, who were shipped to Germany.

Mandel ended up in the VIP section of Buchenwald, along with Léon Blum. Conditions were bearable. He had a little house with a radio and books, and could visit Blum as often as he liked. He maintained his dress code, wearing gloves when he went for a walk and the same high stiff collars he had worn in the Chamber of Deputies. But since there was no starch, the collars drooped. He was arrogant with the guards, which was a mistake, for they held back his packages and mail.

On June 30, two days after the death of Henriot, Mandel was told to pack his bags. He was flown to Reims, and from there driven to Paris, where the Germans kept him for three days while they made arrangements with the Milice to use the same tactic as with Jean Zay—transfer from one prison to the other. On June 7 the Germans took Mandel to Santé Prison in Paris, whose director, Baillet, said he could not keep him there, since Mandel was not charged with any offense. This scenario was of course carefully stage-managed, for Mandel, after being refused admission at the Santé, was to be taken by the Milice to the Château des Brosses, near Vichy. Mandel remained at the Santé for all of three hours. The Gestapo dropped him off at two o'clock and the Milice picked him up at five, led by Darnand's number two, Max Knipping, and an SS officer, Schmidt, Knochen's assistant.

Mandel was placed in a car with three Miliciens, and two other cars followed. They drove to the forest of Fontainebleau, where the lead car stalled. One of the Miliciens said, "Something's wrong with the carburetor." "Maybe you're out of gas," Mandel said. They got out of the car and a Milicien lifted the hood. Mandel was peering under the hood when another Milicien fired a burst from his submachine gun and shot him in the back.

It was the worst kind of lawlessness—to abduct men who had served their country in high positions, and then execute them. Laval was horrified, for he could see that the day was coming when the same treatment might be applied to him. On July 12 the Vichy government held one of its last cabinet meetings, during which Laval brought up the murder of Mandel. When Abel Bonnard, the homosexual minister of education, said something sarcastic about Mandel, Laval retorted, "Be quiet. I knew him better than any of you. I was his friend since he was in Clémenceau's cabinet. He was in my cabinet in 1935. . . . I am against political assassination. . . . All this is abominable."

Laval said that Otto Abetz, who was pushing the idea of "quality hostages," had alerted him that Blum, Daladier, Reynaud, and Mandel would be turned over to the French government to be used in exchange for some pro-Vichy officers de Gaulle had sentenced to death in Algiers. Laval told them he had absolutely refused.

Fernand de Brinon, the Vichy ambassador to Paris, interrupted: "I must tell you, *Monsieur le Président,* that Monsieur Abetz disagrees with you on that point. He says that you accepted the delivery, saying simply, 'this is a gift I can do without.' "

Losing his temper and banging his fist on the table, Laval shouted: "I cannot let you say such a thing. Nothing is more foreign to my character. I have no blood on my hands and I never will have. Mandel was delivered by the German authorities to Monsieur Baillet, who did not inform me, and who did not wish to keep Mandel at the Santé Prison for security reason. . . . The Milice, I think, took him to deliver him to the Château des Brosses near Vichy. Then, I don't know exactly what happened. They say that on the way there was a fight and that in this fight Mandel was killed. I reprove these methods in the most absolute manner."

"We are investigating," said Gabolde, the minister of justice. "Mandel's body, shot six times, was taken to the police station at Bonnelles, near Versailles." Once again, Vichy cabinet ministers were powerless to prevent the murder of their former colleagues.

On July 14, 1944, the last Quatorze Juillet holiday of the occupation, a military band under the trees in the big square outside the Hôtel du Parc played marches as it had every Sunday for four years, patriotic marches such as *"Vous N'Aurez Pas l'Alsace et la Lorraine"* ("You Will Not Get Alsace and Lorraine"), while American planes flew overhead. Pétain went to church to pray for his people.

Assassination was in the air. On July 21, nine days after the July 12 cabinet meeting, Pétain and Laval learned that an attempt on Hitler's life by one of his most trusted officers, Lieutenant Colonel Claus von Stauffenberg, had failed. The bomb in Stauffenberg's briefcase, set down next to Hitler at a conference table, had gone off, but a concrete divider under the table had saved the Führer. The question for Pétain and Laval on that day was whether to send Hitler a telegram of congratulations at having escaped death. The cabinet weighed the pros and cons. "Why should I," asked Pétain, "when he didn't even answer my letter about Oradour?" (On June 10, in the village of Oradour-sur-Glane, north of Limoges, a detachment of the SS *Das Reich* Panzer Division massacred the 642 inhabitants, including women and children, in reprisal for the abduction of a *Das Reich* major by the Maquis.) "I'm obligated to send a rather effusive telegram" Laval replied, "for when I was wounded in 1941, Hitler telegraphed me and offered to send the best German surgeon, Professor Sauerbruch. . . . Too bad he wasn't killed. It would have solved a lot of problems."

Three days later, on July 24, Laval received a letter from Georges Mandel's daughter, in which she wrote: "I'm very small and weak compared to you who have the Germans to defend you. I have the French, it's true, which is why I'm not going to ask you to account for what you did, for they will." The irony was that Laval had had nothing to do with Mandel's death, and that Vichy no longer had anything to do with anything.

George Santayana said that those who cannot remember the past are condemned to repeat it. The action at Vercors was a fiasco that repeated the one of the Plateau des Glières in March, but on a larger scale. Once again, it was due to the mistaken notion that a prolonged defense of a mountain redoubt can be undertaken with a limited number of troops. The Vercors was a big, V-shaped plateau between Grenoble and Valence, with the Rhône and Isère rivers forming the two sides of the V. The plateau was thirty miles long and fifteen miles wide, at an altitude of three thousand feet, with steep limestone cliffs that gave the Maquisards an almost feudal sense of safety, as though they could repel an attack by throwing down boiling oil on their enemies. Deep ravines indented the cliffs like the fingers of a hand, and outcroppings of rocks with strange shapes contributed to the plateau's massive, fortresslike appearance. It was mistaken, however, to think of the Vercors as impregnable, for there were a number of approaches to the plateau, in the form of dirt roads, mule tracks, and mountain passes. The Vercors was a natural fortress, with natural and manmade breaches.

After D Day, the Vercors was considered the Maquis's principal base of operations in France. It was a piece of Free France, a Vercors republic, and the word was out that General de Gaulle would land there and address the nation over the radio. The word was also out that London would drop four thousand paratroopers into the Vercors, and the Vercors would stand and fight. They would have the heavy weapons and the manpower. Drawn by the heroic nature of the event, men began to arrive from surrounding cities, from Grenoble and Romans, from Die and Voiron, even from Lyon. It was an epic in the making. They arrived by twos and threes, including two Red Army soldiers, forcibly drafted into the Wehrmacht on the eastern front, who had deserted. To increase their manpower, the Maquisards sent a raiding party to Lyon, and abducted fifty-two Senegalese who served as orderlies in the German officers' mess. The raiders intercepted the bus taking the Senegalese to work and brought them back to the plateau. By mid-June, there were about five thousand men in the Vercors Maquis.

It was also in mid-June that the Germans reacted, capturing the town of Saint-Nizier, the eastern approach to the plateau, near Grenoble. The Milice pushed further into the region, wearing tricolor armbands such as the resistance wore, and shouting, "Don't shoot, comrades"—then opening fire. The Maquis knew it couldn't hold towns like Saint-Nizier. The obvious strategy was to defend the passes, which took a lot of men, because the Vercors was like an island that could be attacked from all sides. Every day, the

Maquis wired London to send more men and more weapons. The Maquisards were also expecting a team of engineers to build a landing strip, and more radio operators, known as "piano players." But after D Day, London had other priorities. Each night the Maquisards listened for the message that would mean a drop was coming: *Le petit chat est mort* (The little cat is dead)—but the little cat did not die.

On June 22 the men on the plateau looked down and saw troop movements on the ring road, *Départementale* 93. It was one of those clear, sunny days with not a cloud in the sky, where you could see, from the top of the plateau, the shadows cast by the trees on the road three thousand feet below. Beyond what they could see for themselves, the men on the plateau also had a good flow of information from all over the region. There was good news and bad news. The bad news was that German gliders had arrived at the Montélimar airport, using tail parachutes to check their speed on landing. The good news was that on June 25, thirty-six Liberator bombers dropped eight hundred containers near Vassieux-en-Vercors, one of the Maquis headquarters. To celebrate the drop, they held a parade. The nurses from the Vercors infirmary wore their starched caps and aprons.

The biggest threat, the men of the Vercors believed, was that on the western edge of the plateau, near the town of Chabeuil, there was an airfield. The Germans were five minutes from the plateau by air, and could bomb it at will. On June 26, Junker 88s, taking off from Chabeuil, bombed and strafed the Glières. Chabeuil became an obsession. Every day the men on the plateau sent a message to London: "For God's sake, bomb Chabeuil." They now realized that they were surrounded, and at the mercy of bombardments, but they lived on hope—of massive troop drops and of the expected Allied landing in the south of France. They did not know that the landing had been put off until August 15.

The Germans were mounting their biggest operation yet, spearheaded by General Karl Pflaum's 157th Alpine Division, veterans of anti-Maquis mountain attacks, lately of the Glières and Jura actions. In addition, Pflaum had under his command a unit of SS glider troops, led by none other than the head of the Lyon *Einsatzkommando,* Lieutenant Colonel Werner Knab; an elite regiment of Alpine commandos (*Gebirgsjäger*), two batteries of mountain guns, air support from the Chabeuil air base, and tank units from the 9th Panzer division out of Valence—in all, twenty thousand men. The planning was in charge of Colonel Schwehr, who spent long hours in his office in Grenoble staring at the big wall map of the Vercors.

The Schwehr plan was a dawn attack from all points of the compass—from the town of Die in the south up toward Vassieux; from Pont-en-Royans in the west and Saint-Nizier in the east; and over the mule-track passes to the north and northeast. Four hours after the launching of the ground attack, glider troops would be dropped on Vassieux. Then there would be a serious mopping-up operation. Colonel Schwehr had a map of the Vercors water sources, from which the Maquisards would get their supply.

London responded to the pleas of the men on the plateau, in a small way. In early July an OSS team of eleven Americans and four Canadians was dropped, and on July 7 the airstrip team finally arrived. An engineer and his men started leveling a three-thousand-foot runway. The engineer spent his days peering through his surveyor sextant, and promised to have the job done in a week.

On July 12 La-Chapelle-en-Vercors, another Maquis headquarters, was bombed. On July 14 seventy-two Flying Fortresses dropped eight hundred containers over Vassieux in broad daylight, which led to more bombing and strafing. On July 15 the Germans blew up a bridge over the Isère River to the west of Pont-en-Royans, and a tunnel at Engins, and closed off two exit roads. The 157th Alpine Division was on the march from Chambéry to Grenoble, and the Panzer units were moving up from Valence. The artillery, some of it horse-drawn, was positioned near the passes. On July 18 the Germans laid mines, set up their machine-gun emplacements and methodically sealed off the remaining escape routes. On July 20 fifteen heavy guns arrived by train from Lyon.

The men of the Vercors could actually watch themselves being boxed in. They were the observers of their coming demise. They knew that they were about to be attacked by a division-strength force armed with tanks, artillery, mortars, and air cover. Only a massive troop drop or an Allied landing in the south would save them, and it was too late for either.

On July 21 the landing-strip workers were finishing their job outside Vassieux, when they saw forty gliders towed by unmarked aircraft in the sky above them. Just in time, they thought, and took off their hats and cheered and waved, and the anti-aircraft machine guns on the airstrip held their fire. When the gliders were released, they swooped down on the strip, and five hundred SS men jumped out of them, firing submachine guns and flamethrowers and throwing grenades, and quickly overwhelmed the Maquisards in Vassieux, taking control of a central point on the plateau even as it was being besieged from all four sides. This surprise action determined the outcome of the battle, although the Germans took some casualties, including Knab, who was badly wounded as he stepped from the lead glider. As a result of Knab's wounds and Hollert's death in the May 26 bombing, Barbie became the interim head of the Lyon SD office.

On July 22 it was over, and one of the Vercors leaders, Eugène Chavant, sent an angry message to London, charging that the men in Algiers and London, who had refused to help them after goading them on, were criminals and cowards. The engineer and his team had finished the airstrip just in time for the German attack, and on July 22 the big three-engine Junker 88 bombers landed to bring in supplies and take out the German wounded. On that second day of the battle, the line crumbled, the Vercors plateau was invested, and it was every man for himself, as it had been in the Glières, and they all tried to slip past the German patrols over the passes.

One of those who fled was Captain Conus, a strapping, bearded Colonial Infantry officer, who had been a big-game hunter in Chad. On the night of the twenty-first, under a torrential rain, he was heading east toward Corrençon when he saw a German patrol and had to backtrack. The next day, with a guide, he headed south toward the Pas de l'Ane (Donkey's Pass). The guide stepped on a mine and was badly wounded, but Conus continued on his way, spending the night in a shepherd's hut. On the twenty-third, he headed south by southeast, blessing the fog that allowed him to slip by a German patrol. On the twenty-fourth, he was approaching the village of Saint-Guillaume, close to exhaustion, when he was surrounded by Germans and taken prisoner.

These were men of the 157th Alpine, who turned Conus over

to the SD for questioning. The SD took him and five other prisoners to a farm, where he was singled out as the leader. They told
him they would put his eyes out, and jabbed at his face with the
pointed metal tip of an Alpine cane. He bobbed his head so that
the tip bit into his brow. Then they pulled his arms behind him,
dislocating both his shoulders, as they constantly repeated the
question: "Are you from London or Algiers?" At nine that night,
they made the prisoners empty their pockets and put them on a
bus with fifteen German soldiers that took them to an old cement
works outside Saint-Guillaume. Conus realized that the only reason for having that many Germans on the bus was to make up a
firing squad. Everyone got off and walked along the edge of a
ravine until they reached a meadow. The firing squad lined up
sixty feet away, and the *Feldwebel* (sergeant) cried out, "The first
two." Two prisoners rose and walked over to the firing squad.
Conus saw them drop to their knees, then they were shot in the
back. The *Feldwebel* called out, "The next two," and the same
scene was repeated.

Conus had noticed that the German sergeant, after calling out
the victims, put his pistol back in its holster. He told himself the
following: "I am exhausted by the days of walking, my shoulders
are killing me, but I am not going to let myself be gunned down
like a dog." One of the Germans guarding him spotted a medal
around his neck. "Catholic?" he asked, with an accent that Conus
recognized as Slavic. Conus answered "If you fear God, miss me."
The soldier made a sign indicating that he did not approve of what
he was being made to do.

"The last two," the *Feldwebel* called out. Conus pretended that
it was very painful to get up, and waited until the sergeant's pistol
was back in its holster. Then he jumped down the thirty-foot ravine past his guard, who fired without hitting him. Conus's fall
was broken by a tree. He crossed a stream, found a hollow in the
brambles, and covered himself with mud and dead leaves. The
Germans followed and lined up to search the area, but night was
falling and they soon gathered in a circle. Conus overheard them
saying that they were getting the dogs. In the half-light, crouching
in the brambles, he managed to slip by two sentries and climbed
back up the ravine, walking away as fast as he could, heading

southwest toward Oisans, directing himself by the stars as the evening turned into a brilliantly clear night.

He came to a village, thinking, "What a sight I must be." His clothes were in rags, his face bloodied by the cane, his arms and chest scratched by the brambles. He looked like a creature escaped from someone's nightmare. But the local priest took him in and cleaned him up, and delivered him the next day to another resistance group in the area. Conus sent the following telegram to London: ARRESTED. TORTURED. SHOT. IN GOOD HEALTH.

In the first day of the fighting, on July 21, it had been decided to evacuate the field hospital set up by Dr. Fernand Ganimède in a house on the edge of Saint-Martin-en-Vercors, above Vassieux. In this house there were 120 wounded, including some stretcher cases, seven nurses, Dr. Ganimède, two other physicians, Fischer and Ullman, and a Jesuit chaplain, Father Yves de Montcheuil. They all headed south toward Die in buses with the seats removed, somehow avoiding the Germans, hoping to place the wounded in the Catholic hospital in the town. But the Mother Superior told them that the Germans were on the way. Someone thought of the Grotte de la Luire, a huge cavern with a twenty-foot-high ceiling in the side of the Montagne de Beurre, about five miles north of Die. With its extensive network of connecting passages and smaller caves, the cavern was big enough to hide the more seriously wounded. The others, those who were able to walk, took their leave.

Ganimède went back up the twisting mountain road in the bus with the seven nurses, the two other doctors, the priest, and twenty-six wounded, of which eleven were on stretchers. They reached the Rousset Pass at four thousand feet and went onto a dirt road, which became so steep and wooded that they had to walk the last sixty feet carrying the stretcher cases, who were then laid out in the huge grotto on slabs of rock. Among the wounded were four German soldiers—in fact, they were conscripted Poles—and a member of the OSS team, Chester Myers, whose appendix Dr. Ganimède had removed two days before.

The mouth of the cave was hidden by trees. It was an ideal hiding place, and the doctors established as near normal a hospital routine as they could. Water was no problem. It dripped from the ceiling, and could be disinfected with potassium permanganate. For light there were candles. The doctors washed and dressed wounds, administering what medicines they had. Peasants brought food after dark. The nurses changed into ordinary clothes, just in case.

Father de Montcheuil celebrated a candle-lit Mass. With the men on the stretchers, the slow drip of the water, and the candles throwing moving shadows against the walls, it was like a scene from the days of the early Christians who had had to practice their faith in secret.

On July 25 mopping-up operations came close enough to the grottoes that they could hear dogs barking, and at night see flares in the sky and tracer bullets being fired into the underbrush. On the morning of July 27, Dr. Ganimède was awakened by the sound of a Fieseler-Storch reconnaissance plane circling the grotto. It wasn't just passing overhead, but circling back over and over.

As it happened, the Grotte de la Luire was on German staff maps. The plane had been sent to check on reports of activity there, and a detachment that afternoon went up the dry bed of the Luire stream. By following the streambed they reached the cave. At 4:30 P.M., a gray-capped head appeared in the opening to the cavern followed by fifteen more soldiers, visibly nervous, their fingers on the triggers of their submachine guns. The SD lieutenant in charge shouted, *"Tout le monde debout"* ("Everyone on your feet"), which had its humorous aspect, in view of the stretcher cases. The suspicious lieutenant approached one of the men on stretchers and pulled off his bandages to see if they were real.

At the same time, the four German wounded, having recognized men from their unit, began shouting, *"Kameraden"* and *"Nicht schiessen! Hier is eines Krankenhaus! Wir sind gefangene! Sie haben uno gepflegt!"* ("Don't shoot! It's a hospital! We're prisoners! They took care of us!").

Several nurses showed their ID cards, but the SD lieutenant, speaking in French, said: "It's useless to try and explain, your papers are false, you are terrorists, and you will be exterminated, men and women." They were all taken to an abandoned farm in the village of Rousset. There, without further ado, twenty-one of the twenty-two non-German wounded were shot. The stretcher cases were shot as they lay, including one who was pissing blood from a bullet in the groin. Those who could stand were lined up against a wall. The only one spared was the OSS man, who was a curiosity, the first American they had seen in the war.

The SD lieutenant wanted to kill the priest and the doctors and the nurses as well, but a Wehrmacht doctor intervened, pointing out that they had attended to German wounded and threatening to file a report if they were summarily shot. So the doctors, the chaplain, and the nurses were taken the next day to Grenoble for questioning. Dr. Ganimède, who was in his seventies, was released in view of his advanced age, but the two other doctors and the chaplain were shot. The nurses agreed on a cover story. They would say that they had been on vacation in the Vercors when they were forcibly recruited to serve with the Maquis. Cecile Goldet, at forty-three the oldest of the seven, was asked, "Would you nurse German soldiers?" "Of course," she replied. "Then we will send you to be a nurse on the eastern front," her interrogator replied. She and the six other nurses, Rosine Bernheim, France Pinhas, Marie Romana, Suzanne Siveton, Odette Malossane, and Anita Winter, were taken to Lyon's Montluc Prison.

While large-scale battles were being fought in the surrounding region, the city of Lyon, too, was a battleground that summer, and the undermanned German police resorted to free-lance "antiterrorist" teams of Frenchmen, who worked as much for their own profit as for their employer. These men were assorted misfits, often recruited form the *pègre* (underworld) of Lyon, who were only too happy to be empowered do to legally what they had previously gone to jail for, stealing and killing. Under the cover of being true nationalists, that is to say anti-Bolshevik and anti-Semitic, they roamed the city doing the Germans' dirty work and filling their pockets while they were at it. It was the world upside down, where the gangsters had become the policemen.

Chief among them in notoriety and entrepreneurial zeal was Francis André, known as *gueule tordue* (twisted face). As a child, he had been disfigured in a car accident. A facial nerve had been cut, reshuffling his features in a lasting grimace. His left cheek popped out as if it had a golf ball in it, and his mouth was pulled to one side. In school he was so mercilessly teased that he dropped out and became a drifter and a burglar. After two arrests, he joined the Communist party, then made the classic passage from left to right. For he admired Jacques Doriot's neofascist Parti Populaire Français (PPF), and when he met Doriot, and his hero treated him with respect, he was completely won over. He was ready to do anything for Doriot and, while remaining a Communist, he became a paid informant for the PPF. In 1940, having been rejected by the army, André volunteered for the misguided French Legion that fought for the Germans on the eastern front. Returning to his native Lyon in early 1943, he offered his services to the SD, and was put in touch with August Moritz, the head of Section Six (Intelligence and Political Affairs).

Moritz was a short man with thin blond hair and a round, puffy face, who walked with his chest leaning forward. Moritz recognized Francis André as a useful henchman. He was a local boy who knew the lay of the land and could find addresses easily. He had connections in a number of towns. He was unscrupulous, with a kind of low shrewdness, and had a combination of forcefulness and congeniality that would allow him to recruit men like himself and keep them in line.

Moritz funded Francis André to recruit a team, and soon André was making arrests. He made so many of them that in June 1944 he arrested a man in the resistance who had on his person a leaflet with André's photograph on it and the caption SHOOT ON SIGHT. Francis André recruited his team among the criminals serving sentences in Montluc Prison. He recruited René Mazot, who had been jailed in October 1943 for the theft of industrial diamonds. He got Mazot sprung and took him to the Ambassadeurs restaurant for dinner, where he told him: "Since the terrorists are killing our pals, I'm avenging our dead and scaring the shit out of the others. I've got a solid team and my boys don't have to worry about being pulled out of bed by the feet in the middle of the night. And let me tell you that none of those I shot, be they bartenders or senators, keep me from sleeping."

As he drank more wine, Francis André began to brag about his *belles affaires* (big deals). With the Jews, although he turned some over to the Germans, he held others for ransom. "You find a Jew,"

301

he explained, "and you knock on his door, and you say, 'You will have a lot of trouble if you don't get your papers in order.' Usually he coughs up. One of them said his money was in the bank. I took him to the bank and helped him make a withdrawal."

Another recruit was Charles Goetzmann, an Alsatian, twice convicted for theft. He spent some time in the Bron insane asylum outside Lyon. His doctor there got him a job as a baker for the Germans, but he found the work too hard and started forging ration cards instead. He was caught and sent to Montluc, where Francis André found him. Goetzmann and his men were Jew hunters, operating mainly in the suburb of Saint-Fons. His main informant was a Mme. Cassy, a bitter, vindictive woman who had quarreled with her Jewish neighbors and who said, *"Il faut en finir avec cette sale race"* ("We have to end it with this dirty race"). Goetzmann was so low on the scale that he didn't have a car, so he and those he arrested had to take the streetcar back to Gestapo headquarters. He preferred to go after the elderly, because they didn't give him any trouble. After making an arrest, he would loot the apartment. His own apartment had a room stacked with radios. He was paid by the head—five thousand francs for every Jew he brought in . One time he went to arrest a family called Cohen, husband and wife and daughter. The husband slit his throat with a straight razor, saying, "Better to die than fall into your hands." Goetzmann thought, "There goes five thousand francs."

Francis André's right-hand man was twenty-three-year-old Max Payot, known as *le beau* Max, a high-school dropout who had been involved in the black market in 1941. In 1943 he joined André's team, "for something to do." Max specialized in handling informers (*indics*), which gave him a low opinion of human nature, for in his experience people were always selling one another out. He had seen a man sold by his brother for five thousand francs, and another, an unfaithful husband, sold by his wife, who came to the SD office personally to draw a diagram of their house. Another time it was the landlady of a resistance leader, who sold him for five thousand francs and permission to bring him a *colis* (package) in prison. In Lyon in 1944, being an *indic* had become a profession. A Jew had even come to Payot offering to turn in other

Jews. The owner of the La Poterne restaurant, faced with a black market charge, offered to finger some of his customers if the charge was dropped, asking only that they be arrested outside as they were leaving. Informing was a form of currency: "Who will you give us?" A woman, whose husband in the resistance had been arrested, offered to give Payot one of his colleagues if he were released. Payot was certain that he had observed every conceivable kind of treachery, and wondered whether it was the times or the nature of his countrymen.

Now, in August 1944, the SD was concerned about railroad sabotage. With the Allies breaking out of the Normandy pocket and moving toward Paris, German reinforcements had to be brought up by train from other parts of France. It was crucial to the German defense that the rails not be cut, and that there should be enough locomotives, passenger cars, and, even more important, flatcars capable of carrying tanks under bridges from one part of France to the other.

But the *cheminots* (railway workers) were crippling German military movements by cutting the rails, blowing switches, and rubbing abrasive paste into the axle bearings of flatcars, which made them seize up after a few miles. Every railroad yard in France had a sign that read: *AVERTISSEMENT: PEINE DE MORT CONTRE LES SABOTEURS* (Warning: Death Penalty for Saboteurs). And nowhere was rail sabotage conducted on a more intensive scale than in Lyon. In the suburb of Oullins, there was a sprawling SNCF (national railroad) repair yard employing 2,500 workers. Among those workers was a group of about twenty saboteurs who devoted themselves to destroying whatever the other workmen repaired.

On July 30 they blew up the last remaining crane capable of removing an overturned locomotive from the track. A few days later, the sixteen members of the crane crew were arrested, and gave some names under torture. The mission of going to Oullins and arresting the saboteurs was given to Francis André and his men.

On August 9 at 3 P.M., there were knocks on the iron door of the Oullins repair yard, and armed men in blue uniforms entered, flanked by German soldiers who remained as sentries at the gate.

The workers in the shop were brought into the courtyard. Francis André had a list of names and proceeded with a roll call, but after each name he called, there was silence. The workers stood silently, their faces blank, not answering. Francis André told the supervisors to designate the workers whose names he called, or they would be taken hostage. When he called the first few names, the supervisors also remained silent and motionless. Francis André told them he'd had enough. He was going to call out one more name, and if that worker was not identified by his supervisor, he was going to arrest all the supervisors, and they would never see their wives and children again. And he called out the name of Marius Chardon. At first there was silence. André called out his name again. Chardon's supervisor, a man named Hébert, went up to Chardon and said, "They've been calling you for a while, you'd better go see what they want."

Marius Chardon was arrested, but asked if he could go to his locker to change his clothes. He was buying time, but he was also taking a risk, for in his locker there were two detonators. A strike had been called for the following day, and Chardon was planning to blow up the tracks of the Number 26 streetcar line, to give workers an excuse not to come to work. Two of André's men escorted him to his locker, where they found the detonators. Their attention momentarily distracted, Chardon made a run for it, but slipped on the smooth locker-room floor, and was hit with a submachine gun burst and killed.

In the meantime, two other men in Francis André's team had ventured into the repair shop. Marcel Chaffard, who was working there at the time, saw the blue uniforms and thought they were the resistance men he had been expecting to arrive and blow up some of the equipment. "Come on," he said, "I'll show you where it is." The men grabbed him, laid him on his stomach on the marking-off slab, and struck him with a grooved iron bar. When he wouldn't talk, they called Francis André, who told Chaffard to take off his trousers. Then André squeezed Chaffard's private parts in a vise, which he proceeded to twist shut. Chaffard started screaming. Francis André took some combination pliers and tried to pull out some of his teeth. One of the others suggested they cut off his ears, but another observed that it would be too noticeable. André took out his watch and told Chaffard he had five minutes, after which he would be shot. Still Chaffard would not talk, so André's men took him to the Place Bellecour with a few others they had arrested. On the drive in, they searched Chaffard's wallet and found a snapshot of his wife and kids and started telling each other what they would do to Chaffard's wife when they got her alone in a bedroom. After turning Chaffard and the others over to the SD, Francis André told his men they had done a good day's work and took them to the Perroquet for a round of drinks. Then they went to the Ambassadeurs and the Grillon, where they broke the musicians' instruments, tore the place up, and left without paying.

After the war, in 1946, Francis André was captured and tried. At his trial he took a cocky attitude, saying, "There are a lot of people who are going to sleep nights once I'm gone." He also said that "August Moritz was responsible for all the political murders committed in the Lyon region from the end of March 1943 through 1944." And he added: "I also knew Barbie well, who was the real head of the SD in Lyon, a very hard and sanguinary person. He directed most of the operations against the Maquis, and conducted a veritable massacre of peasants and *réfractaires* [STO draft dodgers]." Francis André was found guilty, sentenced to death, and shot on March 9, 1946.

In August, Montluc Prison was overcrowded from all the arrests in the previous months. For the Germans, the end was approaching. The Allies were about to land in the south of France and enter Paris. But with everything collapsing around them, the Germans became more fanatical than ever. They would be leaving Lyon in a matter of days, but in the meantime it was business as usual. On orders from Paris, the deportation of Jews continued. And in August, Barbie's Section Four managed to round up one last train, which they decided to fill with Montluc prisoners to relieve the prison congestion. This departure was organized in spite of the very great difficulties of rail travel at a time of widespread sabotage.

From her cell on the evening of August 10, Harriet Berman, an employee of the UGIF, noticed unusual activity in the courtyard.

Not only prison guards but Gestapo men in civilian clothes who were huddling over lists in their hands. She realized a deportation was in the works, and she found herself hoping that she was on a list. For Barbie had told her that she would be shot, and she preferred to be deported.

At 5 A.M. on August 11, there was an early roll call *avec bagages* for 629 prisoners, including 331 Jews, who were summoned from their cells and lined up in the courtyard, where covered trucks were waiting. Daniel Weill had worked for a furrier in the Croix-Rousse. One day the Gestapo burst into his workplace and made him take down his trousers. When they saw he was circumcised, they slapped him so hard they almost unhinged his jaw. Next to Weill in the *Baraque aux Juifs* there was a badly tortured man who murmured, "I think my misfortunes are over." The following day he was taken out and shot as a hostage. So Weill, standing in the prison courtyard in the summer dawn, was glad to be leaving Montluc because in his mind nothing could be worse than the *Baraque aux Juifs,* where they were all hostages.

For many in the courtyard, deportation seemed like an attractive option, for it meant escape from the prison's jammed, lice-infested cells, escape from the Gestapo and its torture sessions, escape from the firing squads and mass graves. Josette Leroi, who had been arrested on July 15 for hiding Jews, believed they were going to a work camp. She had been taken to the cellar in the Place Bellecour for questioning. She had seen a woman about her age, twenty-four, come into the cellar drenched and bleeding, smelling of alcohol, with no nails on her fingers. The woman opened her shirt, showing cigarette burns on her breasts. The woman had fainted in the *baignoire,* and the SD had given her alcohol to revive her. Then Josette herself had been questioned. The morning of July 15, before her arrest, she had awakened with the feeling of euphoria of someone who feels good about their body, but after being questioned in the cellar of the Place Bellecour, she knew she would never have that feeling again. So now, amid the sweeps in the hallways and the cries of *schnell, schnell,* she thought, "Hope is a thing you can hold in the palm of your hand." When she looked around the courtyard at her companions in misery, she was just as glad to be leaving.

Standing in the courtyard also were the seven nurses from the Grotte de la Luire in striped blouses and clean blue skirts. One of them, Rosine Bernheim, who was Jewish, had been declared Aryan when questioned in Grenoble because of her blue eyes and blond hair. At Montluc she was placed in a cell with a young woman named Monique, who cried incessantly because she had been raped by the Germans and was afraid of becoming pregnant.

Also present was Renée Pin, who had been arrested on June 24 in Villeurbanne because bandages made in England had been found in her apartment. Barbie had questioned her, telling her, "France is the seventh beast after the toad." She had spent two months in solitary, and that morning, August 11, a German guard had unlocked her handcuffs and said, "You are sentenced to death but since we need labor we are sending you to Germany." So she too was relieved.

Renée Belot, arrested on March 27 with her husband, Fernand, who helped put out the newspaper *Combat,* was questioned by Barbie. He told her that her husband refused to talk. She said, "Perhaps he will talk to me." Renée was given five questions to ask him and was taken to his cell. The sentry closed the door to leave them alone, but he was quiet and withdrawn and seemed to resent her having come to question him, which she had only agreed to do so she could see him. "What shall I give as the answers to these questions?" she asked. "Tell the officer that all his questions will be answered after the war," he replied. When she repeated this to Barbie, he said, "If that's the way it is, we'll shoot him." "But why," she asked, "since we are neither Jews, nor Communists, nor terrorists?" Barbie replied, "You are worse than Jews, or Communists, or terrorists, because with your newspaper you are guiding the hands of the terrorists." So that morning in the courtyard, she was looking for her husband, but did not see him. She hoped they would be deported together, but he was not in any of the lines, and she had a premonition she would not see him again. She had not been told that her husband had been shot more than two months earlier, on June 9.

For Isaac Latherman, deportation was a cruel blow. He had been in the Dordogne, hiding out from the labor inspectors who wanted him for the STO. His wife was pregnant, and in July he heard that she was in labor. So when he came back to Lyon to see the baby, the concierge of his building turned him in. Now he was in the Montluc courtyard, about to be deported to an unknown destination, leaving behind his wife and newborn child.

Once the roll call was taken, the 629 Montluc inmates were herded into trucks and driven to the Perrache railroad station, where a train was waiting.

On August 13 Lyon was bombed again; one of the targets was the Bron airport. Two days later came Operation Anvil, the Allied landing in the Provence. In Lyon Barbie and his men were destroying archives. Time was running out and they also had to do something about the remaining prisoners in Montluc so they would not be able to tell what had gone on there. The train that left on August 11 had gotten rid of 629 people, but there were no more trains, and still several thousand inmates.

On August 17 fifty Jews were removed from the *Baraque aux Juifs*. They were told they were being assigned to a work detail at the Bron airport to fill bomb craters from the August 13 bombardment. When they got to Bron they were given shovels, and a truck arrived with a load of soil. Otto Huber, an Alsatian, was detached from the city hall of Décines, the closest town, to act as interpreter. Huber saw a Jew with bandages on both arms, and said to Adjutant Brau, the noncom in charge, "This man can't work." Brau replied, "Tonight, he won't feel a thing."

At 6 P.M. Brau asked for twenty volunteers among the guards to accompany the prisoners, presumably back to Montluc. Otto Huber was surprised by the guards' reaction. They volunteered with enthusiasm, laughing and talking about "making some music." He went home at that point, but the next day he overheard a conversation between Adjutant Brau and a sergeant. Brau mimed the actions of a man who has been hit and whose body turns before falling. Otto Huber understood from the conversation that the fifty Jews from Montluc had been pushed into unfilled bomb craters and machine-gunned. Then a few shovelfuls of dirt had been thrown over their bodies. Adjutant Brau then mimed standing on the edge of a crater and kicking a little dirt in with the side of his foot.

On August 21 Joseph Bouellat, a Bron airport supervisor, was in Hangar 68 with his work crew repairing one of the planes damaged in the August 13 bombing when a truck and a Citroën drove up. A few minutes later he heard the sounds of automatic gunfire, and one of the men in his crew said, "Look boss, they're shooting people." Bouellat went to the open hangar door and saw eight men being pulled out of the truck by their hair and jackets, and thrown into a crater, where they were gunned down. Then some dirt was thrown over the bodies. Bouellat looked no more and went back to his work. Soon a German sentry came over to the hangar, wanting to chat. "It's terrible what they're doing, killing them like that," Bouellat said. "It's nothing," replied the sentry, "it's only Jews, good to make sausage for dogs." Bouellat saw the same thing several times after that: The car and the truck heading in reverse toward Hangar 68, the soldiers standing around a bomb crater, firing their weapons.

After the liberation of Lyon on September 2, a resistance team found the mass grave at Bron airport. Then it was up to the police to identify the badly decomposed remains and notify the families. One of those they contacted was Robert Nathan's mother, who had just given birth to another child. They asked her to identify a belt buckle, the sleeve of a shirt, and a wedding band with the names and the date engraved on the inside. That was what was left of her husband, André, who had been removed from Montluc Prison on August 17 and shot at Bron, four days before the release of the Montluc prisoners.

On December 20, 1940, Césarine Descotte, the faithful maid of Edouard Herriot, the perennial mayor of Lyon, went as usual to get the morning papers, and scanned the headlines as she walked up the cours d'Herbouville in front of his home. Handing the dailies to Herriot, she said, "*Monsieur* will see in the newspaper that he is no longer mayor of Lyon." Herriot knew that Pétain did not like him, but to be dismissed by Vichy and expelled from the Lyon city hall, which he had occupied without interruption for thirty-five years—well, it was a blow. He went to the Hôtel de Ville one last time to get his personal papers, wondering where were all the people who used to fill the hallways asking for favors.

Herriot retired to his country house of Brotel, thirty kilometers east of Lyon, with his wife, his maid, and his spaniel, Fouquet. Shortly afterward, Vichy asked him as former president of the National Assembly (for he was a mayor and a deputy), to make up a list of Jewish deputies. Herriot went to Vichy, asked to see Pétain, and told him: "I don't know any Jewish deputies, or Catholic deputies, or free-thinking deputies. I only know elected deputies."

After the Allied landings in North Africa, Edouard Herriot was sent north to Evaux-les-Bains, a spa for rheumatics, where he either had or feigned symptoms of mental illness, and so he was moved to Maréville, an asylum near Nancy. Herriot was afflicted, or pretended to be, with a particular disorder, the fear of being poisoned. This man with a once voracious appetite now refused to eat. His clothes hung loosely on his shrunken frame.

And now, in August 1944, with Vichy a ghostly presence, Laval was in Paris, his inventive mind still plotting. What if the two houses of parliament, the Chamber of Deputies and the Senate, which had never been formally dissolved, were brought back into existence? What if they met in a formal session in Paris or Versailles and took a vote of confidence that would pave the way for the formation of a new government? It would short-circuit de Gaulle, who was now approaching Paris. Or, once the Germans were gone, it would be a way of forming a coalition government with the general.

And what better person was there to start this process rolling than Herriot, the distinguished president of the National Assembly, who was on good terms with both the Russians and the Americans, and who was up in Maréville pretending to be crazy among those pretending to be sane, which was a sign of great wisdom. So on August 12, Laval personally drove to Maréville, entered Herriot's room at the asylum, and said to him, "You are free." Herriot was completely taken aback. He had always felt a little contemptuous of Laval, of whom he had once written, "His eyelids dropped like the shutters in a brothel." But he was not about to turn down this offer of freedom, and he was willing to cooperate with the Vichy premier up to a point.

Laval drove Herriot back to Paris and put him up at the Hôtel de Ville, as a guest of the prefect of the Seine *département*. On August 15 he told Herriot his plan: to convene the National Assembly, to resign as premier, and to ask Herriot to replace him. Herriot replied that the whole thing was unrealistic. They could not do it without Jeanneney, the president of the Senate. Meanwhile, in Paris, the resistance was concerned that Herriot seemed to be collaborating with the hated Laval. In Germany von Ribbentrop vetoed the Laval plan for a new government, and Himmler ordered Herriot arrested.

On August 16, the day before the Bron airport massacre, as battles were being fought all around them, Laval gave a lunch party at his Paris residence, the Hôtel Matignon. Invited were Mr. and Mrs. Herriot, Otto Abetz, and Laval's daughter, Josée. Laval knew that his attempt to assure a transmission of power by convening the National Assembly was doomed. He knew what was in store for him. He had been ordered to go under German guard to Belfort in eastern France, fifty miles from the German border, where Pétain would join him. After that, he could see, down the road, exile and the firing squad. Herriot would be heading eastward, too, and Abetz was being recalled to Berlin, having displeased his Führer. And yet, on this fine summer day, with the French doors of the dining room opening out on the garden's tended and orderly flowerbeds, cares were momentarily forgotten. Herriot looked out at the garden and said, "The first time I came here, I saw a white blackbird." Abetz asked Herriot if it was true that in Lyon there was a statue of a German. "You're probably talking about 'the Good German' [a famous statue on the banks of the Saône of an unthreatening German civilian]," Herriot replied. "Oh, so there really is a good German?" Abetz rejoined. Herriot recalled that at Oxford in the thirties he had been given a doctorate at the same time as the German scientist Max Planck, developer of the quantum theory. Every word spoken during the ceremony had to be in Latin, and Herriot wondered whether the scientific terms Planck would need for his speech existed in Latin. To his astonishment, Planck began quoting passages from *De Rerum Natura* (On the Nature of Things), in which the Roman philosopher Lucretius argues that everything in man, including the soul, is made up of atoms, so that consciousness ends with death.

The conversation now turned to their imminent departure. The first stage of the trip was Belfort, where Herriot and Laval would join Pétain. Herriot said he would never be able to shake Pétain's hand. "For you, Laval, it's different," he added. "You either liked him or you used him. But for me, to shake the hand of Pétain, never. He is the enemy of the Republic. I have no more confidence in him than I have in de Gaulle. They are both dominated by ambition. That is why I came back to Paris. And now I am being taken away by force."

Abetz seemed suddenly in low spirits, reminded perhaps of his own fate, and so to lighten the atmosphere, they began telling anecdotes. Laval and Herriot recalled statesmen they had known in Geneva during the League of Nations days. Laval pulled out a watch in a platinum case that Nicholas Titulesco, then Roumanian foreign minister and president of the League of Nations, had given him. He remarked with some pride that it was the thinnest watch ever made, and recalled that upon receiving it, he had thought, "After all the trouble Titulesco has caused me, he's giving me a watch—it should have been a grandfather clock." "Yes," said Herriot, his old rivalry with Laval rekindled, "I knew all about the watch, and when I remarked to Titulesco, 'So you gave a watch to Laval,' he sent me one just like it." Not to be outdone, Laval retorted, "Yours isn't as thin as mine. Mine is unique—one of a kind." Laval's daughter Josée wanted to kick her father under the table, but she was too far away. It was a relaxed and convivial lunch, however, with everyone making an effort to be normal in a time of crisis.

On August 17 Laval presided, in Paris, over the last cabinet meeting of the Vichy government. He told the ministers that the Germans were demanding that they move to Belfort, adding: "As for me, I refuse to go to Belfort or transfer the government anywhere. . . . If the Germans want to take us by force, it will be, as far as I am concerned, as a prisoner, and not as chief of the government." But Abel Bonnard, the minister of education, said it was a good idea. To which Dr. Raymond Grasset, the minister of health, replied, "I understand perfectly that you want to go. But I also ask you to understand my state of mind, which is very different from yours." Bonnard said, "It's because of my affection for you that I am telling you that we must go. To stay is to be delivered to the animals. Also, it's cowardly to hide. Only fools think of not leaving." Jean Bichelonne, the minister of production, said with sadness, "We must tell ourselves that we are perhaps leaving for twenty years." To which Bonnard retorted, "Our colleague is talking like a poet, are you not, dear friend?" Gabolde, the minister of justice, added: "Yes, but to stay is to be condemned to live several months in a cave, without a ration card." Abetz's arrival was announced. Laval met with him outside, and returned to tell the ministers that the Germans would take them by force if necessary. The cabinet left on the following day. Only Dr. Grasset refused to go, which was a point in his favor when the Vichy ministers went on trial after the war. Bonnard, whose main achievement was the creation of two chairs of anti-semitic studies at the Sorbonne, regretted bitterly that he could not take along his porcelain collection. Each minister had a car with a German driver, and when Bonnard got into his, he spotted his colleague Paul Marion, the secretary of state for information, and remarked: "That Marion has all the luck. His driver is as handsome as a god."

Pétain and Herriot and the ministers gathered in Belfort, waiting for the next stage of the trip. Herriot was taken to a residence near Potsdam, from which he was freed by the Russians in April 1945, much diminished by his imprisonment. But when he returned to Lyon, his flirtation with Laval was forgiven and he was reelected mayor of the city. Given the speed of the Allied advance that August, the rest of the Belfort group was taken to the Hohenzollern castle of Sigmaringen, a short hop from Belfort, fifty miles south of Stuttgart, on the Danube and close to the Swiss border. Laval refused to cooperate in the formation of a French government-in-exile. In April 1945, with Patton's army approaching, Laval and his wife and two of his ministers, Gabolde and Bonnard, flew to Spain. Franco allowed Laval a three-month stay; then he was flown to the American zone of occupation in Austria and handed over to the French. As for Pétain, in April 1945 he moved to Switzerland. On April 26 he voluntarily returned to France, where he was arrested shortly after his eighty-ninth birthday. He was put on trial in July 1945 and sentenced to death. But in August de

Gaulle commuted the sentence, from soldier to soldier, and Pétain was sent to a prison on the Île d'Yeu in the Atlantic off the coast of Vendée, to finish out his life. He lived on for five and a half years, dying on July 23, 1951, at the age of ninety-five.

On August 19 Max Payot, Francis André's right-hand man, was assigned to an operation in Montluc Prison personally commanded by Klaus Barbie. One hundred and ten inmates were assembled in the courtyard that morning, among them some who had been badly tortured, such as Abbé Boursier, a priest in the resistance who had been arrested in May by André's gang. They had arrived in his church in Villeurbanne as he was saying Mass. They let him continue while they went into the vestry, where they discovered a radio operator with his headset on. In the church organ they found English submachine guns and pistols with silencers. During the questioning, Boursier had his ears cut off and one eye pulled out.

Now, Max Payot was tying the inmates' hands two by two and helping them into trucks. They were told they were being transferred to another prison. The trucks drove to the suburb of Saint-Genis-Laval, a few miles southwest of Lyon, and stopped at the abandoned fort of Côte-Lorette. The passengers disembarked and were herded into an empty guardhouse. Some of the SS went to the upper floor of the guardhouse. Payot stayed in the kitchen, and then led the prisoners up the stairs. Upon reaching the top, they received two bullets in the back of the neck. Payot could hear the bodies falling and saw blood leaking through the planks in the kitchen ceiling. Most of them went quietly, Payot noted, but an old woman with a wrinkled face said to one of the SS, "I'm dying for France, but you, you bastard, you'll rot in hell."

When the upper floor was piled high with bodies, the executions continued downstairs until there was a pile four feet high. Sometimes the SS had to climb up on the pile to finish off victims who were still moaning. Soldiers then brought phosphorus bricks, which they doused with gasoline, lit, and threw on top of the bodies. Payot went outside and watched the house burn. He saw one of the victims, a woman, who had not been killed, appear at the second-floor window with panic on her face, shouting for help.

The Germans fired a few bursts at the window. The woman stood there, her face seeming to melt from her skull like wax, then fell backward. The Germans who had been in the house were wiping blood and bits of brains from their uniforms. Smoke rose from the incinerated house, and Max Payot had to move away because of the smell.

In the meantime, in Savoie, the Maquis was on the attack. The men came down from the mountains and surrounded the German garrisons at Thonon and Chamonix, and the garrisons surrendered on August 17. On August 18 it was Annemasse's turn, and on the nineteenth, Annecy's. The Maquis had practically liberated Savoie. Leading these operations was the unheroic-looking Yves Farge, with his squat figure, thick glasses, disorderly gray hair, and pipe.

Farge, whom we last saw on a streetcar in Lyon in 1940, privately railing against the pro-German proclivities of some of his compatriots, was now a regional commissioner of the Republic. He had been appointed by General de Gaulle to take part in an interim government for the period between the departure of the Germans and his arrival. On August 19, even before the surrender of the Annecy garrison, Farge had more than seven hundred German prisoners in custody. On the nineteenth he heard that the remaining twelve hundred prisoners in Montluc Prison had been divided into two groups, one of which was to be removed. Farge knew that the liberation of Lyon was near. He had heard rumors of atrocities, and wanted to save the remaining prisoners. He drafted a letter to Werner Knab, the head of the SD in Lyon, with three copies, one for the new prefect of Lyon, Boutémy, one for the Swedish consul in Lyon, Robatel, and one for the president of the Red Cross in Lyon, the comte de Loiray. The letter informed Knab that the resistance had taken 752 German prisoners in Savoie, including 420 wounded. "From now on," Farge wrote, "these 752 prisoners will be considered hostages. Their lives will depend on the survival of the patriots incarcerated in the prison of Montluc; any further atrocities committed by the Germans will have serious consequences for the German prisoners in our hands."

Farge did not know at that point about the massacre of Saint-Genis-Laval, but on August 20 he decided to go to Lyon and see the prefect. He did not feel he was running any great risk in view of the prisoners he was holding, among whom were a number of high-ranking officers. When he arrived in Lyon, he heard about Saint-Genis-Laval from his aide, Marc Laurent. Together, they went to see Boutémy, the prefect, who was sheepish in his indecision, not knowing what to do about Farge's letter. Farge urged him to invite Knab to his office. The prefect called Knab on the phone as Marc Laurent listened on the extension. The prefect gave Knab the names of some of the top officers taken prisoner. "He's screaming," said Marc Laurent, "but I think he'll give in. Some of our prisoners seem to interest him."

On August 21 Farge wrote a second letter to Knab: "On the evening of August 20, we now learn, the German police removed from Montluc Prison in Lyon, 80 French prisoners whom they shot at Saint-Genis-Laval. [He had the date and the number of victims wrong.] Consequently, we have ordered our men to shoot 80 of our German prisoners. This order will have been carried out by the time this letter reaches you. . . . In addition, we have now captured a contingent of German police commanded by a certain Buhl and his interpreter Leuman. We consider these prisoners as hostages and inform Colonel Knab that Buhl and Leuman are at the head of the list to be immediately shot if other French patriots are executed." Soon after, Farge learned about the surrender of the Annecy garrison, another twelve hundred prisoners to throw on the scales, including a colonel and a major.

Farge's intervention saved the prisoners of Montluc. There were no more massacres. On August 24 the Germans evacuated Montluc, leaving the keys with the highest-ranking inmate. Yves Farge took over the *préfecture*. He sat at the prefect's empty desk. Not a sheet of paper, not a cigarette butt. He thought of the streets where meetings had taken place, of whispered instructions, and looking over one's shoulder all the time. He remembered that day in 1940 on the Tassin streetcar . . .

The German Nineteenth Army was on the move on both banks of the Rhône, heading north, weighed down by its equipment. Where were the proud and confident warriors who had controlled Europe in 1942? Now their heads were bent and their step was listless. From the hill that prays (Fourvière with its basilica) to the hill that works (Croix-Rousse with its working-class population), the people of Lyon watched them leave. There was no insurrection. It all went calmly, with one exception.

The Germans had a military hospital in a former school in the Rue Tronchet, near the Parc de la Tête d'Or. On August 24 they evacuated the hospital, whose civilian employees began distributing what was left behind. People gathered in the street as hospital workers threw down blankets, bread, chocolate, and biscuits from the windows. Soon a crowd of three hundred, including many women and children, gathered in front of the gray stone school building, which had two entrances, one marked GARÇONS above the door and the other marked FILLES.

The Germans, in the midst of evacuating the city, sent a detachment of troops in a bus to the Rue Tronchet. The troops were let off at the corner of the Rue Tronchet and the Rue Garibaldi. The soldiers calmly and silently approached the school where the crowd had gathered, and began to fire without warning. They had gone berserk in the fury of retreat, of knowing they were beaten.

The crowd dispersed, but many had fallen and were lying in the street, moaning. Soldiers moved among the wounded, finishing them off. One of the wounded was a German woman married to a Frenchman. She saw her husband lying on the sidewalk, playing dead. A corporal approached him, gun in hand, and she dragged herself over, for she was hit in the leg, and told the corporal: "I'm a German. I have a brother in the Wehrmacht on the Normandy front—don't kill my husband." The corporal replied, *"Alles Fransozen müssen erschossen werden"* ("All Frenchmen must be shot") and fired a shot into the man's temple.

From behind barely opened shutters, people living in the apartment houses on the Rue Tronchet were watching the shooting. One of the observers was twelve-year-old Pierre Truche, a schoolboy attending the neighborhood *lycée,* taking German as a first language. His parents had told him not to walk in front of buildings where the Germans had offices since they might be bombed. He was at his bedroom window. His parents, who wondered whether the Germans would start coming into the buildings to kill more people, pulled him away because the soldiers had started firing at moving shutters. The shooting lasted ten minutes, and then the Germans drove off in the bus, leaving behind twenty-six dead and twenty-one wounded. Unarmed civilians had been massacred without any military purpose, in pure crazed, defeat-induced hatred. Pierre Truche never forgot it, and forty-three years later, when he was the prosecutor in the trial of Klaus Barbie in Lyon in May, June, and July of 1987, he felt that even though he had been only twelve then, he had a personal link with the events of that time.

By September 2 the last Germans had left Lyon, after blowing the bridges, and the American VI Corps, under Lieutenant General Lucian Truscott, arrived. The people of Lyon forgot their anger at the Flying Fortresses that had hammered the city on May 26. And soon a purge began, with the arrests of Vichy officials and police inspectors and businessmen who had worked for the Germans. And soon the summary executions began. A woman who had worked for the Milice now offered to point out her former employer to the resistance. She was shot. One of the men involved in the murders of Victor Basch and his wife confessed. He was shot.

On Monday, September 4, the doorbell rang at a fine house on the Avenue Esquirol. An elderly man answered the door, and saw two very young men in civilian clothes, armed, with tricolor armbands on their sleeves. "Are you Marius Berliet?" one asked. "Born in Lons in 1866?" This was the Marius Berliet who had turned the troublemakers in his factory over to the STO. And now, as he opened the door, he thought, "I've been building trucks for half a century and these pygmies come knocking. Look at them! They call themselves fighters, and they haven't even started shaving."

"You're under arrest," one of the young men said. The unthinkable had happened. Berliet, the incarnation of the French *patron,* the top man in Lyon, the man of steel, about as flexible as the frames in his twelve-ton trucks, was under arrest. Berliet threw a cape over his rheumatic shoulders and took a last look at his garden with its lily pond, its blue cedars, and its grove of elms. "Where are you taking me?" he asked. "To Montluc," he was told. Montluc had not stayed empty for long. It was starting to fill up again, and there were already more than four hundred inmates. One of the young resistance men who had arrested Berliet told his friends: "If you'd seen him . . . impressive . . . tall . . . with his hunting jacket and his leggings. You know who he reminded me of? The other one, the Vichy one. Can you imagine when I write my folks that I put Berliet in the jug?" It was true, there was a resemblance to the Maréchal in Berliet's erect carriage, white hair and moustache, and blue eyes.

Berliet was charged with "economic collaboration" and "intelligence with the enemy." He sat in the infirmary, a blanket over his knees, stripped of his authority, a pitiful old man, who told whoever wanted to listen that his only purpose had been to keep his factories open and his workers employed.

The Berliet company was placed under government custody, and was operated by a government-appointed administrator. And what if the purge was something more than a few whores dragged through the streets with their heads shaved? What if it was . . . the start of a new social order? For without the Berliet family, the factory was practically being run by the workers. And the first thing they did was change the order of the letters on the ten-foot-high sign over the entrance of the main plant at Vénissieux so that instead of reading *BERLIET* they read *LIBERTÉ*.

Berliet went on trial in June 1946 and was sentenced to two years in prison, national degradation for life, and the confiscation of his property. He died three years later, and in 1950 the company was returned to the family, and one of the sons, Paul Berliet, took over. End of experiment.

On September 15, 1944, General de Gaulle landed at the Bron airport in his plane with the Cross of Lorraine on it, and was greeted by Yves Farge. What, de Gaulle asked, was the program of the day? "The Maquis leaders will welcome you," Farge said. "Tonight you will have dinner with those who were in the resistance from the beginning." "And the authorities?" de Gaulle asked? "In prison, *mon général,*" Farge replied.

Too old and too stubborn to flee, Berliet stayed home and was arrested. But there were thousands, in the last days of August and the first days of September, who did flee, Miliciens and collaborators and Gestapo informers. Among them was Paul Touvier, who had made a nice sideline out of seizing the apartments and property of the Jews he arrested. On August 24, Touvier found refuge with a right-wing priest, Stéphane Vautherin, who had acted as unofficial chaplain to the Lyon Milice. On September 5 Father Vautherin heard that the resistance was looking for Touvier. He escorted Touvier to the Wilson bridge, hoping that his cassock would get them through if they came on a patrol, and watched Touvier cross the Rhône and vanish up a street and behind a building.

Touvier thereafter lived through a remarkable odyssey, escaping arrest for forty-five yeras, often hidden by friendly priests, until his capture in May 1989. The Touvier case showed that the old divisions of Vichy and the resistance continued to exist in postwar France. Touvier was helped by the remnants of the old Catholic right, which still believed in the values of Pétain, and also by nonpolitical priests acting out of Christian charity, who believed in forgiveness and redemption.

Upon leaving Father Vautherin, Touvier went to stay with his sister Marguerite in the town of Brignais, near Lyon. He had plenty of money, having taken 800,000 francs from the Milice treasury. What he badly needed were papers. His sister's husband, Albert Gaillard, was a prisoner of war in Germany. Touvier assumed his identity. He walked into the Brignais *mairie* and asked for an ID card in Gaillard's name, saying he had come down from the Maquis, and they gave it to him.

Thereafter, Touvier stayed on the move, plugging into the monastery circuit, in which friendly priests and nuns passed him along. He was twice tried in absentia for war crimes and sentenced to death—in Lyon on September 10, 1946, and in Chambéry on March 4, 1947. But he continued to avoid arrest, using the Catholic clergy's underground railroad, and also hiding out in his parent's house in Chambéry. He succeeded in waiting out the twenty-year statute of limitations, which came due in 1967, making him a free man. But then, misguided efforts on the part of a Lyon monsignor, Charles Duquaire, to obtain a pardon for him (because the statute of limitations did not apply to the loss of his rights as a citizen) caused him to be indicted again. For when President Georges Pompidou granted his pardon, there was such a public outcry that he was charged under the new statute of Crimes Against Humanity. In May 1989 he was finally hunted down in one of Archbishop

Marcel Lefebvre's schismatic priories, and although he is now seventy-nine, he is expected to stand trial.

As for Klaus Barbie, he was one of the last Germans to leave Lyon. On August 28 he was wounded in the left foot on the outskirts of the city during a skirmish with the resistance. Barbie was taken to Croix-Rousse Hospital where he was operated on, on August 30. That same day, he took the last train out of Lyon, eventually reaching a military hospital in Baden-Baden, Germany, where he recuperated. On May 9, 1945, the day that Germany capitulated, Barbie went underground. His subsequent activities, as an agent for the U. S. Army Counter-Intelligence Corps, and his escape to Bolivia, where he remained thirty-two years, have been described elsewhere and are not worth repeating. For Barbie was never anything more than a hired hand of the system that spawned him, a henchman, interchangeable with so many others who blindly followed criminal orders. He was ambitious in the thuggish way of such men, and wanted to rise within the system and be mentioned in dispatches. In fact, while hospitalized in Lyon, he was promoted, ending the war as a *Hauptsturmführer,* or captain. But essentially he was a man of little scope, elevated to notoriety because he was more violent and more unscrupulous than most of the others, and because he brought a certain shrewdness to police work, as in the capture of Jean Moulin.

There is, however, a little-known incident that deserves to be told, which took place in April 1946, when Barbie was in the city of Kassel in the province of Hesse. Times were hard, particularly for him, for he was a wanted man and his wife was pregnant and he needed money. At that time he was involved in an activity for which he had arrested people in Lyon; procuring forged ID cards and passports, not for Jews but for former SS members.

He hatched a scheme with two friends, Kurt Barkhausen and Wolfgang Gustmann. On April 19, at 10 P.M., they went to the home of Baron von Forstner at Parkstrasse 43 and rang the bell. When the door opened, Barbie pushed his way in, showing some sort of insignia on the back of his lapel. *"Kriminalpolizei,"* he announced to the Baroness von Forstner, who told him that her husband was not home. "You are accused of hiding a certain Mrs. Kolbenheger, wanted by the police," he said. He and his two accomplices searched the apartment, finding no one there, and then accused the baroness of being involved in the black market.

"I don't need to be," she replied. "I still have enough jewels." When Barbie insisted on seeing the jewels, she went into her room and came back with a little valise. In the meantime, the other two were calling "headquarters" and addressing Barbie as Herr *Kommissar*. Barbie told the baroness that he would have to take her to headquarters and draw up a report, and she would have to take her valise with her. On the stairs, the baroness noticed that she had forgotten her ID card. Barbie, who had the valise, pretended to be annoyed but told her to go back and get it. As soon as her back was turned, Barbie and his friends ran out into the street in different directions. He left the jewels with a woman friend, Maria Becker, who got curious and opened the valise, helping herself to a ring and a bracelet before calling the police. Barkhausen and Gustmann were arrested, but Barbie had vanished. An arrest warrant was drawn up, charging him with fraud and impersonating a policeman.

Owing to postwar confusion in the German court system, the case did not come up before the Kassel tribunal until late 1950. At that time, on October 10, the stolen jewels mysteriously reached Kassel police headquarters and were returned to their owner. The Kassel police wrote in a report: "We know with certainty that the jewels were returned by the American CIC. We already suspected that Barbie was working with the American secret services. These suspicions have been reinforced by the return of the jewels. A written request addressed to the CIC has not been answered."

Barbie at that time was still an agent of the CIC, which hired known Nazi intelligence officers on the pragmatic principle that they were good at their job no matter who they worked for, and reflected a postwar realignment that now regarded the Soviet Union as the enemy. However, since Barbie was becoming an embarrassment to his CIC handlers—in addition to his crime in Kassel, the French were looking for him—they arranged for him to flee to Bolivia in March 1951. But whether in Germany, or Bolivia, or France, to which he was abducted in 1983 to stand trial, Barbie should be remembered as he was in 1946 in Kassel, a small-time hoodlum and con man who gravitated toward a political system that could use his talents.

VII

LAST TRAIN TO AUSCHWITZ

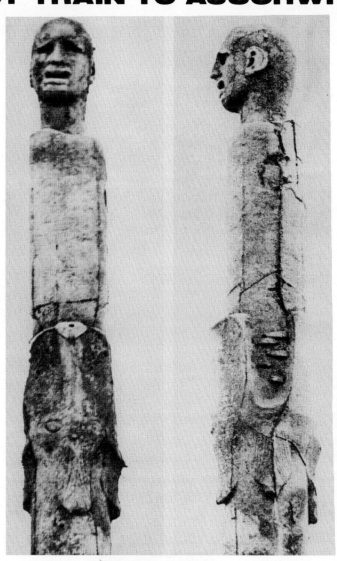

On the morning of August 11, 1944, the 629 inmates of Montluc Prison who had been picked for deportation were taken by truck to the Perrache railroad station where a ten-car, third-class passenger train was waiting for them. One car was for the luggage and nine were for the inmates, who were divided into three groups—331 Jews in the first four cars, 120 non-Jewish women in the next two, and 178 non-Jewish men in the last three. The cars were of a model called *à baïonette,* meaning that they had a door at each end, with nine eight-seat compartments per car. A sliding door closed the compartments, and a hallway went down the length of the cars. This old-model car had wooden benches and a type of window that was raised with a cloth strap. But for this trip the windows had been blocked shut with bits of barbed wire.

The inmates boarded the cars, which had DRANCY written in chalk on the sides, although they would never get to Drancy. As fifteen-year-old Lisette Klein waited in line to board, an SS officer asked her in French, "Do you know where you're going? . . . You will be among yourselves, *en famille.*" And he laughed. The Jews in the first four cars were more cramped than the others, for the normal number of passengers per car was seventy-two, whereas there was a surplus of about ten per car. The non-Jewish cars had seats to spare, but the Germans insisted on racial separation and on treating the Jews more severely than the others. And so, in the Jewish cars, they squeezed in, often ten to a compartment for eight.

Still, it was a great improvement over the sealed and window-less cattle cars that were the usual form of transportation to the camps. There was a guard at either end of each car, and the prisoners were warned that if anyone tried to escape, others in the compartment would be shot. And so they waited in Perrache station, in the stifling August heat, with little ventilation because the windows were shut. But they could open the compartment doors, and if they were near the end of the car, and if the guard was a decent fellow, he opened the door and they got some fresh air. Conversations started up on the reasons for the delay. "The resistance must have cut the tracks, don't you think?" "Or the bridges have been bombed." Then they trailed off into private thoughts. Maybe the train won't get through. Maybe one of the guards can be bribed.

And the morning turned to afternoon, and still they did not leave, and were given neither food nor water. And in the two women's cars the nurses from the Grotte de la Luire, wearing clean uniforms and caps, did what they could to help the elderly. It was a matter of keeping up one's spirits in spite of everything, thought Cécile Goldet, and of being able to see the humor in the midst of discouraging events. One of the women, for instance, was wearing a fur coat in the middle of August, while another took out her makeup kit and applied lipstick, mascara, and eyebrow pencil, the works, as though she were going out for a night at the opera.

In the first Jewish car, Daniel Weill, the furrier from Croix-Rousse, was inwardly bemoaning his bad luck at being in one of the overcrowded compartments. "I don't like to be touching people," he said to himself. "God, it's hot! And smelly, with everyone sweating. Now here's a fellow taking off his shirt, and another pulling out a pack of cigarettes and lighting up. It's like a furnace in here. My lungs are burning. Why don't they open the door at the end of the car?" At that moment, the SS lieutenant in charge of the train, a credit to racial selection in his cookie-cutter blond looks, came through the car. Weill called out, "Could you please leave the door open?" and the lieutenant, without missing a step, made a gesture with his gloved right hand, over his right shoulder, as if he were throwing away as irrelevant what had just been said. And Weill thought, "This is only the beginning."

And then, at four in the afternoon, the train slowly pulled out of Perrache, heading north up the Rhône valley and away from the city, and as it picked up speed, Lisette Klein listened to the clicking of the wheels and heard them saying "to the unknown, to the unknown, to the unknown."

It soon became apparent that this would be no ordinary journey. France was a battleground, with the Allies and the Wehrmacht and the Maquis all over the place, and Allied planes in the sky bombing and strafing anything that moved. Rail traffic was seriously disrupted. The local Maquis, alerted about the train but more concerned about their own people than about the Jews, since they had never tried to stop trains of deportees before, had blown eleven bridges between Lyon and Chalon, sixty miles to the north. So the train pursued its erratic course, stopping and starting, backtracking, zigzagging, looking for alternate tracks and intact bridges, picking its way through the wartime maze.

The first major obstacle came south of Chalon, where the bridge at Saint-Loup-de-Varennes was blown, and the train was stuck in the station at Varennes-le-Grand. After half a day, a secondary track to Chalon was found, where the train was stuck again, right next to a statue of Louis Lumière, inventor of the *cinématographe,* whose birthplace it was.

From Chalon the train was scheduled to head northwest toward Paris and Drancy, but the track was cut in ten places. So, instead of taking the Drancy route, it was decided to go directly to Germany, where the train would be broken up into three sections—the Jews going to Auschwitz, the non-Jewish women to Ravensbrück, north of Berlin, and the non-Jewish men to Stutthof in northern Poland, south of Danzig (then in East Prussia).

And so the train chugged on in the general direction of the German border, up from Chalon through the Burgundy vineyards to Beaune, and on to the mustard city of Dijon, and then farther north to Langres and Chaumont on the Marne. At Chaumont another blown bridge made them backtrack to Langres and head east toward Vittel, another brand-name city, famous for its mineral water.

And all the while, the passengers remained without food and water. In the women's cars, the nurses managed to collect some rainwater in cans with the help of a guard, and dispensed aspirin, which was all they had. They stood out, not only because of their spotless uniforms but because they were young and energetic and healthy-looking and helpful, and had good morale, in contrast to the other women. And this drew the attention of the SS lieutenant who, on one of his inspection visits asked Cécile Goldet, "But what are you doing here?" since the nurses were so different from the others.

"We committed a crime which did not please Hitler," Cécile Goldet replied. "We took care of the wounded." The SS lieutenant went away without saying a word. Cécile Goldet spoke German, so she chatted with the guards and learned that the train was headed for Germany. The rules were that the passengers could only go to the toilet under escort, but after a while the guards let the nurses act as escorts. There developed, over the days, a discreet collusion between the nurses and the guards.

Already, there had been some deaths in the Jewish cars. Some of those who were in a weakened state from their treatment at Montluc did not survive the first days without food or water. Others were seriously ill at the start of the trip. There was a family by the name of Halpern, a husband, and wife, and their fifteen-month-old son, Guy, the youngest passenger on the train. They were separated in Lyon, for families were not allowed to remain together. Mrs. Halpern had a serious asthmatic condition, which the heat and crowding made worse, and she died on the third day. A guard then brought the baby to his father's car. Mr. Halpern saw the baby and knew that his wife was dead. Overnight his hair turned white.

On the afternoon of August 15, the train reached the spa of Vittel. It had taken them four days to cover two hundred miles. Marcel Steff, the stationmaster, wondered what kind of train it could be. He had not seen a train for days. No train of deportees had ever come through Vittel, which was off the usual route. SS guards were keeping everyone away, but Steff approached the train and told them he had to examine the axles. As he busied himself, looking under the cars, passengers in several compartments were able to loosen their windows and raise them a fraction of an inch and drop scrawled messages, which he picked up. Upon reading them in his office, he realized what sort of train this was and called his friend Mme. Bouloumy, the head of the Red Cross in Vittel.

A forceful woman, Mme. Bouloumy went at once to the station and saw that the passengers were in a sorry state, covered with vermin, hungry, thirsty, in distress. Conferring with the SS lieutenant, she offered to set up tables on the station platform and give the passengers a hot meal. Since the train was held up for at least a day while they plotted the best route eastward, the lieutenant agreed.

Mme. Bouloumy marshaled the resources of the community. The spa donated mineral water, local pharmacies gave cotton and medical supplies, and various citizens made soup and sandwiches. To find items unobtainable in the local economy, she went to the Anglo-American prisoner-of-war camp outside Vittel, where she was known for her kindness and zeal, and obtained from the POWs donations of honey, jam, biscuits, chocolate, and cigarettes.

All this took time, and it was not until August 17 that Mme. Bouloumy was able to set up her tables on the station platform. She also enlisted the Vittel fire department to lend a hand, and they arrived with hoses so the prisoners could wash up. They were let off the train in groups of twenty, and after being handed soap and hosed down, moved on to the tables, where volunteers gave them hot soup, fresh bread, sandwiches, and all the other good things that Mme. Bouloumy had been able to collect.

Some of the *cheminots* were helping the firemen with the hoses, and when the furrier Daniel Weill was taking his shower, a *cheminot* whispered that the Allies had landed in the south of France. "Tomorrow," he said, "they'll be drinking *pastis* [a popular anise-based drink] on the Canebière [the main avenue of Marseille]." That bit of good news spread quickly among the passengers, and, along with the unexpected bounty, helped to lift their spirits.

In the meantime, Mme. Bouloumy was talking to Dr. Bernheim, the only doctor in the Jewish group, to whom she gave the medical supplies she had obtained. Dr. Bernheim told her that two passengers were seriously ill, one with tuberculosis, the other with syphilis. She took up the matter with the SS lieutenant, asking that the two be let off. He told her he would wire Paris for permission, but permission was refused. She met Mr. Halpern, whose hair had turned white, and offered to try to get his baby off the train, but he did not want to give up his child. She took letters from some of the other passengers. What a mix! There was a journalist from Lyon, a Polish countess, a Roumanian who had fought in the Maquis, a *lycée* professor, and a ninety-four-year-old Jewish woman.

Mme. Bouloumy saw to it that the leftover food and mineral water were distributed to the passengers, and asked the SS lieutenant one last time to give up the foolhardy enterprise of trying to get his human cargo through. But he was absolutely unshakable in his determination to take the train to Germany, and they left on the evening of the seventeenth, heading eastward toward the town of Épinal. The only thing she could do was call the *Secours National* in Épinal, which sent a team to the station with a hand towel, handkerchief, toothbrush, and toothpaste for each passenger.

In Épinal the tracks north to Nancy and east to Strasbourg were cut, so the train had to head south to Remiremont, west to Plombières, and southeast to Belfort. For several days they picked their way, stopping and starting, making detours. Then in Belfort they got lucky, for the track eastward to Mulhouse was clear, and Mulhouse was right on the German border.

They were leaving Mulhouse, crossing a forested area and heading toward the Rhine, when four British dive bombers came out of the sky, dropping their bombs and strafing. One of the first bombs hit the locomotive, which stopped the train. The guards locked the compartments, then all but a handful of them jumped off and hid in the woods.

In one of the Jewish cars, Antoine Lilienstein and two of his friends found a way to open their compartment door. They knew they were near the German border and that this was their last chance to escape while they were still in France. The three friends decided to draw lots, with the other two giving the one who won their money. Others in the compartment argued against escaping. "The war is nearly over. It's a matter of weeks. so why take risks?" "It's over in France but not in Germany," Lilienstein said. He gave his friend his money, and followed him down the corridor. There was not a guard in sight. The friend jumped off and vanished into the woods as the dive bombers continued their passes overhead, and the cars shook with each explosion, and the air was dense with smoke. For a moment, Antoine Lilienstein wanted to follow his friend, but then he thought he saw a guard and returned to the compartment.

In another car, Charles Lévy, a friend of the furrier Daniel Weill, was trying very hard to control himself. He had felt doomed from the start of the trip. He knew in his gut that they were not going to Germany to work but to die. He had sunk into apathy, resenting the others in his compartment, who were too foolish to see what was really happening. He particularly resented the loud-mouthed Roumanian who sat across from him, Otto Abramovic, who bragged about his exploits in the Maquis and about his physical strength—he claimed that he could lift a 250-pound barrel. And now this. Bombs were exploding outside the window. The noise was deafening. And the Germans had run for the woods. They were sitting ducks, trapped in the compartments. They would be killed on the train, saving the Germans the trouble. As if echoing his thoughts, Abramovic said, "It would be too dumb to be killed by the Brits."

Charles Lévy had had enough. He wanted to find his friend Daniel Weill. He was convinced that if he found Weill things would be all right. Lévy rose from his seat and shouted at Abramovic, "Bastard, why are you staring at me?" "All right, old one, calm down," Abramovic said. But Lévy did not calm down. He broke the glass on the compartment door with his fist, opened it, and ran down the corridor, thinking, "I must find Dan." But there were still guards on the train, and one saw him running and called out for him to stop, and when he kept running, shot him in the back.

The dive bombers finally flew off, leaving about a dozen dead among the passengers, and it took another half day to get a replacement locomotive from Mulhouse. But the bridge over the Rhine at Mulhouse was blown, and the train headed north to Colmar and Strasbourg, where finally it crossed the Rhine. Harriet Berman, who had worked for the UGIF in Lyon and was on the train with her diabetic father, was in one of the bomb-damaged cars. There was broken glass everywhere, and several wounded people in her compartment. She saw that they were crossing an iron bridge over a wide river and thought, "It's funny the noise the train makes on a bridge, like a series of slaps. . . . And now, they've got us on their side of the border." Someone said, "That's not the Rhine, the Rhine is wider." And she sensed that the one who said it was not the Rhine knew that it was the Rhine. And now that they were in Germany, there was a change of attitude, less conversation. There was also a smell of decomposition in the compartment. Someone said it was the sausage they had kept since Vittel and then they realized that it was the elderly lady in the corner, whom they thought had been sleeping. She was dead. Guards came and removed her to the compartment the Germans had emptied to make room for the dead. They had sealed that compartment, and Harriet Berman wondered why—they weren't going anywhere.

The train, now on the German side of the Rhine, headed north toward Karlsruhe and west to Saarbrücken, where the three groups separated to go to their different camps. The prisoners waited on the platform as the cars were being uncoupled, and four uniformed nurses from the German Red Cross offered them bowls of hot soup with white-gloved hands. The two cars of non-Jewish women were attached to a Berlin-bound freight train; from Berlin they would proceed to Ravensbrück. The three cars of non-Jewish men also went in the direction of Berlin, then into northern Poland, toward Danzig. South of Danzig, on the Vistula River, was the Stutthof concentration camp. The four cars of Jews took a more southern route, via Stuttgart, into Czechoslovakia and southern Poland, to Auschwitz, thirty-seven miles west of Krakow.

In Stuttgart there was quite a long wait, and some of the prisoners were let off to fetch water, among them Lisette Klein, who heard loudspeakers announce: "Jewish train, everyone leave the station." But some were slow in leaving, and as she crossed the platform carrying a pail, some German children, not much younger than she was, spat at her.

It was not until August 22, eleven days after their departure from Montluc, that the four cars of Jews reached Auschwitz. It had taken them eleven days to cover roughly a thousand miles.

And now it was over, the *click-clack* of the wheels, the jolts, the long waits, the reverse motion, the *whooshing* through small stations, the red signal lights, the lack of ventilation, the disputes, the compartments stinking of sweat and urine, and having someone next to you die of despair and exhaustion. Of the 331 Jews who had left Montluc, 308 arrived at Auschwitz, and roughly half of the twenty-three dead were victims of the British air raid. This was an unusually high rate of survival, considering the length of the trip, and could be attributed to the relative comfort of the passenger compartments, and to Mme. Bouloumy's ministrations in Vittel, a unique example of how a French community could be mobilized to bring assistance to a train of deportees.

It was night when the train pulled into the floodlight-bathed ramp at Birkenau, also known as Auschwitz II. Through the train windows the passengers could see watchtowers, walls, low buildings, and a long cement ramp, which should have been teeming with the various officials involved in the selection process, but was practically deserted. The deportation system had broken down, for the train was not expected. The lieutenant in charge, who had stayed with the Jews, had to look for an officer in the Admissions Division, to whom to hand his transport list. The admissions officer studied the list, trying to hide his surprise.

Soon SS men with huge Alsatian hounds arrived on the ramp, shouting *"Los, los heraus und einreihen"* ("Get out and form rows"). The *rayés* (striped ones) came aboard to collect the luggage. They were emaciated, hollow-cheeked, like the medieval statues at the portals of Gothic cathedrals, thought Harriet Berman. "Eat your provisions," a voice whispered. "They take everything."

They stood there wondering what was coming next. Daniel Weill kept repeating to himself, "It will be all right, it will be all right." Mr. Halpern stood in line holding his baby, wondering at the strangeness of it all, for the *rayés* didn't seem to be badly off, and even cracked jokes.

The camp administration had been caught napping, and had no place to put these new arrivals. Nor was it ready to carry out a selection, which entailed the presence of doctors and a considerable amount of paperwork. While the camp authorities decided what to do with them, the prisoners waited, not realizing that a breakdown of the system had temporarily saved them from a process that would have sent most of them to the gas chambers.

Finally an officer arrived, resplendent in his black uniform and peaked cap with the skull and bones above the visor, and when Otto Abramovic saw the officer, he recognized him. For Abramovic had been a pharmacist's assistant in the Roumanian town of Ploesti, and had gotten to know the salesman for Bayer aspirin who often came through Ploesti filling orders. The salesman was a hearty, obliging fellow, always ready with a cheerful word or a joke, and he carried a film projector in a case to show a short promotional film. He brought little gifts for the people in the pharmacy, such as notebooks and pencils. And this man, this jovial salesman, Victor Capesius, was now on the ramp at Birkenau wearing the uniform of an officer in the SS. Abramovic caught his eye. He could not be sure but had the impression that Capesius, who used to joke about his Transylvanian origins in Dracula country, had given him a wink.

Eventually it was decided that the 308 unexpected arrivals would be temporarily housed in the Gypsy barracks, recently vacated because the Gypsies had been gassed. Because of confusion at the camp at this late date in 1944, they were kept in those barracks for two weeks, until September 7. During this hiatus, they had a chance to learn a bit more about the nature of Birkenau, for they could see the crematorium smokestacks going full blast day and night, and an unmistakable smell of burning bodies hung over the entire place. They decided that they would destroy their identity papers and claim that they had been lost in the bombardment of the train.

And then, on September 7, they were lined up in front of the Gypsy barracks and asked if any had a non-Jewish parent. Three fourths of them raised their hands and said yes, since they had destroyed their papers and there was no way to dispute it. Back they were taken to the ramp, where Capesius, who was in command of a gang of guards and clerks, announced that whoever was tired or did not feel well should go over to the other side where some Red Cross trucks were waiting to take them to a recovery camp. The sight of the Red Cross on the trucks was reassuring, but there were very few volunteers. So Capesius and several others looked over the group, designating the frail, the ill-looking, the elderly, and the very young. Lisette Klein escaped the selection but Mr. Halpern's baby did not. In the end, 128 of the 308 survivors from the train were selected, and were led away to be gassed. The other 180, 117 men and 63 women, were admitted to the camp (which was a high ratio) owing to their claim of having a non-Jewish parent. Being admitted meant getting deloused, and having your head shaved and your arm tattooed, and as Harriet Berman was being tattooed, she noticed that the woman standing next to her was crying, and she told her, "Keep quiet, don't let them see you crying," but the woman answered, "But how will I ever be able to wear an evening gown again?" And then Harriet went to the clothing room to put on a striped dress when a woman guard said, "Pull up your dress, I want to see your tail." "My tail?" Harriet asked: "Of course. All Jews have a tail, and I want to see it." That was her introduction to Auschwitz.

In May 1940, having risen through loyal service in the concentration camp hierarchy, Rudolf Hoess was sent to Auschwitz, thirty-seven miles west of Krakow, with thirty men, to build what was originally intended as a quarantine camp for ten thousand Poles. This was his first big job, and he wanted to do it right, and he wanted to do it on time.

In the meantime, to raise the sinking morale of his SS *Einsatzkommandos,* whose job was to massacre civilian populations on the eastern front, Himmler, on August 31, 1941, attended the execution of two hundred Jews in Minsk. When he saw the result of the first volley, he almost collapsed. Karl Wolff, the head of his personal staff, propped him up, saying under his breath: "Good for him to see what he expects people to do." Himmler said that a new method of killing had to be found, and someone thought of a truck with a sealed body into which carbon monoxide from the diesel engine could be pumped. This method was adopted, even though it was slow.

Himmler visited Auschwitz and told Hoess to expand the camp into the swampy area between the Sola and Vistula rivers. The inhabitants of seven Polish villages, including Birkenau, which means "in the birches," were resettled. The camp now covered an area of seventeen square miles, and its main function was changed from quarantine to extermination.

Hoess complained that he had to build the big camp at Birkenau with twenty thousand Russian prisoners of war who had arrived exhausted after a forced march and could hardly stand. How did they expect him to do it? No one looked at it from his point of view. No one saw his difficulties, the lack of cooperation from the Fleiwitz depot where the barbed wire was kept, the utter indifference of the Concentration Camp Inspectorate to his needs. And because of the rotten weather, the camp was a tract of mud at the start of autumn and spring.

In November 1941 he went to Berlin to confer with Eichmann on logistics: the housing of prisoners, the supply of trains, the planning of timetables. Eichmann said that the *Einsatzgruppen* were still using the diesel exhaust from trucks to gas Jews, but that it was less than suitable. The Jews would start arriving soon, first from Upper Silesia, the Polish border zone with Germany, then from other parts of Poland, then from Czechoslovakia and Germany, and finally from Western Europe.

Upon his return to Auschwitz, Hoess learned that his deputy, Fritsch, had experimented on Russian prisoners of war with a brand of prussic acid called Zyklon B, which was used to fumigate buildings and ships. There was a supply of the stuff in the camp for use as an insecticide. Hoess watched a killing in Block 11. The gas paralyzed the lungs, and death came quickly before there could be any convulsions. Hoess breathed an enormous sigh of relief. His greatest concern upon being told that Auschwitz was being turned into an extermination camp was that the victims would have to be shot. He had heard Eichmann's descriptions of Jews being mowed down by the *Einsatzgruppen*. The men in those squads consumed amazing amounts of alcohol. If he had to do the job that way, he would have morale and discipline problems.

Thanks to Zyklon B, Hoess was able to build first a gas chamber that could handle eight hundred people a day, then another that could handle twelve hundred. At first they burned the bodies in open trenches on wood pyres, two thousand at a time, pouring oil refuse over them. But open-air cremation was not feasible because of the stench and because the Air Defense Services objected that the fires could be seen at night. Consequently, two large crematoriums with their own gas chambers were built in the winter of 1942–1943 in Birkenau. The five ovens could burn two thousand bodies in twenty-four hours. Two smaller ovens, built by Topf of Erfurt, could burn fifteen hundred bodies in twenty-four hours, but they were constantly breaking down, developed cracks in the smokestacks, that sort of thing, more headaches.

Of course Hoess had to appear convinced of the necessity of what he was doing. He had to be cold and indifferent. He had to set an example. He had to go and look, day after day, at the removal and burning of the bodies, the extraction of gold teeth and the cutting of hair, the whole interminable business. He had to look through the peephole in the gas chamber and watch the process of asphyxiation. One thing he had to admit—he seldom found anyone who wanted to swap jobs with him.

By contrast, Hoess had a happy family life with his wife, his children, their two horses, their dogs, their garden, and their house on the river, beyond the camp. That is, it was happy until someone slipped and told his wife at dinner what the true nature of the camp was. Thereafter, his wife insisted on separate rooms. As a result of his wife's growing contempt for him, Hoess took up with one of the inmates, Eleanor Hodys. He needed female companionship, even if it was with a certified enemy of the people. Since this affair could not be kept quiet, particularly when Eleanor Hodys was found to be pregnant, someone informed on Hoess to the SS corruption court. Hoess was questioned, but got off with a transfer to an office job in Berlin. Eleanor Hodys, being an embarrassment, was killed.

As commandant of Auschwitz, Hoess was privy to the struggle going on in the highest councils of the SS over the purpose of the camps. It was a struggle between the purists, led by Eichmann, who wanted only to carry out the Final Solution, and the pragmatists, led by Oswald Pohl (head of the Economic and Administrative Department of the SS, or WVHA), who sought to run the camps on a sound, profit-making basis by using the inmates as unpaid labor.

Pohl, who came from Kiel and had been a navy paymaster, had

the soul of a corporation executive. He wanted to turn the SS into a conglomerate. He was a numbers-cruncher, happy with his charts and diagrams, who wanted better treatment for the inmates so he could get a day's work out of them. He had Himmler's ear, and advised the elimination of arbitrary handling, warmer clothing in winter, better hygiene, and a better diet. An austere man, he wore a simple uniform without decorations until Himmler ordered him to wear his War Service Cross.

To turn the SS into a corporation, Pohl simply expanded the already existing SS businesses—the German Excavation and Quarrying Company, consisting of fourteen brickworks; the German Equipment Company, which provided bakeries, carpentry shops, and iron foundries for the camps; the German Experimental Establishment for Foodstuffs, a favorite of Himmler's with his interest in herbs and nutrition; and the Society for the Exploitation of Textile and Leather Work, which produced uniforms for the SS.

Pohl adapted a capitalist device, the holding company, and established interests in fringe areas of the German economy under the umbrella of German Industrial Undertakings, or DWB. He started buying up mineral-water firms until in 1944 the SS controlled 75 percent of the German market. Other firms came into his hands through the expropriation of Jewish property, as for example that of Emil Gerstel, the largest furniture maker in Czechoslovakia. Thus, the SS went into the furniture business. Also, because of all the camp construction, Pohl got into building materials in a big way. East German Building Materials Limited owned and operated 313 ex-Polish or ex-Jewish brickworks, and had a cement company in Upper Silesia.

This corporate network of holdings grew in directions that had nothing to do with the needs of the SS, such as estate management in Russia, jam factories, the Allach porcelain works, and the publishing firm Nordland Verlag. Under Pohl's guidance, the SS became an authentic multinational corporation. It was not generally known that the SS owned these companies, for the board of directors gave no affiliation and all SS involvement was concealed—they were presented as ordinary companies under civilian ownership.

Pohl's importance grew until he was second only to Himmler in power and influence. In 1942 he was placed in charge of the 20 concentration camps and 165 labor camps. He was in charge of all SS construction, and all SS economic enterprises. On April 30, 1942, Pohl wrote Himmler that the war effort required the mobilization of all prisoners. The camps must be transformed, he said, into organizations capable of meeting economic and wartime requirements. Himmler agreed, and the prisoners now became a useful commodity. In the death camps like Auschwitz, this led to the selection on the ramp. Arriving prisoners were divided into those able to work, who would be admitted to the camp, and the rest, who were taken directly from the train to the gas chamber.

Under Pohl's tutelage, the camps were now supposed to be run on a practical and humane basis. But he had to fight the resistance of the Final Solution stalwarts, the corruption in the camps, and the ingrained belief that improved food and treatment for the inmates was pointless since they were destined to die anyway. Pohl enlisted other officials to support his view. Richard Gluecks, head of the Concentration Camp Inspectorate, wrote in the summer of 1942 that "it is axiomatic that it is forbidden to strike, kick, or even touch a prisoner." Himmler himself approved Pohl's aims, and suggested that hardworking prisoners should be held up as examples for the listless majority. On December 28, 1942, he circulated an order headed: THE REICHSFÜHRER HAS ORDERED THAT THE DEATH RATE ABSOLUTELY MUST BE REDUCED.

In March 1943 Pohl formed Eastern Industries in Poland, appropriating Polish businesses to employ inmates of the various death camps. There was a brush factory in Lublin, an armaments factory in Radom, a peat-cutting business and a tannery on the Baltic. But the Final Solution purists fought him on the grounds that he was releasing prisoners from the camps. One of them wrote, in a note from Warsaw, "Eastern Industries! I only have to hear the word 'industry' to become nauseated." In this instance, the ideologues won out, and the "Eastern Industries" Jews were claimed by the gas chambers in November 1943. Max Horn, the deputy director of Eastern Industries, complained that "as a result of the withdrawal of Jewish labor all our work of organization and expansion has become totally valueless.'' In the rivalry between those who wanted to employ the prisoners and those who wanted to liquidate them, each side scored points. But from his vantage point in Auschwitz, Rudolf Hoess knew that Pohl was in the stronger position, for the simple reason that Germany had an ever more urgent need for arms and munitions. In fact, there was a separate armaments program under the direction of Hans Kammler, who in 1943 employed 175,000 men from the camps. Kammler was building not only arms factories, but an underground headquarters for Hitler in Thuringia, underground hangars for plane assembly, and launching ramps for the V-1 and V-2 buzzbombs. All were built with camp labor.

To Pohl, the camps were a business, to be run in a businesslike manner. He might have paraphrased the motto of ''Engine Charlie'' Wilson, ''What's good for the concentration camps is good for Germany.'' In his communications, he referred to the camps as a business, as in a progress report to Himmler, which concluded: ''Just such examples show how our business has grown.''

It was Pohl's idea to promote the camps to Germany's industrial giants, such as I. G. Farben, Siemens, and Krupp. He did this in exactly the same way that rival American states compete for a defense plant that will create thousands of jobs, by promotion and lobbying and by a tax-break incentive. To I. G. Farben, he recommended Auschwitz as a site with plentiful water and coal, good transportation, and abundant cheap labor. In 1944 I. G. Farben built a synthetic rubber plant in the satellite camp of Monowitz, three miles from the main camp, also known as Auschwitz III. Siemens came in too, building an electrical-appliance plant that began production on May 20, 1944. And when the Krupp fuse plant in Essen was bombed, the remains of the factory were moved to Auschwitz.

Pohl was so successful in drawing German big business to Auschwitz that in Monowitz in 1944, in spite of fifty thousand workers, there were labor shortages. At that time, massive numbers of Hungarian Jews arrived at Auschwitz, and Pohl on May 24 asked Himmler if he could use some of the Hungarian women for heavy construction work. This astounding reply, in a harebrained, cut-off-from-reality manner, came from Himmler: ''My dear Pohl, of course the Jewish women are to be employed. One will have to worry only about good nourishment. Here the important thing is a supply of raw vegetables. So don't forget to import plenty of garlic from Hungary."

The arrival of big business in Auschwitz was by and large beneficial to the prisoners, for corporate logic is amoral. Corporations will cover up a harmful flaw in their product and lay waste the environment (at Auschwitz ground water was actually polluted as a result of cadaveric poisoning. The fish in the ponds and rivers were dying). At the same time, it is in the corporate interest to improve the lot of the workers, making them more productive. The aim of the Siemens and Farben foremen was to reduce absenteeism and sickness. Accordingly, vegetable gardens and infirmaries for the workers were provided as a matter of corporate policy. The Farben workers were given an extra bowl of soup at lunch. Albert Krauch, head of the "Special Tasks" Department at Farben, said there was no difference between Auschwitz workers and other foreign workers.

Yet there was a difference, an enormous difference, which was the high death rate that continued to prevail at Auschwitz, through disease, malnutrition, and brutal treatment. In Auschwitz there was a factory that operated more efficiently than either Farben or Siemens, and that was the death factory. So in reality, the change in the orientation of the camps resulted in reconciling the two rival concepts of killing the prisoners and providing labor, thanks to a third concept—extermination through work.

When the 308 Jewish passengers on the last train from Lyon arrived at Auschwitz on August 22, Rudolf Hoess had been replaced as commandant, and the expanded camp was divided into three parts: Auschwitz I, the old camp, primarily for the men; Auschwitz II (Birkenau), three miles away, where the trains arrived and ramp selections took place, which also served as a women's camp, a quarantine camp, the Gypsy camp, and an additional men's camp; and Auschwitz III, or Monowitz, the industrial center.

For the SS guards, both men and women, Auschwitz was considered front-line duty, and anyone asking for a transfer would either have it refused and/or be sent to the eastern front. Several doctors, refusing to serve on the ramp, volunteered for the eastern front. Several guards, horrified by what they were ordered to do, also asked for transfers. But these were rare exceptions in a guard population of more than two thousand for an inmate population of sixty thousand. And now, in the late summer of 1944, some of the SS officers had feelings of unease as they sat in their mess eating Greek figs and Hungarian salami, listening to the radio give the latest news of the Russian advances. They began to curse the insignias tattooed on their arms (the one thing they had in common with the inmates) and to destroy camp records. They became a little more lenient with the prisoners, letting the women grow their hair and allowing work details to seek shelter in barns when it rained. Vigilance was to some extent relaxed. At Birkenau, where the men were separated from the women by a high-voltage fence, prisoners were now talking across the barbed wire that would kill them if they touched it; in the shadow of the ovens, they were chatting like housewives across a backyard picket fence, making plans. It was against this fence that men and women threw themselves in despair, and from this fence that their bodies were removed by squads carrying hooked sticks.

Auschwitz, as the 180 survivors of the initial selection among the passengers of the last train from Lyon came to realize, was a complicated and paradoxical place. In Auschwitz, you saw daily executions, and orchestras and soccer games. You saw men so undernourished that they collapsed at roll call, and well-fed, healthy-looking men who bragged about their sexual exploits. You saw a man waiting for another man to be shot so he could inherit his shoes, and you saw examples of generosity and sacrifice that were unmatched in normal society.

The essential fact was that those who had escaped the initial selection and were admitted to the camp had a theoretical chance at life. The survivors were the ones who best understood the nature of the system. For the business mentality so evident in Oswald Pohl's administration of the camps was duplicated among the inmates and guards, who developed a camp society that was Darwinian and entrepreneurial in the extreme.

This society operated according to a definite inmate hierarchy, as in the animal world where larger and stronger animals prey on weaker and smaller ones. At the top of the heap was that semi-officialdom known as the *Prominente* (notables), broadly defined to include the elders, the block leaders, the *Kapos,* the clerks, those with good jobs, those who brokered and operated, the "organizers," great and small. At the bottom of the heap were the *Muselmänner* (Moslems), skeletal, vacant-eyed, zombielike, constituting a doomed underclass. At Auschwitz, as in normal society, there existed every element of entrepreneurial activity, that is, barter and bribes, brokers and middlemen, credit and fraud, partnership and rivalry, loan-sharking and bankruptcy. Inmates sold grain futures—"my next Monday's bread ration." Middlemen arranged the trade of a comb for a potato, extended credit, offered better merchandise, stockpiled cigarettes to use as currency. It was not a society that rewarded scholarship or contemplation, but one that favored hustling, salesmanship, and wheeling and dealing.

The relations between guards and inmates ranged from gratuitous brutality to secret collusion. Here is the story of a pair of trousers: An SS guard gave the trousers to an inmate working in the kitchen in exchange for a pound of sugar. The inmate gave the trousers to one of the asocial females in exchange for sex. A guard confiscated them, and gave them to a second whore, who exchanged them with the block leader for a bottle of schnapps. The block leader gave the trousers to another kitchen worker for a kilo of margarine. It was an Auschwitz version of Schnitzel's *La Ronde*.

Appearance was destiny, for if you washed regularly and wore a clean uniform and looked less than cadaverous, you might avoid in-camp selections and luck into a better job. It was a society based on commerce and favoritism. The block leader who distributed the food could cut sausage into slices of varying thickness, could dole out different portions of the marmalade made from beets, could serve soup from the fifty-quart kettle either by not quite filling the liter-sized ladle, or by filling it from the dishwaterlike upper part, or by scouring the bottom for the thick, nourishing peas-and-potato-laden part.

It was a society where the schemers survived, the entrepreneurs survived, the lucky and the plucky survived, but the meek and the others mentioned in the Beatitudes did not necessarily survive. As for escape, with the high-tension fences, the watch-towers, the searchlights, the dogs, the certainty that capture meant death, and the Polish civilians who would turn you in for a five-zloty reward, it was not in the cards.

Upon admission to the camp, Otto Abramovic was given an IOU for twenty-eight zlotys in exchange for the francs that were taken away from him. His head was shaved, kerosene was rubbed on various parts of his body, the number 193122 was tattooed on his arm, and he was given a uniform and a flat-topped hat, which inmates had to wear at roll call. With the help of Capesius, who in the old days of the pharmacy used to send him a Christmas card each year that said *Molti Anni,* and who had recognized him, he was assigned to one of the best jobs in the camp, the *Effekten-kammer,* known to the inmates as "Canada" (a vast place of un-limited natural resources).

The deportees, not knowing where they were being sent, took their furs and their jewelry with them; all their clothing and be-longings were confiscated upon arrival and sent to Canada. It was property worth millions, and there was so much of it that a sec-ond warehouse, Canada II, had to be built, where inmates worked day and night sorting everything out. They were given the tops of sardine cans to cut through clothing to find hidden jewelry and cash; tens of thousands of hundred-dollar bills were collected, which were packed in trunks and sent to the *Reichsbank* in Berlin. The clothing went to German welfare organizations, which turned it over to victims of air raids. The watches were sent to Sachsen-hausen, where they were repaired in a shop employing hundreds of inmates, after which they were sent to front-line troops.

The conversation at Canada I and II was like a Brechtian re-frain: "What did they bring today?" "A rich transport! You should see the lingerie! And the shoes! Can-a-da, Can-a-da, oh moon of Can-a-da." Abramovic realized at once that Capesius had done him a great favor. For a work detail made all the difference. A work detail could kill you or save you. In that sense, the sign above the entrance gate, ARBEIT MACHT FREI had a specific meaning. It was important to avoid *Aussenarbeit* (outside work), which was useless, back-breaking, nonsensical labor, such as moving rocks from one place to another and then moving them back, or digging pits for unknown reasons.

At the Canada warehouse, you worked indoors, under a roof, protected from the rotten Auschwitz weather, and you dealt in valuables, and you soon learned to steal what you could and smuggle it out, which was the beginning of commerce, of being "organized." You had to buy the goodwill of the guards who conducted the searches. If you spoke German, which Abramovic did, you got to know them. Otto Abramovic, who in a sense had been recommended by Capesius, established a system of connivance with one of the guards. When the prisoners finished work, he would go up to the guard to be searched, whispering, *"Linke Tasche für Sie"* ("Left pocket for you"), and the guard would find his bribe and let Abramovic through, not looking in the right pocket. In this way, Abramovic was able to enter the barter economy—a diamond ring for a potato.

Lisette Klein had just turned fifteen when she entered the camp and was assigned to a block. She was told that the famous Dr. Mengele had rid the women's camp of lice, at least for a while. He had achieved this by sending 750 women in the first block to the gas chambers. He then sealed and disinfected those barracks with the same gas, Zyklon B, that was used in the gas chambers. Then the women from the second block were deloused and moved to the first block, and so on down the line. There were degrees of death, according to an SS guard, who told her, "The Jews have to die, the Poles are supposed to die, and the Germans are allowed to die."

The block leader was a ferocious Polish harpy whose terms of endearment were *du Mistkäfer* (you dung beetle), *du alte Kuh* (you old cow), and *du Krematoriumfigur* (you crematorium creature). The block was a horrible cramped place where Lisette Klein slept on a dirty straw mattress. The food consisted mainly of vile turnip soup she would not have touched had she not been so hungry. The toilets were cement trenches with boards across them. There were so many regulations that you could be punished for doing something that seemed quite reasonable, such as adding a pocket

345

to your camp uniform. There were signs all over the block concerning proper conduct: *HALTE DICH SAUBER* (Keep Clean); *RUHE IM BLOCK* (Quiet in the Block); *EINE LAUS—DEIN TOD* (One Louse—Your Death); *ACHTE DEINE VORGESETZTEN* (Respect Your Superiors).

Too young to have any influence and find a good job, Lisette was assigned to a labor pool that did various kinds of outside work. For weeks she cleaned bricks knocked down in air raids. At four in the morning, three whistles wrenched her from sleep, then she had to stand for hours during an interminable roll call in the dark, leaving for the work site as the sun rose. One day, as she was carrying a burlap bag full of bricks, she tripped on a half-buried stone, fell, and pulled a ligament in her knee. She was confined to barracks while her knee healed.

An electrician came by to fix the wiring in the block, one of the rare men allowed in the women's camp. He was a French-speaking Walloon Belgian, and he and Lisette started talking. He told her he had actually seen the gas chamber, having been summoned to fix some overhead light sockets. The vestibule was a long white-walled room with metal benches along the walls and a large red arrow pointing to the entrance over a sign in six languages: TO THE BATHS AND CLOTHES DISINFECTION. "But you know what?" the electrician said. "Never does a drop of water come from those shower heads."

He pulled a potato from his pocket and gave it to her, and then sat down on the bunk where she was lying and stroked her cheek and said, "It's strange, even though you have no hair and are dressed in rags, there is something very desirable about you." She began to cry, thinking, "How can he talk like this when I have lost my entire family?" The electrician pulled the potato out of her hand and said, "All right, little one, no more food. With the little I have I must get my women. In this misery, we need them more than in normal life. In a while you will understand."

And then, after an Allied bombing destroyed the camp brothel, the girls were temporarily relocated in the other women's blocks. A few of them were in Lisette Klein's block, and went out every night on dates with the SS guards after a hair-dresser had given them a shampoo and a set, and after getting dressed up, for they were allowed to keep their clothes. Their first night in the block, there were catcalls and insults, but one of the influential women, a professor of some kind, said, "They are working exactly as you are," and after that there were no more remarks.

The blocks were overcrowded, so one day an SS detachment arrived to remove the women who were not on work details, most of whom were *Muselmänner,* older desiccated women. Lisette Klein was taken along with the rest, but as they marched in step down the *Lagerstrasse,* a woman guard spotted Lisette and yelled, "What are you doing with that *grünes Gemüse* [green vegetable]? Get her to the *Revier* [infirmary]." And in this way she was taken to the infirmary and her life was saved.

It was the smell that bothered Daniel Weill, the furrier from Croix-Rousse, the unwashed bodies, the moldy food, the corpse stench from the crematoriums, and the general dampness that hung over everything. In the block a new arrival was out of luck. Cliques had already formed, particularly those who were friends with the block leader, Emil Bednarek. You could see it when Bednarek passed out the soup, not quite filling the ladle, those missing fractions added up. And then he skimmed from the top, while Weill and some of the others cried, "Stir the soup, goddammit"; Bednarek would give the ladle a good swirl, careful not to go too deep so the best part would be left for him and his cronies.

In a man like Bednarek, thought Weill, there was a complete twisting of the psyche, for he was an inmate who had come to emulate the traits of the dominant class, the SS, so for him compassion was weakness, brutality was obedience, and killing was duty. But even Bednarek, who was at the feet of the SS and at the throats of the inmates, was not consistently malevolent, Weill realized. That November, when they were on crematorium duty, hauling ashes into a truck, he let them warm themselves in front of the crematorium.

Behavior was never consistent but changed constantly, and you always had to be on your guard. All reason was suspended during the lineup for work at dawn; on one side executed prisoners were lying on wooden slabs, on display as a deterrent, and on the other side a band was playing *"Wien, Wien, Nur du Allein."* Even Stefan Baretzki, one of the most dreaded SS officers, was inconsistent in his behavior. He had invented something called the "knick-knack," which was a pole that he placed over a prone inmate's throat—then he stood on the pole, balancing himself, and swung back and forth. This criminal, who enjoyed killing inmates by this patented method, had once ordered Weill's work detail to follow him to the block leader's room. They were expecting the worst, but Baretzki took out a sausage, cut it into ten slices, and handed out the slices, saying, "Off with their skins." It was incomprehensible, except in terms of the basic pathology of the camp.

When it came to work details, Weill was out of luck. His skills as a furrier would have made him perfect for Canada, which processed thousands of fur coats, but he didn't have any influence. Soon after his arrival, while still in quarantine, he got a package from the Red Cross, and traded his cigarettes for a spot on the potato *Kommando*. However, the very first day he was caught stealing a potato and was transferred to the cement *Kommando*, where he carried big bags of cement. The only thing you could "organize" from the cement *Kommando* were the bags, which could be torn in strips for toilet paper and had a low trade value. So each evening Weill came back to the camp with a cement bag under his shirt, which was also good insulation against the cold. But Bednarek caught him and whacked him across the back with an iron bar, and moved him to a *Kommando* that dug up unexploded bombs. You were given a long metal rod to poke in the ground until you hit something, then you dug up the bombs with a spade. Surprisingly, none of the bombs exploded. In November the ground froze, and his clogs were stolen. He wrapped his feet in rags, but came down with frostbite in one foot. He went to the infirmary, where the doctors had orders to amputate. But it turned out that his doctor had been to Paris and spoke a few words of French, and said, "I'll try to save your foot, I won't cut it." With an old razor blade, the doctor sliced into Weill's foot and drew out a cupful of pus, which he continued to do three days in a row, saving the foot. And then the last week of November, Weill was put on the ash detail.

Daniel Weill had been back in the block no longer than a week when the accursed Bednarek became the instrument of his good fortune by asking for German-speaking draftsmen for the Siemens plant in Monowitz. Weill spoke beginner's German and knew nothing about draftsman's work, but what he did know was that he would not survive the winter in an *Aussenarbeit* detail. So he volunteered and was taken to an office and interviewed by a Siemens personnel man, who called him by his name instead of his number, politely. He was astounded. It was like being in the outside world again. His heart sank when he was told that he would have to take a test, but on the appointed day he found himself sitting at a table in an office in the plant. Behind the table there was a window, and out the window he could see the crematoriums, belching fire and smoke, which lent a certain urgency to the test.

The examiner, an engineer named Heinzel, asked him to make a simple mechanical drawing, which of course he was unable to do. Heinzel said, "Man, you can't even draw." Weill said he hadn't worked in a long time. "Don't get excited," Heinzel said. "I am willing to talk to each one of you." Looking at his file, he said, "It says here that you have a wife and child—where are they?" "Perhaps over there," said Weill, giving a shake of his head toward the window. At this point, an SS officer who had been hanging in the background came up, all gruff irritability, saying, "If this guy is no good, throw him out." "What do you mean, no good?" Heinzel said. "This man is an expert, he is one in a hundred." Then, turning toward him, Heinzel said, "All right, Mr. Weill, as agreed, you'll be working on the polishing machine."

Daniel Weill had never seen a polishing machine in his life, but he muddled through with the help of the other workers, some of whom were proficient. One morning his work detail arrived at the plant to find the same SS officer who had observed his test waiting for them. The officer began selecting a few *Muselmann*-like men in the detail. He took them out of the line and ordered them into trucks. But then Bundus, the chief Siemens engineer, came running out of the building and said, "These are my Siemens people and you are not taking them." There was nothing the SS officer could do because the men were listed as Siemens employees.

There was more trouble from Bednarek, a former coal miner who seemed to resent the factory workers. One day when they got back to the block, he said, "You think because you work at Siemens you have special rights, but don't forget that you have to submit to camp discipline like everybody else." When he distributed soup, he hit them over the head with the ladle and made them do deep kneebends while holding their full bowls of soup so that some of the soup spilled. But Weill realized that there were small ways in which you could resist. To obtain a spoon so that you didn't have to lap your soup like a dog was a small victory. Anything you did in defiance of the camp routine was a victory.

When Harriet Berman was admitted to the women's camp in Birkenau, she was separated from her father, who was sixty and diabetic. She worried about him, but there was no way of finding out more. An officer came around to her block, asking, "Who knows typing, shorthand, and perfect German?" Well, she didn't know perfect German, but she knew some and raised her hand. She went to the camp headquarters for the test. She was asked to write the following sentence on the typewriter and complete it: "What I want for Christmas is . . ." She typed in "my freedom." Harriet was accepted in the Auschwitz typing pool, in the *Schreibstube,* or secretariat. This was part of the *Politische Abteilung,* which was divided into four sections: the *Registratur* (of which the Secretariat was a part), the *Standesamt* (Recorder's Office), the *Aufnahme* (Reception), and the *Krematoriumwaltung* (Administration of the Crematoriums).

Harriet Berman soon saw that the job had many fringe benefits, that simple things like a knowledge of German and typing skills were worth more than all the wealth in Canada. She was moved from the block to sleeping quarters in the basement of the main office building, thereby escaping ill treatment by the block leader. This was a health measure, since the typists shared offices with SS men. Harriet was given a clean uniform, and a white kerchief to cover her bald head, and the food was better. It was a giant step up from ordinary camp life.

The *Schreibstube* was a little green barracks employing half a dozen typists under the command of Unterscharführer Hans Kamphuis, a brutish, bull-faced man and confirmed anti-Semite who nonetheless had a proprietary attitude toward his typists. He gave them paper to practice on and would leave his half-full canteen for them "to clean." He was pedantic. Every *i* had to be dotted, and if there was a single spelling mistake a letter had to be typed over. It was odd, thought Harriet Berman, that these people, who were so cavalier about life and death, should be punctilious over small things. But Auschwitz was full of paradoxes. Millions were gassed, but one girl with tuberculosis was taken to the hospital for a pneumothorax procedure, and her life was saved. Another girl suffered a head wound from an Allied bombardment and was hospitalized until she had recovered.

Harriet Berman's job was to type index cards for those who had been given "special treatment." Using information taken from the transport lists, she typed up cards with the notation SB *(Sonderbehandlung)*. Sometimes she typed N&N *(Nacht und Nebel)*, and those people were assigned to the worst work details, or *Rückkehr Unerwünscht* (Return Undesirable). In addition to the index cards she typed up death certificates for people who had died in the camp, based on reports from the infirmary, and letters to the next of kin if the deceased was Aryan. In writing out the death certificates, she chose one of five approved causes of death: pneumonia, tuberculosis, edema, uremia, and shot while trying to escape. She was relieved that her father's name did not show up, which meant that he was still alive.

One day a skeletal person came into the office. Harriet recognized one of the women from the train. She asked Hans Kamphuis to save this woman. He took up the matter with her block leader, who told him the woman was unable to work. Kamphuis came back to Harriet and said, "The *Blockalteste* does not want to leave her on the block, so I cannot help. But what does it matter, one week more or less." Harriet did not want to become like that woman. The secret of survival, she thought, was to live minute by minute, to use every means to stay alive and to believe in the element of paradox, which might save you. For instance, take the story of Rudy Friemel, which was part of the lore of the *Schreibstube*. Friemel was an Austrian veteran of the International Brigade in Spain. He and his wife had been in Auschwitz since 1940. They had been married in Spain in a civil ceremony, which was not recognized by Austrian authorities. Friemel's father lobbied Himmler, who allowed, "for humanitarian reasons," a marriage ceremony to be performed at Auschwitz. One of the girls in the *Schreibstube* made out a document unique in the annals of the camp—a marriage certificate. Rudy Friemel and his wife were given one of the rooms in the brothel for their wedding night.

You never knew what to expect from these people. Harriet was surprised when another SS man in the *Schreibstube,* Anton Brose, told her, "It is not your fault that you were born Jewish, just as I cannot help that I was born German." His remark emboldened her to ask him why he had joined the Gestapo. "I could not say that I wanted out," he replied, "as they would have liquidated me at once. How do you call it? *Mitgegangen, mitgefangen, mitgehangen.*" ("Walked along, got caught along, got hanged along").

As for her boss, Hans Kamphuis, he was not the worst in the hierarchy of rats. He did little favors for "his girls," giving one, on her birthday, candy received from his wife and wishing her a happy life. One day, Wilhelm Boger of the security detail, who *was* one of the worst, came in and searched the office, pulling drawers from the desks and, finding a few biscuits and lumps of sugar, became livid, shouting, "You dirty Jews, stuffing your bellies while our brave soldiers at the front have nothing." He stomped around the room cuffing the girls, but Kamphuis, alerted by the din, arrived on the scene and warned, "If you hit my Jews, I am going to hit your Jews."

One day Harriet Berman wrote a little poem and unthinkingly left it in the typewriter when she went out for a lunch break with the others. When they got back, Kamphuis made them all stand at attention in the courtyard. "Who wrote this?" he asked, shaking the sheet of paper with her poem on it. No one answered. "If the person who wrote this does not step forward at once, every fourth person will be sent to Birkenau." They all knew what that meant. Harriet raised her hand. Kamphuis took her into his office and delivered a lecture on what happened to people who wrote poems on office time. "Well, what should I do with you?" he asked. "I don't know, Herr *Oberscharführer,*" Harriet replied. Kamphuis took his cane and started hitting the table with measured blows, as Harriet Berman stood at attention and watched.

"Why don't you scream so that those outside can hear you?" Kamphuis asked. She screamed each time he hit the table.

There was a lot of work to do because so many died, and death certificates had to be typed up with seven copies. The letter to the next of kin of Aryan dead was accompanied by a form letter inviting them to buy the urn containing the ashes of their dear departed, another profit-making Oswald Pohl sideline. One day, Kamphuis asked Harriet Berman to come with him and a couple of guards to the old crematorium on the edge of Auschwitz I, gave her a broom, and told her to sweep the dust from the crematorium floor into urns held by the guards. She filled the urns, which the guards carried back to the office, where they were sealed and stamped with the names and dates of death. She realized then that the business of selling urns was completely fraudulent. Sometimes, when she recognized a name on a death certificate as someone who had been on the Lyon train, she felt as she was typing that she was conducting a kind of ceremony, the only burial that person would get.

Shortly after Harriet Berman's visit to the crematorium, a bureaucratic foul-up occurred. A number of gassed inmates were not reported, and the *Schreibstube* did not have the data to draw up the death certificates. Kamphuis asked Harriet to accompany him to the gas chamber and help him record the tattoo numbers on the corpses. She followed him from body to body, writing down the numbers as he called them out. The seventh body they came to was her father's. She did not cry, but continued to register the numbers on the other bodies. However, she kept walking back to her father's body. "Have you lost anything there?" Kamphuis finally asked. "Why do you return to the same spot?" "Nothing, Herr *Oberscharführer*," Harriet replied. "Only my father." Kamphuis tapped her on the shoulder and said, *"Mädchen,* here you are not allowed to think or feel. Here you must function like a machine." And Harriet thought of a line in the poem she had left in the typewriter: "That stoneless graveyard where a man is worth less than a soiled shirt."

In November the Birkenau crematoriums were destroyed, and the ground where they had stood was covered with a lawn. An SS man came by the *Schreibstube* and asked Harriet if she could mail a letter for him. The letter was unsealed, so she read it. "By the way," it said, "the bathing establishments at Birkenau are disappearing and we will be angels again." Yes, she thought, angels in heaven, for in Birkenau the gas chamber was known as the *Himmelfahrtblock* (cabin for those who are climbing to Heaven).

It was December 1944, and Otto Abramovic had been in Auschwitz four months, and reflected that it was a place without precedent in the human span of time on earth. He had seen things he would not have believed if someone else had told him. He had seen one of his Canada teammates smuggle out his sardine-can razor, approach a pile of corpses on the way back to the block in the half-light, cut himself a piece of buttock from one of the corpses, and eat it. He had seen captured Russian soldiers (for the Russians were closing in) taken out to be publicly hanged, kicking away the stools on which they stood before the Germans could pull them away, their last act of defiance. He had seen a woman spot her husband and go up to the fence charged with 60,000 volts that separated the men from the women. Two SS guards told the woman, "Go kiss your husband," and as she advanced toward the fence, they shot her, and laughed as they did so.

He had gone to the *Revier* (infirmary) to see Capesius, who supervised an inmate staff of licensed pharmacists, and realized that the infirmary was actually a killing station. An inmate would be brought before a medical officer. If his file was returned to the clerk rather than to one of the doctors, that meant that his case was considered hopeless, and that he had been selected to be injected with phenolic acid. And there was Capesius, looking relaxed and jovial in his white smock, overseeing the giving of injections by the inmate pharmacists, which he called "spritzing." Since the victims' veins were hard to find, the injections were given directly into the heart. An inmate, who thought he was receiving something beneficial, willingly complied when Capesius asked him to raise his left arm and place his hand behind his head so the injection could be administered to the heart more easily, between the ribs. A moment later, he would be removed on a stretcher.

Capesius explained to Otto Abramovic that he had no choice—the *Revier* was overcrowded, and they could only admit those inmates who had a chance, and dispatch the others. The *Revier* was, in effect, a postramp selection. With camp conditions, the vermin, and the malnutrition, it was not surprising that infectious diseases spread. There was also, Capesius explained, a term that covered everything: *Allgemeinekörperschwäche* (generalized physical weakness). If Capesius didn't do the selection, Dr. Mengele would, saying in his low, melodious voice, like a kindly invitation, *"Alles herunter"* ("Everyone come forward"), and dispatch the entire *Revier* to the gas chamber. So Capesius felt that his way was more selective.

Capesius asked Abramovic for his number—193122—and told him to come back in a few days. This was at the end of December. Poland had been invaded by the Soviets, and Auschwitz was soon to be overrun. When Abramovic returned to the infirmary, Capesius handed him an envelope and said, "This is for you—it may save you some trouble." It was a death certificate. Officially, Otto Abramovic no longer existed. His name would no longer be called at the *Appell* (roll call). He just had to stay out of sight, which was not such a problem in these last and confused days of the camp.

And because he was officially dead, Otto Abramovic's name was not called on January 18, 1945, when Auschwitz was evacuated and the inmates were taken on a death march to the north. He hid out in the area around Canada, which he knew well, and when the Russians arrived on January 27, he was there to greet them, for he spoke some Russian. He became their guide to scenic Canada, with its mountains and rivers—mountains of clothing, mountains of shoes, rivers of hair, rivers of gold teeth.

Lisette Klein, the pulled ligament in her knee improved, found a spot on the nursery *Kommando,* working in the Auschwitz greenhouse under a head gardener. It was one of the better details because the gardener looked the other way when they worked in the vegetable garden. It was there that she heard the story of Lily Toffler, which was the epic romance of Auschwitz. Lily Toffler was a very pretty Slovak girl of twenty, who had a *kochany* (boyfriend) named Josef Gabis, to whom she wrote letters. He had an office job in the camp commandant's office. She worked in the greenhouse. One day two inmates came to the greenhouse to pick up a floral arrangement for the commandant's office. Lily Toffler hid a letter in the bouquet, but it fell out and was retrieved by a guard. And for this Lily Toffler was questioned for four days, refusing to give the name of the letter's recipient. Lily Toffler was taken to the black wall, stripped, and shot, as a "carrier of secrets." All because of a scrap of paper that said, "I cannot give you any news. Encouraging rumors are circulating among us. When I think about whether I could go on living after all the things I have seen, then . . . I am awaiting your reply."

Christmas was approaching, and in the greenhouse they were making wreaths from pine and holly branches. A tall spruce had been installed near the entrance gate in honor of the season, and Lisette Klein was told that it had been placed over a six-foot-deep pit where 250 Jews had been executed in the early days of the camp. In her block there was another seasonal occurrence when one of the recently arrived Hungarian women gave birth to a baby girl with blond hair and big brown eyes. The mother had no milk, so the block "organized" some milk to feed it, keeping it out of sight. But Dr. Mengele got wind of it. He arrived at the block one day, found the baby, and took it away. An hour later he came back and threw the baby's clothes at her mother. Lisette thought, It's not enough to have blood circulating in your veins to qualify as human.

At this time, there was another outbreak of typhus in the camp, and Lisette had the symptoms—spots and a high fever. She went to the *Revier,* where a woman doctor took pity on her and put her down as having the grippe, for people with typhus were given Capesius's famous "spritzers." She stayed in the infirmary into January 1945. One night the woman in the cot next to hers died without having eaten her bread ration. Lisette reached over to take it, thinking the others were asleep, but voices arose in the dark room, saying, "She didn't give it to you, you have to share." Then they began to hear artillery in the distance, and someone said, "It's the Russians, they'll kill us," and someone else said, "What if they don't?" On January 18 most of the inmates were evacuated, but the ones in the infirmary stayed behind, which was a blessing, for ten days later the Russians arrived.

As for Harriet Berman and the other typists in the *Schreib-*

stube, instead of typing death certificates, they were now asked to assist in the destruction of the Auschwitz files. The SS were burning papers by the carload. One day around Christmas, a drunken Kamphuis came into the office and said, "Now you are the prisoners and we are the free ones. Soon it will be the other way around." And then on January 18 they were marched in bitter cold to Loslau, where they were put on trains to Ravensbrück, near Berlin, where the liberating Russians arrived on May 1. Harriet Berman was interviewed by a Russian officer, and when she told her story, he commented, *"Niemetzkaya kultura"* ("German culture").

Daniel Weill's factory job came to an end when the camp was evacuated on January 18, and they started on a forced march—a long line of men in striped suits, walking at a slow pace. Stragglers got a bullet in the head. The guards were not in a charitable mood. But when they went through villages, women on doorsteps offered them milk and potatoes—so, Weill thought, they were back in that part of the world where human pity existed. Continuing across a snowy plain, they stopped at noon in a cluster of farms, then continued their march, past military convoys camouflaged in white. Every few minutes there was a shot, another fallen comrade, one of the *Marschunfähig* (those incapable of walking).

On the second day of the forced march, an SS guard ordered Weill to carry his heavy suitcase. He tried changing hands, but carrying the suitcase soon became intolerable. It seemed to weigh as much as he did, which was about eighty pounds, half his normal weight. He was falling behind, and he knew what that meant. So he moved to the other side of the column, away from the guard, put down the suitcase, and ran into a wooded area, where he fell into a snow-filled ditch. He expected at any moment to hear, *"Du, komme hier,"* but he heard nothing, and the column of marchers went on without him. He spent that night in the ditch, thinking that he would probably freeze, but shook himself awake the next morning and went back to the road, where he saw some villagers in horse-drawn carts fleeing with their belongings piled high and talking to each other about the Russians. He took the road in the opposite direction, and came to a village, which seemed deserted, and walked into an empty house, where he found a coal stove to warm himself by, food to nourish him, and an eiderdown to sleep under.

When the Russians arrived at Auschwitz on January 27, and were sifting through the debris of the camp, they came upon a metal soup bowl with a picture of a boat dancing on top of the waves scratched on it, and the words in German, "don't forget the forlorn man."

When the 178 non-Jewish men from the August 11 train arrived in the village of Stutthof on the afternoon of August 21, SS guards with dogs were at the station waiting for them. The passengers were not allowed to disembark from the train until nightfall. The men were marched in the dark to the camp, a couple of miles away, while the houses on the route were ordered to close their shutters and turn out their lights.

Stutthof was in East Prussia (now part of Poland), in a forested area on the Vistula River, between Danzig (now Gdańsk) and El-blag. In the second half of 1944, the camp was badly overcrowded with 27,000 men and 9,000 women, mostly Poles. The number of inmates had doubled, the number of guards had stayed the same, and the food rations had been cut by half. The guards were jittery, as though already smelling Russian gunpowder. There was unrest among the prisoners, and the commandant, Major Hoppe, gave all new arrivals a brief lecture, which ended with these words: "The crematorium is good—it makes smoke out of loafers."

For Gaston Bonnat, a *lycée* teacher who had joined *Combat,* the underground group, and had been captured in a sweep of Cler-mont-Ferrand, the worst moment of the train trip had come during the first stop after crossing the Rhine when, on German soil, one of the SS guards had told him to shine his boots. He entertained the thought that it would be preferable to die, noticing as he knelt before the boots that the guard was missing a thumb, and wishing he had a knife to cut off all his fingers. Now, at the camp, he felt that he and his resistance friends had a chance, because they were disciplined, and formed a team, and could help one another. He was given a registration form to fill out, and wondered what to say under the category of profession. Was there some skill that the Great Reich needed at which he was semicompetent? Finally he put down "carpenter," and was promptly assigned to the gravel-shoveling detail in the fishing village of Stutthof. The gravel was brought over by barge from the other side of the Vistula. One of the old-timers told him, "Work with your eyes," which meant watch out for the guards.

Siegfried Szemendera, a Pole who had emigrated to France in the thirties and who had been in the resistance in Grenoble, had thought several times during the trip that he could have escaped, when the train slowed down to five kilometers an hour or during the bombardment, but he had been put off by the warning "If one person in a compartment tries to escape the others will be shot." Also, he thought, the war would be over soon, so what was the point? But he was not prepared for conditions at Stutthof, where there was nothing to eat. The inmates grabbed everything they could get their hands on. They chewed old coffee grounds retrieved from the garbage or munched on charcoal. Half of the people in the camp were sick. It didn't take much—a sip of dirty water, a mouthful of potato peel, and you came down with dysentery. Szemendera soon had dysentery himself, and could not move from his bunk. His friends brought him soup with milk, and managed to steal a bit of opium from the *Revier,* which he was sure saved his life. He got better, and when a package arrived, his spirits lifted. Who could describe the profound joy of a canned sardine, the matchless satisfaction of one's first puff on a Gauloise? Thanks to the cigarettes, he bought a spot on the garden detail from a friendly *Kapo.* He spent his days spading and weeding in the camp's vegetable garden, and taking a carrot or a turnip when the guards weren't looking. Angora rabbits were also kept there to make mittens and scarves for the SS. Szemendera and the others on the detail ate the mush intended for the rabbits.

The friendly *Kapo* was a green triangle from Berlin, but civilized, not a troglodyte like the pimps and thieves of the Berlin underworld. A con man who had swindled women of a certain age, he felt that he had been unjustly treated and went on at length about his case. "Can a man be called a criminal just because he tries to make some woman's life a little more pleasant? And a single woman at that, with no hope of marriage whatsoever? My God, man, that's not a crime, it's an act of Christian charity. And in any case, it's a private matter and no one else's business, certainly not the state's."

In December, with the cold, conditions got worse, and the combination of dysentery, typhus, short rations, and freezing weather was killing hundreds a day. The small Stutthof crematorium was cracked from overuse. You had to walk over unburied bodies to get from block to block. Russian divisions were poised on the East Prussian border. As if to counter the mood of impending defeat, the Stutthof authorities became obstinately more punitive. A portable gallows had been built by the carpentry shop and was set up for public hangings on the parade grounds and then dismantled, but now there were so many hangings that they just left it up. The entire camp population had to watch these executions. To Siegfried Szemendera, they became part of the order of events in the daily schedule. The sentence was read aloud by an SS officer, the condemned man climbed the steps to the gallows, and the noose was slipped over his head, the trapdoor dropped, the body jerked, the shoulders heaved, the arms thrashed, and then the body was lowered and disengaged from the rope.

One day an inmate escaped, but was recaptured two days later. He had headed east, trying to reach the Russian armies, but had run into a German patrol. The escape was baffling. There was no break in the barbed wire. The ground was covered with snow, but there were no footprints leading from the camp perimeter. None of the guards in the watchtowers with their Zeiss binoculars had seen anything. No dog had barked. No tunnel had been dug. It was as if the man had simply dematerialized.

The SS officer who questioned the man, a Pole, told him: "If you tell me how you escaped, I give you my word as a German officer that you will not be punished." The man explained that he had been the pole-vaulting champion of Poland, and had represented his country in that event at the 1936 Olympics in Berlin. He worked at the Stutthof sawmill, where he was able to make himself a perch, which he smuggled into the camp in pieces. One night he simply pole-vaulted over the electrified barbed-wire fence to freedom.

The SS officer broke his word, and the next morning, on the roll-call square, the escapee in his zebra-striped uniform was presented to the assembled inmates with a placard around his neck that read *Ich Bin Wieder Da* (I'm Back again). It was announced that he would be whipped, forty strokes, in front of the inmates. And, according to camp tradition, an inmate would do the whipping. Gaston Bonnat, who had been singled out for his unsubmissive attitude, was chosen to carry out the order. He was called from the ranks and told to administer the forty blows. But when he was handed the whip, he refused. The SS officer screamed that he was insubordinate, and that he would be punished for refusing to obey an order, but Gaston Bonnat simply repeated "I refuse" and stood at attention, not saying another word. "Return to the ranks," the SS officer shouted. "We will see what happens."

The SS officer then called one of the *Kapos* from the Berlin underworld, who did not refuse as the Polish escapee called out the number of each lash, *ein zwei* . . . The *Kapo* did not pull his strokes, and after seventeen the young Pole stopped counting. After twenty, a doctor was called to take the pulse of the now unconscious man. Szemendera shut his eyes, finding himself unable to watch. The count from twenty-one to forty seemed to last an eternity; in fact it was less than a minute, and it was impossible to tell whether the young Pole was alive or dead. As for Gaston Bonnat, no punitive measure was taken against him. Less than a month later, the Russians were at Elblag, ten miles from the camp, which was evacuated in utter confusion, and the white flag was raised over the entrance. Siegfried Szemendera, thinking that he would not survive evacuation, went into the frozen vegetable garden and hid in a big pile of compost until the Russians arrived. Then he emerged, feeling no joy, or exultation, but dismay. For some reason, it was upsetting to leave the camp.

The two cars carrying the 120 non-Jewish women from Montluc Prison had been uncoupled from the others on the German side of the Rhine and were added on to a Berlin-bound freight train. From Berlin the cars continued northward to Fürstenberg on the Havel, a tributary of the Oder River. After a forty-minute march through the woods under escort, the women arrived at the camp of Ravensbrück, which means bridge of crows, on August 20.

What a vision of hell, thought Cécile Goldet, one of the seven nurses captured in the Grotte de la Luire, as she saw outside the camp a column of skeletal women with vacant faces, ageless and indistinct, pulling a heavy length of cement pipe. And Josette Leroi, who had been arrested for helping Jews in Lyon, now saw, as they entered the Ravensbrück courtyard, women with their heads shaved, scabs covering their legs, marching in step to music with shovels on their shoulders, like rifles. When the train had been delayed in Vittel, Josette Leroi had flushed a note down the toilet for her husband, hoping that a Red Cross nurse would pick it up and send it. Later, when the women were searched, she put her wedding ring under her tongue, but during the second search it slipped out and she lost it.

Built in 1939 on reclaimed swampland fifty miles north of Berlin, Ravensbrück was the principal concentration camp for women. It was situated in a hollow, and to the north rose sandy land upon which grew a few stunted pines. Ravensbrück was conceived as a model camp, and an effort was made at landscaping, with flower beds, and gravel paths, and well-kept lawns fringed with silver firs. The inmates wore white kerchiefs and dresses with broad blue and white stripes and dark blue aprons.

In 1942 the camp was expanded to thirty-two blocks in order to provide labor for the factories being built on the outskirts. With overcrowding came vermin, typhus, a drop in living standards, and a rise in the mortality rate. Between 1939 and 1945, an estimated 123,000 women were registered at Ravensbrück. Ninety thousand of them died, or roughly three out of four. Although Ravensbrück was not a death camp, a gas chamber was built there in 1944, and the system for gassing inmates was to list them as "transferred to the rest camp of Mittwerda-in-Silesia," a place that did not exist. Older women were taken away, those over fifty, those who had gray hair. Women with grey in their hair made a paste of water and soot to dye it. A crematorium was built, then a second one, to handle the bodies that piled up, not only from the gassing but from disease, for 1944 was the year of typhus, tuberculosis, and pneumonia, and also the year of a new cause of death, Allied bombing. In the early days, before the crematorium, a Fürstenberg undertaker named Wendland had contracted to remove the dead. He came to the camp in a horse-drawn cart filled with pine coffins. The bodies were so emaciated he could fit two to a coffin. Josette Leroi, being told this story, dreamed that Herr Wendland had come for her, looking so friendly in his cap with earflaps and his duffel coat.

The same triangle system existed in Ravensbrück as in the other camps: red for politicals, green for criminals, black for asocials, purple for the *Bibelforscher* (Jehovah's Witnesses), and yellow and black for the *Rassenschande* (literally, "shame to the race," Aryan women married to Jews). Josette Leroi, since she had a Jewish husband, had to wear the yellow and black, although she insisted she was a political. She was assigned to a block of black triangles, mostly prostitutes, who were depressing to be with because they were shirkers and snitches and thieves. She had to sleep with her clogs under her pillow at night. The block was dirty, the beds were badly made, and no one wanted to clean up. The women were constantly bickering and exchanging insults, usually about lack of discrimination and low rates in their former line of work. "You'd take on two drunks in a doorway for a pfennig each," was a typical observation. There were also haughty ones, who went on about the clothes they had had, the fur coats men had given them, the men who had been mad about them and would buy them anything they asked for. "I never worked with older men," one said, "I chose the young ones."

At first, Josette Leroi was in a labor pool for new arrivals, who were given a variety of hard outdoor jobs, such as leveling dunes or camouflaging anti-aircraft positions near the camp with turf. Then, when she told them she knew how to use a sewing machine, she was sent to the garment workshop, where four hundred women sat stitching SS uniforms. The cutting room delivered parts that were assembled on tables and laid out on moving belts. One inmate sewed a back seam, the next one, a front seam, the third, a sleeve, on down the assembly line until the finished jacket was handed over to the controller, who inspected it for errors. It was a ten-hour shift. Air-raid warnings were welcome because they provided a break, except for one day when the hangar where they were working was hit. During the confusion, two Polish women hid in a refuse bin, which was removed from the camp by truck, and they managed to escape toward Berlin.

With the garment workshop out of commission, Josette Leroi was transferred to a munitions plant, where she filled shells with gunpowder. This was not quite the same as sewing uniforms, for she was directly contributing to the deaths of Allied soldiers. The obvious solution was to work slowly and ineffectually, to sabotage the work without being noticed or reprimanded. The problem was, she found, that she had to force herself to be a bad worker. Doing good work was more in conformity with her nature than sabotage, and she had to guard against an inclination to perform well, to please her employer. There were other women who could not help doing their best. When their machines broke down they wanted to fix them right away. It was true that women who exceeded their quotas were given coupons that could be spent at the camp canteen, but that was not much of an incentive, since there was never anything in stock except salt and fish paste. No, these women wanted the inner satisfaction of a job well done. Whereas Josette told herself that the correct attitude was to screw on the same shell casing over and over, so as to seem to be working. The correct attitude was to mix floor sweepings with the gunpowder, and to mix water with the oil so the machine broke down, and you could call out with an air of resignation: *"Maschine kaput."*

On the way back to the camp in the evening, the women passed a big house where the munitions factory director and his children lived. Sometimes the children were waiting with rocks, which they threw at the column of women as it passed. But that was not the hardest thing for Josette Leroi to bear. Nor was hunger the hardest thing. The hardest, it seemed to her, was the total abandonment of hygiene. It became an act of will to keep clean. It took hours to pick off the lice, which she thought of as multiracial because there were white ones, black ones, yellow ones, and striped ones. You had to fight for space at the water trough, and once a drunken guard vomited in it and ordered her to wash her face. The latrine was a ditch with planks thrown across at intervals, over which they squatted in plain sight. There was no toilet paper, and paper of any kind was rare. Some had a bit of cloth they would wash and reuse. Josette Leroi saw the breakdown of life-long habits of cleanliness. She saw women with diarrhea, too exhausted to go to the latrine, relieve themselves in their food bowls at night. They were starving and suffering from dysentery at the same time. She had diarrhea herself, but went to work, heeding the advice of her block leader, who said: "Ladies, you don't want to go to the *Revier*. Even with a temperature of a hundred and four. Do you understand, ladies?" She understood, particularly when a French nurse from the train who now worked in the *Revier* told her that it was a way station to the gas chamber, and that on the charts at the foot of the infirmary beds was written one word: *Durchfall* (diarrhea). So she went to work, and felt the liquid brown matter run down her legs as though life itself were leaking out of her. Some said, Why wash? Why bother? It's too much trouble. In fact, washing was a condition of survival. A way of showing they had not lost hope. This is one thing I can do to show you I am not subhuman. I am not what you have tried to make me. The appearance of the outer person is the key to the state of the inner person. I will wash my face and body. I will brush my teeth. I will go to the latrine at night rather than soil my mattress or food bowl. I will have a clean kerchief. I will clean my shoes with sand. I will stand up straight at roll call. To show them that they have not defeated me. For Josette Leroi was surrounded by death, those who died of shock, weariness, loss of selfhood, of being in a situation for which nothing in their previous life had prepared them. She saw the *Muselmänner,* the faces with the dead eyes, and said to herself, "I will never be like them." At work, cheating the system by mixing dust with gunpowder raised her spirits. Any cheating operation at the camp was in the name of the life force.

Cécile Goldet, being a German-speaking nurse, was assigned to the *Revier*. She was the only French woman in Block 17, the *Bibelforscher*'s block. The *Bibelforscher,* or Jehovah's Witnesses, had struck a sort of tacit bargain with the authorities. They had succeeded in bending regulations to conform with their beliefs. They regarded the Nazi regime as the work of the anti-Christ, and refused to do anything that was remotely military. They would not even roll bandages for field dressings. They would not stand at attention at roll call, or march in step, or salute, saying that such marks of respect were due to God and not man. They were released from whatever they refused to do. In exchange, they were model prisoners who kept a model block, cleaned the camp, and worked as nannies for the children of the SS officers.

Cécile Goldet found herself in a block that was spotlessly clean, with whitewashed walls and ceilings. It smelled of disinfectant and there were no vermin. All the women had been allowed to keep their hair, and tied it neatly in a bun. At mealtime, under each bowl of cabbage soup at the table, there was a little cardboard mat so the bowl would not leave a ring. The floor was covered with sheets of brown paper to protect it from inmates returning from work details. There were brushes and scrapers behind the door, and towels were hanging on the locker doors at precisely the regulation length. The stools were scrubbed and stacked when not in use. Dust was constantly hunted down as enemy number one, even on the roof beams. The straw sacks and pillows were built up and squared, with defined edges; they were not shapeless lumps as in the other blocks. The blankets were folded just so. On every bunk there was a card with the name and number of the prisoner who slept in it.

Cécile was full of admiration for these women, but also felt that there was a touch of arrogance in their self-sufficient sectarianism. They seemed to be announcing their superiority to the rest of mankind. In Block 17, the model block, there was no shouting, or quarreling, or stealing, or lying, or tattling. The block was at the other end of the spectrum from the world of the asocials. The camp commandant, Colonel Suhren, used to show off the block to important visitors from Berlin. One day he arrived unannounced, wearing his best uniform and all his medals, with some dignitaries who oohed and aahed over the tidiness of the barracks.

At the top of his lungs, as if the importance of the occasion required shouting, Suhren yelled: "Block Senior! How much time have the prisoners between reveille and roll call?

"Three quarters of an hour, ladies and gentlemen," he continued, "and in that time look at what my prisoners can do: bed making, dressing, washing, locker cleaning, coffee drinking, and then roll call. And look at these exemplary beds. Or perhaps you think there are boards under the blankets?" He turned down the cover of one of the sacks and smacked the mattress with his whip.

"Look at that straw sack. See how it's packed? That's merely one of the results of the work we do here to educate the prisoners back to a life of order and cleanliness." Then he strode to a window, out of which could be seen a long line of identical blocks, and with a proud movement of his arm, embracing what he saw, he said, "And all those huts are just as clean and orderly as this one. You can take my word for that." The visitors crowded around and gazed with admiration at the noble work of rehabilitation being accomplished with the enemies of the state. One of them asked to see the toilets. "Why of course," shouted Suhren, "and you'll find the same cleanliness and order you see everywhere else. Block Senior, lead the way." The man followed Suhren and the block senior to a toilet, pulled the chain, and approvingly watched it flush. "At the beginning of the war," the man said, "I was interned in England. The water closets never functioned properly there. It just shows you the difference in culture."

Cécile Goldet found the work at the *Revier* depressing, although it was better than working outside. The tubercular cases spat blood, and others came in so weak you knew they would not last the night. The SS matron, a large blond woman with tight lips and hard narrow-lidded eyes, who wore a field-gray skirt and a forage cap, ruled on each patient. If someone was brought in on a stretcher she shouted, "Corridor case," and the woman was laid out in the hall and given morphine for two days. On the third day she was given a phenol injection in the heart muscle.

When pregnant women were brought in, Cécile helped the Austrian midwife, also an inmate, deliver the babies. The midwife carried away the newborns and drowned them in buckets of water. She said their lung capacity and will to live were such that it took as long as twenty minutes. "I was deported for practicing abortions," she told Cécile, "and now I'm drowning babies." Their mothers had no milk so the babies would have died anyway.

Cécile Goldet learned that suffering did not ennoble you, it robbed you of your dignity. It made you lose hope. She heard a woman say: "I don't even want to see my daughters anymore." One day Cécile took a second look at one of the corridor cases and recognized Odette Malossane, one of her fellow nurses from the Grotte de la Luire. When the matron took her lunch break, Cécile pulled

Odette up from the stretcher, and found her a bed in the *Revier*.

Odette Malossane was a pretty, round-faced, round-eyed, somewhat vague young woman who accepted things as they came. She had had the bad luck of being assigned to a block made up mainly of Polish women. The block leader had a grudge against French women, whom she referred to as "those tarts who rouge their cheeks with beet juice." Consequently, Odette was given one of the worst work details, the one they gave to the *Nacht und Nebel* inmates, the salt mine. It involved a three-kilometer walk in the predawn cold to the work site, then a slow freight elevator ride to the center of the earth, and all day underground in the bad light and the bad air, swinging away at a wall of salt with a pick. Coming back to the camp exhausted, she didn't have the energy to go to the latrine. Eating the turnip soup cooked with potato peels gave her dysentery, and she knew that the only way to relieve the dysentery was to go without soup. But if you went without soup, you starved. She had no sooner fallen asleep, it seemed, than she heard the familiar *Aufstehen,* and had to get up in the cold and put on her blue-striped uniform and white kerchief and go out to roll call, and then it was the hike to the salt mine again. One day the block leader approached her and said, "The camp commandant wants to send you to the front to entertain the troops. You'll have plenty of food and nice dresses." She knew what that meant, and continued to work in the salt mine, but one day she collapsed at roll call and was sent on a stretcher to the *Revier*.

In her infirmary bed, attended to by her friend Cécile, Odette Malossane found that her strength was returning bit by bit. On the third day she was examined by two doctors and wondered, why all the attention? One of the doctors gave her an intramuscular injection, then a subcutaneous injection, and she had no idea why, as the doctors babbled away in German. Then the SS matron undressed her and gave her a bathrobe, and by the time she had the bathrobe on she was asleep.

When Odette woke up, she had a cast on her right leg, and on the cast was the mark III TK. She had no idea what had happened to her, and lay in bed crying and looking out the window at sunflowers and high-tension wires, thinking, "If only I could touch them," meaning the wires, not the sunflowers. Cécile Goldet brought her a glass of milk, but was reluctant to explain what had been done to her. "You're a *kroliky* [Polish for rabbit]," was all she would say. A few days later, the cast was removed. There was a long, open wound below the knee. The two doctors, Karl Gebhardt and his assistant, Fritz Fischer, were conducting experiments on the rate of infection in war wounds, which were simulated with the help of surgery. They had removed part of the tibia from Odette's leg and infected the wound with bacteria. Soon they came to her bedside to see how the bacteria were doing, if the leg was really infected yet, if it had developed gangrene. Then she realized what *kroliky* meant, it meant "guinea pig." She had heard rumors about the "bone people," who were deliberately crippled and infected, and now she was one of them. One day the SS matron came around and asked Odette, not in her usual barking tone, to sign a statement that her scars were due to a work accident. Odette said she was too weak to hold the pen, but the matron insisted and put the pen in her hand, and guided her hand so she could write her name at the bottom of the page. Cécile Goldet brought her milk and hot broth, maintaining a cheerful countenance and telling her she would be all right. But she knew that she would not be all right. She was given injections to ease the pain, and slept a great deal. One morning, hearing voices, she opened her eyes and saw Gebhardt's assistant talking to the SS matron. She caught a few words, and realized that the doctor was asking the matron, "Can you make out a death certificate?" Her eyes filled with tears, and she asked to be returned to the block. A little later, she fell asleep.

In December the cold settled in. Long dismal days and feverish nights. Sunlight in the angle of a wall. Cécile Goldet saw the first cases of frostbite arrive at the *Revier*. The treatment was amputation. There was also a typhus epidemic, and the stretchers were moving in and out as though on an assembly line. At night, as she lay on her straw mattress, she could hear the drone of planes overhead and sometimes spot a beam from searchlights scanning the sky over Berlin. She came down with bronchitis and was coughing so badly one morning that she could not get up. One of the "Bible worms," as they were called, told her to "hold on until evening." The woman returned with some herbs and made an herbal tea and chest poultices, which helped Cécile sufficiently so that the next day she could go to work. She did not even know the name of the woman who had helped her. She didn't understand these Jehovah's Witnesses. They could have left the camp any day they chose by simply signing a form repudiating their allegiance to their faith. Cécile asked the woman who had helped her why she didn't sign the form and leave, since a promise made under duress had no value. The woman replied that to sign the form was to make a pact with the Devil.

When Cécile Goldet and the other 119 women from the August 11 train from Lyon arrived at Ravensbrück on August 20 and saw the conditions there, they had every reason to expect that they would never see their native land again. Although the Allies had landed in the west, and the Russians were pushing the Germans back in the east, Hitler's troops were still fighting fiercely and the war showed no sign of ending. And the longer it dragged on, the worse conditions in the camps became, closing the door to survival. Cut off from the outside world, Cécile and her fellow nurses, whose itinerary had taken them from the Grotte de la Luire in the heart of France, where they had been guilty of no crime other than tending the wounded, to a concentration camp in the heart of Germany, where death was the normal method of departure, heard bits and pieces of news, but nothing that gave them a clear idea of the march of events. And even if they had listened every evening to the radio, they would have had no way of knowing that their fate depended on such things as the neutrality of Sweden and the state of Himmler's stomach. The true march of events takes place along a subterranean route, and so the women did not know that they would remain in Ravensbrück almost exactly eight months, and then their fate would be determined by Himmler, who would commit what was in his own eyes an unpardonable act in negotiating face to face with a Jew.

Far from being a superman, or even a normally healthy man, Himmler was chronically ill. He developed terrible, crippling stomach pains, which nothing relieved. He was sure it was cancer, which had killed his father. He also had headaches, which were so bad they impaired his eyesight. He had boxes full of headache remedies, some of them herbal, for he believed in the curative properties of juniper and gentian. Those were the good old ways, going back to the Middle Ages. Bavarian peasants knew how to poultice their sick horses, and cure their own aches and pains with tea made from wormwood and chrysanthemums.

But for Himmler nothing worked. He tried doctor after doctor, remedy after remedy. Nothing alleviated the constant pain. In 1939 the potash magnate Rostberg told him about a Finnish doctor who was able to treat headaches and stomach disorders through massage. The doctor was Felix Kersten, an Estonian whose family had settled in Finland. He was trained in Finnish massage, and was so adept that he won the highest title in Finnish medicine, *Medizinalrat*. But the breakthrough for Kersten came when he moved to Berlin in 1922 and met a Chinese doctor trained in Tibetan techniques who accepted him as a disciple. For three years, Kersten learned from Dr. Ko about pulses and nerve centers and fingertip diagnosis. Having mastered the technique, he inherited Dr. Ko's practice of wealthy German businessmen. The grateful Rostberg gave him a bonus of 100,000 marks. Kersten, who combined an uncanny ability as a healer with a love of wealth and social position, did well enough to buy a 750-acre estate thirty miles north of Berlin, Hartzwalde, where he stocked the house with art, antiques, and a beautiful wife half his age named Irmgard.

His reputation spread, and in the thirties Kersten was invited to Holland to treat the Dutch consort, Prince Hendrik, spending much of his time at the Dutch court. Then, in 1939, came the offer to treat Himmler. At that time, Kersten was a stout man of forty-one, weighing 250 pounds, with thinning dark blond hair swept back, a large head with a domelike brow, a round, jowly, pug-nosed face, and arched eyebrows over deep-set blue eyes. On March 10 he arrived at the Chancellery in Berlin at 8 Prinz Albert Strasse, and was led into a large office where he was met by a slight, narrow-shouldered man with steel-rimmed spectacles, high cheekbones, and a complexion like beeswax. When Kersten examined Himmler, he saw that he did no exercise beyond the occasional parade goosestep, and had a protruding stomach, the seat of his ailment. This was one of the puniest and most sickly-looking specimens Kersten had ever seen, and he thought, "So this is the man who is a source of terror to every German."

The other doctors had asked Himmler a long list of questions about his medical history, nodding wisely as he answered, but Kersten asked no questions. He got right down to business, locating the combination to Himmler's body with a safecracker's sense of touch, finding the pulses and nerve centers and knots, kneading his stomach, his temples, his feet. The results were immediate and amazing—Himmler felt relief from pain for the first time in days. Where medicine had failed, where morphine has lost its effect, this man, with his two hands, had succeeded. It was nothing short of miraculous.

Kersten became indispensable to Himmler. He became a familiar and a friend, and was invited to Himmler's home to meet his wife, an unpleasant woman nine years his senior, with a thin, dried-up face. Kersten's presence was connected in Himmler's mind with relief from pain. In addition to soothing hands, he had a gift for flattery, telling Himmler that he was a great leader, the equal of Henry the Fowler, the first Saxon king. When Kersten magically rubbed the pain out of Himmler's aching body, the relief was so great that the Nazi leader dropped his guard, confiding his innermost thoughts to this bringer of comfort. He talked about the unity of German life, about historical archetypes reappearing in different centuries, of which he said he was one. He talked about his admiration for Buddhism and the notion of karma. He read the *Bhagavad-Gita,* and never traveled without it.

Kersten had become the confidant of one of the most powerful men in the Third Reich, which was too good an opportunity to pass up. When Himmler was on the massage table, and Kersten was stimulating his circulation, making his stress-stiffened muscles supple, filling his body with a sense of well-being, he was at his most approachable. At first Kersten asked Himmler for personal favors having to do with the management of his estate in wartime. Help was scarce, so he asked Himmler to release five or six *Bibelforscher* from Ravensbrück so they could work at Hartzwalde. Then one day Kersten brought a ham from the estate, which Himmler found delicious. But how did he manage to have a ham in wartime? Because, Kersten explained, he was slaughtering his animals clandestinely, an offense against the food-rationing laws that carried the death penalty. The solution, Kersten suggested, was to have Hartzwalde declared extraterritorial property, like an embassy. Not wanting to lose his doctor, Himmler agreed to have it done.

In May 1940 Kersten was ordered to join Himmler's armored train. He was practically commandeered, as someone necessary to the war effort, and remained at Himmler's disposal until 1943. Kersten soon began to make good use of his privileged access to the man who governed the concentration camps. In August 1940 he obtained the release of one of Rostberg's servants from Dachau. After that, he regularly asked for prisoner releases as a form of payment for his healing touch. In November 1942, while on a trip to Holland, Kersten was told about twenty-eight Dutchmen, several of whom were his personal friends, who had been sentenced to death for a sabotage action they had not committed. "I know that your humane feelings will allow you to sign a release for these men," he said as he massaged Himmler's lower back, and Himmler signed. In December Kersten obtained the release of a second group of Dutch prisoners. He cleverly allowed Himmler to assume the role of "nice guy." Himmler could tell himself and others, "I'm so soft-hearted, Kersten asks me to release prisoners and I do it." He also played on his patient's superstitious side, for Himmler believed in an invisible power to which he would some day be accountable, and this would be a way of putting a few good deeds on the ledger.

Himmler saw himself as a selfless servant of the state who had to take on different tasks unsuited to his humane and sensitive nature. As the pain left his body, so did his stream-of-consciousness thoughts: "I try to reach a compromise in my own life; I try to help people and do good, relieve the oppressed and remove injustices wherever I can. Do you think my heart's in all the things which have to be done simply from reasons of state? What wouldn't I give to be minister of religious matters like [Bernhard] Rust and be able to dedicate myself to positive achievement only! . . . But the present state of things both at home and abroad demands the fusion of *Reichsführer* SS and chief of police—that too is karma, which I must come to terms with and turn to my own use."

Asking favor for favor, Himmler wanted Kersten in December 1942 to treat a man suffering from bad headaches and dizziness. He pulled from his safe a twenty-six-page medical report, and swore Kersten to secrecy. The report was Hitler's: poorly treated at Pasenwalk Hospital in 1918 for injuries sustained breathing poison gas; in danger of going blind; symptoms associated with syphilis, showing progressive paralysis in 1942. Kersten said that Hitler was so far gone he should retire at once and appoint a successor.

After Stalingrad, seeing the way the war was going, Kersten decided to move his family and himself to neutral Sweden. He presented this relocation in a way that would not antagonize Himmler by telling him that he had been called up to be a doctor in the Finnish Army. The Finns, however, knowing of his close ties with Himmler, had allowed him to move his practice to Sweden, where he could treat Finnish soldiers convalescing there. In this way, he said, he would continue to fly from Stockholm to Berlin regularly to treat Himmler.

Moving to Stockholm in September 1943, Kersten installed his wife and son in an apartment, and made contact with the Swedish minister of foreign affairs, Christian Gunther. The Swedes at that time were under increasing pressure to enter the war against Hitler. Wanting to show their good intentions without giving up their neutrality, they decided to mount a rescue operation under the auspices of the Swedish Red Cross, starting with the Scandinavian prisoners in the concentration camps. Kersten agreed to work on Himmler to achieve this end. On one of his trips to Berlin, he told Himmler that the Swedes would give asylum to any prisoners he agreed should be released from the camps. But the initial snag was that the German railways could not provide transportation for them.

While the Swedish plan was momentarily stalled, Kersten continued to persuade Himmler to release specific prisoners. Himmler told Count Ciano that Kersten was a magician, a Buddha, "but our Buddha often causes me great anxiety. He comes to me with a list of names in his hand and asks me to release men who are opposed to the war and to the Führer's great conceptions. Most of them are Dutchmen, Jews, and German traitors. And he's so incredibly obstinate and persistent that I always have to give way to him."

In 1944, after the Allied invasion of France and the Russian advances. Himmler took on additional duties: He became head of the SS and the Reich police, minister of the interior, Commander in Chief of the Replacement Army, and Commander of the Army Group Vistula. This last was his first field command, at which he was totally inept. Himmler's stress became aggravated, so Kersten had to travel to the receding eastern front to treat his harassed patient, following by train as best he could to provide the Nazi leader much-needed relief from head and stomach distress. On July 20 Kersten was in a sleeping car near Himmler's Black Forest command post when Himmler's chauffeur, Lukas, burst into Kersten's compartment crying, "Attempt on the Führer! But he's safe!" They had just come from the Wolf's Lair, Hitler's underground headquarters in East Prussia, near Rastenburg (which Jodl had called "that strange mixture of cloister and concentration camp"). Kersten got dressed and went at once to see Himmler, who told him: "A bomb was thrown at the Führer. But Providence has saved him. The attempt was made by a colonel in the Wehrmacht. Now my hour has come. I will round up all the reactionary gang and have already given the orders for the traitors' arrest."

Himmler began to see, however, that the military situation was desperate. Germany was about to be invaded on the east by the Russians and on the west by the Americans and the British. Prodded by Walter Schellenberg, deputy head of the SD, he considered making some kind of deal with the Allies. The release of concentration camp inmates to the Swedish Red Cross would be seen as a gesture of goodwill. He was also negotiating, through Walter Schellenberg and a former president of Switzerland by the name of Musy, for the release of 2,700 Jews from the Theresienstadt camp in exchange for five million Swiss francs. Himmler thought of the people in the camps as his private property, which he could sell or exchange as he wished.

When Kersten saw Himmler on December 8 at Hochwaldt, his East Prussian command post, he found him in a somber mood. It would be treason to the Führer, Himmler said, to release prison inmates just now. The people in the camps were criminals and enemies of the state. He had already let go far too many. Gradually, however, he came around and agreed in principle to a first shipment of 2,800 women from Ravensbrück—1,000 Dutch, 800 French, 500 Poles, 400 Belgian, 50 Danes, and 50 Norwegians. They would go to the Neuengamme camp, north of Hamburg, not far from the Danish border. Swedish buses could come over from Denmark, pick them up, and take them to Sweden.

In February 1945 the Theresienstadt Jews were released and transported by train to the Swiss border, and Himmler received his payment. In the meantime, on February 13, the British raided Dresden with incendiary bombs, starting a firestorm that killed 135,000. In Stockholm Christian Gunther told Kersten that Count Folke Bernadotte, vice-president of the Swedish Red Cross and a nephew of the king, would command the rescue operation and was leaving for Berlin to discuss a timetable.

On February 16 Count Bernadotte flew into Berlin and paid a courtesy call on von Ribbentrop, who offered him Chesterfields and Dubonnet, and spoke for more than an hour—Bernadotte timed him with a stopwatch, and could not get a word in. How could this long-winded buffoon have been in charge of German foreign policy all these years? Bernadotte wondered as he sat listening to the onetime champagne salesman.

Bernadotte's aim was to see Himmler, which he was able to do on February 19 at the SS hospital in Hohenlychen, seventy-five miles north of Berlin. Bernadotte noticed that Himmler's hands were manicured, although manicures were forbidden in the SS. Himmler was wearing a green uniform and was affable, even jocular. He almost seemed to be enjoying the present debacle. Bernadotte, interested only in Scandinavian prisoners, asked him to free the thirteen thousand Danes and Norwegians in concentration camps, so they could be sent to Sweden and interned there. He also asked that Swedish women married to Germans be allowed to go home with their children. Himmler remained silent for a time, then said: "I don't feel inclined to send German children to Sweden. There they will be brought up to hate their country, and they will be spat on by their playmates because their fathers were German." But Himmler needed an insurance policy. The Russians were on the Oder, the German border with Poland. The Allies would soon reach the left bank of the Rhine. He agreed to release the Norwegian and Danish prisoners. They would be removed from their camps and assembled in Neuengamme, where Bernadotte could pick them up in Red Cross buses. As Bernadotte was taking his leave, Himmler asked one of his aides if his guest had been assigned a good chauffeur. The best, he was told. "Good," Himmler said, "otherwise there might be headlines in the Swedish papers saying WAR CRIMINAL HIMMLER MURDERS COUNT BERNADOTTE."

While Bernadotte was in Berlin, Kersten was in Stockholm, where on March 2 he met a leader of the World Jewish Congress, Hilel Storch, who told him that Hitler had ordered the destruction of the concentration camps and the murder of their occupants. Storch asked Kersten if he would be willing to make a direct approach to Himmler not to carry out that order. On March 5 Kersten flew to Berlin and saw a distraught Himmler, who told him: "If National Socialist Germany is going to be destroyed then her enemies and the criminals in concentration camps shall not have the satisfaction of emerging from our ruin as triumphant conquerors. They shall share in the downfall." But then he relented and agreed not to pass on the order to blow up the camps. They would he handed over in an orderly manner. When the Allies arrived, a white flag would be shown. Kersten drew up an agreement to that effect, which Himmler signed.

On March 12 Bernadotte crossed the Danish border into Germany with 100 white Swedish Red Cross buses to collect the 4,400 Danes and Norwegians who were assembled at the Neuengamme camp after being pulled out of Sachsenhausen, Dachau, Buchenwald, and other camps.

On March 13 Kersten asked Himmler to release the French women in Ravensbrück, since France was no longer occupied territory. By this time Germany had been invaded by the Allies and the American First Army had occupied Cologne. Himmler at first demurred, but finally agreed to release eight hundred French women and allow them to go to Sweden. Four days later, Kersten presented Himmler with a plan for the release of Jewish prisoners. He wanted Himmler to meet Hilel Storch of the World Jewish Congress. Himmler at first refused, saying: "I could never receive a Jew. If the Führer were to hear about it, he would have me shot dead on the spot." "Always this fear of the Führer," thought

Kersten, but argued that Himmler's position as head of the German police, responsible for frontier control, gave him every facility for keeping flights in and out of the country secret. It would be easy for him to arrange a flight that neither Goebbels nor Bormann nor Hitler knew about. Kersten proposed his own home, Hartzwalde, as the site of the talks. When Himmler finally agreed, Kersten said he would need a safe-conduct for Hilel Storch. "Nothing will happen to Herr Storch," Himmler said. "I pledge my honor and my life on that."

Kersten returned to Stockholm on March 22 and went at once to see Christian Gunther, who called the camp rescues "a political event of global importance." How many would there be? he asked. Between 20,000 and 25,000, Kersten said. "These people will all be heartily welcome in Sweden," Gunther said. "I hope to be able to fly with Storch to Berlin next week," said Kersten. He saw Storch the next day, March 23, who told him he was willing to go to Berlin and meet Himmler as long as Kersten came too.

In the meantime, Count Bernadotte made a second trip into Germany, visiting Neuengamme on March 30. He could hear guns roaring in Bremen, to the southwest. On April 2 he saw Himmler at the Hohenlychen SS hospital. Himmler agreed to the transfer of more Danes and Norwegians, and also told him about his agreement with Kersten to release the French women in Ravensbrück. It seemed to Bernadotte that Himmler was subject to extreme mood swings, and that now he was in one of his down moods, since he said: "As for me, well of course, I am regarded as the cruelest and most sadistic man alive. But one thing I want to get on the record: I have never publicly vilified Germany's enemies." Himmler kept his word concerning the rest of the Danes and Norwegians, whom Bernadotte removed from Neuengamme during the month of April.

In Stockholm Kersten had fixed April 17 as the date for flying to Berlin with Storch to see Himmler. At the last minute, Storch said he could not go. He had already lost seventeen members of his family in the camps. But he had a replacement in Norbert Masur, the head of the Swedish Section of the World Jewish Congress, a tall, dark young man with a bony face. They left Stockholm on April 19 at 2 P.M., on the normal Stockholm–Berlin run, but they were the only passengers. The rest of the plane was filled with Red Cross parcels. It was a four-hour flight, and when the plane touched down at the Tempelhof airport, Kersten and Masur were met by a group of Himmler's policemen, who greeted them with *Heil Hitlers*. Norbert Masur removed his hat and responded "Good evening."

As they sat in Tempelhof waiting for their car, they heard Goebbels's high-pitched bark over the loudspeaker: "German people rejoice. Tomorrow, the twentieth of April, is your beloved Führer's birthday." Such was the good news for the starving, bombed-out, defeated German people. By this time the country was cut in two, with a narrow corridor separating the Americans, who were on the Elbe, from the Russians, who were on the Oder. In the middle of the corridor sat a heap of rubble that had once been Berlin. Important cities like Mannheim and Kassel and Frankfurt had surrendered without a fight. German soldiers were throwing away their rifles and running. Elite SS divisions, including the *Lebstandarte,* which had provided Hitler's personal bodyguards, had retreated in Hungary under fire. To punish and humiliate them, the Führer had ordered the officers' armbands removed. In his bunker, Hitler was either on the phone to individual unit commanders or throwing tantrums, shrieking that he had been deserted, moving imaginary battalions, and shouting, "The entire Luftwaffe staff should be hanged." There were riots in Berlin, owing to food shortages, and bakeries and grocery stores were broken into. The Russians had captured Vienna and were poised to attack Berlin, and the Americans had taken Leipzig, about one hundred miles southwest of the city. In the bunker, Hitler was joined by Eva Braun, Goebbels, his wife, Magda, their six children, and others. Magda Goebbels wrote her son from her first marriage, Harald Quant, "Our splendid concept is perishing."

An SS car took Kersten and Masur to Hartzwalde, where they arrived in the evening. SD deputy head Walter Schellenberg soon joined them and explained that Himmler would be delayed, as he had decided to attend Hitler's fifty-sixth birthday celebration in the bunker. Schellenberg had warned Himmler that it was dangerous, for Berlin was under constant aerial and artillery bombardment, but he had insisted because the rest of the old guard would be there, Göring, Goebbels, von Ribbentrop, and Bormann.

On the morning of April 20, a bomb exploded a mile away from Hartzwalde. In Berlin the situation was chaotic, with strafing planes, columns of fleeing civilians, rubble-filled streets, the constant wail of sirens. Himmler picked his way through the gutted marble-and-porphyry Chancellery building, down a flight of stairs to the steel entrance of the bunker with its bulkheads, narrow corridors, and cramped rooms. He lined up with the others in the early afternoon to offer birthday congratulations to the man he had served for fifteen years. They all urged Hitler to leave Berlin and go south to take command of the resistance while an escape route was still open, but Hitler was confident that the Russian armies would be beaten back from Berlin. Many of the guests at this sepulchral birthday party realized that he was no longer in touch with reality. Himmler left when the party was over, but was held up by traffic jams, air attacks, and planes dropping flares over the city.

He finally reached Hartzwalde with Lieutenant General Rudolf Brandt, his adjutant, at 2 A.M. on April 21. Before meeting with Masur, Himmler took Kersten aside and said: "I want to bury the hatchet between us and the Jews. If I had had my own way, many things would have been done differently. But I have already explained to you how things developed with us and also what the attitude was of the Jews and the people abroad."

Himmler then said good day to Masur in a cordial manner, and they sat down to have tea and coffee. Kersten reflected that here in his living room, sitting peacefully across from one another, were representatives of two races, each of which regarded the other as its mortal enemy, a situation that had led to the deaths of milions. The shadows of those dead were also present in every word spoken.

Himmler said that his generation had never known any peace. The Jews had played a leading part in the German civil war of 1918–1919, particularly in the Spartacus revolt. They were an alien element in Germany. "When we took power," Himmler went on, "we wanted to solve the Jewish question once and for all. With this in view, I set up an emigration organization which would have been very advantageous to the Jews. But not one of the countries which pretended to be so friendly toward the Jews would accept them. The English demanded that every Jew must take at least a thousand pounds with him.''

Norbert Masur responded that it was not in accordance with international law to drive men from a country in which they and their ancestors had lived for generations.

Himmler went on as if he had not heard him, justifying his policies: "These eastern Jews aided the partisans and helped the underground movements; they also fired on us from their ghettos and were the carriers of epidemics such as typhus. In order to control these epidemics, crematoriums were built for the countless corpses of the victims. And now we are threatened with hanging for that!''

Masur kept silent.

"If the Jewish people have also suffered from the ferocity of war," Himmler continued, "it must not be forgotten that the German people have not been spared anything either. The concentration camps should have been called training camps, for criminal elements were lodged there besides Jews and political prisoners. Thanks to their erection, Germany, in 1941, had the lowest crime rate in many years. The prisoners had to work hard, but all Germans had to do that. The treatment was always just.''

Masur had been listening to Himmler's diatribe with a straight face, but this was too much, and he spoke up: "It is impossible to deny that crimes were committed in the camps.''

"I concede that it has happened occasionally," Himmler replied, "but I have also punished the persons responsible." He had in mind Karl Koch, the commandant of Buchenwald, who had been shot for corruption. Kersten, who did not want the conversation to turn into a counterproductive debate on the camps, intervened. "We don't want to discuss the past; we can't alter that and we'll only create the wrong atmosphere. We're far more concerned in discussing how much can still be saved.''

"At least," Masur said, "all Jews who still remain in Germany must be assured of their lives, if we want to build a bridge between our people for the future.''

Himmler said that he had arranged for Bergen-Belsen to be handed over to the Allies, but he had been very poorly repaid.

One of the guards had been tied up and photographed with some dead prisoners. These pictures had been reprinted all over the world. "At Buchenwald," Himmler went on, "the advancing American tanks suddenly opened fire and set the camp hospital aflame. Since it was made of wood it was soon in full blaze. The corpses were then photographed and more material for atrocity propaganda against us was provided. When I let 2,700 Jews go into Switzerland, this was made the subject of a personal campaign against me in the press, asserting that I had only released these men in order to construct an alibi for myself. But I have no need of an alibi! I have always done what was considered just, but nobody has had so much mud slung at him in the last ten years as I have. I have never bothered myself about that. Even in Germany any man can say about me what he pleases. Newspapers abroad have started a campaign against me, which is no encouragement to me to continued handing over of the camps."

Masur pointed out that not only the Jews but other countries were interested in rescuing the surviving Jews, which would make a good impression on the Allies.

But Himmler was not to be diverted from his train of thought, and went on about the Jews released from Theresienstadt. "It was a kind of town inhabited exclusively by Jews, who also administered it themselves and managed all the work. We had hoped that one day all the camps would be like that."

They finally got down to discussing the release of inmates from Ravensbrück. At first, Himmler agreed on a figure of a thousand Jewish women. He stipulated that they should be described as Polish women to get around Hitler's order against releasing Jewish prisoners. "Even the arrival of these Jewesses in Sweden must be kept secret," he emphasized.

The talks went on for two and a half hours, ending at 5 A.M. Then Himmler left, saying good-bye to Kersten for the last time. "Petty minds bent on revenge will hand down a perverted account of the great and good things I accomplished for Germany," he said. When Himmler was gone, Masur told Kersten: "That was typical of Himmler, his fear of letting the Jewish women go free under their correct designation." Late in the morning, Kersten and Masur flew out of Tempelhof back to Stockholm. They could hear the Russian guns in the distance. Himmler drove from Hartzwalde to Hohenlychen, where he had a breakfast meeting with Count Bernadotte concerning the release of the remaining Scandinavian prisoners still in the Neuengamme camp. Himmler was wound up, nervously tapping his front teeth with his thumbnail.

Later, escaping from Berlin, Himmler went to Lübeck, north of Hamburg, where he saw Bernadotte for the last time on April 24. He told the Swedish diplomat about the plan to release Jewish and French women from Ravensbrück. On April 30 Hitler committed suicide in his bunker. On May 7 Germany surrendered. On May 20 Himmler, hiding in Flensburg on the German-Danish border, disguised himself in the uniform of a field security policeman, shaved his moustache, and put a black patch over one eye. He had papers in the name of Heinrich Hitzinger, a man who had been put to death by a people's court. Himmler and six others headed through Holstein on foot and crossed the mouth of the Elbe in a fishing boat, proceeding west on foot toward the North Sea port of Bremerhaven. On May 23 a British patrol stopped him and took him to an interrogation center near Lüneburg, south of Hamburg. Himmler had a cyanide capsule hidden under his gum, and bit into it just as his mouth was about to searched.

In Ravensbrück the guards were always saying that none of the inmates would leave the camp alive. By April 1945 Cécile Goldet had begun to believe them. Her friend Odette Malossane was dead, and Cécile did not think she could endure camp conditions much longer, for thousands of new inmates, evacuated from other camps, now made the situation intolerable. On April 25, however, there was a roll call in the middle of the morning, and her name was on the list. She was told to get her things, and she joined a group of about three hundred French inmates, who were escorted to the camp gate by guards, now solicitous and polite. At the gate, where other groups of inmates were waiting, there were ten big buses with a red cross painted on the side. They got into the buses, hardly able to grasp what was happening, and crossed the border into Denmark, and then continued by train and ferry to Sweden, where they were welcomed by Count Bernadotte and taken to a rehabilitation camp in Göteborg.

It took time for Cécile Goldet to realize that she had survived

Ravensbrück. She felt as though she were impersonating some-one, that her real self was still at the camp, still standing in line with an empty bowl, still shivering at roll call. She knew that the camp would continue to exist within her, that there was a stag-gering amount of suffering that could never be made up for, and that nothing else that ever happened to her would seem as real as camp life. It could never be erased, it would rise up and fill her mind, stronger than memory, stronger than imagination, stronger than the beat of her own heart.

That April in a Germany in chaos, invaded on two sides, there were quite a few people who were eagerly trying to get out. Ger-man soldiers were under orders to fight the invaders, but many of their leaders were slipping through the lines and out of Germany. One of these was Rudolf Rahn, German ambassador to Italy, who had been in Berlin for consultation and was now trying to get back to Italy through Switzerland. It was a fantastic, end-of-the-world spectacle he saw as he crossed Germany from northeast to southwest: wandering columns of camp inmates in striped suits, open coal trucks loaded with corpses, trainloads of prisoners shunted onto railroad sidings and left there, deserters in groups of two and three, fleeing the Russians. A woman sitting on a tree stump singing to her dead child. Families on the road, as in the French *exode* of 1940, pushing baby carriages stacked high with belongings. Rahn finally arrived at a deserted strip of border to the west of Lake Constance, near the Swiss town of Diessenho-fen. Night was falling, and as he stood on the edge of a pine grove in the snow, seeing Switzerland on the other side of a field, it suddenly occurred to him that he was doing exactly what thou-sands of Jews in the last four years had tried to do—escape into Switzerland. He thought: "Are we now going to share the fate of these unfortunate people? Will we be dispersed in all directions, to give of our tenacity and ability for the welfare of other na-tions—only to provoke their resistance? Shall Germans too be fated to be at home in every place and welcome in none?" The Nazi diaspora had begun.

In March 1943, Léon Blum, the Popular Front premier of the thirties and the first Jewish premier of France, was deported to

Buchenwald. Still tall and elegant at the age of seventy-one, with a silky moustache and a pince-nez, he was in a section of the camp reserved for important persons, and soon had the company of another Third Republic politician, Georges Mandel. In June someone else arrived at Buchenwald who had asked to join him. It seems incredible, but a woman who had loved Blum since she was a girl had lobbied and pulled strings, not to stay out of a concentration camp, but to be admitted to one. Her name was Jeanne Levylier, whom life had separated from Blum and carried in a different direction. She had married a celebrated lawyer, Henri Torrès, later to become a senator, whom she divorced. She then married a department store magnate, Reichenbach, who left her a widow. She decided that she would spend what was left of her life with Blum, the man she had never stopped loving.

In Paris she used all the contacts she had to obtain permission to go to Buchenwald. It took several months, but finally her request was granted, and she arrived at the camp, surprising Blum in his room where he sat on the edge of his bed, soaking lentils. They were married in the camp in a ceremony conducted by Buchenwald officials. The new Mme. Blum was listed as a *Sippenhäftlinge,* a kin-prisoner. The Blums remained in Buchenwald for two years, a couple sustained by mutual devotion and the knowledge that she had given up a life of freedom to be with him in captivity. Blum felt there was a good chance that he would be taken as a hostage, but he wasn't.

On August 24, 1944, Buchenwald was bombed. On April 1, 1945, the American Third Army was in Eisenach, fifty miles away. Blum and the other *Prominente* were taken to the Flossenberg camp near the Czech border. From his window he could see the big firs of the Bohemian forest. From Flossenberg they were moved to Regensburg, in the Bavarian forest on the Danube, where Blum was separated from his wife and locked up in a prison cell. But she put up such a fuss that they were reunited. They were then taken to Dachau, outside Munich, arriving there on April 17.

At Dachau it was a great surprise to see men Blum knew, men he had dealt with when he was in office. It was like time compressed, the past made present. A man with a long face and teeth like a horse came up and asked him, "Don't you remember me?" It was Dr. Hjalmar Schacht, Hitler's finance minister, the economic wizard whom some believed responsible for the rise of the Third Reich. Schacht had been president of the Reichsbank and mastermind of the German war economy. In 1936 he had gone to Paris to discuss the return of Germany's pre-World War One colonies. He saw Blum, who agreed in principle, thinking it might calm Hitler's appetite, but when Schacht got back to Berlin, Hitler was no longer interested. Now, having been involved in the July 20 attempt against Hitler, Schacht was in Dachau.

Blum saw another face from the past, Kurt von Schuschnigg, who had been chancellor of Austria at the time of the *Anschluss*. Schuschnigg had been locked up for seventeen months in the Gestapo headquarters in Vienna, where he was made to clean the slop buckets and latrines of the guards, and then was sent to Sachsenhausen in 1942. In 1936 Schuschnigg, too, had visited Paris and told Blum that he was counting on Mussolini to save Austria from Hitler. Now Blum, seeing him in the Dachau courtyard ten years later, could not resist rubbing it in, saying, "I tried to warn you about Mussolini."

In this camp, with its pompous inscription announcing that work made men free, and its gravel paths bordered with flowers concealing the camp's true purpose (prisoners had once been hung up on hooks on the walls of the courtyard where they strolled), famous prisoners from twenty countries were now incarcerated. One of them was Captain S. Payne Best, a British intelligence officer who had been kidnapped in the Dutch border town of Venlo on November 9, 1939, by Walter Schellenberg and his men. In one of the stranger incidents of the war, Best and his fellow officer Major R. H. Stevens had been blamed for the assassination attempt against Hitler on November 8. This was a propaganda ploy trumped up to show the German public that British agents were trying to do away with the Führer. At the camp, too, was Vyacheslav Molotov's twenty-two-year-old nephew, Wassili. Also present was Fritz Thyssen, head of the German steel trust, and an early backer of Hitler. There were several anti-Nazi generals who had been involved in the von Stauffenberg coup, including General von Falkenhausen, once military commander of Belgium, who wore his Pour le Mérite order on a red silk ribbon around his neck. The generals, still in uniform, followed the progress of the war on outspread maps, drawing the battle lines. Schacht and Falkenhausen were fond of reciting Homer's *Iliad*— both had a stupendous memory. Blum and Schuschnigg spent many pleasant hours reminiscing. Blum was a great European, thought Schuschnigg. He almost wanted to thank the Gestapo for having arranged their meeting.

Every day, someone vanished. Schuschnigg told Blum that one of the SS men had in fact shown him the list of those who on Himmler's orders, were to be liquidated before the camp fell into Allied hands. Both he and Blum were on it. What irony to have survived this far only to be taken "to the woodpile," as the term went, with the Americans approaching. On April 25 they were twenty miles away, and on April 27 the *Prominente* were evacuated on crowded buses. Also released were the regular Dachau inmates, some 35,000 of them, in striped garb and on foot, who all stopped and saluted as the buses passed. The *Prominente* drove off through the ruins of Munich, and south through Innsbruck toward the Austrian Tyrol. Their SS guards seemed bewildered, unsure of where to take them. The buses climbed the road up to the Brenner Pass to the village of Niedendorf, five thousand feet high in the south Tyrol. There was snow on the ground. The prisoners stayed at the Pragser-Wildsee Hotel on a clear mountain lake, with the cliffs of the Dolomites as a backdrop. Blum found himself next door to the great anti-Nazi pastor, Martin Niemöller. To pass the time, the prisoners formed a "Little League of Nations," with a "Permanent Council" and a "General Assembly," which met in the hotel lobby.

One of the anti-Nazi generals was able to make contact with the Wehrmacht commander in the area, an old friend, who was in the Italian city of Bolzano. The next day a Wehrmacht detachment arrived in Niedendorf, surrounded the Pragser-Wildsee Hotel, and disarmed the SS guards. It was to be one of the last engagements of the war in Europe, pitting the German Army against the Nazi party army. The officer in command, Captain Count von Alvensleben, told Blum and the others that they were now under the protection of the German Army. Saved by the Wehrmacht, thought Blum, the surprise ending to a nightmare. It was as though he were back in the days of the Kaiser, when there was such a thing as military honor and courtesy was shown to one's enemy, before Dachau, before Hitler. On May 4 Blum was turned over to the Americans, and on May 14 he was back home in Paris with his bride.

They had left by train, and now, in 1945, they were returning by train, those to whom fate had given a round-trip ticket. In Lyon the social workers who had set up receiving booths on the platforms at Perrache station still did not know what had gone on in the camps, and were shocked to see the survivors disembark. Many of them wore their striped uniforms, and all were emaciated, with blank faces, hardly speaking, seemingly catatonic. When you saw them, thought social worker Yvonne Ditche, who had volunteered to welcome "the manakins," you understood what was behind such names as Ravensbrück and Auschwitz.

At the end of April, a train arrived at the Perrache station in Lyon at midnight with 235 women from Ravensbrück and other camps, among them Josette Leroi, who had been arrested in July 1944 for hiding Jews and whose husband was Jewish. Josette, who had received no mail at Ravensbrück, was sure that her husband was dead, and so was not surprised that he was not there at the platform to greet her. But one of the social workers, upon taking her name, told her that her husband had gone to the other Lyon station, Brotteaux, not knowing at which station her train was arriving. At that her heart lifted, and yet . . . In the camp she had thought, every hour of every day, "How wonderful it will be. There will be French flags everywhere. There will be a band playing the 'Marseillaise.' There will be crowds cheering." But there were no flags and no band and no crowds. Deportees and prisoners of war had been coming home for months now, and people were used to it. She wanted tenderness, she wanted compassion, she wanted human warmth, and what she got was a sandwich and a glass of wine. She looked around at her fellow passengers, the sad faces, the shadowy figures of those with memories they would never be able to share, and she thought: "It will be them and us." For she knew that there were things that she would never be able to discuss, not even with her husband, for no one would believe her. They would think that she was hallucinating. But as she waited

for her husband to arrive, and as she tried to surmount her disappointment, she saw something different on this gloomy cement
platform, with the social workers and their lists and their perfunc-
tory greetings, and the *rayés* as they waited, arranging themselves
in rows from force of habit—and what was different was that there
were no German uniforms on the platform, and in that at least
they had succeeded.

ACKNOWLEDGMENTS

I would like to thank Serge Klarsfeld for his wise counsel; Alan Williams, my editor, for his dowser's touch; Elena S. Danielson of the Hoover Institute for her help; Renata Propper for her expertise in German; Jacqueline Williams for her assistance with the Bolivian and other research; Eileen Bresnahan for her research in Lyon; and Robert S. Taylor for the Barbie statement.

NOTE ON SOURCES

In May, June, and July of 1987, the author covered the trial of Klaus Barbie in Lyon for *The New York Times Magazine*. In the French criminal justice system, there are no grand jury proceedings to determine grounds for indictment, Instead, there is a *juge d'instruction* (examining magistrate), who single-handedly does the job of the grand jury, hearing witnesses, taking depositions, and sending roving commissions to foreign countries to interview those who cannot come to him. The result of this very detailed and comprehensive inquiry is called the "Instruction." In Barbie's case, the indictment was limited to three specific "crimes against humanity," a type of charge that was thought up at the Nuremberg trials to cover conduct so odious that it went beyond the category of war crimes. Barbie had of course committed other crimes, but in France war crimes have a statute of limitations, which had run out by 1981, while crimes against humanity never run out. The three crimes he was charged with were: the raid of the Jewish welfare office (UGIF) in Lyon on February 6, 1943; the raid on the children's home at Izieu on April 6, 1944; and the deportation by train of 629 persons from Lyon to Auschwitz on August 11, 1944. The Instruction, however, ranges much further afield than these three incidents, and includes hundreds of depositions concerning a multitude of other events. Barbie was brought back to France from Bolivia in 1983, and it took the *juge d'instruction* four years to complete his job, which gives some idea of how thorough the investigation was. The final product amounts to some ten thousand pages of depositions and documents. It should be added that the Instruction file is secret. Its circulation is restricted to the trial judges, prosecution counsel, and defense lawyers. The author was able, however, to obtain a copy of it, upon which a great deal of this book is based.

Abbreviated Titles of Frequently Cited Sources

INS: Instruction
BT: Barbie Trial
CH: René de Chambrun collection, Hoover Institute, Stanford University, California

NOTES

CHAPTER I: **LYON '87** INS and BT.
CHAPTER II: **THE FUNNY WAR**

On the Maginot Line, see *The Maginot Line,* by Anthony Kemp, N.Y., 1982.

On the reason why the French left the Maginot Line unfinished, Trumbull Higgins interview.

On the Koestler episode, see *Scum of the Earth,* by Arthur Koestler, N.Y., 1941.

On the prewar French government, see *The Collapse of the Third Republic,* by William L. Shirer, N.Y., 1969; and *Les Fossoyeurs,* by Pertinax, N.Y., 1943.

On Bullitt, see *For the President, Personal and Secret,* by William C. Bullitt, N.Y., 1972.

On de Gaulle, see *Dossiers Secrets de la France Contemporaine,* vol. 4: *Le Désastre de '40,* by Claude Paillat, Paris, 1982.

On André Devigny, see *Je Fus ce Condamné,* by André Devigny, Paris, 1978.

On the *exode,* see *L'Exode,* by Jean Vidalenc, Paris, 1957.

On Georges Villiers, see *Témoignages,* by Georges Villiers, Paris, 1978.

On René Cerf-Ferrière, see *Chemins Clandestins,* by René Cerf-Ferrière, Paris, 1968.

On the situation in Bordeaux, see *Episodes,* by Edouard Herriot, Paris, 1946.

On Mandel, see *Life of Georges Mandel,* by J. Sherwood, N.Y., 1975.

On Pétain, see *Le Maréchal aux Liens: Le Temps du Sacrifice,* by Jean

Tracou, Paris, 1948: *Pétain, Hero or Traitor,* by Herbert O. Lottman, N.Y., 1985; and CH.

On Jean Moulin, see *Jean Moulin,* by Laure Moulin, Paris, 1959; and *J'étais la Femme de Jean Moulin,* by Marguerite Storck-Cerruty, Paris, 1976.

On the Saumur cadets, see *Les Cadets de Saumur,* by Élie Chamard, Paris, 1948.

CHAPTER III: **VICHY**

On the meeting in Bordeaux, see *Episodes,* by Edouard Herriot, Paris, 1946.

On the armistice and Alsace-Lorraine, see *La Grande Histoire des Français Sous l'Occupation,* by Henri Amouroux, six volumes, Paris, 1975–1983.

On the Valence and Saint-Malo incidents, see *Vichy Année 40,* by Henri Michel, Paris, 1966.

On Laval, CH and *Tout ce qu'on Vous a Caché,* by Jacques Baraduc, Paris, 1949; *The Diary of Pierre Laval,* N.Y., 1949; and *Pierre Laval and the Eclipse of Power, 1931–1945,* by Geoffrey Warner, N.Y., 1968.

On the assassination attempt against Laval, CH and Barragué deposition.

On Laval's meeting with Stalin, CH and Bout de l'An deposition.

On Mandel, see *Life of Georges Mandel,* by J. Sherwood, N.Y., 1975.

On the Blum-Laval meeting, see *L'Oeuvre de Léon Blum,* vol. 5, Paris, 1954–1972.

On the end of the Third Republic, see *The Collapse of the Third Republic,* by William Shirer, N.Y., 1969.

On Lebrun, see *Témoignages,* by Albert Lebrun, Paris, 1947.

On Jeanneney, see *Journal Politique,* by Jules Jeanneney, Paris, 1972.

On Vichy, see *Neuf Mois au Gouvernement,* by Paul Baudouin, Paris,

1948; *Le Maréchal Aux Liens,* by Jean Tracou, Paris, 1948; *Vichy France,* by Robert O. Paxton, N.Y., 1972; *Vichy, Cinquante Mois d'Armistice,* by Pierre Nicolle, Paris, 1947; *Resistance in Vichy France.* by H. R. Kedward, Oxford, 1978; *La Chronique de Vichy,* by Maurice Martin du Gard, Paris, 1975; *Souvenirs et Témoignages,* by Ivan Loiseau, Paris, 1974; *Le Drame de Vichy,* by Yves Bouthillier, Paris, 1947; *Journal de la France,* by Alfred Fabre-Luce, Paris, 1948; *Commentaires,* by Jean Chauvel, Paris, 1971; *Le Temps des Illusions,* by Du Moulin de la Barthète, Paris, 1946; *Souvenirs de Sept Ans,* by Jérome Carcopino, Paris, 1953; *Le Royaume d'Otto,* by Raymond Tournoux, Paris, 1982.

On Communists in Paris, see *Paris in the Third Reich,* by David Pryce-Jones, N.Y., 1981.

On LVF, see *Les Collaborateurs,* by Pascal Orry, Paris, 1976; and *The Captive Dreamer,* by Christian de la Mazière, N.Y., 1972.

On Darnand, Bruckberger to author.

On Pétain and Bénoist-Méchin, CH.

On Göring and Laval, CH.

On Sauckel and Laval, Baraduc, op. cit.

On Morand and Laval, CH.

On the occupation, see Amouroux, op. cit.; *French and Germans, Germans and French,* by Richard Cobb, Brandeis University, Mass., 1983; and *Life in Unoccupied France,* by Neville Lytton, London, 1942.

On Roger Souchal, BT.

On Gerhard Heller, Pryce-Jones, op. cit.

On the attack on synagogues, INS.

On collaborators, Orry, op. cit.

On businessmen in Lyon, see *Lyon 40–44,* by Gérard Chauvy, Paris, 1985.

On Berliet, see Chauvy, op. cit., and *Nous Prendrons les Usines,* by Marcel Peyrenet, Geneva, 1980.

On the special courts, Chauvy, op. cit.

On Henri Frenay, see *The Night Will End,* by Henri Frenay, N.Y., 1976.

CHAPTER IV: **SONDERBEHANDLUNG**

On the Kaltenbrunner testimony, see *Episodes,* by Edouard Herriot, Paris, 1946.

On *Einsatzgruppen,* see *The Order of the Death's Head,* by Heinz Hohne, N.Y., 1970; and INS.

On Hoess and Eichmann, see *Commandant at Auschwitz,* by Rudolf Hoess, N.Y., 1951.

On the Wannsee Conference, see *Documents of Destruction,* edited by Raul Hilberg, Chicago, 1971.

On anti-Semitism in France, see *Notre Avant-Guerre,* by Robert Brasillach, Paris, 1941; *Journal Politique,* by Jules Jeanneney Paris, 1972; and *Journal d'un Préfet Pendant l'Occupation,* by Pierre Trouille, Paris, 1964.

On anti-Jewish measures, see *Neuf Mois au Gouvernement,* by Paul Baudouin, Paris, 1948.

On Villiers and Pétain, see *Témoignages,* by Georges Villiers, Paris, 1978.

On anti-Jewish legislation, INS.

Documents quoted from the SS office in Paris come from INS; *Le Mémorial de la Déportation des Juifs en France,* by Serge Klarsfeld, Paris, 1978; and *Vichy-Auschwitz,* by Serge Klarsfeld, Paris, 1983.

On Xavier Vallat, see *Le Grain de Sable de Cromwell,* by Xavier Vallat, Ardèche, 1972; *Grands Procès de la Collaboration,* Paris, 1948; and CH.

On Dannecker and Vallat, INS.

On the light penalties and arrests of veterans, INS.

On the creation of UGIF, INS and UGIF archives at Yivo Institute, N.Y.

On Helbronner and Pétain, UGIF archives.

On the shooting party, see *The Kersten Memoirs,* by Felix Kersten, N.Y., 1957.

On the showdown with Vallat, INS.

On the *Nacht und Nebel* decree, see *The Memoirs of Field-Marshal Keitel,* N.Y., 1965.

On Dannecker in Berlin and Compiègne report, INS.

On the first train, INS and Klarsfeld, *Le Mémorial.*

On the arrival at Auschwitz, see *Auschwitz: A Report on the Proceedings Against Robert Karl Ludwig Mulka and Others Before the Court at Frankfurt,* N.Y., 1966.

On the gassing, Hoess, op. cit.

On Bousquet, CH.

On Heydrich, Hohne, op. cit.

On Bousquet and Heydrich, CH and INS.

On the first trains, INS and Klarsfeld, *Le Mémorial.*

On the Drancy report, Klarsfeld, op. cit.

On Dannecker, CH and Knochen deposition.

On the yellow star, INS and Klarsfeld, op. cit.

On the Vichy-SS negotiations, INS and Klarsfeld, op. cit.

On Bousquet and Oberg, CH, and Bousquet deposition.

On Laval at the cabinet meeting, CH.

On Dannecker to Eichmann, INS.

On the Bordeaux SS, INS.

On the cancellation of the train, INS.

On the July *rafle,* INS and Klarsfeld, op. cit.

On Annette Muller, Klarsfeld, op. cit.

On Lazare Pitkowicz, BT.

On Dannecker's trip, INS and Klarsfeld, op. cit.

On Dannecker's departure, INS.

On the Quakers, CH.

On the deportation of children, INS and Klarsfeld, op. cit.

On Cardinal Gerlier, see *Lyon 40–44,* by Gérard Chauvy, Paris, 1985.

On Cardinal Saliège, see *Sous l'Épiscopat du Cardinal Saliège,* by Monsignor J. Chansou, Toulouse, 1978.

On Laval and Rocco, CH.

On Bousquet's phone conversation, CH.

On Garel and the children, Chauvy, op. cit.

On Laval and Oberg, CH.

On Leguay and Roethke, CH and INS.

On Knochen to Eichmann, INS.

On the last trains of 1942, INS and Klarsfeld, op. cit.

On Laval's visit to Hitler, CH.

On the scuttling of the French fleet, Fabre-Luce, op. cit.

On Sauerbruch, see *Von Hassell Diaries,* N.Y., 1947.

On Hitler and Keitel, Keitel memoirs, op. cit.

On Roethke in 1943, INS and Klarsfeld, op. cit.

On the Italian occupation of the Riviera, see "Jewish Refugees on the

French Riviera,'' by Zannel Diamant, *Yivo Annual of Jewish Social Sciences,* 1953.

On Olivier-Martin and Laval, CH and Olivier-Martin deposition.

On the Vichy delays, INS and Klarsfeld, op. cit.

On the Klarsfeld family in Nice, Serge Klarsfeld to author.

On collaborators entering the government, see *Les Collaborateurs,* by Pascal Orry, Paris, 1976.

On Eichmann to Sassen, INS.

On Laval to Boegner and end of Laval, CH.

On the Klarsfeld Nazi-hunting, see *Wherever They May Be,* by Beate Klarsfeld, N.Y., 1975.

CHAPTER V: **LYON, '43**

On the arrival of Barbie in Lyon, BT and INS.

On Barbie's background, BT and INS.

On Barbie's raid on the UGIF, BT, INS, and UGIF archives at Yivo Institute, N.Y.

On Michael Goldberg's trip to Bolivia, see *Namesake,* by Michael Goldberg, New Haven, 1982.

On Pétain's response to the raid, INS.

On the UGIF after the raid, UGIF archives.

On André Devigny and Moog, see *Je Fus ce Condamné,* by André Devigny, Paris, 1978.

On Jean Moulin as a resistance leader, see *Jean Moulin,* by Laure Moulin, Paris, 1959; *The Night Will End,* by Henri Frenay, N.Y., 1976; and INS.

On René Hardy, see INS and *La Vérité aura le Dernier Mot,* by Henri Noguères, Paris, 1985.

On Barbie and René Hardy, see Barbie report, given to the author by Robert S. Taylor.

On the Kaltenbrunner and Flora reports, INS.

On the Hardy trials, Noguères, op. cit.

On Moulin and Pineau, see *La Simple Vérité,* by Christian Pineau, Paris, 1948.

On Moulin's death, see Laure Moulin, op. cit.

On Gertrude Stein, see *Wars I Have Seen,* by Gertrude Stein, N.Y., 1945.

On the Barbie kidnaping of Lebrun and François-Poncet, see INS; *Témoignages,* by Albert Lebrun, Paris, 1947; and *Mémoires d'un Captif,* by André François-Poncet, Paris, 1952.

On Devigny's escape, see *Un Condamné à Mort s'est Echappé,* by André Devigny, Paris, 1947.

On Frossard at Montluc, BT and Frossard to author.

On the Taborin episode, INS.

CHAPTER VI: **LYON '44**

On Sauckel and Laval, CH.

On Sauckel and Abetz, CH and Abetz deposition.

On the twenty-two hostages, INS.

On the Basch murders, INS.

On Glières, see *La Grande Histoire des Français Sous l'Occupation,* by Henri Amouroux, six volumes, Paris, 1975–1983.

On Izieu, Henri Perret to author: INS; BT; and *The Children of Izieu, A Human Tragedy,* by Serge Klarsfeld, Paris, undated.

On Mme. Zlatin, BT and INS.

On the Saint-Claude action, INS.

On Henri Troussier, BT.

On Trouille to Vichy, see *Journal d'un Préfet Pendant l'Occupation,* by Pierre Trouille, Paris, 1964.

On Pétain leaving Vichy, see *Le Maréchal aux Liens: Le Temps du Sacrifice,* by Jean Tracou, Paris, 1948.

On Lyon being bombed, see *Lyon 40–44,* by Gérard Chauvy, Paris, 1985.

On Pétain visiting Lyon, Tracou, op. cit.

On the murder of Jean Zay, see *Les Collaborateurs,* by Pascal Orry, Paris, 1976.

On the murder of Georges Mandel, see *Life of Georges Mandel,* by J. Sherwood, New York, 1969.

On the July 12 cabinet meeting, CH and Grasset deposition.

On Pétain and Laval on July 21, Tracou, op. cit.

On Vercors, INS and Amouroux, op. cit.

On Vercors, INS and Amouroux, op. cit.

On the nurses in Grotte de la Luire, INS.

On Captain Conus, see *Rebelles, Soldats et Citoyens,* by Yves Farge, Paris, 1946.

On Francis André and Oullins, INS.

On the departure of August 11 train, INS and BT.

On the Bron massacre, INS.

On Herriot, see *Herriot,* by Pierre Olivier Lapie, Paris, 1967.

On Laval and Herriot, CH and Josée de Chambrun deposition.

On the departure of the ministers, Tracou, op. cit.

On the Saint-Genis-Laval massacre, INS.

On Farge saving Montluc prisoners, Farge, op. cit.

On the Rue Tronchet massacre, INS and Pierre Truche to author.

On Berliet's arrest, see *Nous Prendron Les Usines,* by Marcel Peyrenet, Geneva, 1980.

On Barbie's larceny in Kassel, INS.

CHAPTER VII: **LAST TRAIN TO AUSCHWITZ**

All the characters in this chapter are real, but several names have been changed, for certain incidents from other sources have been included in their stories in the interest of compression and narrative focus. Aside from the trial and the instruction, these sources are: *Five Chimneys,* by Olga Lengyel, N.Y., 1973; *Auschwitz: A report, . . .* N.Y., 1966; *Contes de Dachau,* by Joseph Rovan, Paris, 1987; *An Ordinary Camp,* by Micheline Maurel, N.Y., 1958; *My Story,* by Gemma La Guardia Gluck, N.Y., 1961; *Under Two Dictators,* by Margarete Buber, N.Y., no date; *The Other Kingdom,* by David Rousset, N.Y., 1947; *Experiments,* by Léon Szalet, N.Y., 1945; and *Secretaries of Death,* by Dr. Lore Shelley, N.Y., 1986.

On the train departure, INS and BT.

On the stop at Vittel, INS and BT.

On the arrival at Auschwitz, INS and BT.

On Hoess, see *Commandant at Auschwitz,* by Rudolf Hoess, N.Y., 1951.

On the camps run as a business, see *The Order of the Death's Head,* by Heinz Hohne, N.Y., 1970.

On the inmates at Auschwitz, INS and BT.

On the arrival at Stutthof, INS and BT.

On the arrival at Ravensbrück, INS and BT.

On the inmates at Stutthof, INS and BT.

On the inmates at Ravensbrück, INS and BT.

On Himmler and Kersten, see *The Kersten Memoirs*, by Felix Kersten, N.Y., 1957.

On Bernadotte, see *The Curtain Falls*, by Count Folke Bernadotte, N.Y., 1945.

On Hitler's last birthday party, see *The Goebbels Diaries*, London, 1978, and *The Last Days of Hitler*, by Hugh Trevor-Roper, N.Y., 1947.

On the French inmates' departure from Ravensbrück, INS and BT.

On the Léon Blum odyssey, see *L'Oeuvre de Léon Blum*, Paris, 1954–1972.

INDEX

408

Index

Belot, Fernand, 307
Belot, Renée, 307
Benito Cereno (Melville), 177
Benjamin, Walter, 95
Bennett, Robert J., 283
Bentitou, Raoul, 274
Bergen-Belsen concentration camp, 213, 381–382
Berliet, Jean, 120
Berliet, Marius, 119–120, 318–319
Berliet, Paul, 319
Berman, Harriet, 305–306, 331–332, 333, 335, 350–357
Bernadotte, Folke, 376–377, 378, 383
Bernard, Tristan, 180
Bernheim, Dr., 329–330
Bernheim, Rosine, 307
Best, S. Payne, 386
Best, Werner, 115, 139
Beuys, Joseph, 9–10
Bezinenski, Lev, 17, 18
Bichelonne, Jean, 118, 313
Birkenau concentration camp, 333–335, 336–337, 341, 342, 353
Birreshorn, Marianne, 153
Bismarck, Otto von, 34, 36
Blardone, Mario, 22
Bloch, René, 151
Blum Jeanne Levylier, 385
Blum Léon, 36, 40, 56, 59, 85–86, 132, 137, 290, 384–388
Boegner, Marc, 194–195
Boger, Wilhelm, 352
Bohnke, Alfred, 280
Bollaert, Émile, 65
"bone people," 369
Bonnard, Abel, 107, 291, 312–313
Bonnat, Gaston, 358, 361
Bonnet, Georges, 43
Bordes, Hans, 156
Borgel, Henri, 270
Bosse, Roger, 235
Boucher, François, 94
Bouellat, Joseph, 309
Bouloumy, Mme., 329–330, 333
Bourdon, Lucien, 268, 269, 270, 272, 273
Boursier, Abbé, 314
Bousquet, René, 146–148, 154–155, 162, 167–170, 182, 191
Bouthillier, Yves, 48, 98, 99
Bouvier, Marcel, 268, 270
Brandt, Willy, 189, 203
Brasillach, Robert, 132
Brauchitsch, Walther von, 76, 106, 123
Braun, Eva, 379
Breitscheid, Rudolf, 95–96
Bretty, Béatrice, 55, 83
Bron airport, mass grave at, 308–309
Brose, Anton, 352
Bruckberger, Raymond, 104–105
Brunner, Alois, 192, 271–272
Brunschwig, Colonel, 30–31, 32, 33
Buchenwald concentration camp, 280–284, 290, 382, 384–385
Buckmaster network, 217–218
Bulawko, Henri, 185
Bullitt, William, 29, 44, 46–47, 53–54

Cagoule, 115
Cambus, Jean, 230
Camus, Albert, 114
Capesius, Victor, 334–335, 344, 345, 354, 356
Carcopino, Jérome, 93–94, 118
Carné, Marcel, 110
Carnet Bille, 77
Catholic Church, 167–172
Caziot, Pierre, 92, 93
Cerdini, André, 15, 16, 25, 26
Cerf-Ferrière, René, 51–52
Chaffard, Maurice, 304–305
Chaillet, Pierre, 170, 171
Chambard, René, 277–279
Charbin, Paul, 92–93, 98
Chardon, Marius, 304
Chautemps, Camille, 54
Chauvel, Jean, 53
Chavant, Eugène, 296
Chenaut de Layritz, M., 168–169
Chennault, André, 186
Chevance, Maurice, 223
Churchill, Winston S., 37, 53
Ciano, Count Galeazzo, 99, 141, 142, 179, 374
Clémenceau, Georges, 31, 36, 42, 82, 104
Clor, Robert, 22
Clouzot, Georges-Henri, 110–111
Collette, Paul, 78, 79
Combat, 124, 169, 220, 221, 222, 223, 228, 234, 248, 307
Comintern, 80
Commission for the Organization of the *Rafles,* 157
Commune of Paris, 34
Compagnon de la Libération, 160–161
Compiègne concentration camp, 138, 141, 144, 157
concentration camps, 335–341
    camp society in, 342–344
    Eichmann's views on, 161, 337
    French, 96–97, 138
    Himmler's responsibility for, 335, 338, 339, 340–341, 352, 370–383
    Hitler's order for destruction of, 377
    negotiations for release of inmates from, 370–383
    see also individual camps
Conus, Captain, 296–298
Corap, André-Georges, 39, 44
Corbeau, Le, 110–111
"corbeaux," 110
Cot, Pierre, 59
Courvoisier, André, 22
Creyssel, Paul, 108

Dachau concentration camp, 385–387
Daladier, Édouard, 40, 42, 46, 47
Dannecker, Theo:
    Eichmann's support for, 136, 144, 145, 151–154, 155, 193, 194
    "great Parisian action" prepared by, 156, 158, 161, 194
    Jews deported by, 144, 145, 148–149, 150, 151–154, 155, 173, 193, 203
    Vallet's opposition to, 138, 142
Darlan, Jean, 72, 87, 92, 93–94, 100–101, 106
    assassination of, 177
    as head of Navy, 118, 176–177
Darnand, Joseph, 104–105, 117, 190–191, 261, 289

409

Index

Index

Jewish deportations (*continued*)
  Nussbaum and Winkler killings as pretext for, 180, 181, 182
  police assistance for, 88, 92, 146–147, 148, 149, 152, 153–154, 158–159, 161, 175, 176, 182, 185, 190, 192, 249–250
  public opinion on, 152, 154, 155, 174
  rate of, 149–150, 179, 184, 191–192
  as *Sonderbehandlung*, 129–130, 351
  trains provided for, 145, 149, 152, 156–157, 161–162, 173–174, 193, 206
Jews:
  in Bordeaux, 156–157
  census of, 134, 138, 157, 175, 186
  children of, 155–156, 159–161, 165–167, 191–194, 212–213, 216
  confiscated property of, 121, 139, 284, 319–321
  definition of, 134
  denaturalization law for, 183–185, 190
  discrimination against, 131–133, 142–143, 325
  Dutch, 131
  fines for, 139–140
  foreign vs. French, 131, 138, 148, 150, 153, 154–156, 157, 162, 173–174, 179–180, 194, 206
  German laws against, 135–136, 138–139
  in "great Parisian action," 156, 157–163, 164, 194
  Greek, 175, 176
  Himmler's order for release of, 370–383
  as hostages, 143, 145, 246, 247
  hunters of, 301–303
  informing on, 110, 111, 267, 272–273
  in Italian-occupied zones, 180–182, 186, 239, 265, 267
  in Izieu, 24, 263–275, 276
  legislation against, 121, 133, 134–136, 152, 183–185, 190
  in Montluc Prison, 246, 247–248, 306, 308
  in occupied vs. unoccupied zones, 154–156, 162, 163, 167, 193
  in Paris, 114–115, 136, 142, 143, 144, 146, 151, 152, 156, 157–163, 164, 194, 379
  Pétain's views on, 133–134, 140–141, 154, 167, 184, 185
  as refugees, 207–211
  in Riviera, 180, 186
  Roumanian, 174–175
  in Switzerland, 207, 212, 375, 376, 382
  as war veterans, 150–151
  yellow star ordinance for, 152, 154, 157
Jouhaux, Léon, 221
Journal Officiel, 93, 134, 184

Kaltenbrunner, Ernst, 129, 233–234
Kammler, Hans, 340
Kamphuis, Hans, 350, 351, 352–353, 357
Katz, Leah, 210
KDS (*Kommando der SIPO und SD*), 201, 335
  organization of, 201–202
  Section Four of, 203, 206, 207–208, 212, 249–250, 257–258, 276–277, 305
  torture used by, 202
Keitel, Wilhelm, 111–112, 115, 123, 143, 178
Kersten, Felix, 141–142, 371–376, 377–382
Kiep, Otto, 253
Kiesinger, Kurt-Georg, 188–189
Klarsfeld, Beate Kunzel, 188–190

Klarsfeld, Serge, 131, 186–190
Klein, Lisette, 325, 327, 332, 335, 345–347, 355
Knab, Werner, 202–203, 256, 260, 261, 294, 296, 315, 316
Knipping, Max, 290
Knochen, Helmut, 115, 136, 151–155, 158, 174–176, 179, 182, 206, 207, 290
Koch, Karl, 381
Koestler, Arthur, 39–40, 50
Krauch, Albert, 341
Kremer, Johann, 167
Krochmal, Liane, 274
Krochmal, Renata, 274
Krupp plant, 340

Labroue, René, 118
Lambert, Raymond-Raoul, 216
Lassagne, André, 227, 230, 235, 236
Latherman, Isaac, 307–308
Laurent, Marc, 316
Laval, Josée, 311, 312
Laval, Pierre:
  anti-British attitude of, 53
  attempted assassination of, 78–79, 103, 292
  Blum and, 85–86
  character of, 76–82
  as "Chief of Government," 107, 285, 290, 291
  execution of, 195
  as foreign minister, 80–81
  as German collaborator, 75–76, 78, 81–82, 85–86, 91, 94, 99–100, 108, 172, 183, 191, 195, 216
  Göring's meeting with, 106–107
  Herriot and, 310–312
  Hitler and, 82, 99, 106, 177
  Jewish deportations supported by, 79, 153, 154, 155, 156, 167, 169, 172–173, 181, 183, 184–185, 192, 193–194, 195
  "*la relève*" policy of, 107–108
  Lebrun as viewed by, 42
  pacifism of, 77, 80
  Pétain and, 54, 57, 76, 79, 86, 87, 90–91, 99–100, 107, 190
  as politician, 77–78, 85
  resignation of, 100
  return to Vichy government by, 106–107, 146
  scheming by, 79–81, 107–108
  Stalin and, 80–81
  as vice-premier of Vichy government, 88, 90–91, 99–100, 106–108
Lebrun, Albert, 42, 48, 54, 72, 85, 87
  arrest of, 240–243
Leca, Dominique, 53–54
Lécussan, Jean, 257, 258
Lefebvre, Marcel, 321
Legion of French Volunteers (LFV), 78, 102–103, 105, 301
Leguay, Jean, 153, 162, 173, 182, 184
Léon, Georgette, 20
Leopold III, King of Belgium, 62
Leroi, Josette, 306, 362, 363–365, 388–389
Les Mille concentration camp, 96, 171
Le Troquer, André, 71, 87
Levaux, Gilbert, 53–54
Lévy, Charles, 331
Lévy, Gilberte, 212–213
Lévy, Jacques, 176

412

Index

Index